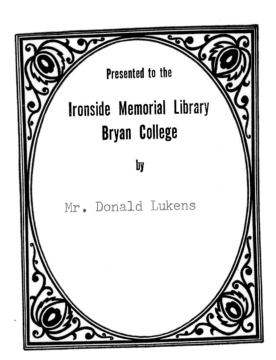

Odyssey *of a* Liberal

Memoirs

Odyssey *of a* Liberal

Memoirs

BY
FREDA UTLEY

Washington National Press, Inc.

128 C Street, Northeast

Washington, D. C. 20002

37433

AUTHOR'S NOTE

Three decades have passed since I wrote *The Dream We Lost** telling the story of my life in Russia in the 30's, and describing the new system of exploitation developed by the Communist totalitarian dictatorship. Since then I have completed my circuit of the political spectrum and learnt that there is all too little difference between the North Pole, where liberal aspirations are blasted by the icy breath of Communist tyranny, and the South Pole where conservatism hardens into reaction or the cold immobility of uncharitableness and fearful concern only for the preservation of possessions, privilege and power.

In now writing my memoirs which cover my life before and after my disillusionment in Russia, I still find no words more relevant to our times and my experience than the quotation from William Morris's *Dream of John Ball* which I put on the fly leaf of my old book:

> I pondered all these things and how men fight and lose the battle, and
> the thing they fought for comes about in spite of their defeat; and
> when it comes about it turns out not to be what they meant, and other
> men have to fight for what they meant under another name.

My life's story is that of the education of a liberal in our time, although it may be that neither my critics to the "Right" or to the "Left" regard me as anything of the sort.

Old political labels have become so confused by passion and prejudice, or so outdated, that they have become irrelevant to our age.

Yet the old landmarks still stand despite the wrongly labelled signposts which confuse and lead astray the generation which has come of age as I overpass the Biblical limit of threescore years and ten.

In writing my memoirs I am not attempting to provide wisdom for the ages, but I hope that in recording my far ranging experience as a participant observer of the history of our times I can contribute something of value to an understanding of the problems of our time. Solutions consonant with liberal aspirations will never be found unless those who strive to make a better world free themselves of the illusions which thrive among those whose personal experience, unlike my own, has been too fortunate for them to appreciate the grim realities of the struggle for survival which is still today man's fate in most regions of the earth.

The belief that we can ourselves create a better world makes life purposeful and worth living—however dim the hope becomes as we grow old. Thus, I suppose I am still a liberal within the original meaning of that much-abused word, although having learned through experience more than is dreamed of in the philosophy of most Western liberals, I no longer share their faith in the inevitability of progress and the perfectibility of man through the creation of a better material environment.

F.U.
Washington, D.C.
November 1969

---

*John Day, 1940. Subsequently republished in abbreviated form as *Lost Illusion* in 1947. Reprinted in The Henry Regnery Co.'s Gateway edition of Classics.

CONTENTS

Page

Chapter 1   As The Sparks Fly   1

Chapter 2   Beginnings   6

Chapter 3   Continental Interlude   15

Chapter 4   My English School   23

Chapter 5   War Years   31

Chapter 6   Travelling Left In Bohemia   43

Chapter 7   Marx, Freud, Love, and the Libido   54

Chapter 8   Remembering Russell   64

Chapter 9   I Take the Plunge   74

Chapter 10   Russia in Rose   81

Chapter 11   Off to the East   87

Chapter 12   Honeymoon in Japan   97

Chapter 13   Working for the Party 108

Chapter 14   Interlude With Temple 114

             Epilogue 125

Chapter 15   The End of My Life in Russia 128

Chapter 16   Return to the West 142

Chapter 17   Bertrand Russell, George Bernard Shaw, and

             the Case of Berdichevsky 152

Chapter 18   Russell in America 167

Chapter 19   My Indian Summer in China 184

Chapter 20   Portrait of Agnes 200

Chapter 21   China Experts Then and Now 210

Chapter 22   I Discover America 220

Chapter 23   Away to the New World 225

Chapter 24   Emigration to America 234

Chapter 25   Friends in the Village 244

Chapter 26   Failure of the Dream 255

Chapter 27   Ordeal of a Premature Anti-Communist 270

Chapter 28   Back to an Office Again 280

Chapter 29   The Political World is Also Round 302

Chapter 1
AS THE SPARKS FLY

In my early teens, at boarding school in England, I cut out the word SOPHROSUNE in Greek letters on my pencil box. Why, I cannot now imagine, since this precept, usually translated as meaning moderation, or nothing in excess, was alien to my temperament. Far from observing the Golden Mean, I have spent most of my life recklessly committed to causes I believed in. Since I either became disillusioned or lost interest in these causes when they prevailed or became popular, I have never ridden the tide which, taken at the flood, leads to success. I should have been more prescient had I carved, "Born to trouble as the sparks fly upward" on the bright polished surface of that light colored wooden box which I can still see clearly in the eye of memory, when so much else has been forgotten. Yet in attempting to analyze the motivations which have shaped my life, I realize that in spite of always having been *engagé*, it was the Greek principle of restraint, or balance, which compelled me to throw my weight on the opposite side of the scales when the oppressed became the oppressors, as so often happens in the course of human events.

Although I never heard of James Russell Lowell until I came to America, his lines express the feeling which has consciously or unconsciously motivated my life:

> Right forever on the scaffold,
> Wrong forever on the throne . . .

Anatole France, with whose writings I became familiar in early youth, expressed the same idea in his *Révolte Des Anges*, which ends when Lucifer refuses to lead an assault on heaven by the angels whose fall was due to their compassion for the sufferings of mankind, because he foresees that:

> *Dieu vancu deviendra Satan; et Satan vanqueur deviendra Dieu.* *

Men are men and there is no innate virtue in the oppressed. On the contrary, as Bertrand Russell pointed out long ago when underdog changes places with upper dog he proves to be more ruthless because he has learned, while underneath, to scratch harder in the battle for survival.

Since, either instinctively or by reason of the sense of proportion which is the essence of the classical concept of beauty, I have tended all my life to throw my weight on the weaker side of the scales of power, perhaps I was not so wrong when I carved SOPHROSUNE on my pencil box when I was 14 or 15 years old.

Unfortunately in my personal life and behavior I have paid little heed to Goethe's dictum that the essence of wisdom is to know when to stop. By expressing my views too sharply, or by carrying my arguments to a ruthlessly logical conclusion, I have failed to influence as many people as I might have done had I been more temperate or restrained and less combative. I have alienated some friends and lost potential allies by turning my back upon those, who by their refusal to go all the way with me in a battle against odds, seemed to me to be cowards unwilling to stand up and be counted when they were in

---

*God conquered will become Satan; and Satan victorious become God.

1

reality only displaying greater political sagacity than myself. Yet despite my all or nothing attitude in the heat of controversy, I have found myself unable to remain long in the company of extremists on any side.

One's character, no doubt, is one's fate. But no one knows the extent to which character is determined by heredity or by environment. Nor is it until late in life that one can dimly perceive how the influences of childhood and youth have shaped one's destiny, and continue to determine one's philosophy and behavior until the curtain falls.

These influences in my case were liberal, socialist and free-thinking, strongly colored by the poetry of revolt and liberty and legends, stories and romances of heroism and adventure upon which I fed in childhood; not without a tincture of Gallic realism, but basically English. I was conditioned by the empirical attitude of mind inculcated in me by my father; and my upbringing, despite the absence of religious instruction, was anchored to the basic tenets of the Puritanism which produced the first English radicals in the 17th century, the Pilgrim Fathers who emigrated to New England, and the Nonconformists who founded the British Labor Party two hundred years later.

The environment which shaped me was in many respects different from that of others of my generation but I am a product of the heyday of the liberal era, reared in its faith in infinite progress through freedom from superstition and by means of the scientific discoveries and their technical application which were expected to make man master of his fate. I am, or was, a child of the age of reason—of that new age of faith when it was believed that freed from "the shambles of faith and of fear" a vista of infinite progress would open to mankind.

Thus I was imbued at an early age with a consuming desire for the emancipation of mankind, or for justice, which is perhaps the moral reflection of the desire for harmony and beauty. I believed, thanks to my rationalist upbringing, that mankind requires only freedom from superstition or from the bonds of established religion to acquire the knowledge which, together with release from a narrow regard for material self interest, could lead to heaven on earth. The libertarian values implanted in my mind which have consciously or unconsciously motivated me all my life, were to cause me to recoil in horror from the Soviet dictatorship when I came intimately to know it. It was a passion for the emancipation of mankind, not the blueprint of a planned society nor any mystical yearning to merge myself in a fellowship absolving me of personal responsibility, which both led me into the Communist fold, and caused me to leave it as soon as I learned that it meant submission to the most total tyranny which mankind has ever experienced.

Many of my contemporaries and those who came after me were to follow the Red Star because of an unhappy childhood, or frustrations of one kind or another, or failure to make a place for themselves in the competitive capitalist world. But I came to Communism via Greek history, French Revolutionary literature, and the English nineteenth century poets of freedom—not in revolt against a strict "bourgeois" upbringing, nor on account of failure to make a place for myself in the "capitalist" world, but profoundly influenced by a happy childhood, a socialist father and a continental education. I am perhaps proof of Arnold Toynbee's contention that Communism is a "Western heresy."

When I came to study ancient history my heroes were Pericles, the Gracchi, and Julius Caesar. From an early age I could recite long passages from Shelley, Swinburne and Keats extolling man's eternal striving for freedom, beauty and justice. Swinburne's love poems I rejected as incomprehensible aberrations from the glorification of freedom and the denunciation of tyranny and superstition which I loved. I thrilled to such lines as:

2

Pride have all men in their fathers that were free before them,
In the warriors that begat us freeborn pride have we;
But the fathers of their spirit, how may men adore them;
With what rapture praise who bade our souls be free.
Sons of Athens born in spirit and truth are all born free men;
Most of all, we, nurtured where the North wind holds his reign.
Children all we sea-folk of the Salaminian seamen,
Sons of they that beat back Persia, we who beat back Spain.*

Today I realize that I ought not to have been so unprepared to learn the facts of political life as might seem from my account of the influences of my childhood and youth.

Like a discordant note or muted theme in the first movement of a symphony, there were other early influences in my life which should have prepared me for the disappointments and disillusionment which awaited me, not only in Soviet Russia but in later years in the Free World. In childhood and youth I had imbibed not only classical and romantic literature and the poems of Shelley and Swinburne, Matthew Arnold, and other poets who sang of freedom and inspired belief in the coming of a Golden Age when men would be freed from the chains of superstition and fear. I was also well acquainted with the writings of Shaw and Anatole France, read and enjoyed Voltaire's "Candide" and "Zadig" and was to win a prize at school for an essay on Machiavelli.

If heredity also molds character I must take some account of the combative and adventurous spirit of my father's Viking freebooter ancestors, who settled in Yorkshire before William of Normandy conquered England. Utley is a Danish name derived from the words out-leigh or out-lee, meaning beyond the moor, and there is still a remote small village called Utley in the West Riding where my paternal ancestors were blacksmiths for many generations.

Many of the Utley's had gone a'roving in their time which accounts for the fact that there are far more of them in America than in England.**

My mother, who came from Lancashire where the Celtic strain is strong, was a woman of charm and wit as well as beautiful, and may be partly responsible for the romantic streak in our characters which led my brother to voyage from England to the South Seas in a small sailing boat, while I sought a false Holy Grail in Communist Russia.

In my brother Temple's view, it was our Utley inheritance combined with the romantic stories we had read in childhood which shaped our lives.

Writing to our mother from Suva in the Fiji Islands in 1934 shortly after the birth of my son in Moscow he said:

---

*Swinburne *Athens.*

**I knew from my father who, while at college in Manchester, won a money prize for amateurs tracing their ancestry, that in the 17th century four Utley brothers had emigrated to Massachusetts. Since it struck my childhood imagination I also recall that the wife of an Utley who was a cavalryman in Wellington's army had accompanied him on the campaigns in the low countries and crossed rivers hanging on to his horse's tail. After my 1936 book, *Japan's Feet of Clay* was published in the U.S.A. I received several letters from American Utleys including one from a man who had made a hobby of tracing Utleys and sent me a long list of them. Unfortunately I have lost this but I remember it included the name of an Utley who had been the champion boxer of the British Navy. In Chicago in 1939 when speaking for the Council of Foreign Relations at the invitation of Clifton Utley I was to find rows of Utleys in the telephone book whereas there had been only myself and one other listed in London. At this time I disabused Clifton Utley of the notion that the Utleys stemmed from Wales.

3

... Freda's letter to me was in tone and spirit very sweet. We neither of us quite seem to have found our new world. Moral—do not read your children romantic tales in their infancy. However hard-boiled they may become afterwards, the original taint remains. Tell Freda to teach Jon to lisp the Maxims of La Rochefoucauld as his first primary. Freda at eleven and I at fourteen learned them too late.

The Songs the Syrens sang for us were not the same. I became a "political animal," travelling ever Left in search of the ideal society which never was, or probably can be, on land or sea. Temple came to seek escape from civilization by venturing on perilous seas in a small sailing boat to seek his dream islands in the South Seas. He was to be more fortunate than I although he died young. While I was passing through the Valley of Despair in Russia in the early 30's, Temple had found his Pacific Islands "just as they should be—of an incredible beauty."

Today I find myself wanting to write about my brother before recording my own story. Perhaps because I now begin to understand that Temple and I in the drama of our lives were like strophe and antistrophe—or thesis and antithesis according to the Hegelian philosophy, eventually to be united in a synthesis of understanding.

Both of us were reared in the liberal philosophy of our time and were subject to the same childhood influences. But whereas I was to follow Marx and Lenin's teachings, Temple's views were more akin to Rousseau's and Bakunin's. He came to believe that freedom and happiness are to be found by escaping from modern industrial civilization which, even when it provides material comforts and security, deprives man of the satisfaction of basic needs of his nature. I imagined that a better organization of society could create conditions in which men would be free while voluntarily submitting to the demands of the state intended to ensure justice for all.

Our lives perhaps exemplify the split in the liberal personality between the extremes of anarchy and statism. Temple took the high road and I the low, or vice versa according to one's prejudices, in our life's journey from the "banks of Loch Lomond."

In a later chapter, I shall have more to tell concerning my brother's life and death. Here I only quote, with wonder at Temple's insight, a passage from a letter he wrote when he was 35 years old on the eve of sailing from Colon to the Marquesas Islands.

> There is a sort of lethal factor in us Utleys which inhibits success. Both
> my father who was, and my sister who is, much cleverer than I am,
> always missed it. You see they, who could have got it easily, never quite
> believed in it. I, who would find its attainment much more difficult,
> believe in it rather less.

Unlike my brother, I was ambitious. Although I was never able to surmount the "lethal factor" in the Utleys which inhibits us from paying the required price for success, I longed for it. And time was when thanks to my having acquired inordinate confidence in my abilities, thanks to my easy academic successes at school and college, I imagined I would be one of the "movers and shakers" of the world. My faith in human reason, inculcated in me by my upbringing, combined with what Bertrand Russell called my incurable political romanticism, impelled me to continue to believe, even when my views were most unpopular, that if only I could write well enough, I could convince the world of the truth as I saw it.

No doubt one gets what one wants most in life if one tries hard enough, but one cannot have everything. The cost of freedom comes high and one cannot expect to enjoy it, least of all in the world of letters, if one desires fame or security more. Of course, one

4

always goes on hoping to enjoy both. There have been times when I railed against my fate and considered myself ill-used because the world failed to award me fame, fortune or influence and I found myself reviled for expressing my deepest convictions regardless of the consequences. On one such occasion Edith Hamilton, who died in her 94th year in full possession of her faculties, gently reproved me for feeling sorry for myself following the failure of my 1949 book, *The High Cost of Vengeance*,* to win a wide circulation. "My dear Freda," she said, "don't expect the material rewards of unrighteousness while engaged in the pursuit of truth." Nevertheless I often did, continuing to yearn for the success which I occasionally glimpsed but never quite achieved. Even when one of my books was a success I went off on another quest.

Like my father, I did not "stick to one last," as they express it in North Country England. I dissipated my energies and endeavors in too many directions, wanting to be both scholar and journalist, politician and preacher, crusader for the causes I believed in and seeker for the truth. Desirous of success but unwilling or unable to pay the ultimate price, I could not devote myself to the goddess who, although not the bitch she has been called, demands wholehearted devotion to herself alone.

Thus, I was destined to become a Communist when it was most unpopular to be one, and an anti-Communist during the years when its false promises were generally believed by Western "liberals." Too fast, too soon. The way to success as I have painfully learned, is not to learn too much too soon. It pays to be wrong when everyone else is deluded and woe betide all Cassandras, or anyone else who learns and speaks truth before the public is prepared to listen. The best reputations are gained by those who change their opinions just before the midnight hour when it is usually too late to change the course of human events.

I might have a man's mind—which was the compliment I most relished—but I could always be accused by my opponents or detractors of being too emotional, as perhaps I am, because I am a woman. And in the struggle for existence in which I was to be engaged at an early age, I had to shoulder the financial responsibilities of a man while also meeting the domestic demands of a woman.

Whether or not I ever deserved the following tribute paid me by Pearl Buck in her review of my 1940, *The Dream We Lost*,** her words are apposite to the struggle all women who strive to overcome the initial disadvantage of not being born men.

> This is one of the richest books I have ever read. It is more than an unassailable indictment of Russian Communism. It is a strongly dramatic story and one interesting enough to make a major novel, the story of a brilliant mind, rigorously truthful in its working, though born unhappily in the body of a woman. For even in the best parts of the world a first rate mind is still hampered if it happens to belong to a woman. Nevertheless, this mind was born, and it is to its honor that Freda Utley has simply borne with the disadvantages of being a woman without allowing them to influence her thinking. (*Asia,* October, 1940)

---

*Henry Regnery Co., Chicago, 1949.

**The John Day Co., 1940.

Chapter 2
BEGINNINGS

Temple and I were both born under our different stars just before the turn of the century, he on June 10, 1895, and I on January 23, 1898, at Number I Kings Bench Walk in the Temple, London. It was exceptional, if not unique, for married couples, much less children, to be permitted to live in those renowned legal chambers and take the air in the beautiful, ancient gardens above the river Thames.

My father, studying for the bar while earning his living as a journalist, had somehow persuaded the authorities to let him continue living in the Temple after his marriage. Although later my parents were to live very comfortably in large houses and luxurious Continental hotels, they remembered those years in cramped quarters, lacking most of the facilities of modern living, as perhaps the best of their lives.

Son of a Yorkshire blacksmith, my father, Willie Herbert Utley, had obtained his education on scholarships from technical secondary school to Owen's College (subsequently renamed Manchester University) where he became an undergraduate at the early age of sixteen. With a voracious appetite for knowledge in every sphere of human questioning and endeavor, my father alternatively or simultaneously studied science and mathematics, languages and the humanities, and thus never obtained an academic degree. But his versatility and wide-ranging knowledge were subsequently to prove of greater advantage to him than any handle to his name when he got to London and started on a successful career in journalism. Thanks to the catholicity of his interests and his literary talent, he was able to write on scientific and economic subjects, as well as on literature, politics, art, drama and music. For instance, when Marconi first demonstrated wireless, he was assigned to Ireland to report this new scientific marvel for a number of newspapers which had no other adequately equipped reporter. Thus, my mother, in London, was one of the first people in the world to receive a radiogram.

My father had secured his first journalistic assignment when he presented himself at the office of the *Morning Leader*, the leading Liberal newspaper of the time, and was told to sit down and write an editorial on some political topic of the day. Having done this with ease, he was accepted as an editorial writer.

When the *Morning Leader* subsequently merged with the *Evening Star*, be became assistant editor and music critic of the *Star and Morning Leader*. George Bernard Shaw was its drama critic but, according to my mother's recollection, their friendship began while my father was financial editor of Frank Harris' *Saturday Review*, a journal that helped make Shaw famous as one of its contributors.

Many years after his death, while doing research for my M.A. thesis at the British Museum, I was asked by the oldest of its librarians whether I was the daughter of Willie Herbert Utley. When I said I was he told me that my father had at one time translated old English medieval manuscripts in the basement of the British Museum in order to earn money, not only for himself but also to help Bernard Shaw and other impecunious friends of his when they were especially hard up.

G.B.S. and my father were both contributors to Annie Besant's publication, *Our Corner*, and were friends of Charles Bradlaugh the famous free-thinking M.P. who directed the Hall of Science school on Fleet Street. Here, when he first came to London at the age of 19, Willie Utley lectured on physiography, according to an old prospectus for the session 1886-7 preserved by my mother and still in my possession.

In his teens he had spoken from the same platform as Friedrich Engels in Manchester, as I learned long after his death from documents I saw at the Marx-Engels Institute in Moscow. Subsequently, in London, he had taken part in the labor struggles of the late eighties and was arrested with John Burns in Trafalgar Square at a demonstration of the unemployed, although spared from imprisonment on account of his youth. For some months he was acting secretary of the Fabian Society founded by Beatrice and Sidney Webb and, had it not been for my arrival, he would have stood for Parliament in the Socialist interest. But M.P.'s were not paid in those days, and with two children to support he perforce abandoned a political career. Even so, in order to earn enough money for all of us, he was on the staff of both a morning and evening newspaper at the same time, besides contributing to weeklies and engaging in unpaid political activities. He worked so hard, slept so little and expended himself so generously that it was not surprising that when I was nine years old, he contracted the tubercular lung infection to which he finally succumbed ten years later.

During my infancy and early childhood my parents had gone through some bad times, as for instance when my father started his own liberal weekly magazine only to have it fold on account of the Boer War; and later, when, after having written the first "Motoring Handbook" published in England, he was compelled before publication to sell the valuable copyright of this future best seller in order to meet a note at the bank he had guaranteed for T.W.H. Crossland, a friend who, like some other well known literary figures, lacked the bourgeois virtue of paying their debts.

Following, or in consequence of these setbacks or disasters, my father turned his talents to financial journalism and business investment advice and started making so much money that my earliest recollections are of life in a big house in Hampstead with servants and governesses, first at 67 Finchley Road and later at 33 St. Johns Wood Park. (Queer that now in my 70's I can still remember the addresses of the houses in which we lived when I was less than ten years old! It is a curious fact that as the shades of the coming night of one's life deepen one retains a better memory of details of the distant past than of more recent events.)

The Utley's would have become really rich had my father's partner, a man called Hannay, been ready to go all out to back my father's conviction that a rubber boom was coming thanks to the invention of the motor car. It was Hannay who supplied the capital for their joint venture in publishing a financial newsletter and investing other peoples money in what is today called a mutual fund but was then frowned on as a "bucket shop."

Notwithstanding the ease with which my father seems to have made money once he set his mind to it, and the affluence which surrounded my childhood as I remember it, I was reared in the socialist beliefs which were to shape my life. A life which was also to be powerfully influenced by the impression made upon me in youth by the tender, passionate and enduring love of my father and mother for one another. Despite the Bohemian world in which I was to take my place in my 20's, I sought to find the same rare and true love which is:

7

> . . . a durable fire,
> In the mind ever burning,
> Never sick, never dead, never cold.
> From itself never turning . . .*

My parents had first met and fallen in love when they were 17 and my father was brought visiting to my grandfather's house by Edward Aveling, Karl Marx's son-in-law and translator. In old age my mother was to recall with pride that Dr. Aveling had introduced my father that first evening as "the most brilliant boy and coming man he knew."

The course of my parents true and life-long love had not run smooth, and they were not married until many years later, mainly because of my grandfather's opposition but also, I surmise, on account of my father's roving, adventurous temperament which led him to spend several years wandering abroad.

My mother's father, Joseph E. Williamson, a prosperous Lancashire manufacturer, was a free-thinker and a republican who was proud to tell that his wife's mother had hidden the famous Chartist leader, Fergus O'Connor, under her bed while pretending to be sick when the police were searching for him. He liked to entertain the prominent or promising radical political "intelligentsia" of his time, but he was far from inclined to believe in the equality of the sexes and was also opposed to any of his daughters (he had seven) marrying an impecunious young man. He had refused to let my mother continue her education to become a doctor, as she passionately desired, and had instead set her to boiling jam in his factory to put such nonsensical ideas out of her head.

After my father came courting following their first meeting, my grandfather ordered my gentle, obedient Williamson grandmother never to leave them alone. They surmounted the obstacle of her presence by my father giving her Ouida's romantic novels to read. These so absorbed her that she paid no attention as they sat together in the parlor of my grandfather's mansion, The Grange, in the Manchester suburb of Stretford, whose gloomy interior I came to know well when I was in my teens.

I narrowly escaped being named "Cigarette" by my mother after the heroine of Ouida's famous book *Under Two Flags*** about the French Foreign Legion in North Africa, this being one of the novels which so absorbed my grandmother as to leave my teenage future parents free from her chaperonage. Maybe also because my mother was an inveterate smoker, as I, alas, was also to become after I went to live in Russia. She had first acquired a taste for smoking in her teens when promised a complete set of Shakespeare's works by her older brother Len, if she could smoke four cigarettes in succession—a feat she accomplished although it made her sick.

Among my precious possessions today is a three volume edition of *The Complete Poetical Works of Percy Bysshe Shelley* published in 1881, given to my mother by my father "on her 18th birthday, October 1883."*** Below the inscription "To Emily Williamson by W.H.U." penned in beautiful script in India ink, my father wrote:

> *A vous mes pensees*
> *Pensées aussi a moi.*

---

*Anonymous 16th Century poem included in the "Oxford Book of English Verse."

** Stein & Day, N. Y., 1966.

***John Slark, London, 1881. "The Text Carefully Revised, with Notes and A Memoir by William Michael Rossetti. Dedicated to Edward John Trelawny, Who loved Shelley, Traced out his corpse, and Snatched from the fire the heart of hearts, This Edition of the imperishable poems is by permission most respectfully dedicated."

Determined to pursue her vocation if only in the secondary role of a nurse, mother eventually ran away to London to become a probationer at St. Thomas Hospital. Meanwhile, my father, despite his love for her, had gone off to Greece to be tutor to the son of a wealthy family on the Island of Andros. Here, as he told me in my childhood, he walked down marble steps to swim in the warm Aegean Sea, and had on one occasion almost been drowned because of his short-sightedness, having lost sight of land one evening when he swam too far out.

Subsequently he had wandered all over the Balkans, learning to speak Turkish as well as Greek and earning his living in diverse ways, mainly as a free lance journalist. His adventures in Eastern Europe were no doubt the equivalent of my brother's voyages in the South Seas many years later. But he had eventually been pulled back to England by his love for my mother.

My mother was exceptionally attractive—indeed, quite beautiful to judge from her photographs and she had many suitors. But she waited for my father in the confident belief that he would eventually come back to her from his roaming abroad. All of which sounds like a 19th century romance but is true. They loved each other passionately and cherished one another all their lives, in poverty as in prosperity, in sickness and in health, until parted by death. During my father's last long illness prior to his death in 1918, she nursed him devotedly in conditions of extreme poverty in a two-room cottage in Cornwall which was so primitive that she had to fetch water with a bucket from a well and cook on a wood stove. But she never let drudgery or poverty get her down. She was still lovely in middle age, slim and supple all her life, and managed somehow to look elegant whatever her circumstances. She was loyal and loving and never reproached my father for their fall from affluence to penury during the last years of his life although, as I came to realize when I grew up, she had little fundamental understanding or sympathy for the ideas which I inherited from him.

She was all woman—more concerned with human relations than with ideas; passionate and charming, unselfish but demanding, jealously possessive in her love for both my father and my brother, but also ready to make any sacrifice for them without complaint.

We could not have been more different. Not only was I never beautiful, I scorned to be feminine. I wished I were a boy and have always felt most flattered when told I have a man's mind. Nevertheless, it was no doubt mainly due to my mother's influence that I was to reject second best substitutes for love. I waited long to find my own true love because I dreamed of the perfect union which my mother and father enjoyed. I could not accept any substitute for the rare love of my parents which had illumined my childhood. Puritan or romantic, or a combination of both, I was to reject the easy fly-by-night liaisons of my contemporaries in the Bohemian world in which I took my place in London in the 20's.

My father's love for my mother was as constant as her's for him. They were lovers in every sense of the word in middle age as in youth. I possess none of the letters she wrote him, but have several which he wrote to her both in their years of prosperity before the 1914 war, and during the disastrous years which followed before he died, destitute in Cornwall, in January 1918. Writing, on October 27, 1911 from our home at Ken Court, Tatsfield to mother visiting my sick grandmother in Manchester, he tells her how "dreary" life was without her and that "In my loneliness last night, I thought I would play the claviole but we could not find the piano key anywhere. My dearie I love you alone and utterly and life is not life when you are away. Goodnight sweetheart. Ever your true lover, Willie."

9

Other passages in my father's letters recall the dimly remembered days of my childhood and early teens when, incredible as it now seems, we lived in such comfort that two servants did not suffice. "I am putting an advertisement in the Globe for a man and wife," he writes, "because, Florence does not want to be a parlor maid and the girl who wrote wants only a housemaid's place."

Florence, whose kind, ugly face and tall angular figure I still remember, was our loyal "retainer," more friend than servant. When bad times came she wanted to continue working for us without wages and offered her own savings to my parents to help out. Back in 1912, she was busy bottling plums and pickling cauliflowers and cucumbers and enjoying herself generally. Recalling the distant days of our prosperity before the 1914 war, Temple was to write on June 3, 1934 from Suva, after the birth of my son in Moscow:

> My Dear Mother and Grandmother,
>
> Queer to think of you as the latter, for I see you more as the Mother I remember, carousing with Lockoff and Madame von Klockner at Arosa, or drinking Chartreuse—French, pre-expulsion of the monks—at Ken Court, Christmas, 1912. Those days when we were young and rich, when property was so secure that people laid down wine cellars and the 'lower orders knew their places'. Little did you think that twenty-two years later you would be grandmother to a little revolutionary in Moscow. It is a pity Dada cannot see the joke, it would have stirred his sense of irony. Well, dear, you have had a life; but really, on the whole, it must have been good. I don't think that at the age of sixty-nine I will be having a little revolutionary grandchild, in what capital shall I suggest?—say, Chicago.

Even in her old age in America Mother was to remain charming and attractive. In 1941 when she was in her seventies George Calverton shortly before his death wrote to her from the offices of *The Modern Quarterly* in the Village:

> Dear Emmie:
>
> Just a little note to say I hope you are feeling well and spreading your radiant personality over Westport.
>
> I've missed you, those minxish eyes of yours, that fine clear English speech, and your infectious laugh, lovely as the song of wind in gentle spring.

Other friends in America, still alive, recall Emmie Utley's beautiful voice and the exquisite diction of her speech which was the more remarkable since her father had denied her the education he could easily have afforded to give her.

In my late teens I came to know my Williamson grandfather as a tall, handsome patriarch who bullied the two of his daughters who had not married but had devoted their lives to looking after their parents. He had cut off my mother without even the proverbial shilling when she married my father. But years afterwards when my father was prosperous and we lived at Ken Court my grandfather had been glad to let my mother nurse grandmother in our home for six months during her fatal illness. When she died, my grandfather did not even offer to pay the medical and funeral expenses. A decade later when my father was dying of tuberculosis in poverty, my grandfather grudgingly allowed my parents ten shillings a week—no doubt well content that he had proved so right in having opposed my mother's marriage to a man who ended his life as he began, in poverty.

10

Following my father's death in January 1918, my grandfather was to cut off even the pittance he had allowed my mother during the last year of my father's illness, leaving me to support her while my brother was fighting in Mesopotamia.

I remember my mother's mother as a small, shrunken old lady with scanty white hair covered by a lace cap, clear blue eyes, a delicately tinted complexion and a tremulous smile, her hands folded in her lap as she sat in our garden at Ken Court with a rug over her knees. She was a sweet and gentle person who let her husband dominate her to such an extent that she had never dared to stand up to him even in order to help their daughters.

My Utley grandmother, whom I knew only from her portrait, must have been a forceful and ambitious woman. She had done everything possible to help my father surmount the handicap of poverty to secure an education. She had succeeded in spurring my Utley grandfather into raising himself from the status of contented blacksmith in Yorkshire into the ranks of the lower middle class by securing for him the management of a small hotel in Manchester.

She had failed to make him a successful inn-keeper and had died comparatively young, leaving her husband to become my father's pensioner; but she must have had the satisfaction of knowing that her talented and energetic son would fulfill her ambitions. I imagine that it is from her that I inherited the drive, as also other unfeminine qualities and defects that have both helped and hurt me during the course of my life.

My father's father, although poor and improvident, was a most happy man, loved by his wife and son. He may have been a financial burden and a failure but he contributed to their lives, love and gaiety and enjoyment of music and art.

He remains in my childhood memories as a hale and hearty, rosy cheeked and whitehaired, cheerful old man. His main interest in life had always been playing the violin and painting pictures of no artistic value, which no doubt afforded him the pleasure of satisfying his creative impulses.

He was so robust and healthy that he had never taken to his bed in illness until he died in his 80's in full possession of his faculties. No doubt, I have owed to him and our Yorkshire yeomen ancestors the vigor, energy and good health I have enjoyed for most of my life. My brother, who like my father, developed tuberculosis and died young, may have derived from our Utley grandfather the sanguine temperament which, as Temple used to say, contrasted with his pessimistic philosophy.

My Utley grandfather gave me a violin when I was a child and insisted that I should learn to play it, and he also endeavored to teach me to draw and paint. Although I was never really musical I tried hard and was most happy when chosen in my teens to play in the school orchestra at my English boarding school.

I also tried my hand at painting and wrote romantic plays which my brother and our friends acted, rigged out in homemade costumes. These plays of mine usually had tragic endings, as did the one we performed while staying at the Hotel Grison at Arosa in Switzerland, in which all the main characters ended up dead on the stage. I was furious when Temple made comedy out of my tragedy by getting up before the curtain fell to sound the hearts of the other "corpses" with a stethoscope.

As I write, memories revive of days when my imagination and interests were unconfined by experience or too great preoccupation with politics. When, although I already had a "social conscience" awakened by my father's teachings, I could indulge my romantic imagination and enjoy all the wonder of the world.

Somewhere along the line of my ancestry or environment, I acquired a Puritan streak which made me take life all too seriously, in contrast to my brother who enjoyed all the pleasures and joys life offered, but who could also laugh in the face of danger or adversity. Temple never experienced the brief religious phase I went through, perhaps induced by one of my governesses at the age of seven or eight, when I prayed every night on my knees beside my bed without, as I imagined, anyone knowing. But my reason, or the logical thought developed by my upbringing soon reasserted itself, bringing my very short "age of faith" to an end. I remember going to discuss it all with my father, telling him that I realized that a just God would not punish man for doing the evil which his Creator must foresee he would do if He were omniscient as well as omnipotent. And if God were not just, he was not God; i.e., did not exist.

As I dimly remember, my father explained his agnostic philosophy in simple terms by saying that if told there was a tiger on the roof he would go up and find out. But no one could verify the existence of a God in heaven.

I wrote stories or fairy tales from an early age and can recollect the main outline of one whose hero was called Cass. Maybe I derived his name from the French verb *casser*—to break—for my story started by telling how his mother and father, realizing that their children, if they lived, would surely sin and go to hell, killed them all in infancy. But baby Cass, having willfully knocked over and smashed his cup of milk, thus already committing a sin, was permitted to live. This is all I remember of Cass's story. A psychologist could no doubt find all sorts of interesting explanations for my remembering even this much.

It was perhaps because he wanted to save me from premature preoccupation with sin and death and religion that my father gave me Fitzgerald's translation of *The Rubaiyat of Omar Khayyam* to read. I was so enthralled by the lyrical beauty of Fitzgerald's rendering of the Persian poet's verses that, when eleven years old, I learnt them by heart—nor have I ever forgotten them entirely. Like the poems of Shelley and Swinburne which enchanted me later, I can still recite verse upon verse of the *Rubaiyat* from memory.

Recently I became acquainted with Omar Abou Riche, a famous modern Arab poet who was Syria's Ambassador to Washington in 1962. When I asked him whether any of his poems had been translated into English or French, he replied, "yes," but went on to remark that very few translations of poems are worth reading, the great exception being Fitzgerald's rendering of Omar Khayyam's *Rubaiyat* which, he said, is not properly speaking a translation, but a free rendering of the spirit and meaning of the original.

As I learnt only then from Omar Abou Riche, it was Swinburne, my favorite poet, who acquainted Fitzgerald with the works of the great Omar and induced him to give the Western world knowledge of the *Rubaiyat* in verses as immortal as the original Persian text.

Perhaps it is no accident but *kismet*—the Arab word for fate—which, by bringing me recently in contact with new friends from the ancient but reborn Middle East, has helped to revive memories of my childhood and youth when the Greco-Roman heritage we share with the Arabs colored and inspired my imagination.

Since he died before my twentieth birthday and long before I learned the facts of political life through experience, I do not know whether it was disillusionment or his love for my mother and desire to give her and their children a good life, which caused my father to devote his talents to making money soon after I was born. But it is clear to me from my memories of him and from the fragmented record of his life, which is all I possess, that like William Morris he was in revolt as much against the sordid ugliness of industrial civilization as against the iniquities of the "Capitalist System" of his time.

He loved music and poetry and beautiful things; was a connoisseur of wines; spoke several foreign languages fluently; loved to swim and sail, and enjoyed driving fast cars although this made my mother very nervous. In general, he had a great zest for living, and revelled in the athletic, as well as the intellectual pleasures of life. My earliest recollection of him is of a slim, trim man of medium height with broad shoulders, fine soft golden hair brushed back from a high wide forehead; clear blue eyes behind gold-rimmed pince-nez glasses perched on an aquiline nose above a reddish drooping moustache partially concealing a full lipped smiling mouth with prominent front teeth. And my happiest memories are of summer holidays in Sussex or Devonshire when Temple and I swam with him and he taught us to row and sail small boats.

I cannot remember ever having not known how to swim and read, but can recall being forbidden by my mother to read in bed, lest I "ruin my eyes"—an injunction which I cannot have paid much attention to because I have a distinct memory of lying in bed, early in the morning, reading a "Told To The Children" illustrated version of Lamb's *Tales from Shakespeare*.

Among the illustrations I can still dimly see Rosalind and Touchstone in the Forest of Arden. Perhaps because Rosalind, disguised as a boy and behaving like one, in contrast to the womanly Ceilia who aroused my contempt, appealed to me who during my childhood longed to have been born a boy.

Apart from shortsightedness my eyes have never troubled me. Mother used to insist that I take off my glasses in company in order to look pretty. She also insisted on putting my straight hair in curl papers at night. I remember an evening when she reproached me for having caused a quarrel between her and my father—a most unusual occurrence—because I had appealed to him to stop her forcing me to endure this discomfort. Also my father telling me in an endeavor to use his influence to support my mother: *"Il faut souffrir pour être belle,"* and myself in tears in a tantrum yelling "I don't want to be beautiful," which of course was not true. But my reaction to my mother's emphasis on my handicaps: shortsightedness and straight hair, as against her perfect sight and lovely naturally curly hair was, of course, to pretend that I was not interested in my appearance. At that early time perhaps I really did not care, being far more concerned in keeping up with my brother in sports and studies in spite of being a girl and younger.

Temple, two and a half years older than I, received a letter on his 18th birthday which conveys some idea of our father's personality and philosophy.

From our home at Ken Court, Tatsfield Surrey to Temple at Trinity Hall, Cambridge on June 9, 1913, he wrote:

My dear Boy,

May this, your eighteenth birthday, be a happy one, not because of anything material that may come to you upon it, but because you feel that you are making progress toward the responsibilities of manhood, because you feel your own powers developing within you, because your inward vision is embracing a wider view of the two worlds, the one which is inside and the one which is outside yourself. You are practically a man already, though for me always my dear boy, and I am happy to see you developing your own personality and being yourself. Whatever may come to you in the future, whether it be of good or ill, this is the greatest of all, to be yourself and no copy of anyone else at all times under all conditions. But for one's own satisfaction it is necessary that the self you are shall be such a self as you can be proud of yourself to yourself, not to other people. "*Il faut cultiver son jardin*" is the French phrase. The garden to be proud of is the garden that produces beautiful flowers, abundance of fruit, a sufficiency of humble necessary vegetables (without which you won't be able to cultivate your garden) and the fewest possible weeds. Alas! there is no garden quite free from weeds. The mistake is to take them for beautiful flowers and it is a mistake quite easy to make both for young and old. It is also a good exercise in philosophy, ethic and aesthetic, to examine what is a weed, what a beautiful flower and what a choice fruit.

I have every confidence in you, dear boy, and in your future. I won't say to you: "think high thoughts," but rather: "Think deep and wide thoughts and do clean deeds." Cleanliness is far above Godliness.

So long, old man. I shall be glad to see you at home again. It seems a very long time since you went away.

Chapter 3
CONTINENTAL INTERLUDE

My brother's and my upbringing was unusual; mine in particular, since as a child I attended the same boy's school as Temple: Peterborough Lodge on Finchley Road in Hampstead. The headmaster's daughter, Cynthia Linford, and I were the only girl pupils. I don't know how her Father had been persuaded to take me but it was Temple who had insisted that I enjoy the same advantages as himself. As I remember, or was told later, he had found I was being very poorly taught at my girls' school: "Memorizing the names of headlands on the West Coast of Scotland when she doesn't know what a headland is," had been his indignant comment.

When I was nine years old my father, who had contracted tuberculosis, was ordered to Switzerland and we all went with him to Arosa. There and in Italy for two years, we children had a wonderful time skating, skiing, and bobsledding in winter, climbing mountains and swimming in the lakes and sea in summer. We spent part of each spring and summer on the Italian lakes and Riviera, where we "discovered" Portofino, as yet barely known to tourists. There the fishermen's wives and daughters sat outside their whitewashed houses on steep narrow streets in the bright sunlight making the exquisite laces my mother loved to buy. Also there was San Frutuosa, lost little town approachable only by sea. One glorious summer we spent two months in Corsica travelling about that wild, romantic island in a horse-drawn carriage, but spending most of the time at Ajaccio where Temple and I swam naked on a deserted beach to which we walked along a road lined by marble tombs.

Rapallo, Santa Margharita and Sestri Levanti, Genoa and Milan, Pisa and Livorno, Lugano, Como and Lake Maggiore; driving by carriage and walking long stretches over the Simplon Pass from Domedossela, whose hotel had, I thought, the unique name "Run to the Post" (*courir a la Poste*) but actually must have been Couriers of the Mail.

Bright unforgotten distant years of my most happy childhood spent in some of the loveliest places in the world, giving Temple and me lasting memories of beauty to carry with us the rest of our lives.

We attended no schools but were taught for an hour or two a day in winter by an old German-Swiss tutor in Arosa. Our father spending his days on a chaise longe on the veranda was always there to answer our questions and impart knowledge which we could never have obtained from a formal education. We read books and we listened and learned from the talks and discussions of our parents with friends and acquaintances from many lands in the cosmopolitan atmosphere in which my multilingual internationally minded father fitted so well. Since we were never repressed but only taught good manners Temple and I had no inhibitions to make us feel awkward or shy and speechless in the presence of our elders.

Unforgettable among my father's friends in Arosa were Herr Lockhoff, a jovial Dutch artist and the dainty fair and smiling Baroness von Klockner from Dresden, who herself resembled one of that city's famous porcelain statuettes. Lockhoff whose tuberculosis was incurable was to die soon after we returned to England. Irene von Klockner lived long but disappeared without trace in the senseless Anglo-American bombing of the open city of Dresden in 1944 which burned alive more civilians than the atom bomb dropped on Hiroshima. Just before the Second World War, Mother and I were to meet her for the last time in London.

In late summer Temple and I climbed quite high mountains alone with a Swiss guide, once reaching the peak of the Aguille de Tour, ten thousand feet above sea level. In winter, besides skiing and skating and playing ice hockey, we took part with adults in the two and a half mile races on our bobsled named Mephistopheles, clad in white wool jerseys with red flannel devils on our chests and caps. Temple sometimes steered, but we won our notable victories when piloted by Mrs. Moreland, the sporting wife of a New Zealand doctor, with Temple and me as crew and a man called Bray as the "break." I still have in my possession a silver beaker inscribed with our names on the memorable occasion when, in 1909, we won the Lucy Challenge Cup, to the amused surprise, friendly applause or outrage of the competing adult teams.

I cannot have made much, if any, contribution as "crew" to our triumphs, far out as I see myself leaning in an old photo as we rushed around the most dangerous corner of the course; or by energetically throwing my slight weight backward and forward to help accelerate speed on the straight. It was probably due to my brother's insistence that I was permitted to participate in these races which actually filled me with a dread I never admitted to Temple, whose belief that anything he could do, I could do, too, spurred me on.

Writing to me a quarter of a century later from the Fiji Islands to congratulate me on the birth of my son in Moscow, Temple recalled my "winning that ice-axe for me" at Champex, where I had outraced the Swiss girls who competed in the two mile race around the Lake.

When my father was sufficiently cured to return to England Temple and I were left at school on the Lake of Geneva. The original intention had been to leave only Temple, but as usual I wanted to do whatever he did. As I recall, at Sestri Levanti on the Italian Riviera in 1909, I had become more and more restless, so that one evening after the usual happy day swimming and basking in the sun, I solemnly informed my parents that it was high time for me to go to school and start studying. Maybe it was the first stirrings of what my brother used to call my "Puritan conscience." Or perhaps it was simply because the joyful, easy, carefree life we children had for so long enjoyed had begun to pall. As Swinburne wrote in Temple's favorite poem, *Faustine*, "To feed a while on honeycomb is sweet," but man tires of the repetition of accepted rhyme.

So, when eleven and a half years old, I became a pupil at La Combe, Rolle on the Lake of Geneva, with my brother at school half a mile away across the fields at the Chateau de Rosey. By special dispensation I had the run of this school where I went for fencing lessons as well as to visit my brother.

The first summer of our separation from our parents I spent three weeks with Temple and the boys of his school in the Swiss Alps, dressed in boy's clothes and climbing the same mountains as teenage youths. Mixing with English, German, French, Swiss, Italian, and other nationalities, soon learning to speak French fluently and German fairly well, I was little aware of national barriers. I acquired an international outlook which neither my father's influence nor theoretical socialist teaching alone could have given me.

So long ago and far away and yet so well remembered, the two years I spent at school in French Switzerland were one of the happiest periods of my life.

16

At first I was the only English girl at La Combe and later one of two. I was also the youngest. The majority of the pupils were German girls in their middle or late teens "finishing" their education by studying the French language, literature and culture. The atmosphere was not unlike that of my home environment; studious, tolerant, kindly and with equal emphasis on study and physical fitness. We skated in winter, swam and rowed on the Lake of Geneva in summer; bicycled and went for long walks, picked narcissi in the fields near Montreux on spring expeditions to such historic sites as the Chateau de Chillon. For a fortnight each year the whole school moved to the Alps, where we climbed mountains and trod the lovely green valleys studded with flowers between the mountain peaks, picking Edelwiss on the few occasions we found this rare flower and chanting French songs. Indelibly imprinted on my mind is a vision of the glories of an Alpine sunset as I stood shyly among my new companions somewhere in the mountains, on the first evening of this happy holiday tentatively attempting to join in the singing.

Sport at La Combe was regarded as a pleasure, not a duty, and study—really hard study—was expected of us all ensured mainly by pride in achievement. Most of the girls came from middle-class German Rheinland and Ruhr families which had made sacrifices to give them their year or two of "finishing school" in Switzerland. In contrast to the English school where I went later, it was considered shameful at La Combe not to work hard and take advantage of the opportunity afforded us to learn all we could from teachers who loved to teach and whom one hated to disappoint.

The headmistress of La Combe, Mademoiselle Marthe Dédie, was a cousin of Monsieur Henri Carnal, the headmaster of my brother's school, and everyone expected them to marry. A handsome woman, I remember her best for the marvel of her long, lustrous and luxuriant black hair which reached almost to her feet and which she braided in thick coils in a crown on top of her head. Perhaps she was too strong-minded and independent for Monsieur Henri who was himself as handsome as a movie star and eventually married an American heiress.

The Chateau de Rosey in later years was to become a favorite school for gilded youth from all over the world, including the present Shah of Iran and other royal personages, besides sons of wealthy American families. In my day it had only one American pupil, a youth of about seventeen whose name I have forgotten, but whom I remembered because of the various troubles he got me into. He took me riding in his newly acquired automobile and promptly ran us into a stone wall. On another occasion he so outraged me by kissing me that I seized his best Panama hat and doused it in the fountain in the Chateau de Rosey courtyard. Once he induced me by the bribe of a carton of Nestle's Swiss chocolate bars to carry a note from him to one of the girls at my school.

This shameful episode is the more inexcusable because, when Temple and I were first left at school in Switzerland, our parents arranged credit for us at the grocery store in Rolle. Unlike Temple, I had refused this opportunity to buy chocolates or anything else, not wishing to enjoy special privileges denied to the other girls at my school. Yet in my second year I succumbed to the lure of a dozen large chocolate bars as the price for delivering a love note, or maybe an invitation to an assignation, to one of my classmates from a rich, young American. I never really liked him but he tempted me and I fell.

This incident is one of the most painful recollections of my childhood because of the feeling of guilt it gave me for long afterwards. I realized that I had betrayed the trust reposed in me by Mademoiselle Marthe who, because my brother was there, permitted me, unlike the other girls at La Combe, to visit the Chateau de Rosey whenever I wished.

My favorite among Temple's classmates was Jimmy Reiss, an intelligent witty and sophisticated Jewish boy from Manchester who was to remain my friend for many years. I still have a photo of him in a Chateau de Rosey performance of "*Le Chapeau de Paille d'Italie*"—a musical farce, two lines from which I was to remember all my life when enjoying myself too much. "*Mon cher mais c'est atroce/Nous faisons touses Les jours la noce.*" Which roughly translated means: My dear it's terrible, we're having a ball every day!

A decade and a half after our school days in Rolle, I was tempted to marry Jimmy because I was very fond of him and he was well-to-do, while I by that time was exceedingly poor. Temple used to say how nice it would be to have a brother-in-law with a wine cellar, and Jimmy and I had much in common. But in the 20's in London I had not given up my hope of romantic love. Besides, Jimmy seemed too "bourgeois" for me much as I enjoyed his company. He never did marry and probably had grave reservations in courting me since he thoroughly enjoyed his foot-loose life. But he was to give me help and comfort when I returned from Russia in 1936 with my political hopes and personal life alike shattered.

La Combe today, although still a more modest establishment than the Chateau de Rosey, has likewise become a fashionable modern school, as I found when I briefly revisited it in 1953 when driving through Switzerland from Germany to Italy with my son. The bedrooms now have running water and there are plenty of bathrooms, whereas in my day we each of us took our turn once a week for a hot bath in a cold outhouse. But the same solidly constructed, cream-colored, two-story, many windowed building still stands looking out upon the same distant view of the Lake of Geneva shimmering in the sunlight. The same *sentier* leads along the railroad line to the Chateau de Rosey along which I trod or bicycled so often.

There is the same tinkling of pianos in practice rooms; the same calm, studious atmosphere; the same lovely gardens shaded by ancient trees; the same flagstoned terrace in front of the main building where we sat in late afternoon embroidering or stitching as we listened to reading aloud of French classic literature. And, no doubt, there is the same curriculum demanding the same conscientious study and endeavor as in the days of my childhood, when we walked up and down in the early morning in the open air learning our grammar lessons from Larousse or memorizing French prose pieces, before classes began.

I can still recite the opening passage of the piece by Alphonse Daudet which begins: "*Les chèvres de Monsieur Seguin s'en allez tous dans la montagne,*" telling the tale of the beautiful little white goat who, despite the love and care lavished on her, was eventually gobbled up by a wolf because like Monsieur Seguin's other goats she would not stay in his lush pastures but sought adventure in the mountains.

So unchanging, widespread and influential are the disciplines of French education and the patterns of French culture that, in Algeria in September 1963, driving in the countryside where goats abound and conversing with my young Arab Moslem chauffeur, I started to quote the above passage and found that he, too, had learned by heart the same Daudet story about Monsieur Seguin's beloved little white goat!

Our places in school each week were determined by the "Dictée" which started classes. By my second year I was often at the top, and always near the head of the class, being able to take French dictation almost without spelling mistakes. I had perforce learned French fast since during my first year there was only one other girl who spoke English. Her name was Gretel Muthmann and her mother was an Englishwoman who had married a German velvet manufacturer from Crefeld in the Ruhr. Gretel helped me and cherished

18

me like an older sister and we have remained close friends until today, in spite of the two wars which split our worlds into contending halves, and in which she suffered both physical and mental anguish.

Whenever I now cross the Atlantic to Europe I visit Gretel, my oldest friend in all the world. During the Second World War she lost her husband and was twice bombed out of her home in Cologne where she practiced as a dentist. After taking refuge with relatives in East Germany she fled before the Red Army with her teenage daughter who was wounded by machine gun fire from an American plane. At the Elbe, in 1945, like so many other thousands of German women and children seeking escape from the Communist terror, they had waited in vain for permission from the U.S. Army to cross over. Luckier than most, thanks to being able to claim kinship with relatives in England, Gretel and her young daughter were eventually permitted to cross over the Elbe to safety. And her English relatives helped them with food packages to survive the hunger years which followed during the Allied Occupation.

Gretel's daughter, Liligret, is today the only woman musician in one of West Germany's most famous orchestras. Gretel herself is slowly dying from an incurable disease, having been finally laid low after her long and gallant fight to survive the vicissitudes of her life.* Today I remember her best in the role of Cyrano de Bergerac as performed at La Combe before an audience which included the staff and boys of my brother's school, the townsfolk of Rolle and leading representatives of the landed aristocracy of the vicinity. Gretel gave a superb and unforgettable performance as the swashbuckling Gascon hero of Rostand's famous play, shocking some of her audience by her fluent colloquial use of French swearwords which she added to the text. The play was not in any case one calculated to uphold the chaste principles of a school for young daughters of the respectable middle classes. Gretel, carried away by her exuberant interpretation of her role, and fortified by champagne, made it even less suitable. But she brought the house down in roars of applause.

It is not possible to remember what one was like in childhood. Nor are the memories of old friends reliable since they are prejudiced in one's favor. But perhaps one's best aspirations are mirrored in what one would like to believe is true according to their recollections. When visiting Gretel in Braunschweig in 1960 I asked her to help me understand myself and the course of my life by telling me what kind of a child I was. She said: "Even as a little girl, you seemed to me to be motivated by a passion for justice." Which reply, I realize, may be due not so much to Gretel's recollection of me at La Combe, as to the books I have written.

Gretel was not the only friend of my childhood days in Switzerland whom I still know, or with whom I have renewed contact in recent years. Following the publication of *The High Cost of Vengeance*** in the U.S. in 1940 and in Germany two years later I received many letters from Germany thanking me for having written this book in which I pleaded for justice and mercy for the defeated Germans and argued that only the Communists would profit from the dismantlement of German industry. Among the hundreds of letters I received from Germany several said: "You must be the Freda Utley we once knew at La Combe." Thus, forty years afterwards, I renewed contact with German friends of my childhood.

Best of all was to receive word from Madmoiselle Marthe Dédie, already in her eighties,

---

*Gretel, whose married name was Mohr, died after the type was set for this book.

**The Henry Regnery Co. Chicago, Noelke Verlag, Hamburg.

congratulating me on the publication of *The High Cost of Vengeance*, and telling me she was proud that I had been one of her pupils when I was a child.

On the other side of the ledger, I was attacked and smeared as "pro-German" or even as an apologist for the Nazis, by most "liberal" and even some conservative publications in America. It was then considered outrageous to insist that the Germans were no more inherently wicked or aggressive than other peoples, nations or races. I, with my experience of the kindness of my schoolmates at La Combe could not believe in the myth of German beastliness, and I knew too much history to accept the thesis of Germany's especial aggressivness.

Peter Blake, himself of German Jewish origin, (and today editor of *Architectural Forum* in New York) gave me much consolation when he wrote in Don Levine's *Plain Talk*: "It is said that cruelty is the result of fear; perhaps Freda Utley's great compassion is the result of her courage."

I should like to think this is true but in fact my compassion for the Germans arose from my own experience. Having myself not so long before lived under the shadow of terror in Stalin's Russia, I understood how dreadful had been the situation of the Germans under Hitler. Unlike most Americans or English I knew that the subjects of a totalitarian state cannot revolt, without outside help, and that the Germans during the war had had no choice but to fight for their country under the Nazi regime, or submit to Communist conquest. "There but for the Grace of God go I" was a precept I could never forget after my experiences of the terrible compulsions exerted on its subjects by the modern totalitarian state.

In 1952 and subsequent years when again visiting Germany, I found some of the dimly remembered friends of my childhood in comfortable circumstances, while others had barely survived the Nazi era, the war, and its aftermath. But our class of 1911 still managed to meet, occasionally, at some place on the Rhine. Moving spirit of these reunions, until she died in 1959, was the fair haired, blue-eyed and still comely Liselotte Euler, from Bielefeld, who had written in my "Birthday Book":

> *Tout change dans ce monde*
> *Vie, plaisir, climat*
> *Seul, mon amitié pour toi*
> *Ne Changera pas.*

Liselotte's son, at the age of sixteen, had been mobilized during the last months of the war and taken prisoner by the French, who sent him to do forced labor in the Lorraine coal mines where he was overworked and underfed for two years before being set at liberty. Visiting her together with my Prussian friend, Count Joachim Kalckreuth who had for four years been a starved prisoner of the Russians in worse conditions, we both vainly tried to persuade Liselotte's son that he should adhere to the West. He repeated the German equivalent of the American expression, "I've had it. Don't talk to me about democracy, or try to tell me there can be anything worse than being a prisoner of the French."

In contrast to Liselotte's bitter young son, there was Else Wollstein-Stolberg, who had been my companion at weekly riding lessons in Geneva, and who being Jewish, had suffered terribly during the war. She and her non-Jewish husband, who stuck by her, had survived, thanks to peasants, who hid them in a "fowl house," to use her own English description of their refuge. I was deeply moved when Else thanked me for having written *The High Cost of Vengeance* and glad to learn that her husband had been reinstated in the important job in the Cologne Municipality from which he had been ousted by the Nazis.

20

I was in my thirteenth year when, in 1911, I left La Combe to return to England. The four years I had spent on the Continent at an impressionable age were to have a lasting influence on my outlook. They were golden years of happy memories of a time when the world had seemed a most friendly place and I was little aware of national barriers created by ignorance, pride and prejudice. Never in the future would it be possible for me to think that my own country, or any other country, was the repository of all virtues, or to believe that "my country right or wrong" is an admirable sentiment. "Menschen sind menschen," as the Germans say—meaning that humanity the whole world over is much of a muchness. In short, my "Continental Interlude" had for good or ill given me an international outlook for the rest of my life. Like Tom Paine, who said, "Where liberty is *not*, there is my country," I came in later years to identify myself with those struggling for freedom and justice anywhere or everywhere on the globe.

No doubt I was spoilt at La Combe. Not only because I was a precocious child among teenagers and for most of the time the only English girl. There was also the fact that my parents were then rich, or seemed to be so, since my father spent his money as easily as he then made it. No other parents in those days came to visit their children in Switzerland in an automobile driven across the continent. As Gretel has told me, my handsome father and my beautiful mother dressed to perfection, made a terrific impact on La Combe, which gave me a special status of which I was totally unaware.

I remember only that the special privilege I asked for, by cable to my parents during my first days at La Combe, was that I should not be compelled to consume soup or drink wine at dinner!

How strange this sounds today when I like nothing better than wine with my meals! In those days on the continent half a century ago the purity of water was not taken for granted even in Switzerland, and wine, or wine and water, was the customary drink for young and old.

My father and mother, besides ensuring my freedom from alcohol later interfered with the disciplines of La Combe by objecting to the system which was so effective in forcing us all to learn French. This system seemed abhorrent to my liberal parents because it entailed "spying" and "denunciation." There were some dozen "billets" which one passed on to anyone one heard speaking their native tongue—meaning generally German but in my case English. Anyone in possession of one of these tokens at mid-day dinner time was kept in to write in full every conjugation of a French verb—which task, including I, thou, you and it as well as we and they in every tense, took most of the afternoon.

My parents' moral objections to this most efficacious system for forcing us all to learn French eventually persuaded Mademoiselle Dédie to abandon it for a short time during my last year. Instead of a hectic scramble to get rid of the "billets" before noon, we were put on an honors system of reward. Once a week, anyone who could get up and say "Je jure devans tout le monde"—swear to the world—that she had not spoken anything but French for the past seven days, received a cheap paper copy of some masterpiece of French literature. By this time French had become almost my native tongue so that it was all too easy for me to collect a book every week, thus acquiring a small library of French classics. The rules were therefore changed in my case to ensure that I should speak German, which I spoke very imperfectly. This created such confusion that the new system was abandoned before I went home to England.

Temple had not been as happy at the Chateau de Rosey as I at La Combe. He had come "to hate the food, the cold and the discomfort" and with the departure of Jimmy

Reiss and his Latin master, Mr. Hammond, he would have "no one in the whole world to talk to." Suggesting that Hammond be engaged as his "tuteur" Temple then aged fifteen wrote:

> I find him one of the nicest men I know, he is very interesting and very well read, an atheist, a liberal and his socialism is the same as ours, and he is not at all fast. He does not want at all a big salary. This is my suggestion, not his.

Following our return to England our situations were to be reversed. I was to endure four generally unhappy years at boarding school in England. Temple escaped a "public school" education and was tutored at home before enjoying a year at Cambridge University before the 1914 War.

Chapter 4

MY ENGLISH SCHOOL

The plunge from Switzerland into the frigid, unkind and alien atmosphere of an expensive English boarding school no doubt helped to lay the psychological foundations for the militant communism which, a decade later, was to supplant the vague academic socialism of my early youth.

Prior's Field, Godalming, Surrey, had been founded by Julia Huxley, granddaughter of the renowned Dr. Arnold, Headmaster of Rugby, niece of the poet Matthew Arnold, wife of Leonard, son of the famous Thomas Huxley, and mother of Aldous and Julian Huxley of future fame.* Mrs. Huxley was dead, but her school headed by Mrs. Burton Brown, had been selected by my parents on the confident assumption that it would provide as congenial an atmosphere as La Combe, where I had been educated beyond my years while uninstructed in several basic subjects. Instead, it proved to be no better than a British "public school" for boys.

There was no "fagging" nor infliction of corporal punishment by seniors on juniors, nor hazing of the weak by the strong. Instead there was mental, or perhaps one should call it social, bullying equally effective in enforcing conformity. Such offenses as studying hard, showing originality in dress or any peculiarity of speech or behavior, were punished by mockery or contempt and, worst of all, the loneliness which comes from alienation from the community, particularly hard to bear when one is homesick. Realizing I was having a bad time my parents offered to remove me during my first year, but, thinking that Prior's Field was typical of English schools, I saw no point in this and decided that I must endure it.

I was handicapped from the start by my slightly foreign accent as well as by my un-English upbringing. My "r's" were French "r's" and I recall my acute embarrassment when made to stand up to say "stirrup" over and over again, unable to pronounce it in an English accent while the whole class laughed.

Other disadvantages due to my lopsided education abroad had to be overcome. At La Combe there had been no mathematics classes, only optional bookkeeping courses for older girls. So although I had a wide-ranging acquaintance with French and English literature and considerable knowledge of European and ancient history, when it came to arithmetic I did not even know what LCM (Lowest Common Multiple) or HFC (Highest Common Factor) meant. And with regard to geometry and algebra, I had to start from scratch. Since I also knew no Latin, I was assigned during my first term to the lowest form with the youngest girls in the school.

Because I had acquired the habit of study, and was blessed with an excellent memory, I quickly caught up and rapidly advanced from class to class winning more prizes than anyone else, and arriving ahead of my time at the sixth, or top form.

---

*In Ronald W. Clark's book, *The Huxleys*, McGraw Hill 1968, there are many pages about Prior's Field where Aldous Huxley was a pupil when seven years old together with the original six girls.

My scholastic achievements counted for less than nothing in the opinion of my classmates, who gave me the nickname of "Brainy," in no complimentary sense. After I was chosen for the tennis and swimming teams which competed with other schools I was tolerated, if never fully accepted, as a member of Prior Field's "ruling class." But I continued to be a non-conformist. I won a prize for botany because collecting specimens of wild flowers enabled me to go for walks and escape playing cricket. La Crosse, which was played in winter, I enjoyed, but I only made the second team. I had from the first refused to wear a black or brown ribbon to bind up my hair, preferring a colored one to match the smocks which we wore over the regulation white blouses and skirts into which we changed each evening from our daytime grey tunics.

Accustomed at La Combe to associate with girls older than myself on terms of equality, I had no inkling of my social misdemeanor when, at the beginning of my residence at Prior's Field, I talked at length with two older girls sitting together on the "horse" in the gym at a Saturday night dance. This "horse" I should explain, was a leather upholstered contraption above which we vaulted with varying degrees of success during our daily mid-morning's gymnasium exercises which included climbing up bars and ropes besides marching and running in step. All of which muscle-building and posture exercises were one of the best sides of the curriculum.

My sins against the social code, at first unconscious, became deliberate. The spirit of rebellion was awakened in me as I opposed the social hierarchy and the conventions of my school. In later life the girls of Prior's Field came to symbolize for me the "imperialist British bourgeoisie:" class conscious, insensitive, sublimely self-assured, scornful of learning, and confident in their divine right to order the universe.

The profound changes brought about by two World Wars and England's loss of her Empire have since my day transformed the atmosphere of English private schools, as also the composition and outlook of English ruling circles. But, "the Establishment" as it is now called, endures.

I made some friends but they were either rebels like myself or passive non-conformists, or victims of 'the system,' whom I tried to help or protect after I had myself achieved the status of a prefect. One among the former was Margaret Waley, cousin of Arthur Waley, the famous sinologist whose translations of Chinese poems are widely known. Margaret, however, was one of those rare characters who are impervious to their environment. She walked alone and did not care whether she was popular or not, whereas I yearned to be liked and appreciated, although unable to make the concessions necessary for social acceptability.

Among other friends there was Nora Buchan-Sydserf—an unforgettable name—who, being Scotch, was better educated than most English girls, and had an amused contempt for the "sassenach" hierarchy which ran our school. Small and wiry with beautiful long, naturally curly golden hair and bright blue eyes, Nora's appearance was marred by a brace on her front teeth, prominently displayed as she laughed in unconfined enjoyment of her mimicry of the silly pretensions of the "tyrants" who dominated our lives. Tough, intelligent and witty, and still alive today, she was one of those who, in Voltaire's phrase, see life as comedy because they think, instead of as the tragedy it seems to those who mainly feel.

Another well remembered friend, with whom I have kept some contact over the years, was Dorothea Bluet from Buenos Aires. A short, fat girl with mousey straight hair and pale round face with no pretensions to beauty except for large sparkling black eyes, she was to marry a rich rancher and is today a happy grandmother in the Argentine. Neither "brainy" nor athletic, Dorothea was amiable and full of fun and uninhibited either by her teenage roly poly figure or her inferior status as "colonial" British. I can still see her in my mind's eye, dumpy, small body shaking with laughter, white teeth gleaming, eyes twinkling and moon face crinkled with mirth as our small group sat on the grass in a secluded corner of the playing fields on the edge of the woods sheltering violets, bluebells and primroses, in Surrey in the springtime after lunch. Here we played the "truth" game, asking each other searching, embarrassing questions which one was honor bound to answer unequivocally.

Others I remember are the older girls who befriended me during my first year at Prior's Field, Beata Crook and Phyllis Vickers. Beata who looked rather Rossettish inspired me to make such efforts in my attempts to play the violin that I became a minor member of the school orchestra—an achievement which filled me with greater pride than my success in classes, although each time I played my heart palpitated with the dread engendered by my consciousness of my inadequacies as a musician.

Phyllis, after a brilliant career at Cambridge University became a Factory Inspector in the Labor Ministry and was a most helpful friend in my days of poverty in London during the 1914 war.

I was on good terms with Margaret Huxley, sister of Julian and Aldous. I remember her brothers only as young men who, on the rare occasions when they spent a weekend at the school from which they derived their income, sat in state at the headmistress' table at Sunday dinner.

As I write and call to mind these and others who were my friends at Prior's Field, I wonder whether my years there were really as unhappy as I used to think.

During my last year I even became friendly with the girl we called "Carrots," a tall superbly built redhead with a freckled face, snubnose, bright blue eyes and engaging smile displaying perfect teeth, who was both the all round athletic champion and head girl. Her name was Mary Cooper, and I had originally hated her as the "boss" of the school and embodiment of all I most disliked at Prior's Field. Carrots, whose leadership I had for long defied, was extremely nice to me after the descent of my parents from affluence to penury. This is perhaps not so strange because today I can appreciate the virtues as well as the defects of the erstwhile British ruling class. As my brother Temple was to write two decades later from Suva, despite our being "intellectuals" we both liked "the barbarian English from the best schools."

Let me not forget in recalling my school impressions of half a century ago, my tennis partner, Marjorie Clemence Dane. A tall, sturdy blond girl with few, if any, intellectual or political interests, but with a good brain and a headstrong and romantic temperament, she was to become my close friend years later in London.

The only child of a "widow of high degree"—at least in her mother's own estimation—Marjorie had never met the "lower classes" until I stayed with her one summer in Sidmouth in Devonshire in the early Twenties. Accustomed from childhood to fishing and sailing whenever I could, I naturally made friends with the local fishermen, and Marjorie and I spent many a night "mackerel drifting," and helping to haul in the nets at dawn.

To me this was just the kind of sea-going holiday I had enjoyed in childhood. But to Marjorie it was romance. She fell in love with a fisherman who was squat and dark and muscular and almost ugly except for his large, black, long-lashed eyes—inherited perhaps from some Spanish ancestor cast upon the Western shore of England after the defeat of the Armada.

25

"Ern" Jenkins was not very bright and his political opinions of the day depended on whether he had just read the Conservative "Daily Mail" or the Labor "Daily Herald." He was far less interesting and attractive than "Stan" Harris who could neither read nor write but who had opinions he had thought out for himself, and whose physique was that of a legendary Norseman or Greek God. Stan was married to a wonderful girl called Kathie who was pretty and witty and well educated and who never let the hardships of a fisherman's wife get her down. They had a charming child called Peggy and theirs was a happy, life-long love. Both of them recur often in my story since they became and remained dear friends long after Marjorie and Ern had parted.

Marjorie's mother called in the Bishop of London to try to stop the marriage and took her on a sea voyage round the world on a luxury liner to cure her of her infatuation. It was all in vain. Although, as my brother observed at the time, if Marjorie's mother had not skimped on this voyage and had taken her on a P. & O. instead of a Japanese boat, she might have met a man who would have made her forget poor Ern.

Marjorie had £500 a year of her own—a not inconsiderable income in those days. She could afford to play at the simple life in a comfortably appointed cottage in Sidmouth after she married Ern. He, unfortunately, had all the "petty bourgeois" prejudices of the respectable British working class and this ruined their marriage. Marjorie had fallen in love not so much with him as with his way of life. But as soon as they were man and wife, he stopped her going out fishing with him at night, insisted on her wearing a hat and stop wearing shorts or slacks, and in general made her life so dull that she yearned to return to London.

Eventually they divorced with Ern keeping the house and being paid quite a bit of "alimony." Marjorie later married my college friend, Robert Ryan, a clever, sensitive and poetical Irishman in delicate health. This proved to be a most happy marriage, but he died soon after.

I owe much to Prior's Field. Not only did my experience there temper and steel me to resist and defy the powers which at all times and places in all societies endeavor to enforce conformity by one means or another. The teaching was also excellent. The trouble was that neither the headmistress nor the staff, with the exception of the games mistress, had much influence outside the classroom.

History, which was my favorite subject, was particularly well taught. At Prior's Field in my early teens I learned more history, ancient, medieval and modern, than most American college students. We were also given some understanding of political realities and the facts of power, so conspicuous by their absence in liberal academic circles today. For instance, it was impressed on me that Magna Carta which in later centuries came to be the Great Charter of English freedom, was nothing of the sort in 1215, at Runnymede. It marked instead, as I learnt at Prior's Field, the success of the feudal aristocracy in wresting back from a cruel and foolish king its own special privileges—then called "liberties"—curtailed by Norman kings seeking to establish a strong central government ensuring law and order and the protection of the weak against the strong. It was not until many centuries later that Magna Carta was transformed into a charter of liberties for all Englishmen. (In parentheses, I must here remark that a minor lesson impressed on me at Prior's Field is never to mix Latin and English by calling the Great Charter Magna Charta—a mistake so general that typists or typographers almost always get it wrong.)

History as taught in most American schools and colleges only briefly scans, or passes over as dark ages of little or no interest to the modern world, the millenium between the fall of the Roman Empire and the Rennaissance and Reformation. This general ignorance of medieval history seems to me the main reason why Americans in general, despite their good will and desire to help, fail to appreciate the problems of government in "underdeveloped" or backward countries. "Democracy" in such countries almost inevitably entails giving a free hand to the rich and powerful, just as in Thirteenth Century England, Magna Carta meant restoring to the Barons their "liberty" to oppress their vassals and serfs without fear of the Crown oppressing them or bringing them to justice.

Many years after, lessons I learned at Prior's Field, and subsequently at London University, enabled me to realize that China in the aftermath of the war against Japan was at about the same stage of political development as England and France in the Middle Ages, when the great need was for a strong government to enforce law and order and defend the country against its external enemies.

It seemed to me absurd and self-defeating for America to demand "democratic" government in China, when the real need was for an effective administration able to curb the centrifugal forces and enforce reforms. As I wrote in my 1947 book, *Last Chance in China*:*

> To call the Kuomintang Government "Facist" is the very reverse of the truth. Its powers are not limitless but far too limited. In war it lacks entirely the simian efficiency of the Nazi, Japanese and Soviet States. It interferes with the individual too little, not too much. Its sins of omission are far greater than its sins of commission. Its gravest fault is the ineffectiveness of its administration, and its failure to force through necessary reforms. It is too soft, not too hard.

Naturally, my political realism in writing that "an economically and politically backward country such as China requires an authoritative administration," called down on me the opprobrium of American "liberals" who accused me of a preference for tyranny even while they themselves were equating willingness to collaborate with Communists as the hallmark of a "democrat."

Owing to this confusion or the ignorance of most Americans of history prior to 1776, we "lost" China. This is a later story which I tell in my 1951 book *The China Story*.** Here I have digressed to show that in spite of my own foolishness in drifting into the Communist camp in the late Twenties, I never quite forgot fundamental historical lessons learned half a century ago at Prior's Field.

On the other side of the ledger, so to speak, I remember a talk given to us in 1913 by Mrs. Burton Brown, in which she compared Lloyd George's reforms with those of the Gracchi who had been murdered for their attempt to remedy social and economic injustice and thus 'save the Republic.' Conservatives who fail to see the need for change and the remedy of abuses pave the way for dictators who abolish all our liberties.

"B.B.," as we called our headmistress, was a great teacher and a scholar who related the lessons of the past to the present. She was a liberal in the true and original meaning of that much abused word, but also a realist without illusions concerning the facts of power and the basic motives of men, ancient, medieval or modern.

Few among her pupils appreciated her great qualities or liked her much. She was a big, heavy, majestic woman with a rugged masculine countenance, thick eyebrows and heavy jowels, who inspired awe, not affection. She was too remote to know how little effect

---

*Bobbs-Merrill, Indianapolis, 1947.

**Henry Regnery, Chicago, 1951.

either her teachings or her personality and high-minded precepts had on the conduct of her pupils. We were all afraid of her, and it was with a beating heart that we obeyed a summons to her book-lined, chintz-curtained study whose French windows looked out on a garden glorious in early summer with deep blue delphiniums and other brilliant flowers. Even I, one of her favorite pupils, vividly recollect that to be called to B.B.'s study in the early morning made my heart palpitate with nameless dread.

B.B.'s daughter, Beatrice (whose shortened name of Bice we pronounced bitch) was a thin-lipped spinster with an artificial smile who was actively disliked for what we instinctively recognized as only a veneer of sweetness, light and charity covering her lack of warmth and humanity, and the conceit which then as now is the besetting sin of class conscious liberal intellectuals.

"Bice" gave me individual instruction in Greek to enable me to acquire sufficient knowledge within a year to pass the Cambridge "Little Go." She spent most of the time trying to inspire me with a vision of Socrates in the false image of a non-conformist parson. The fact that I actually passed Cambridge University's entrance examination at the age of sixteen, in Greek as well as Latin, was due to my excellent memory. I memorized the English translation of Plato's *Apologia* and Zenophon's *Anabasis*, and learned just enough Greek to recognize which passages had been given for translation. However, I owe it to "Bice" that I learned by heart some lines from Plato's account of the death of Socrates in the original Greek, which I can still recite by rote.

My knowledge of Latin, unlike my Greek, was not synthetic. I really learned Latin at Prior's Field, thanks mainly to our Classics teacher, Miss Richards. She was a neat, small, reserved woman with a well-developed sense of humor who never curried popularity, or like the games mistress and some others, sought to stimulate endeavor by arousing inordinate affection—a "pash" to use our word for the unhealthy, adolescent adoration of pupil for mistress in our exclusively feminine society. I remember Miss Richards although I have forgotten the names and faces of other mistresses at Prior's Field, because she was an inspired teacher who could make even Latin grammar and composition interesting, and the reading of Roman poetry and prose an absorbing pleasure instead of a chore.

I can no longer read it with ease, but my good grounding in Latin syntax and logic, and the clarity of expression required by the exigencies of the Latin tongue, together with my earlier French education, taught me to endeavor to express my thoughts succinctly and logically instead of taking refuge in the verbosity and ambiguity, or mushiness, which in our day and age enables many writers to hedge on their convictions. I do not pretend that my writings have measured up to classical standards, but I have always endeavored to express my meaning clearly and unequivocally.

Long before I went to Prior's Field my thoughts and aspirations had been colored by Greek and Roman myths, legends and history.

One of the first books Temple and I read was an abridged version of Chapman's translation of the Iliad and Odyssey, with illustrations by Flaxman copied from Greek vases. The garden of the Hesperides, the siege of Troy, the wanderings of Ulysses and Aeneas, the battles of Marathon and Salamis—the whole beauty and wonder of Greek myth, legend and history, had given me visions from childhood of a lovely land of marble temples and sunlit seas where men first dispelled the mists of superstition, ignorance and fear.

But, until I came to Prior's Field I had no more than a romantic vision of the glory that was Greece or of the lasting contribution made by Rome to the foundations of Western civilization.

28

Thanks to Mrs. Burton Brown, I also acquired some appreciation of the connection between art and religion, politics and philosophy, truth and beauty. One evening a week in the winter and spring terms, "B.B." lectured to us on Greek, Roman, and Renaissance art. Her lectures were illustrated by slides, and although I can recollect little of what she said, I can still visualize some of the photographs of temples, statues and pictures shown to us on the screen. Mrs. Burton Brown gave me the small measure of understanding of art of which I am capable, together with a deep and enduring appreciation of the Greek genius and its lasting influence.

Temple always said that my artistic tastes depended on my political and ethical values, meaning that I had no pure aesthetic appreciation of art. Which is no doubt true and explains why I have no appreciation of most 'modern art' which to me conveys only confusion. Seeking and admiring clarity of thought and expression, I can see no sense in pictures without meaning, or whose meaning is deliberately obscured.

The classical influences of my childhood and youth stayed with me all my life. For some twenty years, until her death in 1963 at the age of 93, I was privileged to count Edith Hamilton among my friends. This outstanding American classical scholar comforted and encouraged me in Washington decades after I was a child at Prior's Field when I was cast down by the failure of my best books. She chided me gently, saying that if one is determined to "witness to the truth" as one sees it, it is inconsistent to yearn for the fruits of the transitory success which come to those who seek popularity. "The excellent becomes the permanent," she wrote, quoting Aristotle, in her inscription to me in one of her last books.

Edith Hamilton also tried to instruct me as to how to get my views heard by a wiser presentation than was my wont.

Mrs. Burton Brown's lectures on history and art compensated for much else lacking at Prior's Field. Now that I am much older than she was when I listened to her with rapt attention, I recognize my debt to her teaching and can forgive her for having failed me at a critical period in my life.

I was one of her favored pupils, not because she had affection for me, but on account of my scholastic record. I won more prizes each year for proficiency in more subjects than anyone else. I even won a prize for Divinity, although I was a free thinker, exempted from church attendance. I acquired a leather bound volume of Meredith's poems, which I still possess, for general knowledge of the Bible, in April 1913, when I was fifteen years old and in class VB. (Lower Fifth) The following term, summer 1913, I won the school "Essay" prize for a dissertation on Machiavelli. This time the book given me was Cary's translation of Dante's "Inferno," which was a more fitting choice as my reward than Meredith's "Poems" may seem as a Divinity prize. In my essay on Machiavelli, I argued that there was not really such a disparity as generally supposed between the Florentine's advice to tyrants, as expressed in his "Prince," and his eulogy of Republican Virtues in his "Commentaries on Livy"—the Roman classical historian. As I saw it, when fifteen years old, men are usually ready to condone, or even approve, actions taken by their state or country which they condemn when taken by an individual, so that what seemed admirable "virtue" in the Romans was regarded as wickedness in an individual Italian prince.

I wish I still had this old essay of mine. All I can now remember is its main argument that Machiavelli's precepts for Princes—his description of how tyrants maintain their power, which came to be called "Machiavellian,"—was not different in essence to the precepts and practices of the Roman Republic or modern nation states.

Mrs. Burton Brown, expecting that I would reflect glory on Prior's Field by future academic achievements at Cambridge University, gave me special facilities for study. She lent me books and during my last year installed me in a room of my own in the hospital annex where I could read late or early instead of being subject to school rules. But in the end she let me down so badly that she did more to awaken my budding revolutionary outlook than anyone else in my early life.

When the war came in 1914, my father was ruined. I was sixteen and had just passed the entrance examination to Cambridge University. Mrs. Burton Brown, confident that I would win laurels for Prior's Field, gave me a year's free schooling. I began working for the Cambridge "Higher Local," an additional examination which women candidates were also required to pass, but it soon became clear that I should not be able to take advantage of the scholarship which I was almost certain to secure, because my father would be unable to contribute anything to my support. Instead of arranging for me to go to London University—where, as I learned years later, I could have obtained a scholarship sufficient to enable me to continue my studies—"B.B." cast me off, as no longer of any interest or value to Prior's Field. Nor did she let me down gently.

She made it brutally clear to me that my presence at Prior's Field was no longer desired, and caused me acute shame by letting it be known that I was at school free because my parents could no longer afford to pay my fees. When I passed the Cambridge "Higher Local" with flying colors "B.B." reserved her congratulations for the girl who had passed with lower marks but had the financial means to continue her education.

Today, six decades later, I remember the shock and disillusionment of the discovery that Mrs. Burton Brown had never had any personal regard for me, having all along been concerned only with the academic laurels I was expected to win for her school. After I was precluded, on account of poverty, from being of any value to Prior's Field, she cast me off without compunction or compassion.

Thus in the summer of 1915, I left school with few regrets and some bitterness, thanks to the personal experience which taught me that the social system could fling one into poverty from security, and prevent one from continuing one's education whatever the proof of one's mental qualifications.

Chapter 5
WAR YEARS

My departure from Prior's Field in August 1915 marked the end of my *jeunesse dorée*. I was plunged from affluence and security into poverty and a hard struggle for existence. Nor was the transition made by slow and easy stages. It was more like the abrupt expulsion of Adam and Eve from the Garden of Eden they had failed sufficiently to appreciate.

My last year at school had been darkened by the money worries of my parents. We had pawned my silver and ivory-fitted monogrammed dressing case to pay my fare back to school and provide me with a little pocket money for my last term. But I had continued to live in comfort, eat well, study and play games as also to believe that my father's financial difficulties were only temporary. I still expected to get to college. But after I came "home" to find we no longer had one, my great expectations faded fast.

My parents were now almost without resources and my father was beginning to succumb to the tubercular infection which had been only partially cured in Switzerland. His precariously restored health depended on his continuing to live in the country which he could no longer afford to do. Our beautiful house and garden at Ken Court had been given up, our furniture sold, and the proceeds used to pay off business debts. Mother's jewels and furs, if not already sold or pawned, were gradually being disposed of to pay for groceries and the rent of the furnished lodgings in Hampstead where we now lived. My brother, who had enlisted in the army in August 1914 after a year at Cambridge had by now received a Commission in the Connaught Rangers and was soon to be fighting in France.

I was seventeen years old when I left school and was flung upon my own resources to earn a living. The only way open seemed to become a governess in the old tradition of decayed, or decaying gentlewomen. First, for a few months, I stayed in my Williamson grandfather's house, where my mother and father, together or separately, briefly took refuge.

Grandfather was looked after by my two maiden aunts, Flossie and Nelly. I remember Flossie as a thin emaciated woman with huge cavernous dark eyes below a high, pale forehead surmounted by abundant plaited braids of silver streaked dark brown hair. Her smile was beautiful but her nervous fingers clutching mine aroused aversion instead of love and made me want to escape from her bedside. She was a typical unselfish and self-sacrificing Victorian spinster who let herself be bullied by my tyrannical Grandfather, a tall, majestic handsome old man with a long white beard and hawk-nosed face who could have served as a model for one of the formidable and self righteous prophets of the Old Testament.

Flossie had inherited some money from their elder brother Len, and during the last destitute years of my father's life it was she who kept the wolf from our door. Besides providing my parents with 10 shillings a week from her own small income, she occasionally managed to extract a few pounds from my Uncle Ted, who was carrying on the family business. She also induced my grandfather to make us some small loans, all of which were carefully recorded in his will as debt against anything my mother should inherit from him.

My Aunt Nelly, baby of the family, was vivacious, vain and pretty with a trim figure, curly dark hair and sparkling eyes, fun-loving, dainty and elegantly dressed. She ought to have married well and been happy. Frustrated by my selfish grandfather whose daughters were expected to devote themselves to serving him, she had sublimated her longing for a husband and a home of her own, into a passion for cleaning and polishing and keeping things orderly and tidy. Nelly liked to sing and the only amusement I remember in the large dark living room was striving to strum the piano and sing with her in tune. Both of my mother's spinster sisters adored my Uncle Ted, youngest child and only surviving son of my Grandfather's nine children, whose occasional visits and many children supplied the main comfort and joy of the barren lives of my aunts.

My favorite aunt was Fia who, after marrying a not much good husband called Arthur Daggett, had become a successful saleswoman in women's lingerie in London. Mother, although letting Fia help us out with gifts of clothes and food, did not really like this energetic aunt of mine, who in appearance most closely resembled my Williamson Grandfather and had inherited his business sense. To me, she now stands out as the only one of my many aunts with whom I had a certain affinity because she had the guts to battle the world despite the handicap of being a woman. She was fond of me and gave me lots of beautiful underwear and nightgowns as a trousseau when I went off to Moscow in 1928 to live with Arcadi without benefit of clergy.

The oldest of Mother's six sisters, Bessie, was plump and prosperous and exceedingly respectable and conventional. Her eldest son Tom, a tall, heavy set, amiable young man, flirted with me, flattered me and occasionally took me out to dine and dance, bringing a little gayety into my life during this dull and dolorous period of my teens.

There was also Maudie, the black sheep, or whatever the equivalent term is for a female. The widow of an actor, she had three beautiful children and little visible means of subsistence besides the charity of her sisters until her daughter Doris became a show girl.

Lastly there was Minnie, a professional invalid who spent her life in bed expecting everybody to be sorry for her and provided with a generous allowance by my grandfather. Indeed my bevy of aunts ran the whole gamut of Victorian and Edwardian female types.

I should explain how it came about that my father was ruined and unable to restore our family fortunes.

Shortly before the war he had invested all his capital in an agency for Austro-Daimler cars—precursors of today's universally known Mercedes Benz automobiles. The Balkan war had hit the agency hard and the 1914 war finished it. He would no doubt have recovered from this misadventure, as from others in the past, had his tubercular trouble not been revived and aggravated by worry and London fog.

My father's hobby was mathematics and his bedside reading the Differential Calculus. He had become absorbed in the discovery, or mathematical working out, of a new curve making possible the construction of a rotary pump without the usual valves and springs. This "Utley Curve" as it came to be called could have made our fortune had it not been for the War. As my father now painfully discovered, no new, unproven invention could secure either government backing or private financing in England at that time.

After the war, when my father was dead, although Temple and I with great difficulty managed to keep up the patent payments for some years, we eventually lost out and my father's invention profited only others.

In a printed prospectus issued by the Kitson Engineering Company, which developed my father's invention and put it on the market in the Twenties, the KITSON-UTLEY ROTARY PUMPS were shown to "derive their superiority over other pumps from the Utley Curve," which "is not a circle but its shape is such that both edges of the blade or impeller maintain contact with the curve continuously when the rotor is rotated and the sliding movement of the blade through the rotor is uniform for each degree of rotation. These Pumps have neither valves nor springs, consequently they work for long periods without repairs."

Arthur Kitson, as far as I know, derived as little benefit from the Utley Curve as the Utleys. A dynamic and successful American engineer and businessman, his main interest was currency reform and abolition of the gold standard. He was a "Douglasite," if anyone still remembers them. This is probably the reason why he failed to make money for himself or for us and lost control of the Kitson-Utley Pump through bankruptcy. I have a dim recollection that my mother received two hundred pounds from Arthur Kitson as a down payment but that was all we ever got. For many years, however, we were to retain, if no longer the dream of revival of the Utley fortunes, the hope that Mother would eventually receive some income from my father's invention.

My letters to Mother through the years contain frequent references to "the pump"—accounts of interviews with lawyers when we expected to be able to sue with success to obtain payment of royalties from those who had acquired the design of the "Utley Pump;" fleeting offers of settlement which never materialized; the recurring difficulty of raising the money to retain our patent rights. We finally lost out because we did not have the financial resources needed to fight. My father's old solicitor friend, J. J. Edwards, at 28 Sackville Street, who helped us without charging a fee, was either just too old or too lacking in experience in this field of law to protect our patent rights.

Life in my Grandfather's gloomy mansion, where he was eventually to die in his nineties, soon proved as unendurable to me as to my parents. I found a job teaching, which paid me enough to rent a small furnished room of my own and to buy a modicum of food and some badly needed clothes. I lived largely on bread, margarine and marmalade. Fortunately, one of my school friends, Sybil Hesse, lived not far off in the pleasant suburb of Didsbury and I was always welcome at her parents' home to spend a night or a weekend—have some fun playing games, enjoying good food and beautiful surroundings. I had befriended Sybil at school when she was having a hard time on account of her shyness and the fact that she enjoyed an egg at breakfast by special request of her parents who thought she was delicate. Her parents, with typical Jewish generosity, offered me a home in their house if my Grandfather would pay my fees to study at Manchester University. My Grandfather, now in his eighties, refused, not having changed since the days when he had denied my mother the education he could easily have afforded to give her. Sybil, whose parents in 1915 changed their name from Hesse to Hescott on account of the hostility during the 1914 war against anyone with a German name, has remained my dear and loyal friend although nowadays when we meet in England we have little in common besides the memory of times shared in our distant youth. In London in the twenties, I emancipated her from her wealthy Christian-Jewish bourgeois environment, and the domination of her beautiful and imperious mother, by getting her a job with the League of Nations in Geneva. There she blossomed out, made many friends and enjoyed herself immensely before getting married—inevitably, perhaps, to a prosperous Jewish businessman despite her longing to break away from her original environment.

In 1916 I left Manchester to take a job as a resident governess in Hampshire where I coached a boy called Ian for his private school entrance examination. There I lived very comfortably but was bored and lonely, so that early in 1917 I was glad to become a clerk at the War Office in London at a starting salary of only 35 shillings a week. This enabled me to be re-united with Mother and Dada in the small house they had managed to rent in the suburb of Lewisham and furnished with little besides beds, a few chairs, and packing cases which served as kitchen, dining and writing tables. My memories of this short interlude with my parents are few. The most vivid one is of a night when having got water heated for a bath, the air raid warning sounded and the lights went out. This did not mean much or any danger in those days and I did not abandon the rare luxury of wallowing in hot water by candlelight to go down to the cellar.

I also recall, I know not why, waiting for my father to board a bus in Whitehall after he had told me how nice I looked in the new thin, dark blue Voile dress I had just bought for ten shillings, out of the first money I earned at the War Office. When so much else of far greater importance has been forgotten, I can still see in my mind's eye the texture, color and form of that dress as well as remember how little it cost.

With shame I also recall the irritation I all too frequently showed at home at Dada's coughing. I must have realized that he could not help it, but I could not help wanting to escape from the sound of it. He was a very sick man endeavoring by the utmost use of his will power to overcome the disease that incapacitated him.

My father's gallant spirit shines through in the letters he wrote during the 1914 war while he was in London vainly endeavoring to market his invention and Mother was enduring the cold charity of her father's home. They are replete with assurances that "the outlook is very promising." Old friends or former colleagues, now Members of Parliament or in important government positions, are giving him introductions and backing, leaving little doubt that he will "get a good job either in the Inventions Bureau or in Munitions." In June 1915 while I was still at Prior's Field, he wrote to Mother:

> Dearest:
> I am feeling very much better and my voice is very much better too, so do not feel uneasy about me. I am resting thoroughly, going to bed early, not smoking, drinking no whiskey, taking my eggs and Horlick. In fact doing all I ought to do and nothing I ought not. I am really better, dear, coughing less and feeling stronger . . . .
> My darling, I am unhappy that I have made your life so miserable. I cannot be happy until I have got life straight again for all of us and it is hard to do so as things are, but I will do my best.
> I love you, dearie, now as always . . . .
> If only I were well and strong again, things would soon go right. As it is, bear with me and know that I think all day long of your courage and your devotion to me.
> Goodnight, sweet.
>
> Ever your true lover,
Willie

Although my father's friends among "the high and mighty" did little more than give him introductions which led only to unfulfilled promises, he, like my brother, aroused affection among all those among whom he dwelt.

While his wealthy friends such as Reeves Smith, managing director of the Savoy Hotel Company, and his fashionable wife "Maudie," did no more than occasionally invite him to dinner at the Berkeley where they lived, the landlady of his Hampstead lodging house on Crossfield Road was so generous and kind that she charged him no more than it cost her for the meals she provided.

In spite of his illness, my father had written, "a number of letters to everybody I could think of who could possibly help" and had "some nice letters back." Sir Sidney Oliver, Secretary of the Board of Agriculture, had replied saying he would see what he could do to help. "The fact is, however," my father wrote:

> You never saw anything like the confusion and chaos there is in all the Government offices I have been into. Everybody seemed to be running up and down doing nothing, nobody ever knows where anybody else is or what they are doing. One day one man is doing one job in one department and the next day he is in some other department doing something else. It is heart-rending to see so much muddle and to think of the men at the front dependent on such an organization. I don't think much of Lloyd George's management of the Munitions job. Everybody tells me it is the same thing all up and down the country—muddle and mess everywhere, five men doing one man's job in one place and in a few places one man doing the work of ten men. The Inventions Bureau itself seems to be overstaffed—that is, they have too many men there already, but they are most of them totally unfit for the job. The Secretary practically told me so himself, and said I was just the sort of man he would like to have there. The difficulty was to make room for me. Anyway it is evidently only by hammering again and again at different doors that one can hope to get in. The difficulty is that I have not much strength to do the hammering with, especially when the weather is so beastly as it has been this week.

By 1917 my father's spirits had begun to flag as his health deteriorated at an ever faster pace, and his hopes of either a job or the adoption of his invention by the Munitions Board sank to zero. But he was as ever more concerned with my mother's unhappiness in Manchester than with his own "tiredness" and "the cold East wind" which had compelled him to rest at home.

Now that I have for many years been a citizen of the United States, and for years before a foreign resident in this generous country, I realize that it must seem incomprehensible to most Americans that neither my father's wealthy friends nor those whom he had helped in former years, gave us any material assistance in those days of adversity. It was not in the British temperament or tradition to give or receive "charity." You kept "a stiff upper lip" and starved or died quietly.

Former friends of my parents would occasionally invite us to a luxurious lunch or dinner—but none of them ever thought of helping us financially. Perhaps this was also our own fault since my parents pride forbade their asking or taking help from well-to-do friends.

At the time, all this seemed natural. The contrast with America, which I came to know many years later and where I have experienced great kindness and generosity, is so striking that for all her faults, the United States will always remain my chosen country.

My father's health continued to deteriorate and we knew he would soon die unless he went to live in the country. My school friend, Phyllis Vickers, lent us her family's summer cottage in South Cornwall where the mild climate offered hope of preserving his life. When my father and mother went there in the fall of 1917 I was left in charge of their few remaining salable possessions consisting of some rare books. I remember going off

35

during my lunch hour at the War Office to sell a vellum-bound edition of the original text of Burton's *Arabian Nights* while Zeppelins were hovering over London. The policeman at the side entrance warned me to stay under cover and when I refused, told me that my blood would be on my own head. Of course, there was little real danger. It was child's play as compared with the bombings of World War Two. In any case, I was too intent on meeting the bookdealer who would enable me to send some desperately needed money to my parents to heed the friendly advice of the Bobby outside the War Office. It is a measure of my preoccupation during the war with pressing family cares that I remember this incident so clearly, but have forgotten the immediate impact made upon me by the Bolshevik Revolution which occurred at about this time.

Temple, unaware of quite how bad things were with us, was enjoying the war as he enjoyed all life's experiences.

After being wounded on the Somme in 1916 he was sent to Mesopotamia in command of a draft of the Connaught Rangers. Writing to us from the Durban Club in Natal in June, 1917, before sailing further East, he told us that his long stopover at the Cape had been "one of the best times of my whole life, which you know is saying a lot." He had seen in the newspapers that the 16th division, in which he had fought in France, had gone "over the top at the Messines ridge show," and hoped we had sent him the casualty list. "I wish I had been there," he wrote from Durban, "really and truly I do." He had been "lazing about aboard ship, lying in the tropic sun" while his friends had gone to their death and it had made him feel "absolutely mad at the time."

"It is so funny," he wrote, "how I always get soft and easy times shoved on me against my will—yet this has been a wonderful time. This is a lovely country and I am coming back here sometime. How my wretched draft can still sigh for England is beyond me. India is even more fascinating we are told. I do not think I could ever stop wandering now. I always had a tendency that way, and the sort of life that has been thrown at me has developed it beyond all bounds. I think I had better become a naturalized gypsy.

"You know I was complaining when last at home that I was getting old and slightly tired. All that feeling has died away and I have recovered that old primitive *joie de vivre*. Life is a good game played quickly. Incidentally I must quote you some verses of Robert Service I have just come across:

> This out of all shall remain
> They have lived and have tossed
> So much of the game shall be gain
> Though the gold of the dice has been lost.*

"Shall we adopt this as a family motto?"

* * *

The death of my father in January, 1918, brought me the first great grief of my life. I had loved him dearly, and thought him the most wonderful person in the world—wise, tolerant, kind, never ill-tempered, and until the last absorbed in the course of history rather than in himself. Arriving in Cornwall on leave from my job at the War Office in London I saw him choke to death as his exhausted heart could no longer pump blood through his diseased lungs. The night before he died, when half conscious, he pronounced his own epitaph, saying: "I, Willie Utley, born Skipton in Craven—just missed being great."

He had missed becoming great, or even successful, because he used or dissipated his

---

*Identify.

exceptional intelligence, talents and energies in too many endeavors; or perhaps because he loved life too much and had savored it too fully to pursue only one objective. Before he died he murmured Shakespeare's lines about the undiscovered country from whose bourn no traveler returns, and said he was curious to know whether he had been right in thinking that death is nothingness.

Among the cherished letters which my mother preserved through the years there is one from Temple dated December 1, 1917 from Mesopotamia, the land between the Euphrates and Tigris rivers now called Iraq, written in pencil on sweat stained green paper, a few months before my father's death which contains passages which express better than anything I can write today, an epitaph on the life of my father and mother as well as Temple's sanguine temperament:

> Really though, Mother, horrid as things are now, don't you think that taking yours and Dada's life as a whole, you have had more of the good things of life than the average? You have had some real joyous times. You have had some most wretched times, but adding them together, is not every moment of pain canceled by a moment of pleasure, and a surplus of pleasure left? That is more than can be said of most people's lives.

> At the bottom of your heart, would you not sooner have had your life and your present condition, than say the life of Mrs. Reeves Smith. Dada and you have played high, won greatly and lost greatly. You might have played low and won little, and lost little. You were greater than that though.

> Do hang on both of you. You mean more to me perhaps than you imagine. You are the only permanent thing in my existence. The only two human beings I care a fig for. I have a great many pals, but of all who have been killed, not one has made me drink a whiskey more or less to their memory. For all my buck and bravado, home, which means no country, but you and Dada, is a great deal to me. You see you are the only home I shall ever have, for I am quite convinced that I must never marry. First, because I would make a wretched husband; secondly because all women that attract me physically would make most wretched wives. Moreover, I value my freedom and my solitude too much. And as I live my life I could not afford to give any hostages to fortune. So please remember that you are the only thing without myself, without you I would become a complete egoist.

> I think I will shut off the self-revealing emotional stuff now.

The entire population of the Cornish village where my father died came to his funeral. Many of them had done all they could to help my mother while she nursed him in the two-room cottage which had been their last refuge. Some had fetched water for her from the pump across the road; others had carried groceries from the nearest shops several miles away, or brought gifts of cooked food. And when I arrived at midnight from London two or three days before he died, I was met at the nearest railroad station and accompanied on the three-mile uphill walk in moonlight to the lonely cottage where my parents lived.

The pastor whose last services my father, still an agnostic, had rejected, blessed his grave. We had no money for a tombstone, and in any case this seemed as unimportant to me as it would have seemed to him. He had been born in obscurity in Yorkshire and lies

37

in an unmarked grave in Cornwall, but he lived a full life and left to his children an abiding memory of a man who, even though he "missed being great" had the quality of greatness.

My Williamson grandfather, who had grudgingly allowed my mother ten shillings a week during the last year of my father's life, cut off even this pittance after he died. I brought mother to London where we lived in a small cold water flat on the £2.10.0 that I was by then earning.

With a rent of sixteen shillings a week and war prices for food we had a hard time. I used to walk to work to save twopence in bus fare, and eat a meager lunch most days at "Sebastian's" in Soho where a substantial ham sandwich cost only six pence and a cup of good coffee only a penny or two. I greatly appreciated the boon afforded to my young appetite by Mrs. Williams Ellis, who worked under me at the War Office and provided sandwiches of bread and jam in mid-afternoon with tea. She was comparatively rich, being a "grass widow" with an allowance from her officer husband. She was, no doubt, a lady of very easy virtue, but she was generous and kind, and sufficiently competent in her work for me not to feel that I was being bribed by jam and bread to cover up for her.

I was starved for other things than food during this period of my life. I could not afford pretty clothes and I had few opportunities to enjoy myself. Mrs. Ellis invited me to parties where the company she kept may have been rather vulgar and was certainly not intellectual, but was jolly and kind. I spent Armistice night with her and her friends in gay and riotous fashion but in those days I was very abstemious and unlike the others ended up sober.

My first "romance," if it can be called anything of the kind since it never got beyond the stage of lunches and dinners, holding hands and a few kisses, was with an Indian Army officer called Farrell. By this time I was a section head with a semi-private office and he frequently came visiting for the ostensible purpose of consulting me on questions of payment to officers of the Indian Army who came under the jurisdiction of my section of "Finance 2." Captain Farrell was a tall slim, black-haired, violet-eyed, beguiling Irishman who in his courting used the gambit of having a wife who misunderstood him. Thanks partly to the warnings of Mrs. Ellis, who was as wise in the ways of men as I was ignorant, I failed to succumb to his charm although I was greatly attracted to him. He was good for my morale at a time when I was lonely and poor and out of my element and had no confidence at all in my feminine allure.

My last recollection of the debonair Captain Farrell who could well have been the hero—or villain—of a Kipling story or a Ouida novel, is his "Indian Gift" of a gold wrist-watch. After having delighted me with this wonderful present prior to returning overseas, he took it back a day or two later, telling me that his wife had found out about it and raised hell. Today, I wonder whether the real reason for his strange behaviour was my failure to "fall"—in other words, be seduced. Which episode recalls to me a story my father liked to tell about his bachelor days. His "laundress," as the Temple charwomen were called, had come to him one day with a woebegone face and said: "Sir, you have seen my pretty daughter?"

"Yes and a nice attractive girl she is."

"Well Sir, a terrible thing has happened; she has fallen and I don't know what to do."

After my father had commiserated with her, she remarked with a Juliet's nurse smirk: "She would fall again for a trifle, Sir."

In later years I often recalled this story because it seemed so apposite to the behaviour of many liberal "fellow travellers" of our time. After first falling for the lure of communist promises of a good time to be had by all and later disillusioned by "Uncle Joe Stalin" after the war, they are still today all too ready to "fall for a trifle," whenever it suits the Kremlin's purpose to appear conciliatory.

While resisting the blandishments of Captain Farrell, I began an enduring friendship with Walter Field and Russell Green who were my "opposite numbers" at the India office on the other side of Whitehall. I knew them first only as voices on the telephone, in arguments as to whether their office or mine was responsible for this or that officer's pay on this or that duty, in this or that theater of war. We became personally acquainted after Russell Green and I began swapping Latin quotations, and engaging in discussions on the classics in which we vied with one another in displaying our erudition, thus wasting government time in conversations which bore no relation to the war effort. Walter for his part, delighted me by his flippant remarks concerning the bureaucracy in general and War Office versus India office in particular.

Soon Russell and Walter were "dating" me or, more accurately, Russell did the dating and Walter the paying when we all three dined together either at Walter's club in Whitehall Court, or at some Soho restaurant. Walter who had been rejected for military service on account of his bad eyesight, came from a well-to-do Jewish merchant family from Glasgow and lived with his parents in Hampstead. He later became my brother's closest friend. There was to be a time when I thought I loved him and he was to remain my friend all his life until he died in England in 1959.

Russell Green, who was of proletarian origin, his father being a factory foreman, had obtained his school and University education on scholarships and had won the Newdigate Prize Poem at Oxford where he was a friend of Aldous Huxley's.

He had married young and was separated from his wife who came from the same "working class" background and who must have had a hard time living with Russell who was as unhappy as only a selfish class conscious intellectual can be.

Russell Green imagined he was in love with me and used to send me poems which flattered my ego but failed to inspire any physical response in me. I never took him seriously, although I pitied him and had an affection for him without believing his sorrows were any more real than the love he professed for me. I laughed with Temple at the ardent verses Russell addressed to me expressing his love and his "faith that from betrayal breathes again," and was flattered rather than offended by the contempt and despair he voiced at my frivolity or cold-heartedness when I made fun of him.

I should be grateful to poor Russell Green whose great expectations of his own genius were never to be fulfilled. He gave me sorely needed confidence when I was "young and twenty." Together with Captain Farrell and Walter Field he dispelled my fear engendered at Prior's Field that to be "brainy" was tantamount to being unattractive as a woman.

Among the few relics of my youth in printed or written form which were neither confiscated in Moscow in the 30's nor destroyed in London in the Blitz, there is a slender volume of Russell Green's poems, published in 1923 on the flyleaf of which is written:

> To Freda Utley,
> Indescribably yours,
> Russell Green

Below this is written: "What was that superb impromptu euphuistic epigram? 'The hobby horse of your discontent becomes the Pegasus of your ambition?'—Ah God, the tragedy . . . . there was a King in Thule . . became a clerk in Whitehall."

Russell Green, although an egotist and an inveterate poseur, had the redeeming quality of being able to mock himself. Maybe, he might have been a "King in Thule"—meaning a great bard—had he been born in another age instead of driven by economic necessity to become "a clerk in Whitehall." But had the divine spark of poetic genius burned brighter in him, it would not have been drowned in self-pity, or stultified by his need for security, and he would not have sunk into obscurity after his brilliant beginnings.

Today in my seventies, I can perhaps take pride that I once inspired some quite good verses by a minor poet, as when he wrote:

> When time and change have taken me from your eyes
> And I am home again in solitude
> Think of me not as one whose heart pursued
> Each sudden fire that on the marshland flies.
> Not as the reckless fugitive from despair
> Caring not of the road of his escape
> From the impending shadow of the shape
> Of love betrayed and of the lost betrayer.
> Think but of one adrift in the storm of time
> Who saw the cloudwrack sundered by a star
> And with a new faith followed from afar
> The light untrembling in the air sublime.

In the same volume of his published poems, he included one written when he was mad at me because, when rejecting his daily demands to see me, I had capped one of his classical quotations by citing Juvenal's lines that pleasures are best enjoyed if rarely indulged in. As printed it reads:

JUVENAL

> (Who said:
> *Voluptates commendat rarior usus*
> Which she quoted)
> He had lain at feasts that toiled from sun to sun,
> Drunk daylong draughts of brute oblivion,
> Drowned spirit in the dead sea of desire,
> Parched even sense to dust in sensual fire,
> Withered his heart in the burning sand of remorse
> Till age came limping on . . .
> This senile raker of imperial styles
> Prying about with scatologic eyes!
> This bombous crater of exhausted force!
> Shall he suffice to curb the youth in me?
> This desiccated dotard! Shall I see
> The pure and vernal passions of my brain,
> The faith that from betrayal breathes again,
> The ardours I imagine—all that I am,
> Butchered to make a Roman epigram?

Today I read with a smarting of the eyes close to tears Russell Green's outpourings in verse—sublime or ridiculous. I am no judge of modern poetry which has no rhyme or reason or makes much sense to me, so I conceive it possible that some of his poems are more beautiful and express more than many written in our time by poets who have achieved greater fame. Russell Green lacked the good looks or the charm which make women and the world fall for even second rate poets and other literary characters of small talent but great pretensions.

40

Meeting again in the late thirties after my return to England from my experience of love and terror in Russia undreamed of in his small world, I found Russell Green complaining of his mistress's unfaithfulness and failure to understand him just as formerly he had complained of his wife's shortcomings. I have long since lost touch with him and do not know if he is still living, but the truth of his line that "the hobby horse of one's discontent becomes the Pegasus of one's ambition" is incontrovertible.

During the war years the international outlook I had acquired form my father's teachings and my continental education prevented me from becoming a 'war patriot'. I could not hate the Germans, among whom I had dear friends and who had been so kind to me at La Combe, and my knowledge of history precluded me from believing the war propaganda which represented them as being a peculiarly aggressive or wicked nation. Then, as in later years, I always enquired, how come, if the Germans were so aggressive it was not they, but we, their Teutonic English cousins, who had acquired an Empire upon which the sun never set?

I had some prejudice against the French as the most chauvinist and military-minded nation in Europe, as a result, no doubt, of the overdose of French literature I had swallowed while at school in Switzerland, which had given me a conception of France as a nation eternally seeking *la gloire* and honoring the Napoleonic tradition above the revolutionary. But I had in general no national or race prejudices and believed that men are much of a muchness everywhere in the world.

My good grounding in history at Prior's Field also caused me to distrust the League of Nations as an instrument to ensure peace and democracy. I can remember mustering the courage to get up at a public meeting in 1919 to suggest that the League appeared to be one of the victors against the vanquished and might prove to be no better than the Holy Alliance set up after Napoleon's defeat to preserve the *status quo*.

Among my vivid memories of this time is the profound impression made on me by Sybil Thorndyke's performance in Euripides *Trojan Women*, put upon the London stage shortly after the Armistice while the starvation blockade of defeated Germany was being continued in order to force the Weimar Republic to submit to the Versailles 'Diktat'. In this play, written during the war between Athens and Sparta, the victorious Greeks decide to throw Hector's young son Astyanax from the battlements of Troy, lest the seed of the Trojan hero survive to menace their hard-won victory. And the child's mother, Hector's widow Andromache, awaiting her fate as a Greek slave among the other Trojan captives exclaims:

> Ah, ye have found an anguish to outstrip all tortures of the East, ye
> gentle Greeks.

Time was in my youth, after the first World War, when all who claimed to be liberals opposed the peace of vengeance which was to make a second World War inevitable. I lived to see the contrast when, during and after the Second World War to "make the world safe for democracy," many of those who claimed to be liberals but were racists at heart, not only demanded the unconditional surrender of our enemies, but favored the Morgenthau Plan for the starvation of millions of Germans and the conversion of what remained of Germany into a "goat pasture."

O tempora, o mores, as the Romans said. Or better to quote one of the many memorable sayings of the greatest of all historians, Thucydides, who in recording the decline of Athenian humanitarian virtues during the course of the Peloponnesian War, wrote: "War, teaching men by violence, fitteth them to their condition."

Today, surveying the wreckage of hopes for an enduring peace which followed both

World Wars, it seems all too clear that those who lack the compassion and intelligence to spare their defeated enemies can never know peace. In 1919 an unjust peace imposed according to the precept 'woe to the vanquished' created Hitler and the Nazi movement. Today we have to contend with the vast power and ruthless will of our erstwhile 'ally,' Soviet Russia, whom we ourselves enabled to become a colossus bestriding Eurasia by our unprincipled and cruel demand for the unconditional surrender of our German foes.

Time was when the mills of God ground slowly, but in our day and age they grind exceeding fast.

Chapter 6
TRAVELLING LEFT IN BOHEMIA

Before the war ended I had attained a position of some responsibility as a "Junior Administrative Assistant" at the War Office earning a salary of £250 a year which rendered life easier for me and mother before my brother came home from the war.

Temple, after returning from Mesopotamia on leave following Dada's death, had been posted to France where he was wounded and gassed at Le Cateau shortly before the Armistice in November 1918. Discharged from hospital early in 1919 he joined us at 68 Jessel House, Judd Street, opposite St. Pancras Station.

His experiences and mine since our childhood and early youth had been so different as partially to account for the divergent paths along which our destiny or our characters were to lead us in the years to come. He had escaped my bitter experience at an English boarding school and had enjoyed a year at Cambridge University before enlisting in the army at the beginning of the 1914 war. Subsequently commissioned as an officer and posted to the Connaught Rangers, he had lived under the shadow of death, been wounded twice, and suffered far worse deprivations than I while fighting in the mud and cold of the trenches in France and in the desert heat in Mesopotamia. But his worst periods of danger and discomfort had been interspersed by joy and ease, love and laughter, whereas my life had been drab. Untroubled by our mundane cares he had enjoyed the war in spite of hardship, danger and wounds. Having faced the ultimate test life seemed wonderful to him as to others who have escaped death. As he was to write years later on his hazardous voyage across the Atlantic in a small sailing boat, the most wonderful feeling in the world, bar only the ecstasy of love, is that following escape from danger. In Edmond Spencer's words:

Sleep after toyle, port after stormie seas,
Ease after war, death after life, does greatly please.

Now, together, again, after his high key and my low key sufferings, we confronted the difficulties and uncertainties of life in post-war England without money.

At the War Office I had become a branch secretary of the Association of Women Clerks and Secretaries. Through this trade union I obtained, in 1920, a bursary from the Ministry of Labor made available to war workers who could prove that their college education had been prevented or interrupted by the war. Thus, five years after I left school, and six years after I had passed Cambridge University's entrance examination, I became a student at London University. Temple, a year previously, had obtained a grant from the Ex-Officers' Fund to resume his university studies, and I now joined him at King's College.

Neither of us was really unfortunate in having had to wait so long to get a university education. The intervening years since Temple had left Cambridge and I had left Priors Field, had taught us both, through a variety of experiences, lessons rarely learned in the academic world. And because we had both had to wait so long to get our university education, we appreciated our opportunities more than most college students.

43

The Librarian at King's College told me that Temple and I were continually astonishing him by the variety of our interests. For both of us it was wonderful once again to be able to satisfy our hunger for knowledge, irrespective of whether the books we read would help us to pass examinations.

Originally, my bursary of £2 a week covered only two years of study, which did not permit me to enroll for the B.A. degree. So, like Temple, I started work for the Journalism Diploma. Both of us specialized in psychology and attended most of the B.A. Honors lectures in this subject along with our regular journalism courses.

Here I might mention a striking illustration of the difference between Temple's mind and temperament and my own. One night during my first year at King's College I had got home at 1:00 a.m. from a dance, to be told by Temple that our class would have a psychology test that morning. For an hour he coached me and I did so well that I gave 97% correct answers in our written test and came out top of the class. But Temple, who had enabled me to achieve this success in competition with a lot of Divinity students, got a rating of only 70%. The difference was that the challenge of an examination brought all my faculties to the highest pitch, whereas Temple was stymied by his greater and more profound knowledge of the subject, as also perhaps by lack of the competitive spirit which was highly developed in me. Moreover, he could not write as fast as I could because he had lost the use of one finger of his right hand when wounded in 1917 on the Somme.

It is easier to answer questions when one does not know too much, as I have long since realized. Yesterday, I could write articles and books very fast. Today, I take much longer because I have learned enough to need to pause and reflect and ponder what I really think or believe. And, of course, today I no longer possess the exceptional memory of my youth.

Encouraged by Temple, who believed I could do anything I set my mind to, and determined that after having at long last got to college I must obtain an Honors degree, I entered for the B.A. Intermediate examination in the Spring of 1921, without having attended the preliminary courses.

For a few weeks I mugged up on my Latin and other subjects not included in the Journalism course, and thanks to the good grounding I had acquired at Priors Field, passed this preliminary first year B.A. examination. A feat which so impressed the King's College authorities that they induced the Department of Labor to extend my scholarship from two to three years, thus enabling me two years later to obtain my B.A. degree in History with First Class Honors.

Temple had tried to persuade me to take Honors in Psychology but I was more interested in history, economics and politics. He, having studied history during his pre-war year at Trinity Hall, Cambridge, had become interested in psychology during his years in the Army. But coming to realize that psychology without a knowledge of medicine was of little use, he became a medical student, after obtaining his Diploma in Journalism. Like my father, my brother was always as interested in the sciences as in the humanities and possessed a rare combination of "literary and scientific aptitudes" to quote from a testimonial given him by King's College recommending him as a "stimulating lecturer alike in history and in elementary science."

Although we profited in other ways from our Journalism courses, neither Temple nor I ever learned how to make easy money by catering to popular tastes. We both had a try at writing stories for magazines but they were always rejected. I remember endeavoring to get a soap opera type of story of a poor girl gets rich boy accepted under the pseudonym of Felicity Fitzmaurice. My failure was no doubt due to my story sounding too much like a parody of popular fiction. Temple with memories of his pre-war years at Cambridge when he had been influenced by the literature of decadence and had been able to indulge his love of beauty and "gracious living," fine wines and foods and furnishings, wrote stories in a neo-Oscar Wilde or early Waugh vein. His efforts were no more successful than mine for much the same reason since they read like a burlesque of such books as "The Portrait of Dorian Grey" and "Vile Bodies." One of his stories I remember involved a millionaire aesthete who had his bathroom fixed up with two tubs enabling him to plunge from warm scented water into an icy tub—a procedure supposedly calculated to restore his sexual virility following a drunken orgy the night before.

One writes well only when one writes as one pleases, not in conformity with actual or imaginary popular taste. Many years later, reviewers of the book Temple's widow and I compiled from his log book jottings and letters, written while sailing across the Atlantic and Pacific oceans on a small yacht*, praised the charm of Temple's fine writing which showed "the heights to which Utley might have risen had not death taken him."

Since my brother and I were supporting our mother, our bursaries were not sufficient for us to live on. We both gave lessons in English to foreigners, helped by our knowledge of French and German. We only got five shillings an hour and had to travel long distances by tube or bus to earn it in the late afternoon or evening after a day's work at college. But we were lucky in that our pupils were interesting people with whom we established friendly relations and whom it was a pleasure to teach. Temple had pupils at the Czecho-Slovak Legation—his "Checks" we called them—with whom he was brought in contact by his friend George Silva, translator of Kapeck's famous play, R.U.R., which gave the word "robot" to the English language. I taught Russian employees of the Soviet Trade Delegation and of Arcos, the equivalent of Amtorg in America.

During the war years I had been more concerned with my own and my parents' struggle for existence than with the class struggle or Socialism, or any idealistic notions of how to establish a more just and rational social and economic order. But once at college I began to take an active part in politics, becoming secretary of the King's College Socialist Society, and later chairman of the London University Labour Party. I joined the Independent Labor Party and became well acquainted with Fenner Brockway, Jimmy Maxton and other dedicated Socialists who led, or inspired, this Left Wing tail of the official Labor Party and opposed its underlying imperialist concepts.

As yet, I had no more knowledge or understanding of Communism and Marxist theory than the "Parlor Bolsheviks" or "Park Avenue Pinks" of the 30's and 40's. Nor did my first Russian pupils enlighten me. They were high Communist Party officials out to enjoy life in the "capitalist world" after the rigors of the "Workers Paradise" and for the most part confined their propaganda to jokes about England where they were enjoying the best years of their lives.

Then I met Plavnik, an old Bolshevik who had lived long years in exile in Germany after the revolution of 1905. To him Bolshevik theory was the breath of life. He was honest and sincere, although extremely vain. His English lessons usually became my German lessons and instruction in Marxist theory. Boris Plavnik was the best type of "Old Guard" Communist: courageous and sincere and self-sacrificing in contrast to the hypocrites and self-seekers who assumed leadership of the Party following Lenin's death. He was honest even in analyzing himself, which is a most rare quality. One evening he took me to listen from the gallery to a meeting of Russian Mensheviks in exile in England.

A Modern Sea Beggar, Peter Davis, London, 1938.

The speakers were Abramovitch and Dan, leaders of the Social Democratic minority which had split with the Bolsheviks in 1905. As we listened to the speeches, Plavnik got more and more excited and finally exploded to me: "He is a very *bad* man." "Why bad?" I replied. "Of course you disagree with him fundamentally, but that does not prove he is a bad man." Plavnik kept saying that he *knew* Abramovitch (or was it Dan?) was *bad*, *bad*, and I kept on saying, "How do you know he is a bad man?" Finally Plavnik replied, "Because he does not like me."

All of us are inclined to see evil in those who dislike us, but how few are candid enough to admit it!

Although so honest about himself, Plavnik shied away from realities when it came to his beloved Party. Whenever I pushed him into a corner by demonstrating the inconsistencies or contradictions of the "Party Line" he would tell me I had no understanding of dialectics. "Sprechen sie bitte dialektisch", he would adjure me, looking at me severely down his long nose when I argued that it made no sense to attack and undermine the British Labor Party as "social fascist" while also hoping for a Conservative defeat.

Plavnik was the most humane of men, and later on in Moscow where he and his devoted wife remained my friends, he sank more and more into his shell, unable to defend, but unwilling to condemn outright, the atrocities committed by Stalin. Like others among the best of the old Bolsheviks, he could not bring himself to face up to the fact that the revolutionary movement to which he had given his whole life had failed and degenerated into Stalin's tyranny. As the years passed, we saw less and less of him because meetings were too painful between friends who dared not speak their thoughts to one another. Plavnik was lucky enough to go into an insane asylum just before the great purge began; at least that is where he was supposed to be in 1935, and we knew his mental faculties had been failing since the death of his beloved wife a year or two before.

Shortly before my graduation in 1923 I defended the Soviet Union as the college speaker in a debate on Russia with H.N. Brailsford as the guest speaker on my side. Our opponents were Sir Bernard Pares, a "White Russian" emigré who had won high academic honors in England, and Cecil H. Driver, a fellow history student, who in later years became a Professor at Yale. When I next met Pares, thirteen years later, he had become a defender of the USSR, while I, back in England after my disillusionment in Russia, was holding my tongue for my husband's sake, but hating Stalin's totalitarian tyranny. The change, it seemed to me was not in us but in Russia. Like some other distinguished exiles Pares patriotism caused him to welcome precisely what I abhorred, namely Stalin's transmutation of communism into national Socialism; and of the Comintern into the arm of Russian policy.

Brailsford, meanwhile, standing steadfastly on his liberal principles, had become one of the all too rare British writers who dared to expose the horrors of Stalin's Russia in defiance of the powerful 'Popular Front' of 'Totalitarian Liberals' and Communists which was exerting so great and baneful an influence on Western public opinion and policy.

Cecil Driver's subsequent career exemplifies the academic rewards which accrue to those who never compromise themselves through extra-curricular activity or any expression of "controversial" views. He and I were rivals at King's College where his conservative bent endeared him to the head of the History Department, Hearnshaw, whereas my radical opinions and activities as Secretary of the King's College Socialist Society were disfavored. Yet such was the impartiality in academic judgement which has generally distinguished British universities that it was to me, not to Driver, that Professor

Hearnshaw awarded the Inglis Research Studentship, after I had won higher honors in London University's B.A. examination. Three decades later, invited to speak at Yale University by such conservative stalwarts as Professor Willmore Kendall, William F. Buckley and Brent Bozell, I found Cecil Driver securely ensconced as a teacher of Political Science, in good repute in the liberal establishment. Whereas I, despite my more distinguished academic record, had found myself precluded from obtaining a university appointment in America on account of my strongly expressed anti-Communist views which made me too "controversial." This is a later story referred to here to illustrate the "changes and chances" of life and the ambivalent meaning of "conservative" and "liberal" in our politically rotating world.

The Inglis Research Studentship at King's College paid only £50 a year and required that I conduct a weekly seminar on political theory. But it also gave me the opportunity to coach backward undergraduates for payment.

A year later I was appointed to a resident research scholarship at Westfield College for Women in Hampstead where I enjoyed the luxury of a bedroom and study of my own, besides free meals and a bursary of £100. Of course, I still had to contribute to Mother's support, but I earned extra money teaching Workers' Education Association evening classes, writing occasional book reviews for the *Daily Herald*, and contributing articles to the Independant Labor Party's *New Leader* (which, insofar as I remember, managed to pay only 10/ for an article) but was an influential weekly. Thus, I was enabled to study for London University's M.A. degree which, unlike that of Oxford and Cambridge, is rated as the equivalent of the American PhD.

The subject I chose for my M.A. thesis was research on the "Collegia," (trade guilds) of the later Roman Empire, thus combining my knowledge of Latin and the interest in ancient history I had acquired in childhood and youth with my modern political interests and activities.

During my two years' work for my M.A. degree I spent long hours in the British Museum deciphering collected Latin inscriptions from tombs, studying the Theodosian Code and Gothofredus' Commentaries thereon (available in a huge brown leather bound volume requiring a 2 ft. high stand to prop it up to be read) and reading translations from the Greek of the writings of such early Fathers of the Church as St. John Chrysostom in order to glean information on the status and condition of the workers in the last days of the Roman Empire.

My Director of Studies, Norman H. Baynes, Professor of Ancient History at University College, was the most inspiring as well as profound scholar I ever knew, and had a delightful sense of humor. At his yearly series of public lectures on the Byzantine Empire you could "have heard a pin drop," as the saying goes, except when his audience roared with laughter at his funny stories of saints and sinners, emperors and courtesans, hermits and foolish virgins, bishops and monks, and the 'sports news' in Constantinople where the chariot races between Reds and Greens at the Hippodrome were followed like American baseball games. The story I remember best, (which may be included in the small volume Baynes later wrote on Byzantium in the Home University series), concerned some beautiful girls in a Black Sea Greek City who mocked a Christian hermit who, being a 'fool for Christ's sake,' was revered by the ignorant but regarded as a lunatic by the sophisticated. As I remember the legend, this otherwise kindly old man had cursed the foolish virgins who teased him, and rendered them all squint-eyed. When implored to lift the curse which marred their beauty he replied that it was better for them that he not do so since had they remained beautiful they would certainly have sinned. Being now ugly, they were sure to be virtuous and go to heaven.

Norman Baynes, who died in February, 1961, at the age of 83 after a long illness, combined, in the words of his obituary in the *London Times,* "scrupulously exact scholarship with the gift of an imagination which he was not afraid to use." For this reason, "his lectures and writings have meant so much to generations of undergraduates who were enabled by his bold reconstructions to understand something of Jewish, Greco-Roman and Byzantine life."

Because I had specialized in ancient and medieval history—a rare choice since most students took medieval and modern courses—I had attended Norman Baynes lectures and small seminars as an undergraduate before he became my Director of Studies while I worked for my M.A. degree. It is to him I owe the wide horizons of my historical perspective, as also more inspiration, help and encouragement than from any other Professor under whom I studied. Today I deeply regret having failed to get to England to see him once again before his death, following my extensive travels in the Middle East of recent years when I visited Egypt, Lebanon, Syria, Jordan, Palestine and Iraq; all the lands permanently influenced by Greece and Rome which after they became part of the Arab world preserved much of our classical heritage during Europe's Dark Ages. And which, after having made so great a contribution to civilization in times past, are once again beginning to play an important role in history after centuries of obscurity under Turkish or Western imperialist domination.

My debt to Norman Baynes as an inspired teacher is incalculable. I also owe a great deal to him as a friend. In 1926 after visiting him at his home at Northwood I wrote to Mother, "He was charming, and has made me feel so much happier and less worried. He has taken my thesis to read again in order to help me to put it into final form for publication. He was so nice about everything and so really friendly. Do you know, just because I mentioned earlier on that I had been very occupied with your affairs which were going badly, he said I should remember that if I were in difficulties there was always £50 ready with him for me. Isn't he extraordinary?"

Many years later, after I had escaped from Russia with my two year old son and was nearly destitute in England prior to the success of my book *Japan's Feet of Clay,** Norman Baynes again wanted to help me financially. I can no longer remember whether or not my 'bourgeois prejudices,' not yet quite dead, prevented me from taking money from him, although I think I must have done so. The big thing was that Norman Baynes, the revered and beloved teacher of my youth, still held me in high regard and with considerable affection, despite my having abandoned the study of history to immerse myself in politics. Although he spent his own life in academic studies, he understood and sympathized with my descent to Avernus in the belief that the Soviet purgatory was Paradise, or at least a way station toward it.

In contrast to Norman Baynes, whose profound historical knowledge and perceptive intelligence prevented him from having illusions about Stalin's dictatorship, Dr. Laistner, Professor of Ancient History at King's College, was to shock me when I met him again some fifteen years later in America. In the 20's at King's College he had been a dyed-in-the-wool conservative who disapproved of my radicalism but, like Professor Hearnshaw, did not let his political views affect his judgement of my academic merits. But in 1941 when I gave a lecture at Cornell University where Laistner had become a

---

*Faber & Faber, London, 1936.

professor, he defended the Soviet Union against me. He was, of course, an Englishman and "Uncle Joe" Stalin was by then England's "gallant ally." Laistner was a handsome, blond Aryan type of fine physique, but a colorless personality who never married and lived with his mother. Baynes, rugged face, too wide mouth, beetle brows and angular figure was almost ugly, but his dynamic personality, character and intelligence rendered him singularly attractive.

* * *

Although the perpetual problem of how to get money for Mother still made life difficult for Temple and me, by 1924 we were much better off than when he first came home from the war.

We still lived in a small cold-water, three-room-and-kitchen flat at Jessel House, Judd Street, close to St. Pancras Station on the outer edges of Bloomsbury. But we now had a gas fire in the living room and a bathroom with a geyser to heat water, instead of having to light a fire under the "copper" in the little wash house behind the kitchen and transfer the heated water with a scoop into a tin tub in the kitchen which, when covered by a board served as a table.

Remembering our poorest years as students in London Temple was to write from Suva in the Fiji Islands shortly before his death in 1935:

> I have not to get up on a freezing, foggy London morning and light the copper before I get a bath. I have not to go dashing about all over London to earn 5/- an hour giving English lessons—I am probably a 'spoilt child of fortune' as I tell Zarathustra my half-caste Persian kitten, he is. I remember well that I have now got everything material I used to think I wanted when we could get nothing in Jessel House. Nevertheless, it was more fun in the Galapagos with Brun . . . .

Today, as I sit writing this book in my centrally heated house in Washington, D.C., with the wolf far from my door instead of howling nearby as during many of the years of my youth, I look back on the Spartan years of my life with nostalgia. So true it is that material comforts have little to do with happiness. Many who have always enjoyed them say this without knowing what it means to be without them. But I can claim to speak from experience, having known real poverty in England, and far worse deprivations in Russia than even the most 'underprivileged' Americans can imagine.

Although I was to experience far greater privation and discomfort in Moscow in the '30's, the niggardly poverty of our life in London in the 20's was harder to bear. Not only because it is in youth that one longs most for pleasure, pretty clothes, fun and gaiety, but also because it is far worse to be without money in an affluent society than to share the general poverty of neighbors and friends.

Arcadi, my long lost Russian husband, whose gift of humor sweetened our lives and helped me to make light of hardships and discomforts in Russia, used to say how much easier it was to be happy there than in the "capitalist world" where everyone longed for all sorts of unnecessary things. "Look," he would say with a twinkle in his eye, "in the bourgeois world people are never satisfied, but in Russia one feels fortunate if one manages to get a seat on a streetcar getting to work, or if one's soup at dinner contains a bit of meat."

All values are relative as Hadow, who once loved me, used to say during our student days. Although I have forgotten his first name, I can still hear his melodious Scotch voice with its rolling r's pronouncing this favorite aphorism of his, the truth of which has become ever clearer to me during the up and down course of my life.

49

I have no idea what happened to Hadow or whether he is still alive today somewhere in the vast reaches of the declining British Empire which Scotsmen of his quality did so much to create, develop and sustain. But the memory of his healthy ruddy countenance, vivid dark eyes, thick black hair, warm smile and sturdy figure clothed in an ill-fitting reach-me-down suit, revives in my mind's eye as I distinguish between the dim or well-remembered companions of my youth. He was one of the nicest men I ever knew and he would have cherished me and given me security and his mind was as good or better than mine. But he aroused no spark in me much as I valued his friendship and respected him for his goodness, intelligence and honesty. He was a down-to-earth Scot with his feet firmly planted on the muddy ground of reality who would have held me back from expending much of my life on an abortive quest for justice on earth.

Mother was a good cook who managed to provide us with a tasty and satisfying dinner in the evening during the hardest years of our student lives. Dinners which ended with strong cups of coffee, ritually brewed by my brother from beans freshly ground at the corner of our kitchen-dining-room table. Until this welcome end to the day, Temple and I endeavored to stave off our youthful appetites, unsatisfied by the ham or cheese sandwich, which, with a cup of coffee, was all we could usually afford to buy for lunch at the King's College underground cafeteria, except on the rare occasions when we won a few shillings, sometimes even a pound or two, betting on the horses. Many other students at King's could be found running out into the Strand between afternoon classes to buy a paper giving the racing results. The attraction of betting is, no doubt, greatest among the poor, and in our case we had been lured into temptation by having been given a tip about Spion Kop who won the Derby in 1920 at odds of 16 to 1. Mother and Temple had dared to stake several pounds on this tip, given us by our once-a-week charwoman whose sister's husband worked at a famous racing stable, and they enjoyed a long holiday together in Brittany that summer on their big gains. I, too, had won a few pounds and was able to buy some clothes, although unable to accompany them to France since I was then still working at the War Office.

We occasionally got another good tip from our charwoman and Temple also worked out a "system" which required that he do complicated calculations based on weights and age and past performance of the horses. By and large I think we won more than we lost by the shilling or half crown bets we usually confined ourselves to. The main thing was that these "flutters" added a little excitement to the daily grind, and sometimes enabled us to enjoy a good dinner with wine at some Soho restaurant.

As our economic situation improved we betted less and less and eventually abandoned the futile pursuit of fast horses as a means to make money.

Although I had missed out on Spion Kop there were other summers when I enjoyed a vacation abroad. Temple and I knew how to enjoy a cheap holiday on the Continent by travelling "hard"—third class—with bread, wine and cheese to sustain us on the journey, and finding some *auberge*, or small hostelry in places where no tourists and few foreigners came, and prices were so low that we could afford to pay them.

Speaking French fluently, and feeling ourselves carefree if we had a few pounds and a return ticket in our pockets, we went off together or separately to France or Italy on summer vacations returning home when the money was spent. At Camaret in Brittany, during that Spion Kop summer, Temple and Mother and Walter Field had discovered an inn where £2 a week covered the cost of room and board, including lobster or langouste, almost every day. Here, becoming friendly with the daughter of the house, I went fishing with her and her brothers at the dawn of many a happy day, and learned from them the words of Breton songs, still remembered.

This fishing was quite different from mackerel drifting in Devonshire where one cast long nets at evening and hauled them in at daybreak. In Brittany the fishermen depended mainly on the langouste (crayfish) they caught off the Cornish shores from large sailing boats which spent weeks or even months away from home. The dawn fishing at Camaret was more of a pastime or only a minor means to earn money. Ground bait was cast around the boat attracting multitudes of fish which we caught with small harpoons.

Besides holidays abroad I was lucky to have Marjorie, my Prior's Field friend, whose story I have already told in the chapter entitled "My English School." After marrying her fisherman in 1921 she was happy to have me visit her in Sidmouth whenever I could afford to leave London and enjoy the greatest of all pleasures to me: swimming in the sea. Nor was Marjorie my only good friend in Devon. There was also Kathy and her husband Stan Harris. Kathy was an educated girl whose widowed mother had run a boarding house and who had married an illiterate, but far more intelligent fisherman than Marjorie's Ern whose views reflected those of the newspaper he happened to read that day.

Many of my letters preserved through the years by my mother, now helping me to write this book were written to her while, for one reason or another, she was staying with Kathie and Stan Harris at their house on Old Fore Street, Sidmouth, ostensibly as a paying guest or lodger, but receiving the love and care and sympathy which are beyond price.

Mother accomplished wonders in decorating our small flat, where her "bedroom" with its black silk-covered divan and various-hued cushions was also our living room. We kept open house once a week with only beer or cheap Spanish wine and sandwiches with most of our guests sitting on the floor, but with good conversation and great argument lasting far into the night.

Temple, after passing his medical examinations at King's College, started clinical studies at St. George's Hospital in 1925. One of his best friends was Dr. David Frost, who married my college classmate, Dora, who later became the wife of Hugh Gaitskell, leader of the British Labor Party.

I remember Dora as a petite, very pretty girl with flashing dark eyes and beautiful curly black hair, who aroused the protective instincts of all the young men in our circle, although she was tough-minded, had a sharp and witty tongue and was eminently well able to take care of herself. In 1962 Teddy Joll, with whom I had long lost touch, wrote me a letter telling me about various members of the "Utley Circle" in Bloomsbury in the 20's, and said: "And there is dear little Dora, maybe wife of a future Prime Minister and of an eventual Earl." To judge from which remark, "steady Teddy" Joll, who became Deputy Registrar General of the United Kingdom before his retirement in 1960, and was our neighbor and close friend while he lived with Bobby in Jessel House, still felt protective toward Dora.

David Frost, unlike Dora, was the type of sensitive Jew without money and with an inferiority complex, which may have accounted, in part, for his joining the Communist Party years after I had already left it. After his and Dora's son was born, Temple warned David that he might give the same complexes to their child as those from which he himself suffered. As Temple saw it, Jewish parents were inclined by excess of affection to store up trouble for their children by making them feel themselves to be the center of the universe. Later, confronted with the realities of life, a child thus reared reacts by

51

developing either a superiority or inferiority complex, resulting, in turn, in behavior that alienates friends and creates prejudice.

I don't know what has happened to David and Dora's son. His parents were divorced long ago and according to what Dora told me when I visited her in London in 1953, David had been such a brute to her that she had left him to marry Hugh Gaitskell. Since God works in mysterious ways one can count it a good thing that, thanks perhaps largely to David's behavior to her after he became a Communist, Mrs. Hugh Gaitskell became uncompromisingly anti-communist, and no doubt also influenced her husband in that direction.

Yet, I remember David with affection as a gentle, intelligent and kind young man, and wonder whether if Dora had been less hard and ambitious, although so feminine in appearance and behavior, he would ever have taken the Moscow road.

Because David Frost was one of the most devoted, loyal and helpful friends Temple ever had, I am, no doubt, prejudiced in his favor. There were so many times when David "turned up trumps" when Temple was in trouble that I find it well nigh impossible to believe that he was ever the brutal husband Dora depicted. But I must admit that I never really liked Dora, no doubt because she possessed and exploited to the full all the feminine allure which I lacked. I was no doubt "catty" about her in those distant days, to judge from a letter written to my mother dated 5 July, 1926 in which I refer to "a man called Napier with whom both Robert and Dora have been very friendly but who seems to have fallen in love with me . . . Married of course, still it is quite pleasant and I have annoyed Dora very much." Showing that I was as inclined to female joy in conquest as most women, I concluded my letter by saying: "I am feeling better about life."

There are several other references to Dora Frost in my letters to Mother which revive my memories of this clever and attractive woman whom I knew so well when we both studied at London University and who was to become the "first lady" of the British Labor Party.

Since I am now dropping famous names, I should also mention Elsa Lanchester, another member of the 1917 Club who was a friend of Temple's and came to our parties. Her "boy friend" in those days was a musician singer and comedian called Harold Scott who never won fame and fortune, but helped launch Elsa Lanchester on her successful career long before her association with Charles Laughton. Elsa then was a girl and Harold in his thirties, or maybe even older since he was one of those small, slight, blond, blue-eyed types who never look their age.

Strange that although I never knew him well or liked him much, I can today still vividly remember Harold Scott dressed in grey flannel trousers and a worn tweed jacket, his high forehead surmounted by scanty golden hair and his long, thin nose slightly red at the tip above his full lipped mouth, strumming on the piano and singing a long forgotten song called "Thank God for the Middle Classes," with the refrain:

> If His Majesty the King
> Wants any little thing
> He sends for the middle classes.

One evening at our flat Philip Rabinovitch, chairman of the Russian Trade Delegation in London, "fell for" Elsa Lanchester after she and Harold had delighted us all by their comic skits.

Philip Rabinovitch had been a tailor in New York before the Bolshevik revolution, had a fine baritone voice and enjoyed singing, fun and good company. His rendering of "Black Eyes," and the "Volga Boat Song" (or Vulgar Boot Song as my friend Yaffle, the humorist and cartoonist of the I.L.P. called it) was superb. But he also took joy in singing such silly popular ditties of the time as "When it's nighttime in Italy, it's Wednesday over here." That evening long ago in London he and Elsa Lanchester sang a duet I should otherwise long since have forgotten, in which two derelicts on the Thames embankment tell one another:

The Times, The Telegraph
And all the papers says:
Money is much cheaper today.

Philip Rabinovitch and his wife Sophie, also a Party member, were to remain my friends until the end of my life in Russia. He became a Vice Commissar of Foreign Trade but was never a party snob. He had a sense of humor, courage and a kind heart, and he owed his rise to a leading position in the Communist hierarchy to his great abilities, which was rare, since the road to preferment for most was paved with the bodies of those they had denounced, slandered, or falsely accused.

Whenever in Moscow our housing difficulties were the greatest, Sophie Rabinovitch would invite me and my husband to take a bath in their well-appointed apartment—a tremendous boon in those days. And it was Philip Rabinovitch who secured us a room in the New Moscow Hotel when we were homeless. He respected my husband as one of the best "non-party specialists" working for the Commissariat of Foreign Trade, and there was doubtless an affinity between them since both were former members of the Jewish Social Democratic Bund.

It required both social and political courage in the 30's in Russia for Bolshevik "aristocrats" like Philip and Sophie Rabinovitch to welcome a "non-party specialist" such as my husband to their home. Looking back I realize that they were permanently influenced by the years they had spent in exile in America, where democratic personal behavior comes naturally.

When I finally left Russia in April 1936 following my husbands arrest, Philip Rabinovitch was to send his official limousine to take my son and me to the station, a courageous act in those times when even to speak to someone connected to anyone else arrested in the Great Purge was dangerous.

I do not know what happened in the end to Philip and Sophie or to their lovely daughter Nuria, whose piquant face, sylph like figure, and lovely smile revealing small perfect teeth which really were like pearls, are etched on my memory. She had been married three times before I left Russia in 1936 which was not unusual among the children of the Communist "aristocracy," but she had followed her heart and never became a snob like so many others who married for privilege and status.

Probably they were eventually liquidated since this was the fate of most of the best of the old Bolsheviks. Today, more than forty years after I first knew them in London, I can still hear Philip singing silly songs at Jessel House, in the days when it was still possible to be both a Bolshevik and a decent human being full of the joy of life.

Chapter 7
MARX, FREUD, LOVE, AND THE LIBIDO

Temple and I both belonged to the "1917 Club" on Gerrard Street, which had been founded in commemoration of the Russian Revolution. Its membership in the 20's included Ramsay MacDonald and other right-wing Labor Party leaders, as well as many left-wing intellectuals and politicians half-in and half-out of the Communist Party. It was a meeting place for avant garde writers, poets, artists, University professors and teachers of various hues from red to pink, collectively named "the bloody intelligents" by my brother.

The interest of many of them in the Labor and Socialist movement stemmed largely from their inclination to free love unconfined by 'bourgeois prejudice' or conventions. But among the members there were some outstanding writers and thinkers of our time. Such a one was Henry Nevinson, a grand old man who belonged to the 19th century liberal and classical tradition in which I had been reared. I remember him well as a tall, white-haired, still virile and handsome old man with sad, pale blue eyes and a drooping moustache partially hiding his sensitive mouth. Once after telling me how well I looked upon my return to London, tanned and fit after a holiday in Italy, he remarked: "Man should never have left the Mediterranean Sea, the fount of beauty and of Western civilization," or words to that effect, reflecting our love of Italy and Greece where freedom, love of truth and the concept of government by law were first conceived, and triumphed for a brief period between the long ages of darkness and tyranny before and after.

Describing Nevinson in his paper the *Daily News*, my father's friend A. G. Gardiner wrote:

> He boils with indignation or scorn, and throws discretion to the winds. He has a noble thirst for fighting forlorn battles. He does not care so much about the merits of a cause so long as it is the cause of the underdog. The underdog is always right because he is the under-dog. Let him become the top dog and the Knight Errant's passion for him is chilled. . . . This instinct is very apparent in such conspicuous crusaders as Mr. Cunninghame Graham and Mr. Nevinson. They bring into life a fine, uncalculating spirit of chivalry, the one touched with ironic scorn, the other charged with a fury of indignation; but both entirely unselfish and elevating, and both a little inclined to regard the question of odds as more important than that of merits. They love to be on the side of the failures, and distrust all success as, *ipso facto*, a little squalid.

Nevinson himself repudiated this "panegyric," not, as he wrote, that he would not like to deserve it, but because he saw himself as a man "much too easily appeased, much too considerate not only of my enemy's feelings, but even of his arguments." He insisted that he made up his mind with painful deliberation, so that "nothing but the calmest exercise of reason would ever induce me to take one side rather than another, although the first impulse of every decent Englishman is, of course, to favor the underdog," a remark as revealing about Nevinson himself as concerning the peculiarities of the English who, while generally pursuing their own self-interest with phenomenal success, have also tolerated and sometimes honored the minority among them who champion the oppressed.

In his introduction to his 1925 book *More Changes More Chances*,* Nevinson, with sublime disregard of his own motivations, or perhaps ironically, wrote:

> Guided only too cautiously in my endeavors to discover where reason and justice lie, I have never wasted time upon any lost cause, and indeed almost every cause for which I have contended has already won.

After cataloging these causes ranging from the freedom of Greece from Turkish misgovernment to the overthrow of Russian Tsardom, women's suffrage, Irish self-government and the advance of India toward it, Nevinson proclaimed that all these 'lost causes' or underdogs for whom he had done what he could as a journalist now "stood on top."

Happy Nevinson at that hour. I left England and lost touch with him soon after, so do not know whether, like myself, he realized how right Bertrand Russell was when he wrote that yesterday's underdog when he gets on top is most brutal because he has learned underneath to scratch harder in the battle for survival than those born on top. Yet he surely knew that the battle against tyranny must constantly be renewed in each generation with the enemy always in a different place under a different guise.

There were all too few old vintage liberals such as Nevinson at the 1917 Club fearlessly seeking and fighting for justice, truth, and beauty and an end to all oppression everywhere under the sun.

For the most part, the membership was composed of the careerists and camp followers of Socialism, or girl-chasers masquerading as *literati* or philosophers. Such a one was C. M. Joad who, following the Second World War, was to become for a while a preferred speaker of the British Broadcasting Company. He was one of the nastiest and most phony characters of the Bohemian World which had its center in the 1917 Club in the 20's in London. Joad made his reputation as a "philosopher" partly by lifting passages from Bertrand Russell's books without acknowledgement, or by plagiarizing them, but also by pandering to the need of men like himself to justify their unrestrained indulgence of their sexual appetites by highfalutin rationalization. He was so frankly cynical that when my brother asked him why he was learning folk dancing, Cyril Joad replied that the girls who went to the classes were for the most part intelligent young women yearning for culture, and he found this type most easy to seduce.

It was perhaps because the Bohemian society to which I then belonged outraged my Puritan prejudices or my romantic conceptions of love and politics, that I was to fall so easily under Communist influence. This may sound strange, but in contrast to the London left-wing intellectual society whose *mores* repelled me, the Russians I first met were decent and honorable men with concepts of the relationships between men and women which corresponded closely to my own. Lenin himself had replied to those who said that sex should be satisfied as simply as thirst, by taking a glass of water, by saying, "Yes, but who wants to drink out of a glass soiled by many lips?"

Reared without religious beliefs or fears of punishment for carnal sins, I had nevertheless inherited, or acquired, a view of life which caused me to recoil from easy indulgence in the pleasures of the flesh. Either for this reason, or because the love of my

---

*Harcourt Brace, New York.

mother and father for one another caused me to reject base substitutes, I was repelled by members of the 1917 Club who made casual attempts to add me to the long list of their easy conquests. I was upset, but nevertheless impervious to the argument that there must be something wrong with me physically or mentally when I refused to sleep with them.

Yet I yearned for love, and no doubt my increasing absorption in political activity was to some extent a sublimation of my sexual desires.

Part of my trouble was due to the several radically different environments in which I had lived since childhood. The Bohemian atmosphere of the society in which I found myself in London in the 20's was as alien to me as Prior's Field had been after LaCombe. I had been reared on Christian ethics but without Christian faith; taught to despise conventions but also to discipline myself and behave like a "lady." My mother had a gold cigarette case inscribed with the old French motto "Fay ce que voudra" but she did not really believe one should do as one pleases. Her ideals are indicated in the lines she wrote to me in 1940 when my own son was not yet six years old:

> I have just seen the New Year in. I have kissed Jon. I wish you and Jon the best of all things. I feel I shall not see another year. Do see to his character. He is such, such good stuff. Try and train him to what you call my old fashioned ideals. Your father and Temple were courageous and honest and truthful and had their own fine standards. If Jon will only give you as much joy and happiness, I cannot wish you better. All my love, dearest Fredakin and all my thanks.

I was perhaps a proof of Bertrand Russell's theory that the way to cure a child of undue preoccupation with sex is to give him all the information he wants in a scientific way so that he thinks there is nothing more to know, and that what he does know is uninteresting. I had been brought up with full knowledge about "the birds and the bees," and imagined that I knew everything when I really knew nothing. It was only after I read Shaw's *Mrs. Warren's Profession* in my early teens that I was shocked into awareness that there was something more to sex than I knew from my mother's aseptic teachings. In great distress I had gone to Temple for information, as was my usual practice when seeking knowledge, and he, albeit gently, had taught me some of the facts of life which mother's sense of delicacy and restraint had withheld from me in spite of her conviction that she was a "modern" woman. Yet even in my twenties I was still not only without experience, but also did not know how little I really knew.

Moreover, I had been reared on the works of the great novelists of the 19th century. *Romola* was one of Mother's favorite books and George Eliot's novels made an enduring impression on me. Since the one I remember best is *The Mill on the Floss*, I suppose that the sad fate of Maggie Tulliver, who ruined her life by the sin of loving out of wedlock influenced my own 'virtuous' behavior in youth. In a word, I was at heart still a 'Victorian' in matters of sex, although politically I had no respect for "bourgeois" values or conventions.

Although at Prior's Field I had found English upper class society alien to me, and since then been excluded from it by poverty, I retained some of its prejudices or preferences. As Temple once observed "I like intelligents, English and French—but I also like what David Frost calls the barbarian Englishmen from the best schools, and also Navy officers. Of course, Freda does too, really."

I suppose I did, too, "really," as evidenced by an unforgettable summer in Devon before my graduation. I was 25 then.

Intending to study in Devonshire solitude for my final B.A. examination, I met and fell passionately in love with a "barbarian Englishman." His name was Eric, and he was the games master at Harrow. He was also intelligent and very quick on the uptake without the distasteful characteristics of most intellectuals. He had a delightful sense of humor and was a dear, sweet lovable and kind person with a most happy temperament.

He was in fact everything my romantic imagination could ask for, but, unfortunately, he was married. To Eric, as to me, no "light affair" was possible. He could easily have seduced me but he loved me too much to take advantage of the overwhelming attraction he had for me—the feeling which comes so seldom in life when the presence of the beloved even across a room makes one's heart beat faster.

Divorce would have brought an end to his job or any possibility of another one in England in his profession. The only way out seemed to be emigration to Canada, which we actually contemplated, so that I came near to jettisoning my academic career in the north of the American continent in 1923 instead of in Russia in 1928. Our "affair" was further complicated by the fact that Eric's wife when I met her in London was so very nice to me that I felt ashamed. In the final event, both Eric and I, realizing that the end of an elopement could not be happy, since in spite of the strength of our attraction to one another, we had few shared interests, parted in sorrow.

He was a conservative and I was a radical Socialist, but we both had the same old-fashioned prejudices, or attitudes, about love which, no doubt, was one reason why I loved him so much. He was perhaps the one man in my life besides my future husband, Arcadi, with whom I could have been happy. No one else except Arcadi ever excited me so much, or aroused such deep feelings in me. Feelings which combined a powerful sexual urge with appreciation of the qualities of mind and heart of the man to whom one desired to give one's self.

Today, in my seventies, "with all passion spent," I still have rosy memories of that lovely summer in Devon by the sea when I went to bed each night with thoughts of the joy of meeting Eric early next morning on top of the cliffs which separated Branscombe and Sidmouth, at the trysting place to which we both walked two or three miles in the dawn; of long walks and swims together and of evenings at the "pub" in the small and very old village of Branscombe drinking flagons of home-brewed cider before we parted for the night.

The good constitution and strong muscles I owed to my upbringing had survived the hard years of poverty so that I could almost keep pace with Eric in the sea. That summer I swam the three miles between Sidmouth and Ladrum Cove, emerging so frozen that my limbs had to be rubbed to restore circulation. And I acquired a set of knives and forks as prize for winning the annual long distance women's swimming race at Sidmouth.

Remembering Eric forty-five years after, I can still see the lovable quirk at the corner of his generous mouth when he tenderly teased me. I suppose that his attraction for me was not dissimilar to that of my future husband, Arcadi, despite the differences in their origins, physical appearance, beliefs, and destiny.

Besides looking for a rare or impossible combination of Kipling hero and Socialist idealist, English "gentleman" and intellectual, I was also, no doubt, obsessed with a father-image or whatever the correct psychological term is.

Freud was all the rage in the 20's and I had studied enough psychology myself during my first year at college to be able to diagnose my trouble according to psychoanalytical theories. But I agreed with my mother who, one evening after a lot of talk about the *libido* and all that, exclaimed: "Well, it seems to me that according to Freud everything decent you do is done from a bad motive, while when you do wrong it's fine because you are not repressing yourself."

During this 'Freudian period' my brother fell deeply in love with a psychology student called Dickie, who looked like a Botticelli angel but believed in free love. She and Temple lived together for a year or two 'in sin' and parted in friendship when their passion was spent, Dickie eventually marrying a professor of philology and living respectably ever after. I never liked her much because she mocked my Socialist faith while I regarded her as woefully lacking in social consciousness, or a proper concern for the economic welfare of mankind. To her, as to many others in our circle of friends and acquaintances, Freud, not Marx, was the prophet of our age, and the uninhibited satisfaction of sexual needs the primary requisite for the successful pursuit of happiness.

In spite of my antagonism to the idea that freedom for the *libido* was more important than "breaking the chains of capitalist exploitation," I respected Dickie's courage in defying "bourgeois conventions," by living openly with Temple in a one room apartment in Bloomsbury, and not insisting on marriage as the price for surrender of her virtue. I had already learned that most of the girls who professed scorn for the marriage tie had in reality only adopted a new way to get a husband. By a reverse process to that of the Victorian age when well-bred girls got their man by refusing to give themselves without benefit of clergy, the modern girl who gave herself freely could count upon subsequently making life so miserable for her lover should he fail to marry her, that she achieved the same aim as her Victorian mother or grandmother.

Dickie, in spite of her independence, may have wanted to be bullied a bit, as shown by the type of man she eventually married. His name was Norman and we used to call him "the fascist" because of his Nietzschean ideas and contempt for such liberal ideas as the equality of the sexes. Nietzsche, as my brother liked to quote him in teasing me about my unrealistic views about sex, wrote that "When you go to a woman, take a whip." Temple, despite his appreciation of Nietzsche, was never the type of lover capable of treating a woman with what Michael Arlen in his *Green Hat** described as "a little tender brutality tastefully applied." Either because she was too intellectual, or too feminine, or both, Temple and Dickie soon found life together incompatible and parted in friendship.

Temple's next love affair was with a strikingly lovely brunette who had a profile like Queen Nefertiti and was so passionate that, on returning to London from a walking tour with her in Cornwall, Temple fled from her telling me that loving Bobbie left a man no energy or time to do any work. Bobbie then became the mistress of our sedate and respectable friend Teddy Joll, then already on his way up in the Civil Service to an eminent position. Fortunately for Teddy, Bobbie, after some stormy years with him as our neighbors in Jessel House, left him to marry a Sassoon and lived richly ever after.

Although I loved Temple dearly and we were good friends all our lives, I strongly resented the fact that Mother loved him so much more than me that she was, as I saw it, unfair to me, expecting me to do more than my fair share of household chores although I was contributing as much, and often more, to our living expenses. Today, I realize that he paid a heavy price for her great and all too possessive love for her son. Only his strength of character enabled him to break away and live his own life in spite of his great love for her, since Mother tried hard to shatter any lasting attachment he formed to any woman.

She had no objection to his 'light affairs' which, as a result of her Victorian upbringing she considered unreprehensible for the male animal, and she liked to have him tell her

---

*W. Collins Sons & Co., Ltd., London, June 1924.

58

about them since this assured her that she was in his confidence. But she did not in her heart of hearts really want him to marry anyone, although she never admitted this even to herself.

Although Mother was to make difficulties for me with my husband a decade later, when by force of circumstances she lived with us in Moscow, and although during most of my adult life she endeavored to bind me to her by my sympathy for her loneliness and her financial dependence on me, I now realize that Temple's problem was greater than mine.

In spite of, or because of, Mother's endeavor to keep him forever by her side, Temple eventually married a girl called Robert who was a games mistress with honey-colored hair and features as classically proportioned as her figure, but who lacked the warm human qualities of her sister Jean, whose husband Rab was Temple's close friend and who years later enabled him to sail to the South Seas.

In contrast to Dickie, Robert was so virtuous that she insisted on marriage. She was also, in my estimation, a prude and a hypocrite. Small incidents sometimes reveal most, and I recall one occasion before their marriage when Robert told us how shocked she had been when one of our friends, taking her home in a taxi from a party had made amorous advances. Whereupon I said to her, "Isn't that what you expected? Why else should he have paid for a taxi for the long ride to Hampstead instead of taking you on the underground?"

Maybe today this remark of mine makes little sense. But in those days in London in our circle of students and struggling young professional men, a taxi was a luxury few of us could afford unless absolutely necessary.

Before her marriage to Temple, Robert had professed herself to be an independent woman happy to be earning her own living and not expecting Temple to support her. But she had never really meant it and was continually demanding money from him, both before and after their marriage went on the rocks, following Temple's contraction of tuberculosis and the end of her hopes that he would eventually become a well-to-do medical practitioner.

On their honeymoon in France Robert had travelled first class Calais-Dover while Temple went third class New Haven-Dieppe, meeting her in Paris. During their life together in an apartment in Hampstead, Temple occupied a small room furnished with only his minimum requirements of a bed, table and chair, while Robert furnished her bedroom and the living room with every comfort and all artistry. Temple always wanted to live the simple life, whereas Robert wanted all the luxuries. And Robert, despite her athletic prowess was a rotten sailor who could get seasick even in a rowing boat, and whose conception of a Riviera holiday was far removed from Temple's. Visiting them one summer at Portofino I found Temple so happy to have me with him sailing and swimming and talking that I felt compelled to leave them and go south to Porto de Venere on my own on account of Robert's jealousy.

As can be judged from the foregoing, I disliked my brothers first wife, as much as I came to love his second one, Emsie, whom he met in Barbados in 1930 on his voyage to the South Seas and who was to become my very dear friend after his death.

For both Temple and myself the problem of our mother was not only that of earning enough to support her. There were also the difficulties created by her loneliness and her demands upon our time. Often when I told her I was too busy to talk to her or take her out she would say, "But you went out with so-and-so last night—you always find time for what you want to do." Which, of course was true. Mother would be very good in helping me to 'look my best' when I went out on what Americans call "a date." But she was hurt and resentful when Temple or I went to a party without her. It never occurred to her or to us that, following my father's death, she could have taken a job of some kind or got married again. She was still, in her 50's and even later in her 60's an attractive woman, with vitality and great charm, so much so that Temple's and my friends really enjoyed her company. But this did not mean that she could expect to be invited to all the parties we went to.

Yet she had something of a Ninon de Lenclos about her, in spite of being a virtuous Victorian. Age had not staled, nor custom withered her charms nor the enduring quality of her beauty of face and figure. Had she only had a little money she could still have enjoyed life enormously. But since she had none and Temple and I so little, it was impossible to give her all she needed. I could not buy a dress or a hat without feeling mean unless I could afford to buy something for Mother. And if I had anything nice to wear I lent it to her or shared it with her. For instance, in a letter from Manchester in January, 1926, I wrote: "Dear, it sounds mean, but I am afraid I shall have to ask you to send my black felt hat here. I meant you to use it but I cannot manage here in the rain with only a velvet hat. Could you ask Kathie to send it to me at once?"

Reading my many letters preserved by Mother through the years, I now marvel at myself. They are so full of love and sympathy; concern for her happiness and desire to give her a little pleasure, or some small luxury to compensate for her loneliness. The recurring motif is gifts of clothes or money to buy clothes, or money to pay for a holiday, or to provide for her living expenses. In later years in America, when I had to choose between my son's needs and mother's, I became much harder. But in my youth and during my married life my letters show that I was continually concerned with how to make up to her in material ways for the lack of basic sympathy between us.

I suppose I was driven not only by pity and love but by a feeling of guilt. Whenever Mother was away from me I remembered only that I loved her, felt dreadfully sorry for her and regretted having hurt her. When she was with me I was often cross and irritable and mean to her, so that as soon as she was away I wanted to compensate for having been unkind.

In spite of the temperamental antagonism between us, she knew my heart's secrets, my sorrows, joys and frustrations; my longing to find my own true love and my doubts that I ever should. In a word, there was always trust between us as between her and Temple and myself. We quarrelled but we never doubted the loyalty which united all three of us.

My letters, read again after so many years, recall the time when I had become convinced that I must overcome my Puritan or Victorian inhibitions concerning love without marriage. In March, 1926, I wrote Mother: "Had another long and loving letter from the Czech. He is coming to England May 8 and going to stay a few days to see me. I really believes that he loves me, and dear, I shall give myself to him when he comes. I am beginning to think this is going to be the big love of my life. He remembers every detail and moment of our time together and he understands me and seems to look at things something like me. His letter has made me very happy."

In the final event, I did not "give myself" to "the Czech," whose name I have forgotten and of whom I have no visual memory except, in a dim way, that he was tall and slender, had brown hair and dark blue eyes. Having nerved myself, as for an operation, to consummate the sexual act in the room he had taken for us in the Imperial Hotel on Bloomsbury Square, I frightened him into impotency. So true it is that one cannot go against one's nature however persuasive the psychoanalyst's arguments that freedom for the libido is the way to adjust to life. In reverse fashion to my brother, I had to follow my real will or hurt my soul.

Maybe it was not my instinctive rejection of Freud, who outraged my romantic imagination, but my 'guardian angel' who preserved me that night from "giving myself" on the altar of free love without really wanting to. Because, a few months later I met Arcadi who, soon after our first encounter, convinced me beyond a shadow of doubt that we belonged together.

All my Puritan inhibitions were dispelled as we joyfully became lovers, although it was to be long before we could become man and wife.

Perhaps my enduring love for my mother in spite of irritations and temperamental antagonism was due to my realization that without her influence and example I might not have been able to wait long enough to find the greatest happiness which life can give—to love and be loved utterly.

As I was to write to her from Japan in January, 1929:

> Life now is altogether a different thing, more complete and wonderful than I ever imagined it could be. Even the love I felt for Arcadi a year ago seems a small thing now, I love him so much more. There is really a complete understanding between us and sometimes I feel my happiness is too great to last. You know I have always felt, like the Greeks, that the Gods are jealous of human happiness. But anyhow life is worth having lived for this alone. So you see how I feel, dear, in answer to your birthday letter and whether I am glad I was born. Life seems a wonderful thing now and also I can see that my childhood made this happiness possible. That has given me such great happiness in the end. The memories I have always had of you and Dada which made the substitutes, the second-bests, of no use to me and kept me lonely for so long, have now given me Arcadi and our happiness together. So I love you, Mother dearest, more and more for the happiness you have given me.

Today I realize that I also owe a great debt to my brother for having saved me from becoming the type of unsexed, frustrated or embittered woman who provides dynamic energy to all movements for the regimentation of mankind, whether they call themselves Communists or Nazis or 'progressives.' Thanks largely to Temple's influence my Puritan conscience and sexual repressions did not result in my becoming a Beatrice Webb, a Priscilla Hiss, or an Eleanor Roosevelt type of ambitious woman.

How nearly I came to belong to the monstrous regiment of self-righteous women with cold hearts puffed up by their virtue and supposed dedication to humanity, is revealed by the following quotation from a letter I wrote to my mother in March, 1926 in which I display a priggish attitude toward life, sex, drink and all other pleasures of the flesh, also my too great intellectual class consciousness which is the hallmark today of the liberal intelligentsia of the Western World.

> Back's party on Saturday was very much a drinking, loving party and was very dull. They are no pleasure to me now. Joll was very charming but Molly McClane is simply sucking him under in a sea of sex. Whenever he tried to talk to me or Eleanor she put her arms around him, dragged him to her and began stroking him! She is one of those fat, heavy, odorous people and obviously perfectly inane. Even Mrs. Boothroyd asked me the other day who was the stupid-looking girl Joll

was going about with. I think all the same Joll may marry her. She makes no pretense about her having him, or so the Frosts say.

I am going tonight to dance with Stewart, the Assistant Secretary of State at the India office. I told you, didn't I, that I had met him again at the Hunter's party? He is only 45—at least ten years younger than anyone else in such a position. A widower with two children, but I am not likely to fall in love with him."

I had known Sir Findlater Stewart when I worked at the War Office before he was knighted. He was the second level-headed Scotsman in my life who for some unaccountable reason was fond of me. I remember him best on account of an incident later that year. Philip Spratt had got himself arrested in India as one of the "Meirut prisoners" on account of his activities in the left wing Indian Trade Union movement. Jane Tabrisky tried to get Professor Laski to intercede to get bail for him, but got no help from him. I went to see my conservative friend Stewart who was frank and honest with me saying: "Freda, we know much more about this young man than you do. He is a communist and nothing can be done about it. But believe me, an English prison in India is not as bad a place as you think."

A quarter of a century later Philip Spratt, married to an Indian girl and living near Bangalore, was to write an anti-Nehru, anti-communist book called *Blowing Up India*,* in which he relates how while in jail in India, he had time to think, read, study, learn and reflect, and had thus ceased to be a Communist. As also that the treatment he and the other political prisoners received was so humane that he was "disconcerted" to see a cartoon in the Communist *Daily Worker* picturing them as "emaciated, manacled and starving with horror filled eyes from behind barred windows." The reality more than justified the assurances given me by the Under Secretary of State for India. He writes:

> In the summer we were allowed to sleep in the yard. We were given 12 annas per head per day for food, and were allowed to supervise its expenditure and to do the cooking ourselves, with the aid of two convicts. Needless to say, we lived well. We were also given a clothing allowance. Twice in the hot weather we were taken to jails in the hills. We were allowed to bring into the jail books and papers with scarcely any censorship, and we played chess, cards, table-tennis, cricket and volley-ball. The court was held in a house some distance from the jail and we met visitors there without effective supervision.**

By very different experiences to my own, Philip Spratt and I were to learn the same facts about Communism and become its irreconcilable enemy. But in the intervening years, Laski, who had been anti-Communist until Hitler came to power, had come to exert all his great influence among Western youth in favor of the Soviet Union.

During the Spratt episode Jane and I, and some others, endeavored to check up on Harold Laski. He was well known not only as a namedropper, but as a telephoner-to-important-persons in the presence of his students or petitioners. Several people at the London School of Economics had got suspicious because nothing ever seemed to come of Laski's telephone conservations with "the P.M.," or the Foreign Secretary or other VIP's.

---

*Blowing Up India. Reminiscences and Reflections of a Former Comintern Emmissary, Prachi Prakashan, Calcutta, 1955.

**ibid.

One day it was discovered by a ruse that the telephone operator at the L.S.E. had his line plugged out during one of his imaginary or one-way conversations with the high and mighty.

However Laski was actually very kind and helpful to many students including myself. He strongly advised me to seek an appointment at an American University because it was so much easier there for English scholars to acquire reputation and status. As witness his own experience.

Chapter 8
REMEMBERING RUSSELL

The strongest influence which held me back for a time from joining the Communist party was that of Bertrand Russell. I met him first when he came to speak for the King's College Socialist Society in 1924. Subsequently he invited me to tea at his home in Chelsea. Thus began a friendship which has been one of the precious things in my life. In the Easter vacation of 1926 I spent a month with him and his wife, Dora, at Porthcurno in Cornwall, teaching their young son John in the mornings, walking, talking, and bathing in the afternoons, reading aloud in the evenings.

"Bertie" as I already called him tried hard to convince me that the Marxist theory was untenable in the light of modern physics. I wrote to Mother in April 1926: "Tell Temple I have been driven to try to understand relativity in order to understand what Russell thinks about Russia: I am reading the *A.B.C. of Relativity*,* with Russell sitting near me to explain what I don't understand. He is most awfully kind to me."

Unfortunately, I never understood the theory of relativity. In spite of Russell's patience and the time he spent on my education, my mind could not grasp the basic connection between Marxism and Newton's theory of gravity. Nor could I as yet accept the truth of Russell's *Practise and Theory of Bolshevism.*** Written in 1920, this book was uncannily prophetic of the Russia I was soon to know. Bertrand Russell was one of the very few who, in those early days of the Revolution, was able to perceive what manner of tree would grow from the seed which Lenin planted.

Others have appreciated the truth expressed by Lord Acton that all power corrupts and absolute power corrupts absolutely. But it took such a rare philosopher as Bertrand Russell, who had the faculty of seeing things writ small as well as large, to appreciate the significance of such incidents as his witnessing Kameniev smuggling milk for his children in his Commissar's car during the famine in Russia in 1920. As Russell endeavored to impress on me, the instinct to provide for one's own family would bring to naught all Communism's fine promises of equality and brotherhood. Forty years before Djilas wrote his famous book*** Russell foresaw that the so-called dictatorship of the proletariat meant that of a Communist party élite which could not but lead to the establishment of a new privileged class.

I can of course no longer recall many details of our conversation during the memorable and most happy days I spent with Bertrand and Dora Russell in Cornwall long ago when, as I wrote to Temple, "We talk and discuss everything under the sun." But I well remember how Bertie, one of the very few people who has actually read *Das Kapital* from beginning to end, endeavored to convince me that Marx's philosophy was bound to produce bad results because he was motivated by hate—by hatred of the rich, not

---

*K. Paul, Trench, Trubner & Co., Ltd., London, 1925.

**G. Allen and Unwin Ltd., London, 1920.

****The New Class,* Praeger, N. Y., 1957.

sympathy for the poor, by the desire to punish the exploiters rather than by compassion for the exploited.

I, who had read and thought I understood Anatole France's *Les Dieux Ont Soif* about the French Revolution, as well as his *Révolte des Anges*, failed to heed Russell's warnings concerning the inevitable corruption of the Bolshevik Revolution with its built-in despotism. So true it is that one learns only by experience. I had to find out for myself the hard way that even if Lenin had envisaged human freedom as the goal of the class war, by inflaming the hatreds of mankind he laid the foundations for a more total tyranny than the world had yet known.

One windy afternoon as we walked together on the Cornish cliffs above a turbulent sea, Bertie remarked that since no one can ever be sure of the ultimate result of his actions, one should be guided by realization of their immediate effects, and never inflict a certain present evil for the sake of a doubtful future good. A principle which Russell himself has not always observed, since he came to support the Second World War after it began, and is today aligned with those who are helping to sustain the immediate evil of Communist tyranny for the sake of a doubtful future peace to be achieved by the unilateral atomic disarmament of the West. As Russell himself has written, empiricists should never hold any principle absolutely because there are occasions when the future consequences of failure to act may be predictably worse than the consequences of taking action, however bad or dangerous its immediate consequences. None of us are always logical, or consistent in our beliefs, not even Bertrand Russell, the greatest man I ever knew.

Life in Porthcurno with the Russells that April long ago was like a brief return to my happy childhood. Writing to Mother and Temple during those halcyon days in Cornwall in the springtime, I said: "I like him better and better and feel a little bit like I used to feel about Dada."

My father, as I remember him before his last sad years of illness and hapless poverty, had the same capacity as Bertrand Russell for enjoyment of life and laughter, work and play, strenuous exercise followed by relaxed ease, good conversation and good argument, appreciation of poetry and music and beauty in all its forms, and above all such delight in the company of his children and such an intimate and understanding relationship with them.

Remembering both Bertie and my father, I call to mind lines from Gilbert Murray's translation of the Choruses in Euripides' *Bacchae*, learned long ago and still remembered:

A God of Heaven is he,
And born in majesty;
Yet hath he mirth in the joy of the Earth,
And he loveth constantly
Her who brings increase,
The Feeder of Children, Peace.
No grudge hath he of the great;
No scorn of the mean estate;
But to all that liveth His wine he giveth,
Griefless, immaculate;
Only on them that spurn
Joy, may his anger burn.

Whoever has read, and felt his courage revived by reading Russell's incomparable expression of his stoic philosophy in the essay called *A Freeman's Worship*, must feel how

65

apposite are other verses written by the greatest of the Greek dramatists more than two milleniums ago. Such lines as:

> What else is wisdom? What of man's endeavor?
> Or God's high grace, so lovely and so great?
> To stand from fear set free, to breathe and wait
> To hold a hand uplifted over Hate
> And shall not loveliness be loved forever?

Bertie loved his children far more than any of the many women in his life, continuing to enjoy through his extraordinarily long life the simple pleasures of humanity which many other philosophers have failed to appreciate. He shared their pleasures and romped with them and played with them like a young man, besides talking to them as if they were adults.

When grown to manhood, Bertie's first-born son, John, gave me great pleasure in recalling the impression made on him when he was not yet six years old, by my vivid account of Columbus dreaming as a boy in Genoa of the vast seas he would traverse as a man searching for a Westward route to the East Indies and accidentally discovering the New World.

I myself remember best the remark John made while Bertie was reading the Bluebeard story to him and his four year old sister Kate. At the point in the narrative when Bluebeard's wife, terrified at the prospect of having her head cut off unless her brother arrives in time to rescue her, calls again and again to her sister watching on the castle battlements: "Sister Anne, do you see anyone coming?" John interrupted his father's dramatic rendering of her anguished tones by remarking: "Wasn't she a fuss pot."

During that month in Cornwall Bertie taught me far more than I taught John or four year old Kate whom he was paying me to teach. What I learned from seeing how he was bringing up his own children was to prove important to me a decade later when I had a son of my own to rear without father, husband or brother to help me. Bertie believed that parents must be careful not to impair a child's nerve by letting him know one is fearful for him. He would watch John climbing dangerously on the rocky Cornish coast with anxiety, but determined not to let his son know how fearful he was. Years later in Moscow I was to have arguments with my husband who was all too prone to pick up our baby son from the floor to save him from bumps and scratches or a bad fall when he was showing himself too adventurous in his explorations of the world. And later on in England and America I had to contend with my mother's nervous exhortations to her grandson to "be careful" as against my endeavors never to arouse fear in his heart.

My father's training of Temple and me had been like Russell's treatment of his children. I became a fearless swimmer in my early childhood because my father used to take me far out of my depth when I barely knew how to swim, but trusted him completely. And, when I was ten or eleven years old I had climbed quite high mountains in Switzerland with my brother and a guide, besides being one of the crew in bobsled races along fast courses in competition with adults in the Engadine.

In bringing up my own son I tried to follow the example set me by Bertrand Russell and my father, and was greatly pleased when on his 27th birthday in 1961, Jon wrote me that I had "taught me to live so that I am not afraid to die."

Without courage there can be no virtue, as the Romans, who had the same word *virtus* for both, knew.

Although Bertrand Russell failed to save me from myself by stopping me from joining the Communist party, his influence remained potent.

When I came back to England from Russia in 1931 for a brief visit and stayed with the Russells in Hampshire I believed that the horrible society I was living in was Stalin's creation and that if Lenin had lived or if Trotsky's policies had been followed, all would have been well. Bertie would bang his fist on the table and say "No! Freda, can't you understand even now, that the conditions you describe followed naturally from Lenin's premises and Lenin's acts? Will you never learn and stop being romantic about politics?"

Some of my best friends still like to quote this Russell remark against me, although I think it is no longer true with regard to my political outlook. But if it be "romantic" to believe that man, by exercise of his reason and critical faculties, and by fostering his creative instead of his destructive instincts, could if he would, create a world nearer to the heart's desire, then Bertrand Russell has been the greatest romantic of us all.

The word "romantic" with its connotation of disregard for realities is not the right adjective to describe those who realize that there is an impulse within us, unexplained by the instinct for survival, to seek for truth and justice. It may be an illusion to believe that man has the capacity to attain to stature of the gods in whose existence he has longed to believe since he first came out of brutishness, but if this be romanticism let no one be ashamed of the appellation.

The poems Bertie loved best reveal that despite all his analytical, aseptic or "scientific" dissertations about sex, marriage, morality and libido in his popular books or pot boilers, he was at heart as old fashioned and romantic about love as any Victorian novelist or Elizabethan poets. Remembering his favorite poem, read to me long ago in Cornwall, as "Lady of Walsingham," which is not its title, I have now found it by searching diligently in the *Oxford Book of English Verse*. Included among anonymous 16th century poems, it is so beautiful, so little known, and so evocative of the tender and romantic side of Bertrand Russell's nature that I here reproduce it in full.

As ye came from the holy land
    of Walsinghame,
Met you not with my true love
    By the way as you came?
How should I know your true love,
    That have met many a one
As I came from the holy land,
    That have come, that have gone?
She is neither white nor brown,
    But as the heavens fair;
There is none hath her form divine
    In the earth or the air.
Such a one did I meet, good sir,
    Such an angelic face,
Who like a nymph, like a queen, did appear
    In her gait, in her grace.
She hath left me here alone
    All alone, as unknown,
Who sometime did me lead with herself,
    And me loved as her own.
What's the cause that she leaves you alone
    And a new way doth take,

That sometime did love you as her own,
    And her joy did you make?
I have loved her all my youth,
    But now am old, as you see:
Love likes not the falling fruit,
    Nor the withered tree.
Know that Love is a careless child,
    And forgets promise past:
He is blind, he is deaf when he list,
    And in faith never fast.
His desire is a dureless content,
    And a trustless joy;
He is won with a world of despair,
    And is lost with a toy.
Of womenkind such indeed is the love,
    Or the word love abused,
Under which many childish desires
    And conceits are excused.
But true love is a durable fire,
    In the mind ever burning,
Never sick, never dead, never cold,
    From itself never turning.

Bertie, for all his many love affairs and four marriages, never did find in the words of his favorite poem the "durable fire" of true love, "in the mind ever burning." This failure was not, I think to be ascribed simply to his inability to restrain the abnormally strong sexual urges which were the accompaniment of his great physical and mental vigor rendering him incapable of monogamy. His marriage failures were also due, as it seems to me, who knew two of his wives well, to his longing to mate with an equal. This led him to ascribe greater human qualities and mental capacities to the women he married than they possessed, or could long continue to pretend to have. Since he was seeking for an impossible combination of Cleopatra and Aspasia, Hypatia and St. Theresa, Boadicea and Joan of Arc, and was also drawn to Quakers and other Puritan types as shown by his first and last choice of wives*—his quest for enduring love was abortive. But he would not have made so much trouble for himself had he not so puffed up his wives that they became difficult to live with. Convinced by Bertie that they actually were his equals and collaborators, they acquired an undue influence over him which led him to great follies. As when he let Dora "inspire" him to write several rather silly books about free love which did great harm to his reputation, expressing views which he was to find untenable after she foisted two bastard children upon him. Or when, as today in his 90's he is married to a woman of Bryn Mawr who has no more understanding or knowledge of Communism than a nun in a convent insulated against evil has about the world, the flesh and the devil. I surmise from my memory of a talk with them in London in 1954 that the last Lady Russell bears considerable responsibility for the fact that Bertie in his last decade came to ignore his original acute perception of the nature and aims of the Soviet Power.

Influenced as he was by Dora's free love theories as well as by his own polygamous

---

*The present Lady Russell is not a Quaker but a pacifist of similar persuasion.

inclinations, Russell remained impervious to her arguments in favor of the Soviet dictatorship. He relates in his autobiography that she viewed his revulsion to the "cruelty, poverty, suspicion and persecution in Russia" as "bourgeois, senile and sentimental" while he regarded her liking for the Bolsheviks "with bewildered horror."

I confess that I do not remember much about Dora's political views in 1926 in Cornwall. I must have been too enthralled by Bertie to take note of them, much as they no doubt resembled my own at this time. I remember her as an attractive buxom fresh faced and energetic woman and recall Bertie's remark that living with her was as relaxing as travelling on an express train bearing one to one's destination without effort on one's own part. Dora's main interest in the mid-20's was in birth control and her campaign to induce the Labor Party to go all out for it. One remark of hers stuck in my mind. Telling about a textile trade union worker she had stayed with in Lancashire, Dora, instead of being repelled by her dirty house and unkempt personal appearance had understood that a woman in her circumstances could not possibly do a day's work in the mills and be active politically, unless she neglected her household chores and herself.

Writing to Mother I described Dora as "about the most able all around woman I have ever met." She seemed able to do everything, "is a perfect mother and she writes and runs birth control propaganda" and she was "awfully nice to me."

A decade later I was to accept, all too uncritically, Bertie's charges against Dora. I did not come to realize until the 50's, after his break with his third wife Patricia, Russell's capacity to erase from the tablet of his mind the true record of loves and friendships turned sour.

Today finding a letter I wrote on March 7, 1926, I am amazed to recall that, honored and pleased as I had been, by the Russell's invitation to spend the summer as well as the Easter vacation with them in Cornwall, I hesitated to commit myself to acceptance of an opportunity which many people would have jumped at then as well as today. Not because I did not revere Bertie or was not delighted at the prospect of enjoying the privilege and pleasure of his company. But on account of overriding concern for my lonely mother temporarily "exiled" in Devonshire as a paying guest with our friends Kathie and Stanley Harris. Because while I was in residence at Westfield College and Temple living with his wife in Hampstead, neither of us could contribute sufficient funds to Mother's support and she had sublet the Jessel House apartment. "Dear Mother," I wrote,

> I want especially to tell you about an offer I have had from the Russells, I enclose his letter which you might read first.
>
> I had dinner with them last night and said then I should love to come at Easter but did not like to promise anything definite about the summer, though I thought I could come for a month if I could arrange for you to come to Mousehole so that I could see you often.
>
> Today Mrs. Russell rang up and said she and Bertie did not want at this stage of my career to persuade me into anything but I have been round again this afternoon and have promised to come for April and for July. I saw Temple in the meantime and he seemed to think I ought to go as it *is* rather an opportunity, isn't it? I like the children and shall, I think, enjoy teaching them. Also, Porthcurno is quite near Mousehole and you thought, dear, that you would like to go to Mousehole in the summer and if you came for July I could see you nearly every day.
>
> Let me know what you think, dear? I think really I ought to feel honored.

As it turned out, by the summer of 1926 I was too actively involved in the long losing struggle of the British miners—which followed the collapse of the General Strike—to indulge myself again with the Russells in Cornwall as tutor to their children. I visited them only briefly that summer while accompanying A. J. Cook, Secretary of the Miner's Union, on a speaking tour through the Western Shires to raise funds for the striking miners.

Arthur Cook, who died not long afterwards as the result of his exertions, or perhaps because his heart was broken by his failure to save his people, was a type of labor leader practically unknown in this day and age when high-ranking trade union officials in England as well as America have become indistinguishable in income, mode of living and "status" from the executives of big corporations. A tall, rangy sandy-haired blue-eyed man with a great heart and fighting spirit, he lived almost as poorly as the miners he represented and never spared himself even when sick in his desperate efforts to save his people from destitution.

When we reached Cornwall on Arthur Cook's strenuous speaking tour, during which I occasionally spoke myself but was mainly instrumental in putting him in touch with my fishermen and other "proletarian" friends in Devonshire and Cornwall, I took the Miner's Union leader and his retinue to visit Bertrand Russell at Porthcurno, a small village in a cove some miles beyond Penzance on the way to Land's End. It was an occasion which illustrates Russell's kindness and concern for the practical needs ignored by most philosophers.

It had been raining all day and Arthur Cook was wet and exhausted and so hoarse that he was almost unable to speak after having addressed many small open-air meetings in spite of suffering from a bad cold. While the rest of us chattered excitedly downstairs, Bertie, infuriated by the indifference shown to the Mine Union leader's physical condition by his secretary, who was a hard-boiled left-winger, himself escorted Cook upstairs, carrying a can of hot water, and insisting that his guest change his sodden clothing, put on dry socks and take some rest.

This is one among many small incidents I recall which show Russell's concern for human ills, both great and small. In particular he was always prone to worry about people catching cold through getting their feet wet. At the progressive school which he and Dora established in England in the 30's, it was Bertie who insisted that the children change their socks when they came in out of the rain. And it was Bertie, not Dora, who saw to it that the groceries were ordered and the children properly fed.

How-Well-I-Remember-Bertie could be the title of a book I am unlikely ever to write. His kindness and his naughtiness; his wit and his courtesy and his weaknesses; his enjoyment of family life and his terrific sexual urges which led him to the pursuit of women until long past threescore years and ten. His boyish delight in shocking people by stating his views in the most exaggerated or provocative way possible. His joyful chuckles and the wicked gleam in his eye after making some particularly outrageous statement. The pleasure he took in reducing the sublime to the ridiculous even to the extent of making fun of his own cherished beliefs. His delight in paradox and his facial resemblance to the Mad Hatter in Alice in Wonderland. His logical mind which led him to say B.C.D. down even as far as X, after having once said A, even if the end result was absurd. His courage and integrity, his passionate hatred of cruelty and injustice and his burning sympathy for the injured and oppressed. All his great qualities of mind and heart and spirit uniquely combined with compassion and understanding.

As also the defects which are the reverse side of Russell's genius and humanity. His

70

exaggerated, sometimes ridiculous, overstatements when he refused to make any distinction between the trees and the wood, or to admit that a difference in degree makes a difference in kind. The contrast between his sceptical and stoic philosophy and his behaviour when he became a none-too-scrupulous propagandist for a cause in which he passionately believed. His propensity in the heat of controversy to ignore his own precept that one should always be aware that one may be mistaken. The occasions when his judgment has been warped by some particular personal experience, as when he came to conceive an enduring resentment against America because Catholic pressures in 1940 forced the cancellation of his appointment as Professor of Philosophy at the City College of New York on account of his "immoral" views on sex and marriage. His pride and prejudices as an Englishman and an aristocrat and his fears for his own country which eventually led him to take positions inconsistent with his basic views. His tendency to forget in the heat of controversy his own warning that "opinions that are held with passion are always those for which no good ground exists; indeed the passion is the measure of the holder's lack of rational conviction."

Nor can Bertrand Russell be held guiltless of sometimes shifting the original premise of his arguments without admitting he has done so after his heart or his hopes or his fears had, in fact caused him to change his mind.

Russell's liking for me and my deep affection and admiration for him were perhaps due to some basic affinity in our minds, characters and ideals. I do not, of course, pretend to be in any way his intellectual equal. But both of us had the mentality which pursues beliefs or theories to their logical conclusion, and the temperament which impelled us to commit ourselves unreservedly in defense of our convictions. Neither of us ever paid much attention to Goethe's dictum that the essence of wisdom is to know when to stop.

Lord Russell is an aristocrat by temperament as well as by birth, and, above all, an Englishman who instinctively reacts as such to the crises of our time. I, on the contrary, was to become a citizen of the United States by choice while remaining an internationalist at heart, and am perhaps also, as Bertie used to tell me in explaining my predilection for America, a 'social outcast by nature.' But we shared the same basic values and esteemed the same virtues: courage, honesty, clarity of mind, and the toughness of moral and mental fibre to face reality, acknowledge error, cast illusions aside and yet continue on the quest for truth and justice.

The inexcusable crimes in Bertie's view were cruelty and lying in either great or small matters. Thus, for instance, he broke off relations with Arthur Koestler, who was his neighbor in Wales after the Second World War, because Koestler was unkind to his wife, Mamime, and had lied to Russell on some small matter. And as I shall relate in a later chapter Russell was to sever his long friendship with George Bernard Shaw, over me in 1937, when he found Shaw to be cruel and deceitful as well as very silly about the Soviet Union.

I, too, am all too prone to break off relations with friends who disappoint me by not living up to my expectations of their integrity or courage. I can like and respect people who disagree with me and remain friends with them if they seem to be honest, but I hate hypocrites, humbugs and prevaricators, and despise those who seem to share my convictions but lack the courage to stand up and be counted when it comes to a showdown. Like Dante, I think those who are so indifferent or "tolerant" or cowardly as to have no opinion, deserve to be consigned to Hell's anteroom.

In a word, in my judgement of people I share to some extent Bertie's aristocratic prejudices.

The original Greek meaning of the word aristocrat was "the best"; and the term *noblesse oblige* reminds us that there was a time when the nobility was expected to behave nobly. The aristocratic principle, even if more honored in the breach than in observance by men of high degree, is the antithesis of the "bourgeois" passion for security, and the deification of private property rights.

There could be no greater contrast between an aristocrat in the original meaning of the word and the type of 'conservative' whose main concern is the preservation of wealth, incomes or security. Indeed, as it seems to me, the basic weakness of the so-called 'Right' in America today is its lack of 'virtue'—in the Roman sense of the word, meaning both courage and integrity and a measure of generosity.

This similarity in our temperaments, values, and behavior may account for the fact that my friendship with Bertrand Russell stood the test of time, despite some fierce altercations and temporary estrangements. As also because of his generosity of mind and heart. During the early 40's in America, after Bertie had abandoned his pacifism to support the war against Germany, he was to become infuriated by my arguments which echoed his own former belief that the Second World War would have even worse consequences than the first one. Yet, on one occasion, after we had parted in anger, he told his third wife, Peter, that I had the quality of greatness.

The real greatness was in Russell, who saw his own qualities reflected in his friends and in the women he loved or liked.

I am one of the few, if not the only, woman who enjoyed Russell's friendship for many years who did *not* have an affair with him. Although he wanted to make love to me, as was his nature, and laughed at my 'Puritan prejudices,' he understood me and helped me to understand myself. And it was at least partially thanks to him that when I fell in love with Arcadi, some six months after my vacation with the Russell's in Cornwall, I did not hesitate to consummate our love.

Through the years I was occasionally to be appalled when Bertie's terrific sexual urges, which were the accompaniment of his genius, caused him to assume the repulsive expression of a lustful satyr. My reverence for him as philosopher and humanitarian enabled me to dismiss these recollections from my mind. But buried in my subconscious they can still evoke an all too vivid vision of his hungry lips and avid eyes momentarily blotting out the image of philosopher and friend which mattered most.

I shall have much more to relate about Bertrand Russell in later chapters. At this point I am remembering through the mist of the years the wonderful month I spent with him in Cornwall in the springtime of my life when, if only I had heeded his teaching I would never have become a Communist, and might have saved my husband from being engulfed ten years later by the Red Tide which swept him to death and me to loneliness for the rest of my life.

* * *

After my month with the Russells in Cornwall I returned to Westfield College and my usual practical concerns. With work still to be done on my M.A. thesis I was looking around for a job in the fall, as also endeavoring to raise some cash to continue paying for the patent fees on my father's invention which we still hoped would eventually secure an income for mother. Temple was in a worse situation than myself since I was getting free board and lodging and £100 a year from Westfield College and earning some money by articles and book reviews and lectures for the Workers Educational Association. Writing to Mother in Devonshire from London that spring I say:

Very sorry you feel so lonely and sad. Shall come and see you soon.

Cannot come this weekend because going Cambridge for University Labor Federation meeting.

I can't see how Temple can manage to come. He has absolutely no money at all and is worried about it. Perhaps soon you will be getting money from the pump and will be able to come back, darling. I will look this week for a jumper suit for you.

In another letter concerning her forthcoming visit to London to stay with Temple, I wrote:

I got your letter last night although not posted by 9:30! Today and yesterday I have been chasing round for testimonials for a job advertised in the D. Herald for someone to do Research in a Trade Union Office (£ 300- £ 350 p.a.). I am afraid though, that there are heaps of people in for it—I have met several—and I don't stand much chance without an Economics degree. Baynes has given me a wonderful testimonial; I enclose a copy. Archie (Henderson, Transport Workers Union Secretary) has too, and his may count most. He is still terribly busy and looking absolutely fagged out but he asked after you very particularly.

As it turned out I was soon to be relieved of worry about jobs and money by being appointed to a fellowship at the London School of Economics and Political Science.

Chapter 9
I TAKE THE PLUNGE

The General Strike of 1926 was the turning point of my early political development. The high hopes raised when it began and what then seemed to me the "betrayal" of the workers by the Trade Union Council and the Labor Party, which had backed down in the middle of the fight, led me all the way into the Communist camp. I became convinced of the reality of the class war and of the truth of the Communist thesis that Socialism could not be obtained gradually by Fabian methods. There was apparently no solution for unemployment and low wages under the capitalist system. Only its overthrow by the unity of the workers of the world under Communist leadership seemed to offer a way of escape from poverty in the midst of plenty, gross inequalities in income and opportunity, periodic economic depressions or crises, and "imperialist wars."

The General Strike stirred all my emotions, the more so as I was then living at Westfield College among the most conservative set of University teachers I had ever met. My crude, somewhat childish, but I believe sincere, revolutionary reaction is expressed in a letter written to my mother in Devonshire on May 10:

> I have never lived through such a terrible week. I feel all hot inside and trembling all the time. It is such an unequal fight for us, and I want so much to help. I am speaking tonight at Edgware, I am glad to say. I wish I could speak all day—never was there a more unjust issue and more lies told by a government. Yet the government is so ruthless it may win. It is parading armored cars about and soldiers are all over the place. The buses are running with two policemen on each and volunteer O.M.S. labor. Everything is quite safe for ordinary people like me—I almost wish it were not! I cannot write properly, dear, I am too worried and upset. It is so dreadful not to be able to help and to have to listen to the misrepresentations of the capitalist press. Westfield is impossible except for a few students. I spent last night with the Boothroyds.* I saw Wilmot,** who is half expecting to be arrested for sedition. Anything almost can be called sedition. The Archbishop of Canterbury and the churches proposed terms of peace: withdrawal of both lockout and strike. The Government would not allow the proposal to be broadcast! It would be acceptable to us and not to them.

A few years later I was to realize that the behavior of the British government was like that of a loving mother in comparison to that of the Soviet government toward the Russian working class. But I still remember the passionate anger I felt in 1926 against the "capitalist government" and its most ruthless member, Winston Churchill, who was responsible for the show of armed force and was prepared to have the workers shot at if

---

*Well known humorist and cartoonist under the name of Yaffle.

**Labor M.P.

74

the strike went on. (Fifteen years later Winston Churchill was to become for a while the darling of the Communists and their fellow travelers, as also a hero in American eyes as Germany's most implacable foe. But to me he seemed no more admirable then than in 1926, since he went along with Roosevelt in demanding the unconditional surrender of the German people which led to the Communist conquest of Eastern Europe.)

Today, I also realize how tolerant were the Principal of Westfield College and the staff members with whom I argued fiercely in the Common Room and who appeared to me in the guise of 'class enemies' or bulwarks of reaction. No one interfered with me, even when I took a group of the undergraduates to T.U.C. headquarters to offer our services.

The day I was invested with my M.A. degree was the day the General Strike was called off. After bicycling all the way from Hampstead to the Senate House in South Kensington and sitting impatiently waiting in a borrowed cap and gown to receive my scroll, I tore off to T.U.C. headquarters. The bitterness of defeat and the long agony of the miners which was to follow the end of the General Strike have obliterated from my mind the feelings of satisfaction I must have had in having finally achieved more than even Mrs. Burton Brown had expected of me.

My M.A. degree had been awarded with the coveted mark of distinction and a recommendation by the Senate of London University that my thesis be published, for which purpose £ 50 was made available. This led to my being appointed to the Ratan Tata Fellowship at the London School of Economics and Political Science which was one of the juiciest plums in the academic world of my time since it paid £ 400 a year for two years. I no longer had to worry about how to make enough money to provide for Mother, and a successful academic or political career was open to me. Yet it was now that I prepared to take the fateful step of joining the Communist Party.

The subject I chose for my research and for the book which I was expected to write for publication by the London School of Economics, concerned Eastern competition and the declining Lancashire cotton industry. This may sound an odd transition from my previous work on the Roman Empire, but as I saw it, there was a parallel between the economic and social effects of the competition of slave labor on the condition of free labor in the ancient world and that of cheap "colonial" or Asiatic labor on Western labor standards in the modern world. I had moved from the study of ancient to that of modern imperialism.

The book which I eventually wrote on this subject, entitled *Lancashire and the Far East** was to be published without the blessing of the London School of Economics because its principal, William Beveridge, objected to my indictment of British Imperialist rule in India and insisted on the revision of my chapters on India as a condition for his approval.

Subsequently knighted, Sir William Beveridge became famous as the author of the *Beveridge Report* which laid the foundations of today's Britain's "Welfare State." He was an outstanding example of those, perhaps justly designated by the communists as "social fascists," since his main concern was with the condition of the British working class whose livelihood depended on the preservation of the British Empire and the continued exploitation of its colonial subjects.

Following World War II the United States came to supply the subsidy formerly available for the welfare of the British laboring and middle classes for the maintenance of the standard of life to which they were accustomed.

---

*Allen and Unwin, London, 1930.

75

For the most part, the L.S.E. professors, in contrast to those at Kings College and Westfield, were liberals and socialists. Graham Wallas, R. H. Tawney, Eileen Power, C. M. Lloyd (who was also foreign editor of the *New Statesman*), and above all Harold Laski, to mention only some of the best known names of the lecturers at the L.S.E., exerted far more influence than the few conservative economists and political scientists who taught there.

I naturally felt very much in my element at the London School of Economics and Political Science and soon came to exert some influence there myself, after being elected chairman of the London University Labor Party.

My friend, Jane Tabrisky, who was Secretary of the L.U.L.P., was already a member of the Communist Party, and between us we largely controlled the show. Since London University was a constituency which sent two members to Parliament, our activities and influence had some importance outside college. On one occasion Herbert Morrison came over to address one of our meetings in a vain endeavor to stem the Left Wing tide which I was leading or being led by. This one-eyed right-wing Labor Party leader was a fighter and man of integrity and intelligence besides being a most eloquent speaker, and I respected him even while opposing him. He well deserved to become Prime Minister in later years but was passed over in favor of the colorless Clement Attlee who made no enemies, thanks to his ability to sit upon a fence.

I was also Vice President of the University Labor Federation which comprised the Labor and Socialist Clubs of all British universities. The President was Arthur Greenwood, M.P., a Cabinet Minister in the first Labor government. Elegantly attired, very tall and rather gaunt in appearance despite his liking for liquor, good natured, amiable, and convivial and apparently devoid of strong political convictions, Arthur Greenwood had charm and the impeccable good manners of the British upper class. He frequently invited me and other students to drink a glass of sherry with him on the terrace of the House of Commons, and these social amenities helped him to preserve unity between the warring right and left wing factions of the University Labor Federation. A federation which comprised all the colors of the left rainbow ranging from such avowed Communists as Professor Maurice Dobb of Cambridge, and the aristocratic Irish Earl of Listowel, to Colin Clark, at that time a boyish looking rosy-cheeked and intrepid right wing Labor man from Australia, today internationally known as a brilliant and enlightened conservative economist.

We were a society of 'Lib-Labs' and socialists or 'progressives' who managed to retain a comradely atmosphere in our debates because we imagined that we all wanted to achieve the same end, albeit by different methods. As also because we paid due regard to the old maxim that "the secret of a close community is toleration of each other's idiosyncracies."

Happy days of innocence before Moscow became strong enough to divide the sheep from the goats and the lions, with intent to destroy all who failed to at least act like sheep in the Bolshevik fold.

The majority of our articulate and active members were 'Left of Center.' Among them, the leading light was G. D. H. Cole and his wife Margaret, already well known as economic historians and later also to become authors of successful detective stories. This brilliant and versatile couple wrote humorous verse and staged skits on topical subjects performed by our members. It was largely due to them that the University Labor Federation meetings at Oxford and Cambridge were great fun as well as forums for earnest discussion of the great issues of our time.

By now, besides my stipend from the L.S.E., I was earning quite high fees as a lecturer to extra-mural "Tutorial Classes" paid for jointly by London University and the Workers' Educational Association. I was also making a little money and establishing a reputation as a writer by the articles and book reviews I contributed to such publications as the *New Statesman, Labor Monthly,* and *The New Leader,* and soon also to the *Contemporary Review* and other nonpartisan journals.

For the first time since I left school I had no money worries, and had embarked with a fair wind on the scholastic career which I had hoped to pursue a decade earlier while at Prior's Field. As Arnold Toynbee's future wife, who was at this time Secretary of the London School of Economics, was to tell me in America some twenty years after, it was confidently expected that I would become as distinguished a woman economic historian as Dr. Eileen Power, who was a member of the Board which had chosen me for the Ratan Tata Fellowship against all my male competitors. Such was not to be my destiny. I was too deeply involved in politics, or as I saw it then, in the struggle for the emancipation of mankind. The study of history could no longer satisfy me; I yearned too greatly to take part in making it.

In 1928, two years after I had won the Ratan Tata Fellowship, I abandoned my promising academic career. Forever, as it turned out, since a decade later when I emigrated to America after my disillusionment in Soviet Russia, my anti-Communist views were to preclude my obtaining a University appointment.

In later years I was to regret having so light-heartedly thrown away the opportunity given me long ago to become a professor and make teaching my career, for I liked to teach and was successful with my classes. Moreover, the chance then afforded me to live the contemplative life, which failed to appeal to me in my 20's, seemed very attractive to me in my 60's. Today, I would ask for nothing better than a secure niche in the academic world.

Yet even now, in the evening of my life, I do not really regret having by-passed the opportunity given me in my youth to acquire academic fame and material security. It would be very nice to have them, but I ask myself whether I would consider them worth the loss of the experiences, the freedom, the joys and the sorrows which have made life's great adventure worthwhile, and have given me, if not any great measure of wisdom, knowledge obtainable only in a life of strife and struggle and an unending quest for the unobtainable.

As Temple, my long dead brother, expressed it, "We think there is something on the other side of the furthest ridge. There is not, but a further one. However let us go on looking for something we know is silly from all the viewpoints of others."

The 'motive patterns' of socialism, to use Max Eastman's expression, are various. As also the reasons why at various times and places, one man or woman or another has joined the Communist Party. My own case proves that it is not necessarily, or even primarily, poverty or lack of opportunity which makes Communists, since it was only after I began to earn a good income that I joined the Communist Party.

Nor would it seem to be true, to judge from my personal experience, that sex frustrations, or loneliness, or unhappiness in their personal lives lead both young and old to embrace the Communist faith.

I realize, in contemplating and endeavoring to analyze the motive forces of my life, that my unsatisfied longing for husband, home and children played a large part in impelling me into an increasingly absorbing political life. As also how true it is that, in Russell Green's words: "The hobby-horse of one's discontent becomes the Pegasus of one's ambition." But my decision to join the Communist Party came after I was not only on the way to realizing my worldly ambitions, but had also at long last found a man to love who loved me.

I first met my future husband Arcadi Jacovlevitch Berdichevsky when Boris Plavnik took me to his house on Goldhurst Terrace in Hampstead on a gloomy rainy autumn evening in 1926. I have no recollection of what we talked about as we sat sipping tea through sweets in the Russian fashion around the dining-room table where there may or may not have been a samovar. But how easy to recall and how difficult to convey by the printed word the current which passed between us, the look in Arcadi's expressive eyes which made my heart beat faster, the humorous twist to his generous sensitive mouth, the touch of his hand at parting when we arranged to meet again alone.

We knew we loved one another after only a few meetings, and in the Christmas vacation we journeyed together to Herrenalp in the Black Forest for a premature honeymoon. Premature, since Arcadi was married and it was to take much time, travail and heartbreak before he could divorce his wife and become my husband in the summer of 1928 in Moscow.

Arcadi, whose love was to illumine my whole life, was a Russian Jew, whose family had moved during his boyhood from Odessa on the Black Sea to Lodz in Poland. After studying at Zurich University in Switzerland for his Masters Degree in Economics and Commerce, Arcadi had emigrated to the United States shortly before the first World War. In New York he had married the daughter of a well-to-do family of Russian Jewish extraction. Her name and patronym was Anna Abramovna and they had a young son called Vitia. They had begun to be estranged when Arcadi, in 1920, gave up a $600 a month salary as representative of an American firm in London, to work for only $150 at the newly formed trading organization of the Soviet government known as ARCOS.

By the time I met them in 1926, Arcadi had become Finance Manager of the Soviet Trade Delegation in London, at a salary of $500 a month, which in those days in England enabled him and his wife to live well in a large house with a servant. But he had become increasingly dissatisfied both with his personal life and his comfortable "bourgeois" existence.

Arcadi was not a Bolshevik, but had been a member of the Jewish Social Democratic Party, known in Poland as the Bund, and had retained his socialist ideals. In 1923 he had been asked to join the Communist Party, thus ensuring his future career in the Soviet service. But he had the feeling that since he had played no part in the Revolution he could not join now that the fighting was over and membership in the Party had become a privilege. Also, and basically more important, Arcadi had the same repugnance as my brother to adherence to any creed or dogma. He wanted to believe that the Soviet Government could and would establish a Socialist order of society fulfilling the aspirations of men of good will for social justice, but he was never able to subscribe to the Bolshevik philosophy.

In spite of what Bertrand Russell called my incurable political romanticism, my father's and my brother's scepticism, and the distrust they had inculcated in me of those who profess altruistic motives, were not without influence on me. Arcadi attracted me precisely because he made fun both of himself and the lofty pretensions of the Communist 'Saviors of Mankind,' even while ready to work harder, and make greater sacrifices than most Communists, in order to help build the good society. He was as witty, intelligent, and charming, and far more handsome and virile than Walter Field, whom I had once loved, but who, as he told my brother, had run away from me in spite

78

of wanting me, because he was afraid that life with me would be dangerous and uncomfortable.

Arcadi loved me for the very reasons which, as my mother had so often told me, were likely to prevent any man I liked from wanting to marry me. Far from wishing me to be a 'good wife' subordinating myself to him and my interests to his, Arcadi loved me because he thought I was different from most women. Being an attractive man, he had long since enjoyed a surfeit of feminine women, and was always concerned that I preserve my individuality, go on with my work, and not succumb to the temptation of becoming just another wife and mother.

Anna Abramovna, never having understood or sympathized with Arcadi's socialist aspirations, could not see why he was not satisfied with a comfortable home, a pretty wife, a child and a well-paid job. To the last it remained inexplicable to her why he left her for me, since as she told their friends, I was not pretty and would never make him comfortable.

In the summer of 1927 I was invited to visit the Soviet Union in my capacity as Vice President of the University Labor Federation. My writings had attracted the attention of Ivan Maisky, then Counselor of the Soviet Embassy in London, and I was by this time well acquainted with the British Communist Party leaders. I had met Petrovsky, the Comintern representative in England during the General Strike, and became friendly with him and his wife without knowing his identity or even his real name. He then called himself Max Breguer and was masquerading as a "Nepman"—meaning a businessman—under the New Economic Policy dispensation in Russia which permitted a limited degree of private enterprise. I had accepted him as what he professed himself to be, namely a "good capitalist" friendly to the Soviet Government, and was astonished in Moscow to discover that he was a V.I.P. in the Communist hierarchy and its secret apparatus.

I was regarded, I suppose, as a promising young 'bourgeois intellectual' whose writings displayed appreciation of Marxist theory and whose conversion to Communism would have an impact on British Left Wing intellectual circles. I intended to join the Party as soon as I returned. The propaganda effect would be greater if I joined after, not before, I saw the U.S.S.R.

My excitement at my coming visit to the Land of Promise knew no bounds. My brother from his bed in a tuberculosis sanatorium in Surrey wrote me some words of caution:

> My dear Freda:
>
> This is just to wish you luck in your adventure. I think in one way you are quite right. I would do the same thing if I wanted to, I expect. After all, one must follow one's own thinking and one's own desires. It is an adventure, but I do not expect for a moment that you will find what you are seeking for intellectually. Men are much of a muchness everywhere, and they behave much in the same way whatever they profess to believe.
>
> Of course you will see the country and the people and the society as you wish to believe they are, at first. But later, your scepticism will reassert itself.
>
> But don't join the Communist Party. It seems to me a terrible thing for any intelligent person to adhere to any creed or dogma; to have to say that you accept any empirical generalization as an article of faith. I

do not see why you should not work for them and with them and yet reserve your opinion about their fundamental propositions.

These sweeping generalizations are to be distrusted. Even when you are dealing with a subject like physics–a subject by which human desires and fears are little affected in its findings, as more and more is discovered and its fundamental promises examined, you are all the time modifying and modifying.

And what a phrase that "materialistic conception of history" is: 'Matter'–the word is not really used in Physics. Bodies have mass and the mass of a body is its weight divided by the acceleration due to gravity. That is all Physics knows about it.

Matter psychologically is one's sense of resistance–pushiness–quite different. Matter is also a "banner word," a symbol with emotions attached to it used by various sects to throw at one another.

I must end half finished, or I will lose the post. I need another four pages to explain myself. Anyhow, the best of luck, my dear, and all my love.

Temple

Failing at that period of my life to appreciate my brother's wisdom, I brushed aside his wise counsel as I had Bertrand Russell's warnings. All their arguments seemed abstract. I could not see that they had any relevance to the concrete problem of how to establish socialism. I suppose I was then like a religious convert whose beliefs are no longer susceptible to reason or philosophical argument. I had faith in socialism as the answer to man's age-old longing for justice and a well-ordered universe; I failed to perceive that Communism, with its false hope of establishing heaven on earth, was a substitute for religion, luring men to worship the devil under the guise of a great emancipator. I replied to my brother: "In spite of what you say, I must join the Communist Party. I cannot live without feeling I am doing worthwhile work. I see no hope in the Labor Party. I think the Communist thesis is right."

Thus, I departed on my first visit to Russia in June 1927, full of enthusiasm and willingness to believe that the Communists were in the process of creating the best economic and social system which the world had ever known.

Chapter 10
RUSSIA IN ROSE

I traveled with Ivan Maisky from Berlin to Moscow, together with W.J. Brown, Secretary of one of the most militant trade unions in England, the Clerical Association, whose members were office workers in government service.

Two days after our arrival we stood in the Red Square to witness the funeral of Voikov, murdered in Poland. This was the first demonstration I saw in the "socialist fatherland"; and I vividly recall the exaltation and excitement that filled my heart and mind as I stood close to Lenin's tomb under a blue sky watching the Red Army parade and the thousands upon thousands of demonstrators. My mind in those days was full of romantic libertarian images. I wrote after the demonstration: "People in the street look well fed enough though poorly clothed, and there seems to be such vitality and purpose among the people one meets . . . . The soldiers in the demonstration especially looked so splendid—more like the Greeks of Xenophon must have looked than like the usual wooden soldier . . . ."

I was also enchanted by the as yet unspoiled charm of Moscow which, as Bertrand Russell had told me, rivalled Peking among the most beautiful cities of the world. "Moscow is a lovely place," I wrote to Mother, "I wish you could see the Kremlin across the river and all the domes of the churches. I will bring home some pictures."

Visitors to the U.S.S.R. in those days were comparatively rare. There was no Intourist, and only invited delegates from trade-unions and Labor parties got the chance to travel over Russia. One was lapped around with kindness, hospitality, and good fellowship. Nor were outward signs of prosperity lacking. The market places of Moscow and other towns were overflowing with vegetables, dairy products, milk, and meat. New apartment houses and office buildings built in the severe but pleasing style introduced after the Revolution were much in evidence. There were no queues for bread and other foods at the state and cooperative shops, and one could buy the most delicious pastries for only five kopeks. There was a shortage of manufactured goods even in the cities, but it was not to be compared to the almost total lack of necessities a few years later after the "gigantic successes on the industrial front."

One is tempted to imagine what Russia might have become if the New Economic Policy, permitting the peasants to enjoy the fruits of their labor under free enterprise and thus fructify the fertile Russian soil, had been continued. But as early as 1924 the "Scissors Crisis" (the disproportion between the price of manufactured goods and agricultural produce) had split the Central Committee of the Bolsheviks into left and right factions.

Disagreements began over how much to take from the peasants for industrial development, and ended in the bitter controversy over collectivization. With the aid of Bucharin, Tomsky, and others on the right who maintained that any attempt to force the pace of industrialization would destroy the stimulus to labor, Stalin had overcome Trotsky and was soon to exile him and the rest of the left opposition. Once rid of the

Trotskyists, Stalin, in 1929, was to wipe out the right opposition and embark upon an ultra-left policy of forced collectivization and intensive industrialization.

The U.S.S.R. was soon to become a country of starved peasants and undernourished workers, cowed and whipped by fierce punishments to toil endlessly for a state which could not provide them even with enough to eat. But, unfortunately for my own future, I first saw Russia during the brief period of prosperity which began in 1924 and ended in 1928.

My 1927 visit to Russia was marred only by my fellow guest, Billy Brown, an oversexed left-winger who imagined that in the Communist world he would be afforded unlimited opportunity for the indulgence of his carnal appetites. He had wanted to make love to me before in London, where we were politically associated, but it was not until we got to Moscow that I had difficulty in holding him off. Although he knew I was in love with Arcadi, he fancied that in the supposedly uninhibited sexual climate of the Soviet Union I would naturally sleep with him. When his expectations remained unfulfilled, and he had also found it difficult to find a Russian mistress, he turned nasty. This may all have had the desirable long range effect of souring him on Communism, but at the time he caused me embarrassment.

There was a whole class of hopeful leftwingers whose attraction to Communism was at least partially inspired by their mistaken belief that the U.S.S.R., if not yet all that might be desired economically, was at least the paradise of free lovers. For them, sex and politics were always mixed.

Writing Mother from Moscow in July, 1928, I told her:

> They are sending me to a place in the Caucasus for two weeks and then home by way of Tiflis and Baku which will take a week or 10 days. The original arrangement has been broken up because Brown has had a nervous breakdown. The last few days have been very trying. Billy gradually became impossible and has been very rude and unpleasant to me. It is too long a story to tell you in a letter and how much is due to Billy's nerves and how much to sex, etc., I don't know. Anyway, we have definitely split and are following our different programs. Billy has behaved just like a spoilt child. Everything in Russia has annoyed him especially the unpunctuality—and the food upset him—he was in bed for two days.
>
> But the occasion of things going wrong was his accusation that I monopolized people: the fact is that people have been awfully nice to me and as I speak German and am a woman, I do perhaps get more attention. But the whole business has been childish I think it is his nerves which are wrong; in fact two doctors say he has a bad nervous breakdown. Also there has been this sex business. In Berlin already he was telling everyone he wanted to find a girl and he went off to find a prostitute and came to tell next morning. Also, he had asked me, more or less casually, the first night, if I would sleep with him, and I passed it off as a joke. Then he said quite calmly: "How will you manage so long away from your lover?"

Billy Brown, as I say, was only one among several left-wingers who visited the Soviet Union with false expectations. Years later, when living with my husband in Moscow, I witnessed with considerable amusement the frustrations of an American from Georgia, who came to Russia on a Rosenwald Foundation fellowship, confidently expecting to be

able to indulge his sexual appetites without bourgeois restraints. Unable, to his dismay, to find any girl to sleep with him in spite of the soap, coffee, and other luxuries he had to offer, he married a nice Canadian girl in Paris after six months of sexual abstinence. Admittedly, X, as I shall call him (since he was a nice person and is today not unknown in America), did not know how to go about it. There were plenty of women in the hungry 30's in Russia who were ready to give themselves for "three pairs of silk stockings," to quote the title of a novel at that time, or even for one lipstick, as my husband phrased it. But X made the mistake of imagining that he could find a mistress among the Communist élite who traveled *de luxe* like himself and had no reason to fall for a trifle.

I drove to Tiflis from Vladikafkaz along the fabulous Georgian Military Road built by the Tsars during their conquest of the Caucasus. A road which skirts high mountains rising almost perpendicularly from the river beds, torrent gorges and narrow valleys of the land known to the ancient Greeks as Colchis. How easy to imagine that Prometheus was chained by Zeus to a high peak in this majestic territory to have his heart devoured by a vulture for his defiance of the gods by setting man on the road to progress by teaching him to make fire. Here Jason had come in search of the Golden Fleece. And here, today, there may still remain, in inaccessible mountain Fastnesses, remnants of the many races which have passed through this land bridge from Europe to Asia, still unconquered even by the all reaching Soviet power.

I have forgotten more than I remember about my first visit to Russia when I was seeing everything in rose, or through the spectrum of my romantic imagination which enabled me, incongruously, to regard Bolsheviks and ancient Greeks equally striving to emancipate mankind from what Swinburne called "the shambles of faith and of fear." But I can still conjure up in my mind's eye my first view of the Caucasus Mountains purple dark in the early dawn as dimly seen from the railway carriage on arrival at Vladikafkaz from Moscow. And of the drive along the Georgian Military Road to Tiflis when my heart stood still with dread and wonder as we sped round bends thousands of feet above the river beds below in this majestic and untamed land "half as old as time."

In view of all the legends and stories about "Circassian beauties" captured or sold to become slaves or harem concubines by Persians, Greeks, Arabs and Turks, I was surprised to find in Tiflis that it was Georgian men, not women, who were strikingly handsome. The women of the Caucasus seemed to me less beautiful than Italians and generally far too fat—a defect doubtless remedied soon afterwards by Stalin's economic policies which condemned all but the Communist élite to near starvation. In 1927 I remembered Elroy Flecker's poem, *The Road to Samarkand* in which he expressed the oriental love for women whose hips are "as broad as watermelons in the season of watermelons."

No doubt today the gay, talented, courageous and handsome peoples of the Caucasus, among whom the Georgians take pride of place, have been reduced to the same drab uniformity or conformity as all the other races and peoples subjected to Communist tyranny. But I saw Tiflis before Moscow's heavy hand had extinguished the enjoyment of life and love, laughter and beauty which distinguish the peoples of the Mediterranean world and which tyrants from time immemorial have found hard to drown.

In Tiflis I became friendly with a woman who was a Menshevik but who defended the Soviet regime and convinced me that there was no terror anymore. The time was as yet far off when I was to learn that Communist terror is so all pervading that it forces all its victims to pretend that it does not exist. Perhaps this woman of Tiflis believed what she said to me because she had convinced herself that now, thanks to the New Economic

83

policy, incentives had supplanted brutal compulsions as the dynamic of socialist construction. I was at this time as gullible or ignorant as the rest of my liberal contemporaries in the West who, a decade later, came to exert such direful influence on Western policy during the Roosevelt era. But my brief belief in the Communist Party was before Stalin won absolute power and plunged Russia into the hell of forced collectivization.

My first impressions of the U.S.S.R. were obtained during the all-too-brief period of the NEP policy when the Russian "toiling masses" were substantially better off than they had ever been before or were to be again in our time. (Even if today some few of them have refrigerators and T.V. sets, most would still seem to have less to eat than when I first visited Russia forty years ago.)

Returning from the Caucasus to Moscow I had the thrill of travelling in an airplane for the first time in my life. It was supposed to fly to Moscow from Kharkov but came down with engine trouble in a field half-way. The only other passenger was an amiable Italian businessman, and together with the pilot we made our way on foot to the nearest village, and thence by a horsedrawn cart to a railroad station. The Italian, who was middle-aged and corpulent, made heavy weather of our mishap, but nothing could then daunt my spirits or my enthusiasm about Russia. From Moscow, referring to Temple's plea that I should pause and reflect before joining the Communist Party, I wrote to Mother:

"I am sorry Temple is worried about me. I shall come home, dear, but I hope I shall be able to join Arcadi here next year. I have been making inquiries about the cost of living in Moscow and think we could manage and me send you £ 2 a month."

In a postscript I wrote that it was difficult to write without writing a great deal about Russia, and that I was too busy making notes for articles to write more in a letter. "I do feel that things worthwhile are being accomplished in Russia," I added. "I like the spirit of the people and the look of them. Everyone is simply or poorly clad, but everyone looks well fed. Clothes are just made of anything and one can go out in any sort of dress without exciting comment." How welcome this must have seemed to me who had never had enough money to dress well during my adult life.

I returned to England full of enthusiasm and prepared to tell the world about the wonders of socialist construction in the U.S.S.R. Rejecting an offer to stand for Parliament as a Labor Party candidate in the Rusholme division of Manchester, I publicly proclaimed my adherence to the Communist Party, and addressed meetings all over England.

Archie Henderson, one of the National Secretaries of the Transport Workers Union, told our friends: "Freda always belligerently rolls up her sleeves when she starts to talk about Russia."

I admitted that the standard of life in the U.S.S.R. was far lower than in the Western capitalist countries, but went on to explain that this was because Russia needed to accumulate capital for industrialization. I assured my audiences, that since there was no exploiting capitalist class in the Soviet Union, the burden of saving and investment was being borne equally by all, so that there was no such acute misery in Russia as in the era of the British Industrial Revolution.

"Bliss was in that dawn to be alive," as Wordsworth had thought at the time of the French Revolution. To me it seemed that Russia had unlocked the gates of Paradise to mankind, and that I must help to convince the workers of my own country to enter in by overthrowing capitalism and joining up with the U.S.S.R.

Looking back to that distant time, I now ask myself, did I really believe it? Was I, who had studied history, really so naive? I must have been, else I should never have thrown up my career and encouraged my husband to abandon his comfortable life in the "capitalist world," to go off with me to take part, as we imagined, in the construction of Socialist Society in Russia.

On my return to London from Russia I learned that Arcadi was being expelled from England by order of the Home Office. His expulsion may have been due to the indiscreet letters I had sent him from Russia expressing my complete conversion to Communism. But it is more likely to have been the result of his having been assigned by the Chairman of the Russian Trade Delegation to be one of the small number of Soviet employees permitted to remain on the premises when the British Home Secretary, Joynson-Hicks, raided the Arcos offices in June, 1927.

Although I was flattered to think that I was regarded as a dangerous revolutionary by the British Home Office, it was a great blow to have Arcadi expelled. The Soviet authorities assigned him temporarily to Berlin where I visited him during the Christmas vacation, but he was so busy that we were unable to go off and enjoy ourselves as we had done the previous year in the Black Forest.

Whereas Arcadi had been working so hard on Soviet Government business in Berlin that we had all too little time together, I took my political work so seriously that when, in February, 1928 he was allowed to come to London for ten days to represent Arcos in a lawsuit, I was so busy campaigning as the Communist Party's candidate in the London County Council elections, speaking either to indoor meetings or at street corners mornings, afternoons and evenings, that I did not give up a single evening to him. This was the first election in which the Communist Party came out in opposition to the Labor Party, thus helping the Conservatives to win. Although I had no hope of winning the election, I made a fair showing, gaining a considerable number of votes against both my Labor and Tory opponents.

Two incidents stand out in my memory of my first and last political campaign. One is the remark made to me by a respectable working class wife and mother. "I'm for you and what you say the Communist Party stands for," she said, "but I and many others like me cannot abide those loose-living, hard-drinking, foul-mouthed young men and women of the upper classes who call themselves Communist and support you."

The other is my own behavior on election night when at London's City Hall, after the votes had been counted, the winning Conservative candidate came up to shake hands with me. My upbringing in the traditions of British good sportsmanship warred within me against my belief in the Class War. For a moment I had difficulty in repressing my natural impulse to smile and take his outstretched hand. But ideology triumphed over good manners and I firmly placed both my hands behind my back, albeit with a feeling of acute shame and embarrassment.

Even after I joined the Communist Party I could have continued my successful academic career had I remained in England. Although being a Communist in those days was a handicap, my scholastic record and the tolerant attitude of British Universities toward "heretics" of one kind or another provided that they are "brainy," speak with an educated accent and have tolerably good manners, ensured me a University appointment following the termination of my Fellowship at the London School of Economics and Political Science.

In the 20's, the distinction between a Socialist and a Communist was not clearly demarcated. Most Labor Party and Trade Union leaders had already learned enough through experience to hate and distrust all Communists, but in intellectual left-wing circles they were generally regarded simply as people who wanted to achieve Socialism

85

faster than others, if necessary by revolutionary means. Revolution was only a word to them as to me in those days when like most of my contemporaries I had no conception of what violence meant, or of the horrible "means" or methods which were soon to become standard operating procedure in the Union of Soviet Socialist Republics.

We all laughed and enjoyed the musical skit about my Soviet tour, written and stage managed by G.D.H. and Margaret Cole at a special meeting of the University Labor Federation called to hear my report on Russia at Oxford in the fall of 1927. I remember some lines from some of the songs sung to popular tunes by our members, making fun of my glowing account of the state of Russia. One was called *Come to Prison in Georgia*, where life was just wonderful, and one could meet either:

> Burglar Bill who, flushed with wine
> Murdered his registered concubine.

or:

> Commissar Trotsky, in for life
> Fraction work with Lenin's wife.

The performance ended with myself appointed as Soviet Commissar of Education, while the other members of a U.L.F. delegation to Russia were strung up one by one on lamp posts to the refrain:

> Red, white or pink, no difference can we see,
> So perish all the British bourgeoisie.

There was also a song with a refrain: "Stick to Marx, my hearty, Damn the Labor Party, Keep the hell fires burning for the bourgeoisie."

It could be that Margaret Cole was to be responsible for my husband's arrest some nine years after she and her husband had made fun of my conversion to Communism. For on my return to England in 1936 I learned that she had betrayed the confidence I had reposed in her during her visit to Moscow not long before when I had told her in strict secrecy my real views. She had, I heard, been going around telling people that "Freda was very soured on Russia"—her term for my profound disillusionment. This was surely not because she was malicious or wished to jeopardize my husband's life, but simply because she had remained as ignorant or innocent as I had once been. She simply had not believed me when I told her in Moscow how dangerous it is to speak the truth under a Communist dictatorship.

Still today in the West there are all too many liberal innocents who cannot or will not understand what terror means.

Chapter 11
OFF TO THE EAST

Arcadi had asked his wife Anna Abramovna, to divorce him in January 1927, following our time together in the Black Forest, but his separation from her proved to be a long and painful business, complicated by his expulsion from England in the fall of that year. "Mrs. B," as we called her, had first asked him to wait until she could join either her brother in New York, or her sister in Paris, because she could not bear to have their friends in London know he had left her. Subsequently it became clear that she hoped all along that his feeling for me was a temporary infatuation and that if they continued to live in the same house he would return to her.

Arcadi tried without success to obtain a visa for her to go to the United States where her brother was an engineer with the General Electric Company. And by the time he was able to secure a French visa for her, he himself was being expelled from England. Unfortunately for her own future and that of their son Vitia, she insisted on following him to Moscow after a short sojourn in Paris. Since I remained in England to finish my second year as a Fellow of the London School of Economics and to work for the Communist Party, she continued to hope he would change his mind. It was not until I came to Moscow in the summer of 1928 that they were at long last divorced. Arcadi and I then registered as man and wife in the apartment house where we lived.

I had been too inexperienced fully to appreciate Arcadi's difficulties. At times I had rebelled at his long delay in freeing himself to be with me. I had felt that he should either break with her at once or give up the idea of living with me. I knew that leaving his son was very difficult for him, but I failed to understand that the ties between a man and a woman who once loved each other are hard for a sensitive man to break when the woman tries with every means at her disposal to maintain the old relationship. Moreover, in leaving his wife Arcadi was making a break with the "bourgeois" life he had lived since finishing his studies in Switzerland. For him I was a symbol as well as companion in the new life in socialist society which we both wanted to lead.

Nearly ten years later the O.G.P.U. was to deprive me of almost all Arcadi's letters when they searched our Moscow home. But one he wrote to me during this difficult period of our relationship remained hidden within the pages of a book.

"Darling Fredochka," he wrote,

I suppose you are right in your own way, your brutal way, and that I shall never be able to satisfy you as to the validity of my reason for acting in the way I do.

I shall not pick a quarrel on what you say about my "playing about with the idea of living a different sort of life"; "desiring to go on the same way as before" and a number of other things "read at the bottom of my heart." There is no use to argue about things on which we can never agree, and I shall not appeal to you to reverse your decision until I can tell you that the way is clear for my giving you as much of myself as you can desire. I love you and I cannot and shall not believe that everything is over until you refuse to come to me when I shall ask you to do so on the strength of changes in my family life. There are for me two possibilities only in the future; either I shall embrace fully to the extent of 100 per cent the creed which will keep me going and make me forget you, or I shall accept it partially as I have done until now and you will be my beloved comrade in fighting all doubts which will arise. Nothing else is possible and the "desire to go on the same way as before" is death, which I do not feel I am ready to accept.

Both of us knew that life in Russia would be hard, that living space was difficult to obtain, and that the conveniences and comforts he had for many years enjoyed abroad would not be obtainable in Russia. Also since he was not a member of the Communist Party, he could never rise to a top position in the Soviet State. Arcadi, being well acquainted with both the old enduring Russian character and the Communists with whom he worked in London as a "non-party specialist," realized that my rosy picture of the Soviet Union was naive. But, like myself, he believed that a new and better world was being created in Russia, or could be built, if he and others like him devoted themselves to the endeavor without thought of personal advantage.

When my Fellowship came to an end in July, 1928, I took off for Moscow to join Arcadi, prior to his expected assignment to Japan where I should be able to complete the research work on my book on the cotton industry.

This time no smiling delegation met me at the Moscow station, and no luxurious quarters at the Metropol Hotel awaited me. Arcadi took me to a tiny room, not more than fifteen feet by twelve, with a single bed, a chest of drawers, and two straight chairs. There was not even a table, and I had to cook and iron and write on the wide window sill. But the flat was clean, and there was only one family in each of the four rooms sharing kitchen, bathroom and lavatory. For Moscow that was not bad. Unfortunately the room was not ours, but only lent to Arcadi for a few weeks. During the three months we lived in Moscow that year we moved twice.

Arcadi's salary was only 300 rubles a month, and since we were expecting to leave for Japan at any moment, I could not take a regular job. We just managed to live. Our rent was 50 rubles, meals at a cheap restaurant cost a ruble each. But bread was still cheap; and butter, when obtainable, about the same price as in England. Cigarettes were our greatest extravagance. At the end of each month I used to cart our empty bottles out to sell, or rake through our pockets for forgotten kopeks, to raise the price of a meal.

We were very happy. Discomfort and comparative poverty do not matter much so long as one is in love and has faith. And we both still had faith. Arcadi never regretted his house in London, and I had been poor most of the years since 1914. I wrote to my mother:

> I feel sometimes that having found Arcadi is too good to be true. I feel that the fact that we have been able to be happy together in these conditions argues well for the future. We have begun life together in the worst material conditions instead of the best. All the same, we both look forward to the day when we have a bed each and spoons and knives, and a bath and toilet of our own.

The months of waiting in Moscow were difficult and frustrating. I was kept busy finishing a translation from the German of *The Illustrated History of the Russian*

*Revolution** which I had begun in England, and which I counted on to provide money for Mother. I found it hard to work that summer in the uncertainty of our situation and the physical difficulties of existence. It became clear to us that without a considerable investment we would never get an apartment or even a room of our own. The brutal facts of life in the 'Socialist Paradise' were becoming more and more apparent, although I convinced myself that they were only a passing phase.

As usual I was worried about how to provide money for Mother, who was reluctant to rent out a room in our flat in Jessel House to any stranger.

I had hoped to be able to make some money as an interpreter at the Sixth Congress of the Comintern held that summer, having been recommended by Max Petrovsky, alias Breguer, at that time a big wheel in Moscow. But the deafness which was to afflict me far more seriously in later years prevented me. To mother I wrote: "I tried to interpret into a microphone while the speaker speaks but found my hearing was too bad to manage it. Arcadi is very concerned about my hearing and we are going to try and see a doctor. Also I shall be vaccinated before we leave Moscow and I am arranging to have my teeth done. We have just earned £4 on a Russian translation to pay for it."

I attended the Congress as a translator of written papers; listened to Bucharin from the visitors' gallery; saw Borodin walking in the corridors, already disgraced but still a romantic figure; thrilled at the sight of delegates—white, black, brown and yellow—from every corner of the world assembled in the socialist capital, visible witnesses to the "Unity of the Workers of the World."

Even in those days I had some deviations from "the Party line." My communism was essentially internationalistic and I thought of Trotsky as Lenin's heir. But I did not foresee that Stalin would soon acquire the power to destroy all that Lenin and Trotsky and the other old Bolsheviks had hoped to create. Nor had I as yet any inkling of the fundamental canker at the root of the Marxian doctrine which made the emergence of a tyrant such as Stalin practically inevitable. One believes what one wished to believe, until experience bangs one's head against the wall of reality.

At long last after the O.G.P.U. had fully satisfied itself concerning Arcadi and given him a passport, and the Japanese Government having likewise investigated him and given him a visa, we boarded the Trans Siberian Express. It was already October and we left Russia in the chill, wet Russian autumn, with the first signs of coming hardships already visible in Moscow. For some weeks I had been spending more and more time chasing after food supplies from one shop to another. Rationing had not yet been enforced, but the peasants were already refusing to sell their produce in return for money which could not buy them the clothing and other manufactures they required. Russia was on the eve of the Calvary of forced collectivization.

Describing our hasty departure from Moscow and the first days of our long journey, I wrote to Mother in a letter begun on the train on October 27, 1926:

> I am afraid, I have not written for a long time but you will have had my wire saying that we left Moscow on the 20th. As you might expect with me and Arcadi, we hardly managed to get packed in time to catch the train as we did not begin 'til 1:30 A.M. the night before and then had dozens of things to do the last day. So after waiting five months to be off we only just managed to catch the train on Saturday night, arriving at the station 15 minutes before the train left!! However, here

*London, Martin Lawrence, 1928. Translation from the German made by Freda Utley, M.A.

we are in a comfortable second-class carriage and having a most interesting journey. Only it is tantalizing not to be able to get off and look at all the places. One gets out at the stations for 10 or 20 minutes and runs about but that is all.

It is already very cold in Siberia. Snow in most places and bitter cold but sunny. Very beautiful after Irkutsk but just flat plains before that. We have already been more than six days in the train but it passes very quickly. Each day time changes by one hour, so one puts one's watch forward an hour every night and really feels one is racing across the world.

The most wonderful part of the journey is the Baikal lake. We got up at 5:00 A.M. to see the beginning of it. The train runs by the side of the lake for hours and hours—it is like a sea. Absolutely deserted except for a few tiny villages. A great lost lake in the middle of Asia. The wildness of the land even near the railway is wonderful after Europe. I am out of Europe for the first time.

At Chita, in Siberia, I left Arcadi—he to proceed direct to Japan, I to China. To my great delight the Comintern in Moscow had entrusted me with secret papers to take to China. I was to travel across the Russian border into Manchuria and on to Shanghai alone, so that I should not be suspect, while Arcadi proceeded direct to Japan. For a day before I left Moscow I had hunted in the shops for a corset so that I could hide the papers in approved Secret Agent style. I had never before worn even a brassiere and was extremely uncomfortable all through that long journey, but the thrill of conceiving of myself as a real revolutionary, helping to fan the flames of world revolution and liberate the "oppressed colonial workers" sustained me through the ordeal of wearing what is today called a foundation garment for the first time in my life.

From Chita on October 29 I wrote to Mother with discretion:

Have decided to stop two days here and have a look around. This place is a day's journey from the Chinese frontier and is already very Eastern. It was the capital of the Far Eastern Republic before the Bolsheviks got control. The people here other than the Russians are Mongols. Unfortunately, one can get little information from anyone.

It is a pity Temple is not here to tell me about the races, etc. I wish I remembered more about Genghis Khan, etc. On the train one passes through great stretches of land and over big rivers of which no one seems to know even the name. The unexplored, unknown parts of the world. It is amazing to think that the Russians managed to colonize as far as this.

All I can today remember of Chita is the intense cold from which I sought temporary relief by boiling myself in hot baths, and the memorials of the Decembrists, the 150 exiled revolutionaries of 1825 who had dreamed of liberty, equality, and fraternity under the Iron Tsar, Nicholas I. Only later was it to be borne in me how mild had been the tyranny of the Tsars compared to that of Stalin. Few nineteenth- and early twentieth-century revolutionaries in Russia were executed or herded into concentration camps to do forced labor as under Stalin and Hitler's 20th-century totalitarian tyrannies. For the most part they were permitted to live in exile in Siberia with their families, and could even escape without too much difficulty if they were so minded. In Soviet Russia in later years I was to learn that such comparatively humane and civilized treatment of political opponents makes Tsarist tyranny in retrospect seem almost benevolent.

I was looked after in Chita by a lively, energetic, and cheerful little O.G.P.U. man who had formerly been a sailor on American boats, and whom I was to meet years later in Moscow as a minor and most unhappy official at the Comintern. He was the sort of man who loves being conspiratorial for its own sake, and his manner of putting me on the express train to Harbin, from the tracks instead of the platform, into a specially reserved compartment, should have aroused the suspicion of the Japanese or Chinese spies, if there had been any.

I went through a bad half-hour at the Manchurian border. A young German with whom I had got friendly in the dining car remarked to me while we waited at the passport and customs-control office, that the system was to watch the faces of the travelers rather than to search their baggage carefully. A row of huge "White Russian" guards stood behind the Chinese customs officials watching the passengers. I had an innocent face and a British passport and Marshal Chang Tso-lin's police would need to have been very suspicious to search the person of a British subject, which was the reason why the Comintern had selected me to be its courier. So I really had nothing much to fear and my papers remained safe "in my bosom," as the old novels would have said.

Arrived in Harbin, I had the shock of discovering that Arcadi was still there and staying in the same hotel as myself. Seeing him quite close as I entered the restaurant for breakfast, I veered away and took a seat as far from him as possible, although longing to speak to him. However, it was a comfort to both of us that he should know I had safely crossed the border.

The Comintern, with the inefficiency characteristic of all Russian institutions, had been unaware that the fighting going on in North China had stopped all passenger traffic on the railway to Peking and that I would, therefore, have to get to Shanghai by sea from Dairen. The money I had been provided with for my journey was insufficient to meet the extra expense of waiting in the hotel at Dairen for passage on the crowded boats, and I had hardly a cent of my own. So in order to preserve enough to exist on in Shanghai for the ten days I planned to stay there, I economized in Dairen by eating only one meal a day. I took the table d'hote midday dinner at the de luxe Yamamoto Hotel and ate all through every one of its six or seven courses under the astonished and amused eyes of the Japanese waiters.

Eventually I got a ship to Shanghai where, according to my instructions I registered at the Palace Hotel and telephoned to a business office asking for a gentleman with a German name and telling him I had arrived with the samples of silk stockings he was waiting for. "Herr Doktor Haber," as he then called himself, came over at once and I handed over to him with considerable relief the sealed and silk encased package which I had concealed so long on my person, and which contained I know not what secret instructions for the furtherance of Communist aims in China.

Some days later I was permitted to meet with leaders of the Communist underground in Shanghai in one of their secret hideouts. Our rendezvous was at midnight in a whitewashed cellar somewhere off the Nanking Road in the British concession, to which I was conducted by a devious route lest anyone should be following me. It was very conspiratorial and thrilling and reminds me today of a Hollywood spy movie. For my Chinese companions it was deadly earnest since the British authorities in the International settlement, as well as Chiang Kai-shek's newly establishment government, were intent on rooting out and exterminating the remnants of the Moscow directed Chinese Communist party.

I was probably safe from anything worse than deportation from China, but others were risking their lives.

Most of the men I met that night were not Chinese, but Americans and Germans or German speaking Europeans. The former, like myself, could rely on their governments' protecting them, however reluctantly, against summary arrest, torture or death. But some among those present had become men without a country by reason of their dedication to the Communist cause. Those who came from Eastern Europe or other countries ruled over by dictatorships had no hope of protection from their governments.

They all plied me with questions about happenings in Moscow which I had difficulty in answering. If not crypto-Trotskyists, most of them seemed to be most unhappy revolutionaries who had witnessed Stalin's callous and cynical sacrifice of the Chinese Communists, and were watching with dismay the beginnings of his transformation of the Comintern into a sub-office of the Russian national state.

If I had been able to transcribe and preserve details of my discussions with the Comintern underground leaders in Shanghai in 1928 I could present some valuable historical sidelights on *The Tragedy of the Chinese Revolution.**

Ten years later I was to meet victims of this long drawnout tragedy whom I had briefly encountered in the Communist underground in 1928.

In Shanghai, in October 1938, when about to leave for America after six months as correspondent for the *London News Chronicle* in the Hankow war zone, I was awakened very early by the telephone ringing by my bedside. A man's voice asked me if he could come up but would give no name. I was still half asleep when a white-faced, emaciated and shabbily dressed individual entered the room. I did not remember him but he gave me such full details of my visit to Shanghai in 1928 that I was convinced. He was pitifully nervous, dared not stay long, and begged me to come and visit him and his wife that evening.

They were the once famous couple internationally known under the name Noulens who had been arrested as Comintern agents in 1933 and made headlines when they went on a hunger strike.

I agreed to visit them but I was nervous because Noulens had insisted on my telling no one. For all I knew he might still be a Communist agent or could conceivably be working for the Japanese, and both Moscow and Tokyo would no doubt have liked to have me quietly disappear. So I took my trusted friend Randall Gould, editor of the Shanghai *Evening Post*, into my confidence. He offered to wait for me in his car at the end of the street and come and rescue me if I did not rejoin him in an hour's time.

The Noulens told me they had been released from prison in 1937 following the outbreak of war with Japan and the ostensible submission of the Chinese Communist Party to the Kuomintang government in a joint defense against Japanese aggression. Madame Sun Yat-sen was supplying them with enough money to exist. But they had been warned to see no one—or so they said, and I believed them. They told me they had so longed to speak to someone they had once known and trusted that they had risked asking me to their home. They were obviously terrified. Austrians without passports and with

---

*Title of Harold Isaacs book which in its original edition published in England in 1938 is the best and most fully documented account of Soviet policy in China in the 20's and 30's. The edition published later in the U.S. was expurgated by the author to be less offensive to Stalin.

nowhere to go, they feared liquidation if they returned to Russia because they knew too much. I urged them to meet Randall Gould, who was a liberal and a kindly man and who I knew would try to help them. But they dared not.

Poor devils. I felt full of pity for these two white-faced derelicts of an age in Comintern history long past. They had left one prison only to fear incarceration in another. Rejected by everyone, they were too broken in spirit to save themselves and start a new life. I had known men and women like them in Moscow, old revolutionaries whose hopes were dead but who could not break with their past and waited only for death.

"Dr. Haber" seems to have had better luck and more sense. He had organized a real import business as cover for his Comintern activities and developed it into a flourishing enterprise. Some of his employees acted in the double capacity of traveling salesmen and agents of the Comintern with their salaries halved between Moscow and Haber's business account. According to the account given of him in *Pattern for World Revolution** by the former Communist "Ypsilon," Haber, whom he calls Comrade L, decided in the early thirties that the Revolution was dead and henceforth devoted himself exclusively to the business which was by then netting him a hundred thousand dollars a year profit. He calmly returned the amount of the original capital advanced to him by Moscow, arguing that this was all the Comintern had a right to expect since he had all along paid ten per cent interest besides performing his duties as a Comintern agent.

I lived a double, or rather, a treble life in Shanghai, spending part of my time investigating conditions in the cotton industry; some evenings as the guest of "British Imperialists" at luxurious dinner parties and dancing or going to theaters with them; and others in secret meetings with the Communists.

It was part of the game that I should mix with the "bourgeoisie" and appear quite innocent of revolutionary activity; and my cotton industry investigations were in any case genuine. But, I was not cut out to be a conspirator, being all too intent on testifying to the "capitalists" concerning the rottenness of their system and the wickedness of their exploitation of the colonial workers. Thinking on one occasion to kill any doubts they might have about me, I told a Shanghai dinner party that I was doing some reporting for the *Manchester Guardian*. This was true, and I thought it should establish my *bona fides* in the "bourgeois" world. To my mind, the *Manchester Guardian* signified the "capitalist press," but to my compatriots in Shanghai it was "that Red rag," the paper for which "that awful fellow Arthur Ransome" wrote. All values are indeed relative as Hadow used to say. Five years later in Moscow in one of the periodic purges, or "cleansing of the apparatus," it was brought up against me as a proof of capitalist connections, that I had at one time worked for the *Manchester Guardian*.

Before sailing for Kobe with a batch of letters to be mailed there to Communist agents in Japan, I had myself inoculated against smallpox. Either because it was the first time, or because I went to a careless doctor or the serum was contaminated, or because I got some infection in the cheap and rather dirty hotel in the French concession to which I had moved after completing my mission for the Comintern, the results was so grim as to justify my father's refusal to have me inoculated in childhood when even in England the hazards of vaccination were considerable.

A German doctor in Shanghai after having "done me on the leg" had told me to come back four days later. Finding then that his inoculation seemed to have had no effect, he

---

*Ziff-Davis Publishing Co: Chicago–New York, 1947.

concluded that I was not liable to smallpox infection, and dismissed me without even putting on a piece of clean lint. The old dressing had fallen off before I left Shanghai, but I didn't bother since the doctor had been so casual about it. That night it seemed a bit swollen, so I went to the ship's doctor and he put on a clean dressing. Next day I felt rather bad and had a lump in my groin and the vaccinated part was so swollen that I went to the doctor again and he said not to worry, it was the natural effect of vaccination. That afternoon I went to bed about 5 o'clock and sent for aspirin. I felt very ill and even a bit delirious that night and had to make a great effort to pack and get ashore next morning, but nonetheless did not feel as bad as the night before. I got into a train at Kobe at once for Tokyo where I arrived next morning at 6:00 A.M. I went to an hotel and had a bath but kept my leg out of it, lay down a bit and later on went off to find Arcadi. My leg was by this time very swollen and painful and I put it all down to the vaccination. Arcadi insisted on my going to a doctor at once and I came to a place called St. Luke's hospital run by Americans but with Japanese doctors. At last I was in competent hands in a beautiful clean place. The doctor said I had been infected and had got erysipelas and must go to bed at once as it would be very dangerous if it spread. I was a bit frightened. The inflammation spread up to my groin and when my temperature went up and I felt generally pretty rotten they took me into the hospital where I spent 2½ days and got down the lump in my groin with ice bags. They stopped the inflammation spreading with some thick black ointment and soon there was no more danger. I have been up three days only I have had to go and have it dressed every two days, till the ulcers healed. The worst of the whole business is that it is and has been very expensive. I have not yet paid the Doctor's bill but it is about 6 shillings a time, and the hospital was 24/- a day, and then there is also the waste of time. In a later letter to Mother I wrote: "My leg has cost £11 already apart from the waste of time. Altogether, I wish very much that I had never been vaccinated. Arcadi never wanted me to and now I have worried him so much. He has been very concerned especially, as he says, because it is my leg and he thinks my legs the best part of me!"

Even after I left the hospital I remained separated from Arcadi except for clandestine meetings. As I wrote Mother:

> The worst of it is that at present we are living almost as strangers and only meeting occasionally. This week he is in Osaka and I shall not be seeing him at all. The point is that I must see factories here and be accepted as a research student before I get mixed up with him, he being a Russian. The spying here is terrible and although Arcadi is not a Communist, and I am here for absolutely *bona fide* reasons, it is dangerous for us to be together at first. It is all a damnable nuisance and soon we are going to the same boarding house to lead an immoral life! But for the moment you will laugh to hear that I am living with a missionary! She is a very nice one and has a charming house on the water, and I have a delightful room and good food but I feel a bit lonely after this long separation—more than a month now—and am longing to be with Arcadi again. I am getting this letter posted in Vladivostock as otherwise, of course, the Japanese police would read it. You will also understand why I wired to stop Lily's letters, which are most compromising politically. This is a country in which it is dangerous to be even a liberal. The University here has me under their wing and I have other good introductions and I don't want to spoil it all by association with

Russians until I have seen all I can. Hence my temporary 'divorce' from
Arcadi. So my future letters will be a bit colourless.

It proved as impossible to get some of my English friends to understand the nature of
a police state then as later in Russia. John Strachey's wife was so ignorant or silly as to
send me a letter addressed c/o the Japanese Communist Party, which was of course illegal
and underground—a letter which I naturally never received and learned about only later.

The name of the very nice missionary with the "house on the water" was Miss Henty.
She ran a kindergarten school for poor Japanese children and she was a darling. After I
had confided in her and told her all about Arcadi instead of being shocked she helped us
to meet as often and as discreetly as possible. She also assisted me greatly in my research
by introducing me to Japanese friends, interpreting for me, and putting me in touch with
teachers and social workers in other cities. Thus I stayed mainly with missionaries or in
YWCA dormitories with Japanese girls while busily visiting large textile factories in
Tokyo, Osaka and Nagoya, and small weaving sheds in outlying districts.

But for awhile I was, if not immobilized, considerably hampered by the after effects of
my Shanghai vaccination.

On December 27, 1929 I wrote to Mother telling her that I evidently must have got
"very run down" in Moscow because otherwise the "vaccination business" would not
have developed such complications. "It is nearly seven weeks since it was done," I wrote
on December 27, "and the ulcers have only just begun to heal. Also my teeth have been
all wrong and I have had a lot of toothache." But I add, she should not worry because,
after having just spent three Christmas holiday days at the sea at Atami with Arcadi,
"walking all the time" I am feeling particularly well.

My letters from Japan that lonely December of separation from Arcadi reveal both my
nostalgia for home and my temporary loss of confidence in myself, which was in part the
result of the English Communist publishers of my translation of the *Illustrated History of
the Russian Revolution* having complained of the quality of the work I had done on the
second volume while in Moscow. Today I surmise that the real reason why, after having
been very well satisfied with my translation of the first volume, they were now
complaining and refusing to pay the money due to me, was because of the change in the
'party line' necessitating revision of the text to eliminate Trotsky entirely from the scene.
But at the time I was shattered by the complaint about the quality of my work, and
feared that I had become "decomposed."*

I was soon to recover my self-confidence as I immersed myself in my study of the
Japanese cotton industry and after I had some widely publicized articles published in the
Manchester Guardian. But I retained a lingering fear that I might be becoming
"decomposed," as when I wrote to Mother: "I am living in the present for the first time
in my life and I know it is dangerous."

At the end of January, having accumulated an abundance of data, I went to live with
Arcadi in Tokyo at the small house he had rented at Kogaicho 2, Azabu, near the Soviet
Trade Representation offices. To the letter I wrote to Mother from Tokyo early in the
morning of January 30, 1929, after a long coach journey from Osaka, Arcadi added a
squeezed in postscript:

I bargained with Freda for space but she treats room on her paper as if
it were a Moscow flat. She is rather stingy but it can't be helped. I must

---

*This was my husband's translation of the Russian adjective *rajlajitse* applied to Communists whose
revolutionary energy was sapped by residence among the bourgeoisie. The word implies a general
softening and giving way to the desire for an easy, comfortable life.

95

stand it because she is now such a rare guest of mine! Three weeks in **three** months! I used an extension of space wishing you the best of luck **in** 1929 and all the years to come. My love to Temple and many thanks for the book you sent me. Best of love, Arcadi.

Chapter 12
HONEYMOON IN JAPAN

My Japanese year was the best in all my life. So happy, so well-remembered that I look back on it through the gathering mist of my coming old age with an aching nostalgia.

Arcadi and I were very much in love and enjoyed to the full the great happiness of being at long last together. We were getting to care more and more for one another as we understood one another better and became increasingly intimate both physically and mentally. Life was full of laughter, thanks to his gift of humor and my release for awhile from the nagging money worries of the past. I described what I felt to Mother in sentences I could not improve on today:

> I can realize now the sweetness and joy of your life with Dada and the terrible loneliness afterwards. You, dear, and I think I also, for a time at least—have enjoyed a perfect companionship which simply does not admit of pretenses and squabbles and flirtations, which do in fact come into the life of most people. I waited a very long weary time Mother, and it only came just in time to save me from taking a third or fifth best or, rather, nothing.

We lived very simply, for although Arcadi was earning £100 a month, we hoped to save enough money to buy an apartment in Moscow when we returned—which meant stringent economizing in view of the dependents we both had to provide for. In addition to "Mrs. B." Arcadi had a son in Poland by his first wife whom he was educating, and I had Mother. Besides it hardly seemed worthwhile buying anything but the minimum essentials of furniture and other things since we thought we would be in Japan only a few months.

We went on with one table, two chairs, two knives, two glasses and plates, and that was about all. We slept on the floor as the Japanese do on "foutons" but later an old divan was lent to us. It was a Japanese house in which we had two rooms. It was all made of paper and thin wood. No glass and you could put your fingers through the walls in many places. I kept on making holes in the paper so we had plenty of fresh air coming in! There were also plenty of rats which disturbed Arcadi's sleep but I was too deaf to hear them.

By summer 1929 we had four rooms. We went on existing with two writing tables, one round table and three straight chairs, and were still sleeping on the floor—but had acquired six sets of knives, forks, spoons and china. I could see us going on for years like this, always thinking we were not going to stay put more than a few weeks and then staying months. I didn't really mind. It made life "very simple" and I was far too happy with Arcadi.

Moreover, as compared with earlier years of my life, and the future which awaited us in Moscow, we were in clover. We had plenty to eat and ample living space and no serious money troubles.

In addition, as rarely afterwards in my life, I did not have to do the cooking or washing up. We had acquired a wonderful servant. Arcadi had been joking for a long time that since he lived with me he was kept starving, and after I had been in bed for a few days with an ulcerated throat, we thought we had better do something. So I got rid of my inefficient charwoman and engaged an Amah. After a week she had become a pearl beyond price. She cooked well and was scrupulously clean. We were living as we had never lived. Three regular meals a day! It was too good to be true. Of course, our living expenses went up but we were eating good wholesome food and enough. It was a great change. It was also rather a joke because we had to live up to our servant. She was used to a "proper household." We had to use serviettes, but Arcadi had never accustomed himself to doing without them. Best of all, he was beginning to go to bed earlier. He advanced his usual bedtime from 3:00 a.m. to 12:30 p.m.! We were forced into regular habits. We paid her 50 yen a month (£5) and she lived in but found her own food. I hoped she would stay for I expected we were in for a lot of lean living again in the future, so we might as well live a bit better while we could. However, we still didn't buy a bed as it didn't seem worthwhile.

We surmised that our invaluable Japanese servant was, of necessity, a spy. But she was a very nice one. She became so friendly that she told us she had to report on us daily to the Security Police. This did not worry us since there was actually little or nothing for her to report about either of us.

Arcadi's mission to Japan was for the purpose of investigating the possibilities of expanding the market for "Santonin," a medicine extracted from a plant grown only in Turkestan, which cured the worms which afflict and debilitate the people of all rice culture "night soil" fertilizer Asian countries.

Nowadays there are chemically produced synthetics which are equally efficacious, but at this time Russia had a monopoly on the drug and Japan was the largest consumer, because the Chinese and other rice culture countries were too poor to buy Santonin. Arcadi had to study the market situation and decide whether lowering the price would increase sales in Japan and elsewhere, or whether maintenance of the very high Russian monopoly price would be more profitable.

"Monopolistic capitalist" or "Soviet imperialist" as Arcadi's business activities undoubtedly were, they were no more subversive than my investigations of the Japanese cotton industry.

It was, however, the fixed belief of the Japanese authorities that all Soviet employees must be doubling as Communist agents. So much so that when Arcadi was seeking a Japanese assistant in his Santonin promotion and advertising campaign, a well qualified young Japanese who applied for the job said to him, "I cannot do both." "Both what?" Arcadi asked, "Both business and Communist propaganda," he replied.

Wonderfully naive Japanese, I used to think. But they were perhaps no more naive or misguided than Americans today who imagine that every Soviet technician or specialist abroad is clandestinely or openly engaged in Communist propaganda, whereas the truth in most cases is that he is just too, too, happy to have escaped for awhile from the "Socialist Paradise."

In Japan in 1929 when life in Russia was not nearly so hard as it became later, the majority of Soviet employees at the Trade Representation and Embassy wanted above all to remain abroad.

Of course, they could not say so openly, but it was all too obvious. Those who dreaded most being recalled to Moscow were the men who suspected that their wives had married them only in order to go abroad and would divorce them if they were sent home. A notable case was that of poor Shubin, the middle-aged Counsellor of the Soviet

Embassy in Tokyo whose beautiful young wife was the belle of the diplomatic corps. As only a high grade member of the Communist party could provide her in Russia with the standard of life she had become accustomed to in the capitalist world, she promptly divorced him after they were recalled to Moscow and married Voitinsky, a big shot in the Comintern who later became my "boss" at the Institute of World Economy and Politics in Moscow.

Shubin was a gentle, honorable, and kindly man, a Menshevik who never joined "the Party." Nevertheless, he did not do at all badly for himself on his return to Moscow. After his lovely young wife had duly divorced him to take a higher place in Soviet society, Shubin married Anna Louise Strong, the foremost female American propagandist for the Soviet Union, whose "passionate stupidity" is described in Malcolm Muggeridge's satire on the Soviet Union entitled *Winter in Moscow*.* In Moscow in the 30's, Shubin, who was a small thin man, would appear like a small tug conveying an ocean liner when he accompanied his massively proportioned wife to Moscow parties.**

The intrigues, the calumnies, and the factional struggles which went on in the small Russian colony of employees at the Trade Representation and Embassy in Tokyo should have taught us what to expect in the USSR. But we thought, or continued to kid ourselves, that this was because the Russian colony was composed of "intellectuals" and that in Russia the proletarians ensured a cleaner atmosphere.

Moreover, both the Ambassador, Tryanovsky, and the Trade Representative, Anikeev, were decent men and the same could be said of Ivan Maisky, later to become Ambassador to Britain, but at this time the Counsellor of the Embassy in Tokyo. Maisky's wife and my friend Madam Anikeev were at daggers drawn and once during Tryanovky's absence from Tokyo a telegram had to be sent to Moscow to settle the delicate question of precedence at Embassy dinner parties and Japanese state functions: who came first—the wife of Maisky, the Embassy Counsellor, or the wife of Anikeev, the Trade Representative? As far as I remember, the question was settled in Madam Anikeev's favor, but the whole Russian colony was split into factions by the antagonism between these two women. They were fairly evenly matched, because although Maiskaya was a member of the Party and Anikeeva was not, Maiskaya had not joined the Bolsheviks until 1924, whereas Anikeev was not only an old Bolshevik but was also of proletarian origin, having once been a factory worker in France. Anikeeva being both a beautiful woman and intelligent, became a sort of First Lady, in spite of Maiskaya's "old Bolshevik" qualifications. Tryanovsky's wife, an unassuming lady, played no part in the faction fights of Red society. His first wife had been a Bolshevik when he was a Menshevik, and the story told was that during the civil wars she had condemned her husband to death when he was brought before her as a prisoner. Lenin himself had talked Tryanovsky over into joining the Bolsheviks and saved him from the death sentence imposed by his wife. I cannot vouch for the truth of this story, as whispered to me in Tokyo, but at least it explained Tryanovsky's choice of a non-political, rather colorless lady as his second wife. It is more pleasant to have a wife not liable to shoot one on account of one's political

---

*Eyre & Spottiswoode, London, 1934.

**Shubin was purged in the late '30s and Anna Louise Strong briefly arrested as I learnt on my 1938 lecture tour in America when I met her father, a devout minister, in Seattle, dreadfully worried at his daughter's arrest. Terrified, or clinging to her Communist faith, Anna Louise Strong made all the necessary confessions and is today, in her 80's, comfortably installed in Peking as the grand old lady of Western Communist society among a handful of other defectors.

99

beliefs. (Decades later their son became a familiar figure in the West as Khrushchev's interpreter.)

Soviet society cannot intelligibly be described without some account of the human element. Russian women are just as prone to social discrimination, pride in their social status, love of fine clothes and admiration, as women in "bourgeois" society. Soviet society has its hierarchies and its jealousies and never was composed of simple-minded, ardent revolutionaries with red cotton handkerchiefs on their heads, intent on constructing socialism regardless of personal advancement and the material comforts such advancement brings. The poorly dressed men and women who march in the demonstrations of the proletariat, to the admiration of foreign tourists, are most of them longing to change places with the "boyars of the bureaucracy"* who watch them from reserved seats in the Red Square.

Despite my mainly political interests, I became interested in Arcadi's business activities on behalf of the Soviet government. I followed his negotiations learning something about business and realized that it can be fascinating. At least when it is on a big scale such as Arcadi's work where he had to use so many kinds of knowledge: finance, economics, and psychology. His understanding of people's characters, motives, and weaknesses was astonishing. At the same time he was amazingly young and happy and sometimes absurdly playful. Even as I write of him now, I smile at memories of his whimsicalities.

Arcadi also taught me chess and was anxious that I should learn to beat him. We doubted that I ever would. Our son was to become a good chess player even as a child without benefit of teaching by his father. Today I often marvel at Jon's resemblance to his father in qualities of mind, heart, intelligence, and above all, in understanding of people. Arcadi was a success in private business before he devoted his talents to the service of the first "socialist state," and thereafter became an invaluable asset to his Communist "bosses." Jon, following his graduation from Georgetown University's School of Foreign Service in 1956 was to achieve financial independence by making a success in business in South America.

Morgan Young, publisher and editor of the *Japan Chronicle*, had told me that once my connection with Arcadi was discovered I would find myself in difficulties and that the police might confiscate all my notes. Warned by him ahead of time that the Japanese authorities had caught up with me, I took his advice to deliver them for safekeeping to George Sansom, the Commercial Counsellor of the British Embassy to whom he gave me an introduction.

Approaching the British Embassy with some trepidation as a class-conscious Communist, I was met by George Sansom with the disarming remark, "What a lovely coat you have on"—referring to a dark blue Harris tweed coat which was my pride and joy, but which Arcadi and other Russians thought inelegant!

Years later in Moscow I was to discover in selling old clothes to a Tartar trader in order to buy food, that the garments regarded in England as best because made of handspun and woven material, were despised in Russia where only machine-made stuff, however shoddy, was considered valuable.

George Sansom, having already charmed me by his appreciation of my coat, proceeded to win my further confidence by agreeing to take all my precious notes on the Japanese cotton industry into safekeeping until such time as the danger had passed over. He also

---

*The term used to describe the Communist aristocracy by Boris Souvarine in his monumental and unequaled book, *Stalin: A Critical Survey of Bolshevism*, Secker & Warburg, London, 1939.

100

invited me to have lunch with him and his wife, Katherine, and later they visited Arcadi and me at our home and we gradually became good friends. Years afterwards in England, George (later Sir George) Sansom, internationally recognized as the foremost Western scholar of Japanese history and culture, told me that prior to my coming to see him he had been warned against me as a dangerous Communist agent by the British Foreign Office.

The Sansoms met the Chairman of the Soviet Trade Delegation, Anikeev, and his charming wife at our house, although the Soviet and British Governments and Embassies were not on speaking terms. George and Katherine both became quite attached to my husband, and George and Arcadi were mutually appreciative of each other's qualities and knowledge. Arcadi was as reserved as any Englishman and made the kind of ironical jokes which appeal to the English but were to get him into trouble in Russia.

Katherine, who was quite a beauty and was always elegantly attired although not spending much money on clothes, endeavored in Tokyo in 1929 to improve my appearance. She took me to her dressmaker, and, more important, taught me to use cosmetics. I used powder, although not lipstick, and was not unfamiliar with Pond's cold cream. But it was Katherine Sansom who gave me a pot of lemon complexion cream, took me to the first beauty parlor or hair dresser I had ever gone to, and in general interested me in my appearance—as my mother had tried and singularly failed to do.

Although I was by now living openly in Tokyo with Arcadi as his wife, my marital status was ambiguous. In Temple's phrase, I had the choice between "sin or citizenship." My living with Arcadi without any formalization of our marriage became generally known, and, of course, some people were shocked. George Sansom had known for some time, but he realized that it was only to keep my British citizenship and he was extremely decent. Also, Miss Henty, the missonary with whom I stayed before, was "perfectly ripping" about it. She said that I was really married, that it was just the same thing as if I were.

The Japanese police were naturally suspicious of me because of the secrecy of our relationship. I asked George Sansom for his protection. He told me to refer them to him if I had any trouble. Morgan Young had warned me some time before when I told him about my having a husband to whom I was not legally married that anyone who associated with Russians would be suspect in Tokyo.

The Professor at Keio University to whom the School of Economics had given me an introduction was I wrote "a beautiful example of things here." I didn't know what he knew about my personal affairs but thought that it was probably a good deal. One day when I went to see him, Bertrand Russell's name came up and I saw he was anything but *persona grata*. This Professor had the cheek to say that Russell had shocked the Japanese very much by living there *openly* with a woman to whom he was not married! This, in a country where divorce for men was as easy as in Russia; where it was common for couples to live together for a year without registering their marriage; and where people who made their fortunes out of brothels were respected members of society. I planned to write and tell Russell about it, so indignant was I at his daring to criticize so great a man. Whether he was getting at me or not, I didn't know. Anyhow, I looked forward with great joy to telling the School of Economics about it when I got back because he was the Japanese representative on the Economic History Society Committee.

I must here digress to explain my marital status, or lack of it, as also to pay tribute to the British authorities who both then and years later were as helpful as they could be in the circumstances.

101

According to Soviet law at this time, it was sufficient to register as man and wife with the house management of the block in which one lived to be considered married, and this we had done. The further step of recording a marriage with the district Soviet authorities was extremely simple. As I had seen, when Arcadi divorced Anna Abramovna in 1928, there was a clerk at a table on one side of the room to register divorces and another some few feet away at which to marry. But, had we recorded our marriage at the Soviet divorce and marriage office I would have had to surrender my British passport and become a Soviet "citizen."

Originally, I had wanted to retain my British passport in order not to encounter the difficulties which Soviet citizens experienced in obtaining visas to visit foreign countries. Later it was the fact that I had remained a British "subject" which saved me from being incarcerated forever in the vast prison house which Soviet Russia was to become.

When my son was born in Moscow in March 1934, I registered his birth with the Soviet authorities without giving his father's name, and the British Embassy did me the great favor of inscribing Jon's name on my passport with the proviso that he was not a British subject. And in 1940 in America, when applying for United States citizenship for myself and my son, a sympathetic British consul in New York who happened to have known my brother in the South Seas, gave me the precious document reproduced here:

BRITISH COUNSULATE-GENERAL,
25, BROADWAY
NEW YORK
8th November 1940.
TO WHOM IT MAY CONCERN:

It is hereby certified that the form of marriage which Miss Freda Utley went through in Moscow in the year 1928 is not regarded by His Majesty's Government as binding. Miss Utley is, therefore, considered officially unmarried and she therefore continues to hold a British passport in her maiden-name.

Miss Utley's son, John Basil Utley, was included in her passport at His Majesty's Consulate in Moscow, since she had chosen to register him under her own name, although he is not considered as a British subject for the time being.

(S)
H.B.M. Vice-Consul.

This cleverly worded letter enabled me to escape from my old dilemma of "sin or citizenship" without any stigma of illegitimacy on my son.

* * *

Besides the most useful contacts given me by my missionary friend, Miss Henty, I had introductions from the London School of Economics which opened many doors. And I was fortunate in that on my first visit to Kobe I met and began what was to prove a life-long friendship with Morgan Young, the intrepid editor and publisher of the world renowned liberal weekly, *Japan Chronicle*, and author of several excellent books on Japan. He knew Russell and admired him. He was interesting, intelligent, and humane and was to remain my friend until his death in England at the beginning of the Second World War.

In general I was afforded a rare opportunity to acquire the information I required to write my book and the articles I had contracted to send to the *Manchester Guardian Commercial Supplement* on comparative costs of production in the Japanese and

Lancashire cotton industries. I was hampered only by my lack of any mechanical or engineering training or of practical knowledge of the production process. I had visited a few cotton textile factories in Lancashire while at the London School of Economics but until I came to Japan I had no opportunity to master the many stages of the productive process which transforms a ball of raw cotton into the yarn which is eventually woven into cloth. So I had to pretend to be an expert until I actually became one. This required hard work and constant vigilance lest I betray my ignorance. While posing the questions, noting the answers, and checking them by my own observations of how many workers were standing at each machine producing so much per hour or day from carding to spinning to weaving, enabling me to calculate labor and other costs, I learnt to distinguish one machine from another in the whole complicated process.

I also had to beware of permitting myself to be overwhelmed by Japanese courtesy and hospitality to the extent of neglecting my primary interest in the condition of the Japanese proletariat. It was quite difficult to prevent myself from relaxing after a luncheon with sake toasts, following a strenuous morning walking through the many departments of a textile mill and cataloging my observations and the replies to my questions. I had to overcome both temporary lethargy and a certain reluctance to embarrass my hosts when I insisted on spending the rest of the day inspecting living conditions, and talking to the indentured girl workers who constituted the bulk of the labor force in the Japanese textile industry.

There were some embarrassing times when, myself treated as an equal by my Japanese hosts, I came up against their attitude to their own women. As when the managing director of a big textile mill in Nagoya invited me to dinner bringing his wife with him to the restaurant. I felt very uncomfortable when she knelt in the background to serve us. Or when I was bowed out of a room first while the Japanese women waited to follow the men.

I have never been much of a feminist since I usually like men better than women but I believe in equality of rights and opportunities for the sexes as well as for races and peoples. So I was outraged at the subordinate status of Japanese women in those days, as well as horrified at the exploitation of the women workers.

I remember one amusing episode: in a conversation with an engineer when responding to the usual Japanese enquiry in making social talk, "How many childs have you?" I dodged the question, not knowing whether it was by now known that I was married, and replied with the same query. Whereupon the Japanese engineer replied, "Two, and one in the course of production."

Writing to Mother in March 1929, I say: "I believe I have done some good work. I have just sent a long article to the *Manchester Guardian* on spinning costs. My report goes very much against the Consular Report issued in 1927 and I think it will make a stir. Last Sunday I spent the day with Arno Pearce, the Secretary of the International Master Cotton Spinners whom I got to know in Manchester when the School of Economics sent me there. He was just leaving after three weeks in Japan and although he has not collected nearly so much information as I have—not visited so many mills—his results fit in fairly well with mine. He congratulated me on the work I have done and said it would be a good thing if I could go to India and study the industry there in the same way. I am afraid though that the expense makes this impossible.

"As I gave a good many of my figures to Pearce I am now in a great hurry to get my stuff published, as, although he would be too decent actually to use them, his report will probably be affected by them. So I have already rushed off one article."

In another sentence in this letter which I read today with wry amusement at my attitude toward life in those distant days I concluded:

"Although I had felt that I had wasted a lot of my time here just being happy, I seem really to have done something."

My second article, 5,000 words long on weaving, had really entailed a terrific amount of work. I had been working so hard I had "hardly missed Arcadi!" who had been away in Osaka. I asked Mother to telephone Emile Burns at the Labor Research Dept. and tell him that: "my conclusions show Japanese labor costs in spinning to be about one-half English ones and in weaving about one-third."

My continuing contributions published in the *Manchester Guardian Commercial Supplement* in the spring and summer of 1929, for which I was paid £15 each provided some money for Mother, besides winning me recognition as an expert on the cotton industry at home and abroad. And my book *Lancashire and the Far East** (although not published until 1931 on account of the refusal of Sir William Beveridge to permit the London School of Economics to sponsor it) was also to win me acclaim as the author of a valuable study even by those who disliked my Socialist and anti-imperialist viewpoint.

Once again I was given the opportunity to take my place as a scholar, economist, or expert in the "capitalist world" with a secure and profitable future. But all my life I could never "stick to one last," or "cash in" on the successes I have achieved in one or another field of endeavor. My mental bent was toward research and the quest for facts, truth, and more than superficial understanding in every branch of knowledge in which I became interested. But my temperament impelled me to get involved in political fights which tarnished my reputation as a scholar; and to dissipate or spread my energies in too many different directions.

Happy as I was in Japan, I had a deep conviction that it was wrong to be living comfortably while surrounded by poverty, misery and oppression. Japan was giving me my first experience of a police state. It could not be compared to the apparatus of compulsion and terror I was to know in Soviet Russia, but the regime was sufficiently tyrannical and oppressive to keep my revolutionary fervor alive and make me feel guilty because I was enjoying life so much.

I decided I must tear myself away from Arcadi and return to England to work for the Communist Party. My letters to my mother reflect the conflict between what I conceived as my duty to humanity and the desire of my heart to continue the wonderful joy of life in Japan with Arcadi. In a letter dated July 5, 1929 I wrote:

"I suppose I really am coming back (probably by September). Now it is getting so close I dare not think of it. Forgive me, dearest, I want to be with you *very* much indeed but I can now hardly contemplate life without Arcadi . . . I feel a fierce desire to stay with Arcadi and seize what life offers in the present. And yet I know I must remain Freda and come home to do some work. I even feel and know I should not keep Arcadi's love if I became just his wife."

Two decades later, hearing Marlene Dietrich sing her unforgettable Berlin song with the refrain "Why in this earthly paradise are we in love with pain," I remembered and wondered why I left Arcadi in Japan instead of enjoying to the full as long as possible the wonderful life we had there together.

Of course, no one knows his real motives. Perhaps it was not really my feeling that one has no right to great personal happiness so long as the majority of mankind starve and toil

---

*Allen & Unwin, 1931.

without joy. It may have been ambition or the desire to make my mark in the world, which is perhaps the same thing as love of power, which impelled me to leave Arcadi and return to work in the Communist Party in England. Or it may have been the feeling I expressed in several of my letters that Arcadi's love for me was founded upon his conception of me as a revolutionary, an intellectual, an independent woman, not a "mere wife." I felt that if I lost myself in his love I might lose it, that I must somehow continue being what I had been when he began to love me.

Although he knew he would be terribly lonely when I was gone, Arcadi encouraged me to leave him to go back to England to work for the Communist cause in which I still believed. Arcadi, even as I, believed in what the Webbs called the Vocation of Leadership, meaning the duty of all who long for social justice, to sacrifice personal happiness to political work.

Before tearing myself away from Arcadi to work in England until we could meet again in Moscow, we spent the best holiday we ever had together at Tsuruga on the northwest coast of Japan where we shared lodgings with some Russian friends. It was extremely hot but far better than Tokyo, since we had the sea to cool ourselves in and could go around in the cotton kimonos suitable to the climate. I taught Arcadi to swim and he did his best to improve my chess game.

Arcadi used to call me his 'swan song', meaning then, as I understood him, that after his previous unhappy marriages, he saw me as his last best love who gave him all he longed for in his personal life as both wife and comrade, and renewed his hope in the possiblity of creating a world where there should be no more man-made misery and injustice.

After I lost him, some ten years after we had found one another in London, I realized that he had been more prophetic than he knew, since the swan dies in singing its last beautiful song, and it was I who had lured Arcadi to death or slavery in Soviet Russia by renewing his faith that God's kingdom on earth could be established by adhering to the godless faith of the Marxists.

In 1940 when I wrote *The Dream We Lost** the only letter I possessed from my husband was one quoted at the beginning of the previous chapter. But while writing these Memoirs I found among my Mother's papers a letter from Tsuruga Arcadi wrote to me in London a few days after we parted and I was on the Trans-Siberian Railway from Vladivostok to Moscow on my way home to England:

> My darling Fredochka,
>
> I spent nearly a week in Tsuruga since you left and I have already a slight foretaste of what it will be like in the future. The most important is that however hard I try to adapt myself to the human milieu I find it nearly impossible. Humbug, cowardice and lack of culture, not to say refinement, seem to be all pervading with a few very rare exceptions. It is evident that the only way is seclusion, just as we secluded ourselves from all the world when you were here. This mode of living will secure at least that I shall not feel provoked by stupidity or cowardice to say unpleasant truths which are of no earthly use to anyone. I never had such a clear conception of how much the set habits and conceptions mean in the life of any community, as I learned here.
>
> I shall miss terribly my darling comrade but I hope that you will make it worth while by attending to your hearing and preparing for our

---

*The John Day Co., New York.

future life together. At the same time don't neglect to create for yourself a proper footing in the things that interest you and are essential for you. Your personality should not get dissolved in the small family interests, it would have been too shortsighted, however great may be the temptation to do so.

My darling wife is really very much different from the other women I know, and I cherish that you are so different. I cannot help making mental comparisons and they are all in your favour. My swan song is bound to remain my swan song, however long the separation, and I only hope that you will not forget me. I am with you in my thoughts. I know each day your approximate whereabouts and it gives me some strange pleasure to know which point you have passed already and how far the train has carried you away to a place which will fill you with new joys and pleasure.

I love you so very, very much.

Yours, Arcadi

In reading this letter so many years after, I recall with wonder that I was once so greatly loved by a man with such exceptional qualities of mind and heart as my long lost husband.

Today I regret nothing more in my life than not having savored my happiness to the full and lived out the brief periods Arcadi and I might have had together before we were incarcerated in a purgatory of our own choosing in Soviet Russia. Today, I not only know that the gods are jealous of human happiness but the way to cheat them is not to be afraid of them. To be alive at all is wonderful, and to have known, even for only a short while, the greatest happiness which life can give—to love and be loved utterly—gives life a savor even after it has all vanished with the snows of yesteryear.

To Arcadi, who did not live to see the transformation of the "capitalist system" in the West into a society of greater abundance and opportunities for all than had ever been known anywhere on earth, socialism, even as practised in Russia, still seemed to offer the only hope for the emancipation of mankind from want. He continued to believe, during the worst years in Russia that were to follow our honeymoon year in Japan, that men of good will, even under Stalin's terrible tyranny, could eventually ameliorate the condition of the Russian people and show mankind the way to a better order of society.

Maybe Arcadi with his acute intelligence, sensitivity and lack of illusions would have been as unhappy in any society as he was in Japan after I left him there alone. He needed the sustenance of love and comradeship and faith that somewhere, somehow life can be good and beautiful, which I had given him while I was still young and full of illusions.

Several years later in Moscow he used to say that the position and perquisites of a Communist in the ruling hierarchy depended mainly on how much he had "invested" in the revolution before the Bolsheviks came to power. It is also true that the greater one's commitment to the ideas in which one has staked all of one's heart and mind, the harder it is to cut one's losses. In spite of doubts, I could not let myself believe that the cause to which we wanted to devote our lives was a mirage. Neither I nor Arcadi could quickly cut loose and, by abandoning our tarnished hopes of helping to establish a better world in Soviet Russia, save ourselves.

We had to learn the hard way by bitter personal experience that bad means cannot establish good ends, but by that time it was too late to save ourselves. At various points in our lives it would have been easy for both of us to cut our ideological losses, pursue our

106

personal happiness, and enjoy prosperity and security in the "capitalist world." Particularly so in 1930 when he, still in the Far East, and I in England were both free to go wherever we wished. But like moths attracted to a flame which, considering that we both had better brains and more experience than most moths, we ought to have had the sense not to be destroyed by, Arcadi and I flew back to Moscow's brilliant red light and to his ultimate destruction.

Chapter 13
WORKING FOR THE PARTY

In Moscow for a week or two on my way home to England in the fall of 1929, I became aware of the shadows of terror which were already closing in on Russia. Nevertheless, back in London I threw myself into the work of the British Communist party, and tried to bury in my subconscious my doubts concerning the Soviet socialist new order. I worked for the British Communist party among the textile workers in Lancashire and campaigned for the Communist candidate at a by-election in Sheffield. I became a member of the Industrial Committee of the Party in London and wrote articles for Communist publications. I had won a reputation as an expert on costs of production in the cotton industry by my *Manchester Guardian* articles, and the endorsement of the results of my research by the International Master Cotton Spinners Association. Instead of cashing in on it by contributing well paid articles to the "capitalist press," I wrote a pamphlet for the Communist Party on "What's Wrong with the Cotton Trade."

Arcadi sent me money and I took no payment from the Party. I was able to resume giving lecture courses for the Workers' Educational Association, thanks to Barbara Wootton.* I was also busy on my first book *Lancashire and the Far East*, which I had begun writing in Japan. I read the works of Marx and Lenin conscientiously and thoroughly, and tried to explain in simple language the basic tenets of the Communist faith which, if one could make them clear to the workers, *must* make them see that only through the unity of the workers of the world could living standards be improved and unemployment eliminated.

In speaking to the Lancashire cotton operatives, I came up against the basic dilemma of the Marxist revolution, and also against the obstacle of the Comintern's indifference to the sufferings of the working class.

How could one convince the Lancashire cotton operatives that they should refuse to allow the cotton industry to be rationalized, refuse to work more looms, and go on strike for higher wages, when they knew as well as I did that the immediate result of such action would be more unemployment through the loss of more markets to Japan and other competing countries? To my mind it seemed clear that the basic need was to explain Marxist theory to them, to make them understand the meaning of "Workers of the world, unite" by showing that if all textile workers in all countries got together in one organization they could establish higher wages for all; to make them understand that the capitalist system based on production for profit inevitably doomed them to increasing poverty now that other countries besides England were industrialized, and workers in the East with lower standards of life competed against them.

In my pamphlet** I endeavored to express in simple language the "contradictions of

---

*Now Lady Wootton and a member of the House of Lords.

**What's Wrong With the Cotton Trade: *An explanation of the present depression and the Communist policy for cotton workers*. Published in 1930 by the Communist Party of Great Britain.

the capitalist system" which forced one to the conclusion that socialism was the only way to solve the problem of poverty in the midst of plenty. "Is it true," I asked, "that because more of everything is being produced all over the world, all workers must be made poorer by wage reductions? Is it true that because the total quantity of goods which the world can produce has grown greater, all workers are to have less of these goods?" This I continued, "is actually what the employers—the capitalists—argue and this *is* the position under capitalism . . . ." Because, I explained, giving the classical Marxist explanation, "under the capitalist system under which we live, the workers receive much less in wages than the value of the goods they produce."

I possess a torn and battered copy of this old pamphlet of mine, thanks to my old friend and former comrade in the British Communist Party, Michael Ross, who, after abjuring Communism emigrated to America ahead of me and was foreign adviser to George Meany at the American Federation of Labor when he died in 1964. Reading it now, I consider that I did a pretty good job of setting forth in easily understandable terms the basic Marxist theses which were tenable at that time but which have, happily, been refuted during my lifetime by the transmutation of the "capitalist system," in the advanced Western countries into something far better and more progressive than the sterile and stultifying "socialism" of the Communist powers.

By retaining the profit motive as its dynamo but accepting the necessity for some state regulation or control, the system we still call capitalist has demonstrated its capacity to produce more for more people than the socialist system which, in practice, has been found to require compulsion in order to function, and is consequently as inefficient as slave systems of bygone ages, although likewise formidable in war.

Back in the 20's and 30's, international socialism seemed the only way out, and even today one can question whether, had it not been for the Communist and National Socialist challenge and menace, the "capitalist system" would ever have resolved its contradictions.

It is I think wrong to regard the USSR and the USA today as having developed similar systems from opposite premises because this too optimistic world outlook disregards vital political factors. Despite the resemblance between the ever less socialist Soviet economic set up and the increasingly "socialist" capitalist system, the fundamental difference remains between government by consent of the governed under the rule of law, and that of an autocracy—or communist oligarchy relying on compulsion to preserve its privileges and powers. Nevertheless there is truth in the Hegelian theory of thesis, anti-thesis and eventual synthesis, as applied to the development of the free enterprise and opposing socialist systems of our time.

One can also view the course of human events in my lifetime as illustrating basic truths expressed in the Morality Plays and legends of the "Ages of Faith." Fear of the devil and hell, caused many a king, baron, or knight and others enjoying temporal power, to behave somewhat better to their subjects than they otherwise would have done, just as in our times the fear of Communism leads to reform.

In England in 1930 I found myself up against the Comintern, which was then pursuing an ultra-left policy and insisting that agitation, agitation above all, was the function of Communist parties. No theoretical explanations, no waste of time or energy in exposing the dynamics of capitalism; just tell the workers to strike and strike whatever the consequences. The Comintern, already transformed into an arm of the Soviet government, was not concerned with the livelihood of the workers; it aimed only to weaken the capitalist states by continual strikes and the dislocation of economic life. Its primary objective was the safety of the USSR and it recked nothing of the interests or sufferings of the "toiling masses."

One day in Blackburn, the great weaving center of Lancashire, an elderly textile worker complained bitterly to me that it was all very well for the paid officials of the Communist Party to get themselves arrested for deliberately and unnecessarily holding meetings where they obstructed the traffic, but how could we expect workers with families to do so, since it was an utterly useless performance? He did not know how proud Communist Party members were if, when they went to Moscow, they could boast that they had gone to jail in the class struggle. Such an accomplishment might be held to wipe out the stigma of their non-proletarian origin.

(In Moscow some years later I was to meet again an unemployed worker and his wife with whom I had stayed in Sheffield while speaking for the party. Appalled by the miserable condition of the Russian "proletariat" he went home to affirm that living on "the dole" was preferable to being employed in the "Workers' Paradise." Which reminds me of a joke current in Russia in the hungry thirties. Two elderly women formerly good friends meeting by chance on a Moscow street ask each other how they are faring. One is very poor and hungry, the other tolerably well off. "Is it your son Boris who helps you, or Ivan?" the hungry one asks. "Oh no," replies the other, "Boris is an accountant who can barely provide for his own family and Ivan who works in a factory is even worse off. It's Dimitry who helps me." "Dimitry? What does he do?" "He emigrated and is unemployed in America."

This "joke" was based on the fact that in those days two or three dollars a month in *valuta* enabled one to buy at Torgsin at cheap world prices the butter and eggs and meat unavailable on ration cards.

I can remember once finding two English pennies in the pocket of an old suit and journeying by streetcar with Jane to buy one egg at Torgsin with which she baked a cake.)

Finally I got myself into trouble with the Politbureau of the Party in London on account of an article I wrote which my friend Murphy, editor of the *Communist Review*, had allowed to be published. I had been reading Lenin's writings of the "Iskra period" and had discovered that he condemned the "Economists" who maintained that the intellectual has no role to play in the Party and that the socialist idea can spring "spontaneously" out of the experiences of the working class. Lenin had insisted that the ordinary worker, by the experience of his daily life, develops not a full revolutionary class consciousness but only that of a trade-unionist. Clearly, to my mind, in this period of declining markets for Britain, the workers' trade-union consciousness was likely to impel them to accept wage reductions and join with the bosses in attempting to recapture their markets. I did not foresee that this would lead Europe to a fascist development, but I perceived that, unless the Marxist conception of international working-class solidarity could be put across to the workers, they would perforce unite with their employers against other countries.

Already, during the First World War patriotism had proved more potent than Social Democracy. Soon it was to be demonstrated that Hitler and Mussolini could rouse their people to gird for battle under the slogan of the "proletarian nations" against the "Pluto-democracies." Similarly today the "underdeveloped" countries of Africa and Asia show a tendency to unite against the industrialized West—"Have Nots" against "Haves" in the international arena instead of at home.

Although my article was buttressed by quotations from Lenin, I was held to have deviated seriously from the Party Line by maintaining that theory was of primary importance and that the intellectual should not play at being a proletarian, since he had an important part to perform in enlightening the workers and convincing them that socialism was the only solution for unemployment and poverty in the midst of plenty. I was not directly accused of Trotskyism, but I was held to be slightly tainted with heresy.

Even at this stage of my Communist experience I had not the sense to see that nothing good would come out of the USSR and that the foreign Communist parties were already corrupted and impotent. I had a great respect and liking for Harry Pollitt, Secretary of the British Communist Party, who had been my friend before I joined the Party and now prevented the little bureaucrats in the Agitprop Department from sabotaging my pamphlet and my Party work. To this day I find it difficult to understand how this British working-class leader of Nonconformist Christian background came to subordinate his conscience and sacrifice his personal integrity to become a stooge of the Stalinists. In 1930 the fact that Harry Pollitt who was a principled, kind and intelligent man of integrity and courage led the British Communist Party deluded me into thinking that it was still a genuine socialist working class party. Six years later in Moscow I was to be shocked at Pollitt's failure to make any overt protest when Rose Cohen, his much loved mistress was arrested and condemned to a Soviet forced labor camp. True, she had since then become the wife of Petrovsky alias Breguer, the big shot in the underground Comintern apparatus about whom I have already written. Nevertheless one might have expected Pollitt to make an effort to save her.

My basically liberal aspirations and my false conception of the nature and aims of Communism four decades ago, have relevance today, because so many of those who now control the destiny of the newly independent states of Asia and Africa harbor the same illusions about socialism as I had in the 20's.

Listening to Nehru in the 50's was like an echo of my own youth when I knew and understood as little about Communism as he did until the end of his life. And still today although other leaders of the "Third World" have learned through experience bitter truths about the real aims, methods and practices of the Communists, they still conceive of "socialism" as synonymous with social justice.

When I asked my Indian friends what hold the diabolical Krishna Menon, whom I had known in London as a Communist, had on Nehru, I was told "Just Nehru's belief in Socialism." And as late as 1961, Cheddi Jagan, Prime Minister of British Guiana, the then latest British colony to become an independent state, visiting Washington hoping to obtain money from "capitalist" America, told the National Press Club that "only state control of production and distribution can pull a country up from poverty." Nor did such statements apparently lessen his chances of a loan from the U.S. As why should they, since Nehru, whose disapproval of the West was matched by his soft attitude toward Soviet Russia and Communist China, had been given so many millions or was it billions?

Harold Laski both during his anti- and pro-communist phases was the most widely known of the professors at the London School of Economics who exerted their influence in the socialist direction. They can be held largely responsible for the political illusions of the élite of Asia and Africa, educated in British schools and universities, who now control the destinies of most of the newly independent countries of the former "colonial" world.

Harold Laski is dead and the good he and his disciples did in awakening the social conscience of the Western world to the abuses of the "capitalist imperialist" economic and social system of the past is interred with their bones. But the evil they did lives after them in the influence still exerted by their teachings in the "Third World" and among old American New Dealers.

In spite of the abundant evidence provided by the USSR and the "People's Republic" of China that "socialism," far from offering an escape from poverty and injustice, rivets on those who succumb to its lure a tyranny from which there is no escape, the Asian and African students who were my contemporaries at the London School of Economics in the 20's, and those who came after me seem to have learned nothing and forgotten nothing since their student days. They still see the "capitalist imperialist" world as it was then while viewing the Communist empires through a mist of illusion. They continue to believe that "socialism" is the way to emancipate their peoples from poverty, and ignore the terrible lesson taught mankind by the Union of Soviet Socialist Republics and, more recently, by Communist China.

While the West has developed a new economic and social system which combines the dynamics of a competitive 'capitalist' economy with the major benefits of a "welfare state", the East, in particular India, became worse off under the doctrinaire Socialist Nehru than under the British.

The old proud and unrepentant British Imperial rule over subject peoples in Asia and Africa is gone with the wind. But British socialist influence over the generation of Asian and African intellectuals who now rule their emancipated countries still impregnates their political conceptions like a delayed-action fallout.

In April 1960, in Baghdad I remarked to the British Ambassador, that England had to a considerable extent been successful in substituting London School of Economics graduates, and others nurtured in the Socialist philosophy in English schools and colleges, as the new ruling class in Asia, in place of the princes and "feudalists" who had been Britain's collaborators in the past. Sir Hugh Trevelyan, who is one of Britain's cleverest and best informed ambassadors, responded with an appreciative laugh. Nor did he dispute my surmise that the course of events in Iraq had shown that "tame" socialists nurtured in the Fabian Socialist philosophy, were all too prone to kick over the traces and become Communists or communist collaborators in times of stress. It is of little or no importance to Moscow whether or not their collaborators have aims different from theirs so long as they continue to damn America for being capitalist and imperialist while never condemning Soviet Russia because of its socialist halo.

No doubt it was useful to the British that they had a second string to their bow in Asia and Africa in the persons of the Fabian Socialists they had nurtured in their schools. The British "ruling classes" have continued to demonstrate their cleverness in staying on top whatever economic, political and social system prevails. In ages past younger sons of feudal lords joined the ranks of the rising mercantile class. Today, after education in the best schools and universities, the sons of the privileged become Labor Ministers advocating "Progressive policies."

* * *

While I had been in Japan enjoying the best year of my life, Temple was going through a very bad period of his.

Endeavoring to perform the arduous duties of House Physician at the Metropolitan Hospital in spite of having one lung deflated by a pneumo-thorax operation, he had temporarily lost his usual zest for life, was drinking too much, and seemed not to care if he killed himself.

Temple used to say that one regrets most not the things one has done which might

112

better not have been done, but those one failed to do. So I am happy now to have found a letter I wrote him from Tokyo which, in contrast to my many complaints over the years that he failed to contribute his fair share towards Mother's support, expresses my love and concern and appreciation of my brother. Writing to him from Tokyo in February 1929 I said:

> Since I got Mother's last letter I have been thinking a lot about you and discovering that I love you very much. Although I have seen comparatively little of you these last years you fill a big place in my life and Mother's letter has upset me. You must do your best to live, Temple. You have always found life good. Is it no longer so? Give up this hospital job and get one on a ship or in a sanitorium. It *is* worth caring for yourself, Temple, even if you will never be very strong. You have always found so much in life intellectually and surely this must be more than ever true now? Only a short time ago I wrote to Mother that after all it would be you who did the big things . . . .
>
> You remember how Arcadi said you could never be "decomposed." He meant, I think, that for you, the intellectual, objective interests would never be lost. Arcadi liked you so much, Temple. And I find in him all the things I remember of Dada, plus a lover. I am a little afraid of my happiness—the gods are sure to be jealous. I suppose I idealize, but that does not matter. For me he is the perfect lover, comrade, playmate, and husband. We both want a child but are both afraid of what it may do to me—Arcadi wants me to be the old Freda. It is difficult to try to be the two incompatible things in women. To be a woman and yet to work like a man, to look at life like a man does.
>
> I wish I had you here to talk to, Temple. I understand so many things I never understood before. Take care of yourself Temple—life is good. Even for you, Temple, with one lung. Do be sensible about your work and give up this job.
>
> Write to me if you ever have time and tell me what is wrong. I really do love you very much and I know how much I have learnt from you, some of it unconsciously.

By the time I returned to England Temple had secured an appointment on the staff of Colney Hatch, the famous and largest mental hospital in England. Now as I prepared to leave for Moscow, Temple was about to fulfill his long cherished dream of voyaging to the South Seas.

In recalling nearly 40 years later my last year in England as an active member of the Communist Party, I remember best the last days I spent with my brother sailing along the coast of Devon and Cornwall before he took off on his long voyage to find his "dream islands" in the South Seas.

Chapter 14
INTERLUDE WITH TEMPLE

Originally Temple's voyage had been planned as a joint enterprise with his three closest friends: Rab Buchanan, Walter Field and Gilly Back, who all professed an ardent desire to get out of the rut of their lives in England to sail with Temple to the South Seas. Rab, husband of Jean, sister to Temple's ex-wife Robert, was the most experienced sailor and the only navigator among them. He was also the only one with money and had bought the *Inyala* for their venture.

As Temple told it:

> We four met in a pub in London and decided to sail about the middle of July. There was great enthusiasm. We toasted one another again and again. We were all convinced that town life was just silly. We said that all it amounted to was earning enough money to buy enough beer to deaden the memory of how one earned the money to buy the beer. We damned all civilization and swore we would never come home again, that we would find some obscure atoll and settle, and then spend our lives waiting for the cocoanuts to drop off the trees.

As it turned out, my brother was the only one of them who really meant it. When it came to the point of actually embarking across the Atlantic Ocean in a forty-five-foot yawl-rigged sailing boat, built in 1897, they one after another abandoned the venture for one reason or another. Gilly Back, a doctor working for the London County Council, fell out first, after being offered a job at double his former salary to stay on. In early August the others set sail from Brixham in spite of the dire warnings of the renowned fishermen of that Devon town who ridiculed the idea that the *Inyala* could ever make it across the Atlantic—only to be ignominiously driven back to port in a gale. Rab, incapacitated by sea sickness, had given orders to return in spite of Temple's furious objections and Walter's readiness to sail on although he, too, was feeling ill.

Following this misadventure Rab told Temple that he would not again attempt the voyage from England, but would join him and Walter later in Spain if they could secure another amateur or a paid hand to make the voyage.

Walter stuck by Temple while they endeavored in vain to find anyone else to sail with them, but his morale too gradually seeped away. After Ruby, his mistress whom he later married, came visiting, he too abandoned the enterprise.

Temple would not give up, and Rab now offered to pay the wages of two paid hands across the Atlantic if they could be found. There was no hope of getting anyone in Brixham to sign on since the fishermen there were convinced that no boat as old and with as little beam as the *Inyala* was fit for the voyage. "These Devon men," Temple exclaimed, "admire boats, like some men admire women in direct ratio to the plumpness of their bottoms."

I had better hopes of Cornishmen. I had friends in Newlyn and Mousehole and thought

I could help Temple fulfill his dream in spite of the defection of his friends. Thus it came about that my last days with my brother were spent sailing with him from Brixham in Devon to Mousehole in Cornwall where two fishermen, one old and one young, signed on to cross the Atlantic in the *Inyala*.

Temple and I had been very close to one another in childhood and in youth, but in the twenties had drifted apart. I thought he was too little concerned with the fate of mankind, too cynical and hedonistic. In 1930 when we sailed alone together along the southern coast of England, I had come to be tolerant of his attitude toward life, thanks to the beginning of my disillusionment with Communism and the great personal happiness I had found with Arcadi. We became as intimate and understanding of one another as when we had played together as children and while growing up before the 1914 war. Temple's skeptical outlook on men and politics, his professed lack of exalted motives in doing what he wanted to do, and his carefree zest in the enjoyment of living no longer seemed reprehensible to me now that I had begun to shed some of my political illusions.

I could not accept Temple's epicurian philosophy but I already knew, if I did not as yet consciously admit, that the Socialist reorganization of society could not set men free even if, as seemed more and more doubtful, it could better their material condition. Man's happiness or the satisfaction of his yearning depend only to a minimum extent on his material condition. We do not live by bread alone, although without it we die.

As Temple was to write in the fullness of his joy while crossing the Atlantic:

> I often say to myself when I take the wheel at night, the sky a blaze of stars and the ship cutting a phosphorescent track through the black, 'Where would I sooner be? Who would I change places with?' I tell myself, 'nowhere and no one.' One lives fully like this—doing things and dreaming . . . . One needs beauty but one is not directly conscious of one's need. Without it one is restless and irritated without knowing why; with it one is happy and contented; one is just glad of the moment, demanding nothing more.

In the night watches, sitting together under the stars while I steered under Temple's directions, he warned me of the certain disappointment which awaited me. "You will probably end up in a Siberian prison, my dear," he said to me one night. "But so long as you don't deceive yourself, they will not break you. Only don't ever be a hypocrite to yourself: that is the real sin against the Holy Ghost."

During the bittersweet years of my life in Russia which followed these last days with my brother, I was frequently to recall Temple's words. And, later on, in America, when sorely tempted to compromise with my beliefs for the sake of material advantage or acclaim, I remembered them and put behind me the temptation to deceive myself and by so doing mislead others.

Together we remembered the days when we had played at being Vikings or Greek and Trojan warriors, when I was seven and he nine years old and we lived in a large house at 67 Finchley Road in Hampstead with a big terrace and garden at back ideally suited to our games, and had ourselves fashioned plumed helmets and wooden swords and shields. Temple was to write:

> I remember thinking one night how curiously things work out. The first book I ever read was Nansen's *Furtherest North*. This led to a demand for a Norwegian governess, which was granted. She was a dear and very beautiful, and she used to tell me tale after tale about the Vikings . . . . They superceded Diomedes and Ajax as the heroes of my

childhood. I played nothing but Viking Games, and my cup was full when my governess' father, himself a sea captain, sent me a perfect model of a Viking Ship.

Enthralled by Balentine's *Coral Island* and Robert Louis Stevenson's books, he had dreamed as a boy of voyaging either to the North Pole or the South Seas. Now at the age of 34 he was on his way to his "dream islands" in the Pacific and to enjoy an adventurous life on the high seas.

"How careful parents should be about the first books their children read and the first tales they hear," Temple was to remark in explaining how it came about that he was celebrating Norway's day in the Galapagos Islands in 1931 instead of "looking after lunatics at Colney Hatch and paying income tax."

In childhood and youth Temple and I had both drunk deep of the same wells of legend, history, poetry and romance, but despite the twin sources of our lives, our dreams led us to opposite ends of the earth. Temple, having no illusions concerning the perfectability of man or society, wanted, in modern parlance, to "get away from it all."

I was ambitious whereas Temple had no desire by words or works to erect a monument "more enduring than bronze." It was I who had been able to recite the Rubaiyat of Omar Khayyam by heart when ten years old. But it was Temple who had taken the Persian poet's advice to savor all the fleeting joys and beauty of life without knowing "why, whence, or whither" we have been put upon earth.

Both of us had rejected "bourgeois values" but Temple's denial of their validity was more fundamental than mine. As he was to write to Emsie Phillips, the girl he met in Barbados and later married in Tahiti:

> You see, dear, I do not believe basically as a part of my character, in the values of society. Many people are skeptical about them intellectually, but they are not skeptical about them as a part of their own character as I am .... I believe myself that my own values are based on more fundamental human needs, but nevertheless that is but an opinion, and for certain of them there is nothing to be adduced but prejudice. But I hold them with a whole-hearted fanaticism. A certain number of people in every generation have always thought as I do. The first-rate ones have been poets. The second-rate ones like myself have believed their songs.

To our great joy when Temple and I docked the *Inyala* in Newlyn harbor, Rab was there to greet us. He prepared to sail with Temple at least as far as Spain, but this time with Temple as captain so that Rab would not have the right to order the ship back to port in a storm, should he again succumb to the sea sickness to which he was prone.

Rab, a Highland Scotsman, shared Temple's longing for adventure and would undoubtedly have gone the whole way with him had not the call of his wife and many children pulled him home, first from Spain and later from Panama after he had rejoined Temple in the West Indies. (Which was odd because Rab married four times and was never faithful to any woman until the last one he married when already getting old but still energetic and leanly handsome as he still is today.)

Temple sailed away from Newlyn in Cornwall toward the setting sun one golden August evening in 1930. Most of the population of the small fishing village of Mousehole close by were there to bid him godspeed on his adventure together with the two fishermen who went with him. He had urged me until the last moment to sail with him if

116

only as far as Spain, but as usual I was driven by a nervous sense of urgency which caused me to miss some of the greatest pleasures in life.

I was expecting Arcadi soon to meet me in Moscow from Japan where I had left him nearly a year before, and even if there was time enough for me to sail to Vigo, I felt I could not go dashing off with Temple simply to enjoy myself. Although I had already learned enough to be vaguely apprehensive of the future which awaited us in Russia, love drew me back to Moscow. Yet I was sorely tempted to sail away with my brother, abandoning all else to fulfill the dreams we had shared in childhood and youth, when both of us longed to voyage "beyond the pillars of Hercules."

As the *Inyala* swept by the Newlyn breakwater on which our mother and I were standing, I cried out to Temple: "I must come, too," and he, steering with one hand while he waved farewell with the other, shouted to me: "Jump for the rigging!" As he wrote later in his account of his departure from England, "Freda hesitated, looked as if she was going to, then hesitated again and we swept by."

We never saw each other again. Two weeks after I had hesitated too long to "jump for the rigging" I was on a boat to Leningrad, and wrote from Hamburg: "I am beginning dimly to realize how blind and how much in a rut most people are. They do not want to see everything—it is too dangerous and too windswept and too awful. One must have courage, mentally as well as physically."

How much courage was to be required of me in the future was still unknown to me but I was to learn that it is love which can enable one to endure the death of one's hopes.

Temple, usually as tolerant and understanding of his friends as I have been intolerant when they failed to come up to my expectations, never quite forgave Walter for his defection. Rab he understood and sympathized with and was always grateful to, not only for having provided him with the financial means to enable him to fulfill his hearts desire, but for having been willing to try and try again to sail with him. But for the rest of his life Temple felt bitter about Walter having let him down at the eleventh hour.

"Does Walter ever come to see you or does his bad conscience prevent him?" he wrote to Mother from Trinidad in November 1930. Gilly Back he did not feel so bitter about, there would always be "some divine discontent in him." But Walter would become "a complete little bourgeois" without Temple's influence.

Queer how intolerant I am, he wrote, in a letter recognizing how basically akin we were,

> I have never realized so vividly before as when I was struggling to get
> off, and Walter was struggling to run away, and Freda was helping me
> to get off, how alike Freda and I are. We both try to constrain others to
> our dreams, and we can still dream. And the others just want to be
> comfortable and smug, and go on leading their routine little lives. Then
> we get furious. But how thoroughly infirm of purpose people like
> Walter are.

It was, I suppose, because Temple had more confidence in him than in any of the others and missed his companionship most that he could not forgive Walter. In one of the jottings in his log book, after a big sea had just come down the companionway, Temple noted that although he sorely missed Walter's companionship he would rather be alone crossing the Atlantic than having a good dinner at the Eiffel Tower restaurant in Soho on Saturday night, "listening to Walter talking about the sailing he never eventually did . . . and explaining for the nth time exactly why his delicate nervous system could not stand the strain of waiting." And when 750 miles from Trinidad, he wrote: "Queer how bitter I feel about Walter. Yet I have not even the satisfaction of knowing he will regret it. He will just get more and more verbose and alcoholic and will sail a thousand Atlantics twixt beer and brandy. The trend of his talk will be that he made a 'great renunciation for the sake of his family and common sense.' "

The remarkable thing was that Temple had almost succeeded in tearing Walter away from his secure moorings in "bourgeois" society, and the anchor of his family affection and obligations. A decade before Walter had told Temple that although he was attracted to me I would be too dangerous and uncomfortable to live with. It was of him I wrote from Japan:

> Looking back on things I realize that my unhappy love for Walter made me put all my energies into work, whereas now . . . . I have just received a letter from Walter, by the way. You might tell him what I say. If he admires my brain and capabilities as he says, tell him that he helped me to achieve things by refusing to love me. I can look back on it all very casually now and genuinely say to Walter, "Peace be with you." Tell him there is something in Russell Green's favorite saying: "The hobbyhorse of one's discontent becomes the Pegasus of one's ambition." And yet I am still ambitious only not so vividly so. I enjoy the present too much.

My friendship with Walter was to endure long after Temple's death in 1935 when he wrote that "something gallant and fine had gone out of his life" at Temple's passing. Even after my emigration to America, Walter and I got together in London whenever I visited England until he died in 1958.

Walter, who had almost been my lover before he became Temple's closest friend, combined the endearing Jewish qualities of intelligence, humor and wit, understanding of human nature, kindness and loyalty to friends, wide-ranging intellectual interests and courage in adversity. Temple had enjoyed telling the story of their voyage to Norway with two other amateur sailors in a ramshackle old boat whose mast was shattered in a storm off the northwest coast of Germany. Compelled to take to their lifeboat in raging seas they had stocked it with three ships biscuits and a bottle of whiskey per man, and Walter laughing in the gale when their chances of survival seemed slim, had remarked: "Why so many biscuits?"

It has become a cliché to say "some of my best friends are Jews" usually as preface to some derogatory remark. In my case it is literally true that not some, but most of my enduring friendships have been with Jewish men and women. Both Arcadi whom I married and Walter whom I once loved, had the keen intelligence, wry sense of humor combining appreciation of the ridiculous and the sublime in juxtaposition, and the philosophical detachment to make fun of themselves which, besides loyalty to friends, are among the most endearing characteristics of this many-sided and gifted people. The two of them also represented opposing poles of the Jewish character, outlook and aspirations: the one seeking security or money and devoted mainly to family interests; the other dreaming of international brotherhood or God's Kingdom on earth even while, like myself, believing themselves to be atheists or agnostics.

Stalin was to liquidate the internationalist minded Jews calling them Trotskyists, or to bludgeon them into submission to Russian National Socialism. Hitler made no distinction in exterminating or driving into exile even those Jews who were among the most patriotic Germans as proven during the first world war. The evil both men did lives after them. Today survivors of the Nazi concentration camps, supported by "international Jewry," have themselves become super-nationalists. Convinced that their salvation lies in a "blood and soil" Israeli state in Palestine, founded at the price of expulsion or expropriation of its Arab inhabitants, the Zionists have repudiated the international outlook of the Jews who were my closest friends.

After crossing the Atlantic sojourning awhile in Barbados; being shipwrecked in the Galapagos Islands on a Norwegian boat whose captain was drowned and where Temple himself nearly died of thirst, my brother crossed 3,000 miles of the Pacific Ocean in 22 days with a half-caste Barbadian called Mobile as his only crew, and while himself suffering severely from septic sores. British reviewers of the book which his widow and I composed out of his log book and letters after his death* described this voyage in an old forty five foot yawl as a "heroic feat" entitling him to belong to the "truly great company" of Voss and Alan Gerbault. "It was an amazing feat of endurance," the *Oxford Times* wrote, "for his right lung was practically useless owing to tuberculosis, developed as a result of being gassed in the war. His navigation was faultless and his handling of the boat excellent."

"Queer what a little persistance will do" he wrote from Hiva Owa in the Marquesas in September 1931, "once you have seen these islands, it seems absurd to live anywhere else. Things do not usually come up to one's imagination, but this place is much, much more beautiful that I had dreamt. To live saturated with beauty has a tremendous effect on one's well-being. The sea is in my bones. A good life consists of fight and struggle and anxiety; working twenty-four hours out of twenty-four, with every nerve on strain and death round the corner, varied by periods of complete rest and idleness . . . ."

The governor of the Marquesas was a French doctor . . . . "an intelligent of the kind he liked—" the first civilized person he had met since leaving London. Dr. Benoit had taken him home to lunch when he arrived and given him a "real French meal." Within a few minutes they were "discussing Villon, Baudelaire, Communism, Mussolini, Bergson, Nietzsche."

Two months later he wrote that his first impressions had been confirmed. All he asked was to pass his life in the Marquesas: "Their beauty has not been exaggerated; there is nothing to compare with them in the world. Beyond their beauty there is something else; something which soothes and contents one making all else seem of little worth." Stevenson had written that "Few men who come to the islands leave them; they grow grey where they alighted: the palm shades and the trade winds fan them until they die, perhaps cherishing to the last the fancy of a visit home, which is rarely made and yet more rarely repeated. No part of the world exerts the same attractive power."

"Life was gay then" as Neo, an old Marquesan chieftain said to Temple who commented, "It was a very fair thing which the whites destroyed." Already in Temple's time the old days were vanishing before the march of progress.

The missionaries had not yet suppressed the old ways. A man still married all his wife's sisters and a woman all her husband's brothers. Sexual jealousy was almost unknown. The excess of males to females in the proportion of five to three seemed to "make for happiness." As the chieftain of one of the least civilized and last occupied of the islands said to Temple: "One man no good for a woman, no satisfy. Woman needs three men, taken turn. One sleep, one fish, one gather poi poi. Woman want love and play every night many times. One man not strong enough." No wonder that the Moslems, who saw things the other way round, never converted the South Sea Islanders although they got as far as Indonesia.

A Modern Sea Beggar. Peter Davis. London, 1938. (This publisher when a child was the original Peter of Barrie's Peter Pan.)

119

The governor, Dr. Benoit, and Temple had struck up a firm friendship, but French law did not permit any foreigner to practice medicine so that Temple was precluded from earning a living in the islands. All he could do was to treat patients for free, unofficially helping out Dr. Benoit, who was spending his life "in a desperate fight to protect the natives from traders, missionaries, T. B. baccilli, filarial worms and other parasites."

In Barbados (before sailing on to the South Seas) Temple had fallen in love with a half-English, half-American girl, Emsie Phillips, whom he could not marry since his divorce from Robert had not yet been made absolute. Writing to her from Colon he warned her what to expect if she decided to forsake her own people and the security of her home among the British ruling class of the West Indies, to share his fate. "You know me," he wrote. "Do you really think there is any chance of stability, worldly success or safety with me?" Her mother and her friends were right. She would be undertaking "a frightful risk with all the odds against you." I offer you hardship, risk, discomfort, poverty, sordidness . . . and something which we two alone know between ourselves." He was going off to the South Seas: "because I must. There is no justification or rationalization. I just must—well dearest it will always be the same. There will be a dream and "I must" and then for you it will be pay pack and follow."

After reaching the Marquesas he told Mother he had some wonderful letters from Emsie and knew he would be wise to marry her.

> But I am free and I want to be responsible for no one. If she had only
> grabbed me when she could have done. If she had had the courage to
> send her aunts and uncles to hell and sail alone with me across the
> Pacific, I would have stuck to her for ever and ever. I cannot think of
> any woman who would have done so, except Freda—the older I get the
> more I realize her greatness at a distance.

In spite, or because of, the letter he had written to Emsie, she joined him in the Marquesas nine months after they had parted in Barbados. Later they were married in Tahiti and she voyaged with him as his 'crew' to the Fiji Islands, where they settled and enjoyed for the few years before he died, so happy a union that Emsie accounted herself fortunate among women in spite of her loneliness for the rest of her life.

During the years which followed our last days together Temple and I were as far removed from one another geographically and in environment as it is possible to be. Nor could we easily communicate since I dared not write to him freely from Russia for fear of endangering Arcadi.

Temple sensed my disllusionment. "We neither of us," he wrote to Mother, "quite seem to have found our new world. Freda's letter was very, very interesting and I chuckled and wept and remembered that Shelley used to be her favorite poet."

Recently I have found among his widow Emsie's effects a letter written to them in 1933 while I was in hospital in London following an antrum operation, which I told them to burn but which fortunately she preserved, in which I dared to express my real thoughts:

> " . . . As you will gather I am thoroughly disillusioned. One could,
> stand the material conditions even though they get worse and worse
> (they are infinitely worse than when Mother was out last year) but it is
> the mental difficulties. Hypocrisy, sycophancy, patronage, lying, etc.
> The people at the top get everything and pretend they don't. There is
> nothing of communism or socialism left. I consider there was a
> counter-revolution in 1927 when Trotsky was turned out. It need not

120

have gone this way. When I first went there in 1926 everything was different—in 1928 still. But Stalin thinks he can do everything with the whip and the gun against all economic and psychological forces. He is not a Marxist at all and has reversed all Lenin's principles on which the Soviet State was founded. Consequently again I can't tell you everything I mean in a letter or in fact explain myself really at all. But as the best example of what has happened take the complete mess the Comintern has made in Germany and China. International Socialism has been completely sacrificed to "Socialism in one country"—the very negation of Marxism which taught that the only way out for mankind is international socialism. Consequently we have a Fascist world growing up around us and really by now Russia is herself a Fascist state with an established ruling aristocracy and an ideal of economic self sufficiency.

If I were free I would join the opposition movement of Trotsky and try to restart an international Socialist movement. By free I mean if only Arcadi was not a Russian. As it is he cannot leave the country and I can't leave him. Nor can I speak or write a word of what I want to say. I am always in deadly fear of bringing him to grief by my incautious tongue. I have to pretend and lie and be a hypocrite like everyone else. Being like you of a sanguine temperament I still hope that one day he may get sent abroad again but it is a faint hope because nowadays no one not in the party and not of working class origins is "trusted" to go abroad. The official idea is that they would never come back. One is literally a prisoner. Even I, although English and able to leave the country when I want, feel like a prisoner on parole as I dare not speak and as I am tied to Arcadi whom I love more than ever as the years go on. Perhaps it is the very difficulties and dangers and strain of living which draws us closer and closer. One just turns to each other and no one else. We have lived all this time in one room until a year ago with no servant and me doing all the work. Standing in queue and cooking and washing besides going to the office but we have never quarreled. Arcadi is the most lovable of men and I am still what he calls his "swan song." So that, Temple dear, emotionally I am very happy. Life has given me a lot in giving me Arcadi although it has made me give up everything else I cared about: career, ambition, politics, fortune, Etc.!! I am very anxious to have a child although it will be so difficult. I want a second edition of Arcadi. We have two rooms now since June and if only it weren't for the necessity of bringing Mother here we could be comparatively comfortable . . . .

Will you please *be certain to destroy this* letter as soon as you have read it. Also will Emsie *not* tell her relations anything of what I have said of Russia especially not the political remarks. Mother is so nervous that I am writing it all to you in Suva. But I don't see how it can ever get to anyone's eyes in Russia if you destroy my letter. It is terrible to live under a tyranny—secondly do be very careful to write nothing compromising to me or Mother while in Russia . . . .

This letter shows that I had not as yet disabused myself of the illusion that socialism in Russia would have been different if only Trotsky instead of Stalin had succeeded Lenin.

Later I came to realize that the Soviet System required Stalin or someone like him in order to function. A fact today again becoming apparent by Khrushchev's failure and the reversion to Stalinism.

In this same letter, describing our difficult food and housing situation which made it imperative that Temple help me with Mother, I wrote:

> It has been hard enough in the past but now I am going to have a child and unless the burden of Mother is taken off my hands it will finish me. When my child is born it will be difficult to get the most elementary necessities—milk and fruit—(obtainable for *Valuta*) which Arcadi's savings would have procured if Mother had not had to use them.
>
> I am afraid you will both think I am piling it on but I am not exaggerating things a bit. Our position in Russia is actually comparatively good—many people are actually starving without even enough bread—I don't expect either of you to talk to anyone else about these conditions because by doing so even in Suva you might get me into trouble. An elaborate game of hush hush is played about all the food difficulties etc. and it is a terrible offense to tell the truth about that or anything else.

When Temple died in April 1935 in Suva, I was still living in Russia, held there by my love for my husband, long after my complete disillusionment with Communism, and a year after the birth of my son, Jon, who was to inherit my brother's most lovable qualities as well as resembling him physically.

I recall sitting on a stone bench beside the Moscow river, on my way home from work on the evening of the sad, grey, cold spring day on which I received the news of Temple's death. Vivid memories of our childhood and youth and of our last sail together crowded in on me. I wept not only for his death but for all the lost hopes and lovely visions which had inspired us in our different fashion to follow our heart's desire regardless of the consequences. I was still alive and had a son, a joy he had never known. But I was confined within the vast prison Soviet Russia had become, whereas he had never known anything but freedom and had found and briefly enjoyed his El Dorado in the South Seas. He had ended up "earning bread and butter again, which is very dull; not the earning of it, but the life I have to lead to earn it." But Temple never knew or imagined the terror and hardship of my life in Russia, or had been compelled to bow his head before omnipotent tyranny, as I was forced to do in order to continue living with my husband. In Suva he had found the conventions of the accepted social order tiresome and the people for the most part "deadly dull" and felt dull himself without the "stimulus of other minds," but he had been spared knowledge of the tyrannical compulsions of the Soviet Socialist order under which I was living. And at the end, he could recall the words which he had scribbled in pencil when he thought he was about to die of thirst after being shipwrecked in the Galapagos Islands: "If I have got to die I have had a fine time and thoroughly enjoyed myself."

Long before in London Temple had written to Mother:

> If one goes one's own way, whatever may appear as outward disaster to others does no permanent harm to one's self development, but if one refrains from carrying out one's own will at the bidding of others, or at the bidding of law, custom, morality, material interest, or fundamental weakness, permanent harm is done to oneself, and one's growth is all

122

twisted awry. It is the failure to follow one's will, not failure after one
has willed with all one's power that hurts the soul.

Both of us had "gone our own way" and despite the disappointments of my life in
Russia or later I did not then or after regret having done so.

Temple had gone, in his own words written from the Marquesas, where his "curiosity,
love of beauty and adventure had driven him seeking his heart's desire," and had "found it
many times, gaining much joy and complete satisfaction." Why should he "seek for those
solid things which give me no satisfaction and which, as far as I can see, give no
satisfaction to anybody?"

Reflecting today on my brother's motivations, I can dimly understand the "hippies"
and "flower people" who reject the values of our affluent society by refusing to step on
the treadmill of conformity which ensures security and status and a dull life. Today there
are no longer any "dream islands" in the Pacific, or anywhere else, to escape to, in search
of freedom from boredom or what Temple called the "idiocy of things." Nor are there
today in the West any such burning injustices and inequalities as to inspire the generous
aspirations of youth to sacrifice for an ideal. Turned in upon themselves, precisely
because of the success of "capitalism" in solving its contradictions, some become the
destructive element which has destroyed other civilizations. In 1931 Temple could write
from the Marquesas that Freda was right in thinking that the old world was falling to
pieces and that this meant there was no sense in "piling up treasure, either of money or
position." Today we can see that, far from falling to pieces the "capitalist world" has
created a system so productive and successful that many of the children of the well to do
so long for pain, poverty and struggle that they endeavor to look like unshorn, unshaven
and unwashed medieval peasants.

The Western world has not by any means achieved "Utopia," but has come far closer
to it than past civilizations ever did. With the result that many of its over privileged youth
are finding in Temple's words that "civilization only seems to make life safe at the cost of
making it damned dull." Life deprived of struggle and danger and joy in achievement by
one's own efforts has no meaning and leads to self destruction.

Man against nature is an older story with more universal appeal than the conflict of
nations, classes and ideologies in our industrial age. The "burning heart of man and boy
alike rejoices" in every age in reading tales of courage, endurance and adventure. Hence
the success of Kon-Tiki in our time because it has the same timeless appeal as the voyage
of the Argonauts, the Odyssey, the Norse Sagas and other tales which belong to the
springtime of the world.

Temple, according to his description of himself, was something of a leprechaun in
Aldous Huxley's meaning. He had little sense of responsibility and had left me to provide
for our mother who loved him best. I had worked to support her and was to bring her to
Moscow to live with us in our confined space in two rooms because I could not send her
money out of Russia. Temple, meanwhile, refused, after settling in Suva, to bring our
mother there because he feared she would disrupt his happy marriage by her
possessiveness and jealousy of any woman he loved.

I, on the other hand, was too impatient, or intolerant, or lacking in sympathy and
understanding to give our mother much of my time, while Temple had held her hand,
comforted her, understood her problems and given her the conviction that she was loved
and cherished, which was more important than money. He could steel his heart to leave
her and the girls he loved at various times. But he had given understanding and sympathy
to everyone he knew, or only briefly encountered, whereas I, listening to distant drums,

was more concerned with ideas and prescriptions for the welfare of mankind than with the problems of individual human beings. Like so many liberals and intellectuals of our time, I have been intolerant or arrogant in my convictions, right or wrong. Temple always made a distinction between his critical analysis and his personal affections.

As one of his medical colleagues wrote of Temple, he had "the rare gift of being able to live in peace with other men." A devout old lady in Suva, bedridden in hospital said to her daughter: "I do like seeing my doctors; I've been lying here thinking to myself that I could give them each a new name: Dr. Y's faith; Dr. X, he's hope, but Dr. Utley, he is charity." And one of their friends remarked: "I enjoy going to the Utley's house; you never know who you will find there, from the Bishop to a bum."

"Nobody who knew him could bear the thought of his not having or doing what he wanted," Arthur Ransome wrote in the *London Observer* in reviewing Temple's book, *A Modern Sea Beggar*. "Friends, wife, mother, and chance acquaintances were all at one. One man gives him a yacht, another gives him a share in a medical practice, a third, hoping to sail with him, sells his own boat, takes the engine out of it, puts it into Utley's, and does not complain when Utley changes his mind and takes work ashore. All kinds of people seem to have found themselves more alive than usual when in his presence, and to have felt that they could not do too much for him." His book was "incandescent" with his relish of experience "whether pleasant or horrible" and ordinary human beings "bound hand and foot with cobwebs of memory or apprehension will do almost anything for those who can let themselves go."

The following passage from Dostoyevsky, chosen by Temple's widow and friends as his fitting epitaph, was read at his funeral:

> Here is perhaps the one man in the world whom you might leave alone without a penny, in the center of an unknown town of a million inhabitants, and he would not die of cold and hunger, for he would be fed and sheltered at once; and, if he were not, he would find a shelter for himself, and it would cost him no effort or humiliation. And to shelter him would be no burden, but, on the contrary, would probably be looked on as a pleasure.

* * *

From Moscow, shortly after saying farewell to Temple in Cornwall, I wrote to Mother telling her that I would soon be leaving for the Far East to rejoin Arcadi and sail with him to San Francisco. The Commissariat of Foreign Trade, endeavoring to keep qualified men abroad, offered to pay my fare to go with him to America. We were given a last chance to escape the fate which awaited him in Russia. We did not take it.

Arcadi insisted on returning to Moscow after his long exile, and I did not have the sense to dash off to Shanghai to try to stop him.

I am omitting from these Memoirs the story of my life in Russia from 1930 to 1936, as originally told in my 1940 book, *The Dream We Lost*. In the next chapter I tell only how it ended.

EPILOGUE

Late in August 1936, Arcadi was sentenced, without trial, to five years imprisonment. Vera* telephoned from Moscow to tell me. If I could have got to Russia within three days I would have been able to see and talk to him once more for a few minutes, as Vera did, behind bars separating them by a wide distance. Even this privilege was denied me.

I had tried again and again to secure a visa to return to Russia. Every time I visited my old friend Ivan Maisky, who was now the Soviet Ambassador to England, he received me kindly but told me to be patient and to wait. Either he had been instructed to refuse me a visa, or he feared that if I returned to Russia I, too, would be arrested, in which event he might have trouble with the British Foreign Office. Maisky, with whom I had traveled to Russia on my first visit in 1927, when I was full of youthful hopes and faith in the Soviet Socialist experiment, was a decent and kindly man who had originally been a Menshevik. It is probable that in denying me a visa he thought he was saving me from imprisonment or liquidation. He must also have been motivated by his fear that if this happened he would have some trouble with the British Government. On the morning of my last visit to him to plead for a visa in time to get to Moscow to see Arcadi prior to his incarceration in a Soviet concentration camp, Maisky, pointing to a Mongolian ring on my finger given me by Owen Lattimore, quoted the Chinese saying: "Everything passes." Indeed it does, but in passing it carries with it all that is worth living for. When one reaches the age when one abandons hope for humanity as well as for oneself and has no more tears to shed, one had better die.

From Archangel, on his way to a concentration camp in the far North, Arcadi sent me a postcard, dated 22 September 1936, assuring me of his love and telling me to be cheerful. Early in 1937 I received a second postcard, this time from Ust Usya, in the Arctic regions where prisoners worked in the mines. In May 1937, I received a third and last postcard telling me he was well and he was now doing office work. This implied that he had previously been doing physical hard labor in the mines. I could only hope that his health had not been permanently ruined since his heart was already strained and enlarged from overwork in the service of the Soviet State.

I never heard from Arcadi again. For a quarter of a century I did not know whether he had died from cold, hunger and overwork in the Arctic regions from whence he last wrote to me.

Perhaps of all my many letters and postcards to him none were delivered, and feeling I had abandoned him, he ceased to write. This was the saddest thought of all but I could not believe that he ever doubted my love and my loyalty. The hopes we had shared of a better social and economic order to be created in Russia had gone with the wind long before we were parted. But we had kept our faith in one another and our love had been enduring.

During the long and lonely years which followed the end of our life in Russia, I comforted myself with the thought that if he were still alive somewhere in the vast reaches of the Russian land he would still be making jokes and viewing with tolerant

*Vera Berdichevsky, sister of Arcadi Berdichevsky.

125

irony the crimes, cruelties and follies of mankind, retaining through all his sufferings the philosophical detachment which enabled him to endure and preserve his integrity even under the Communist terror.

His three postcards were full of confidence in our love. In the last one he said that one year of our five years separation had already passed and he was living for the day when we should be together again.

Emma continued to write to me and to send parcels of food to Arcadi until the late summer of 1937. Then I ceased to hear from her for four months. In December I received a letter saying she had been four months in the "Krankenhaus"–the German word for hospital but probably meaning prison–and had been very frightened. Now that she was out she had at once sent Arcadi a food parcel. She also sent me a new address for him. After that I never heard from Emma again.

Perhaps she was arrested again. Perhaps her letters were stopped. She had proved to be the most loyal and fearless of my friends. Only she had dared to go on writing to me after Vera was arrested. Emma had been my last link, my last source of information about Arcadi. After she was silenced, I was as cut off from him as if he were on another planet.

Our Moscow flat had been confiscated and the friends I installed there thrown out. What was left of the money I had left with Vera was taken when she too was arrested. Emma had our clothes, books and other possessions. I had written her to try to keep the books safe but to sell everything else to buy food for Arcadi. I was never able to retrieve our library of several hundred books.

I did not ask the help of the British Foreign Office until 1938 because I feared to harm Arcadi. When I did so, the officials there did all they could to help me, but since my husband was a Russian subject, this was of little avail.

In the summer of 1938, while I was in China, Maxim Litvinov who was at this time the Soviet Foreign Minister told Lord Chilston, the British Ambassador in Moscow that Arcadi Berdichevsky was still alive. But Litvinov offered no proof and it was obviously to the Soviet Government's advantage to keep my mouth shut by an assurance that my husband was still living. So long as I had hope, I would be expected to keep silent and not expose the truth about Russia, which I, having lived there so long as an ordinary Moscow resident knew so much better than other foreigners.

I could not even place any confidence in Litvinov whose wife, Ivy Low, I knew well but who was avoiding trouble by concentrating her energies on the promotion of Basic English in Russia.

Years later in 1956 my friend Isaac Don Levine, visiting Iran on an assignment for LIFE magazine, met a Georgian woman who had escaped from Russia and who had known a Berdichevsky in the Turkestan village in which she and others had been confined in the 40's following the end of their prison terms. This Berdichevsky, we thought, might well have been my Arcadi since she told Don that he spoke English fluently and had known Lenin in Switzerland before the First World War. I was unable to find out by meeting her because, following her arrival in the U.S.A. under the sponsorship of the CIA, she was put in a lunatic asylum and prevented from having any further communication with Don Levine or any other anti-Communists in America. Such were and are the mixed up hopes and fears entertained by the United States Government eternally seeking co-existence with Soviet Russia.

It was not until New Year's Eve of 1963 that I at long last learned that my husband had died on March 30, 1938, at Komi in the Arctic North. Llewellyn E. Thompson, past and present U.S. Ambassador to Moscow, whom I approached at the time of Mikoyan's *visit to Washington, was kind enough to extract this information from the Soviet authorities and wrote as follows:*

Department of State
Ambassador at Large
Washington
December 27, 1962

Dear Mrs. Utley:
Further to my letter of December tenth, the Soviet Ambassador has now informed me that Berdichevsky, Arkady Yakovlevich, who was living at Komi, ASSR, died on March 30, 1938.

Sincerely yours,
Llewellyn E. Thompson

Mrs. Freda Utley
1807 R Street, N.W.
Washington 9, D. C.

Our son Jon was with me to comfort me that New Year's Eve when, a quarter of a century after Arcadi's arrest, my last lingering hopes that he was still alive were finally obliterated.

Chapter 15
THE END OF MY LIFE IN RUSSIA

During most of the years of my life in Russia we had, at best, the use of two rooms sharing kitchen and bathroom with one or more families. This had been our situation when my son was born in 1934 and my mother was living with us.

At long last Arcadi and I obtained our own flat. Paid for years before in foreign exchange and in rubles, and long since due to us by the length of our membership in the Cooperative, we had almost given up hope of ever getting it. Now suddenly it was ours. Not without a struggle, not without another threat by Arcadi to leave Promexport if the Chairman did not help him to secure his rights, but finally ours.

We had to move in the middle of the night because a fight was going on between contenders for our old rooms at Ordinka. Both the Commissariat of Foreign Trade and the Commissariat's Cooperative into whose block of flats we were moving claimed possession. If we didn't let in the people to whom the Cooperative had allocated the rooms, they would not give us the key of our new flat.

So we made a lightning move at one o'clock in the morning. We sent Emma on first with my sleeping son in her arms to take possession and sit on the floor until we arrived with the furniture after admitting the new occupants to our old rooms.

Our new flat had three rooms, a kitchen and bathroom, but alas, no bath. After nearly two years with a bath and no hot water heater we now had a hot water heater and no bath. Such is life, but we were too happy at getting the flat to complain, and a tub was promised "eventually or a little before" to use our favorite Russian expression. We could at least get hot water fast instead of carrying kettles from kitchen to bathroom. We acquired a large tin washtub in which we performed our ablutions and in which I bathed Jon every evening. Promptly at 6 p.m. Arcadi would rush home from the office to be present at this best moment of the day when the sudden appearance of his father's head in the aperture near the top of the wall which divided bathroom from lavatory evoked squeals of joy and radiant smiles from our small son splashing water around the floor of our clean tiled bathroom. Arcadi, who usually expressed his deepest feelings frivolously used to say, "It's the smile that's worth the money."

For the first time in all the years of our life in Russia we could unpack our books and trunks and have ample space for everything. For the first time Jon had a large floor space to play in.

We sold Arcadi's bicycle and typewriter, brought from Japan, to buy furniture. We reveled in our possession of a home all our own. No longer had we to share a bathroom and lavatory, no longer tumble over another family in the kitchen. We ate and slept in a different room. We had real privacy at last. Privacy, the lack of which had been so hard for Arcadi especially to bear. To him, even the presence of a servant was inhibiting, so that he was happiest and most playful on her day off when there was no one to impel him to encase himself in the shell of reserve which protected his too acute sensibilities.

I remember saying to Arcadi after we moved in that, having at last got a home of our

128

own, we should perhaps soon be leaving Russia. All my life I had been uprooted, or had uprooted myself, after a few years in one place. When I was 9 years old we had left our London home to go abroad. In 1914 the war deprived us of our Surrey country home. In 1928 I had left the little flat in London where Mother and Temple and I had lived after he came home from the war, and which we had been able to make comfortable only a short while before I left England. I had left Japan soon after we started living in a little house where we alone were the tenants. Now, after nearly six years of waiting, we had our own flat in Moscow. It would surely be our fate to move again soon. I did not make my remark at this time with any prescience of the disaster which awaited us. On the contrary, I hoped that some way or another we might all three be able to get out of Russia. Expecting soon to visit England to deliver the finished manuscript of my book on Japan to my English publishers, I wrote Mother on February 24, 1936, that I had only one more chapter to write. My conditions of living were so greatly improved I was managing to do much more work. We had acquired an extra maid for the general housework so that Emma (our Volga German servant) could devote herself to Jon and to sewing and mending. It was cheaper in the end for me to be entirely free from housework. I could make more money and had taken on an extra job as consultant on textile exports, besides doing my regular work at the Institute of World Economy and Politics where I was doing the English translation of a book by Eugene Varga. We were sleeping much better now that we had space for separate beds. Our new flat was "not draughty and gets the sun" and Jon was flourishing. It had been terribly cold 25-30 degrees all the time and I had got my nose slightly frostbitten, but it was alright again. With my English ideas I always saw to it that Jon had a walk every day but we rubbed his nose with grease to ensure against frostbite. Fascinated like other parents the world over by what our child did and said I wrote:

A few days ago we wished so much that you were here to see Jon. We were having dinner. First he climbed up on his chair himself, took a plate, put it down in front of him and demanded tatoes (potatoes). He ate them beautifully himself with fork and then, when he had finished, he reached for cigarettes, took one, put it in his mouth and said: "Mak, mak" (match). All perfectly seriously and naturally! So you see what kind of a grandson you have! You always said he should wait to smoke 'til he was 3! It was so funny that we could not stop laughing. He has begun to say quite a lot of words. He still says damn when annoyed. He also says "come here" as Komm (German) Suda (Russian). He speaks a terrible lot—a real Utley says Arcadi—but one can't always tell what language he is trying to speak.

I finished *Japan's Feet of Clay* early in March, but it took me three weeks of wangling to secure good paper on which to have it cleanly typed. Ordinary Russian paper was gray, soggy stuff not unlike blotting paper. I could not obtain a supply of anything better until Eugene Varga himself spoke to a Vice-Commissar at the Commissariat of Light Industry.

On March 10, 1936, we had a housewarming party on Jon's second birthday. Without Jane and Michael parties were not as gay as of yore, but the Rabinovitch's came, and also to our great joy, our dear friend from Japanese days, Dementiev, whom we called Mentich. He was visiting Moscow from the South, where he had recently conducted the U.S. Ambassador, William Bullitt, on a tour of the Ukraine.

"Mentich" was a "Great Russian" both in his geographical origins and in his spirit.

Huge, shaggily blond with pale blue eyes in a pallid face he was ponderous as a bear and somewhat slow on the uptake. But after he got the point of a joke his uproarious peals of laughter were heartwarming. Whenever he came to Moscow I opened my heart freely, knowing he was our loyal and devoted friend. An old Bolshevik who had fought gallantly in the Civil War, he took no pleasure in the material privileges he now enjoyed. He longed for the good old days when a revolutionary's life was honest and hard and dangerous and was trying to get himself sent on an Arctic expedition.

Instead he was arrested not long after our last party. I have often wondered whether this was at least in part the result of the unfavorable view of the USSR which Bill Bullitt acquired at this time as contrasted with his championship of Russia in Lenin's day.

On the night of April tenth, Arcadi awakened me from a deep sleep, saying, "We have visitors."

I sprang out of bed to see a soldier in the hall. Two NKVD officers in uniform were in our sitting room, together with the janitor of the building.

The secret police officers forbade us to speak to one another and started on a methodical search of our apartment. We had hundreds of books, and they went through every one of them, shaking out their leaves and scanning their titles.

They also examined all our papers. They could not read English, and strangely enough they accepted Arcadi's word for the contents of my manuscripts.

When they came across the typescript of a book on Pushkin's life in my desk, written by Mark Kazanin, my closest friend at the institute where we both worked, my heart beat faster. Mark had asked me to take it to England and send it to his brother in America for publication under a pseudonym. There was nothing subversive or anti-Communist in it, but no Soviet citizen was permitted to write anything for publication abroad without rigorous censorship and official permission. Arcadi knew nothing about the book and was not on too good terms with Mark Kazanin who was a class-conscious intellectual who looked down on business executives such as my husband, and who was also rather too fond of me in his own peculiar fashion. Whatever he may have thought after glancing at a page or two of the manuscript, Arcadi convinced the NKVD searchers that it was of no interest to them, and when I left Russia a few weeks later I carried Mark's manuscript with me.

We sat silent and tense. The slight up-and-down movement of Arcadi's right foot crossed over his left alone betrayed his feelings. As the hours passed and the search went on, I said to myself over and over again: "They will find nothing and then they will go. They will find nothing and they will go." Thus defensively did I try to keep up my courage, although I knew only too well that the innocent were just as likely to be arrested as the guilty.

When Arcadi went to the toilet, an NKVD soldier went with him, presumably to see that he should destroy no documents. Emma, indignant and nervous, but as ever unafraid, protested when the noise the officers made searching in cupboards and drawers in our bedroom threatened to wake Jon. Arcadi told her to keep quiet and his authority was more potent than that of the representatives of Stalin's tyranny.

When Arcadi's eyes and mine met, we gave each other a smile and a look of confidence and calm. One must keep calm. Is it a dream? Has the end come? Is this now happening to us which has happened to so many others? Will the nightmare pass, or is this the end of our life and our love?

The dawn came, but the search went on. The officers were polite, silent, methodical. They selected a few books to take away, including a volume of Marx and one of Keynes.

They took my letters from Arcadi, preserved through the years. They took my address book. These, some office papers Arcadi had been working on at home, and the books they packed in a bag. At seven o'clock Jon awakened and Emma gave him breakfast.

At eight o'clock they told Arcadi they were taking him away to be examined, but the search was not yet completed. I made coffee. My mind now was filled with only one purpose: to strengthen him for the ordeal before him.

I knew he was innocent, but I also knew of the terrible, long, exhausting examinations to which the NKVD subjected its victims. Arcadi had been up all night, and might be confused—too tired to think clearly. By this time they allowed us to talk a little. Jon was around the place, and him they could not silence.

I might have asked Arcadi what I should do when he was gone, what I should do if he were imprisoned. But I still hoped he would come home in a few days or a few weeks. I wanted only to give him strength and confidence.

I asked him no questions. I let him rest half-sitting, half-lying on the couch with his head sunk down and his face very pale. I packed a small suitcase with brush and comb, soap, toothbrush, and a change of linen. I also put in a slim volume of Galsworthy stories hoping he might be allowed to have it with him for consolation or distraction.

At about nine o'clock they took him away. We kissed for the last time. At the door I said, "What can I do? To whom shall I go?"

He shrugged his shoulders. "No one can help," he said.

No words of love passed between us. They were not needed. Reserved to the last, he gave me a gentle smile and was gone.

I never saw him again. He passed out of my life on that lovely April morning in his old, Navy blue English flannel jacket, his black head hatless, a slight figure between the two stonefaced, khaki-clad police officers.

Emma was in tears. I sent her out with Jon. I walked from room to room trying to think what I could do, to whom I could go, where I could discover what Arcadi was accused of. Finally I found myself vomiting. Fleetingly I remembered learning in a psychology class that the stomach, not the heart, is the seat of the emotions.

"It must be a mistake," I reasoned. Queer things were going on at Promexport. The manager and assistant manager of a department had been arrested a few days before. That last evening Arcadi had told me about it, but he had not suggested that he himself was in danger.

In order to maintain Promexport's position as the leading export organization, Kalmanovsky, the Chairman, had continued to sell certain goods abroad which should, according to a new policy, have been retained for use in Russian industry. This had just been found out by the "Workers and Peasants Inspection" authorities.

Kalmanovsky had placed the blame upon the manager of the department in question, although this man had only carried out his orders and, being non-Party, would have lost his job had he refused to do so.

As finance manager of Promexport, Arcadi signed all contracts. Although he was in no way responsible for the kind of goods exported, it would have been a more or less normal procedure to rope him in for examination. This was, I believe, from what I learned later, the actual reason for his arrest.

But once you were in the hands of the secret police, they didn't let you go easily. If they found nothing against you on one count, they hunted around for some other charge.

The concentration camps were always hungry for more men, always in need of more labor. Almost every citizen had at some time or another said, or been reported to have said, something critical of the regime, or of the Party line. Moreover, since guilt by association was an integral part of the Soviet way of life, having been associated with a condemned person was often enough reason to get sent to prison.

That first morning I went to the NKVD office in Petrovka, where the officer in charge of the search party had told me I could get information as to the reason for Arcadi's arrest. It was the free day and it was closed. Next day I went again and waited in a line-up with others, only to be told that no information could be given to me yet. I went each day and was always given the same answer.

I went to the Commissariat of Foreign Trade. No one could tell me anything or help me. Philip Rabinovitch, now Vice Commissar under the durable Anastasius Mikoyan told me not to worry; that, of course Arcadi was innocent and would soon be home again. But he himself seemed nervous. When anyone was arrested in the USSR it was as if the plague had struck his family. All were afraid of any contact lest they themselves be contaminated with dire consequences to themselves and to their families.

In spite of the ever increasing miasma of fear in Moscow in 1936, several friends had the courage to see me and try to help me. Sophie Rabinovitch told me to come to their flat, in the same block as ours, whenever I felt like it. Anikeeva, my friend since the days we had lived in Tokyo, tried to give me comfort. Her husband thought it was Arcadi's irrepressible propensity to make dangerous jokes which had got him into trouble.

At the Institute some shunned me, but I was not dismissed. Eugene Varga was kind and tried to get information as to why my husband has been arrested.

One man at the Institute whom I had known years before in London at the School of Economics attempted to console me by showing me that mine was the lot of all. He said, "I don't suppose there is a family in Moscow which has not lost at least one member in the past years either through arrest or typhus."

I went to see Kalmanovsky, the Chairman of Promexport, at his home. He faced me in a dark room lit by a small lamp on his writing table. He was ill at ease and his dark expressive eyes showed panic. I could see he was already afraid for himself, and that no help could come from him. His brother, a non-party man who had been my friend ever since I got to know him in the Caucasus on my first visit to the Soviet Union in 1928, came to see me. He was sunk in the deepest despair at the ever-increasing terror.

I went to see Z. our ex-OGPU friend. He promised to make inquiries. Two days later he told me I had nothing to fear, Arcadi was being held for questioning in connection with the case of the other Promexport men arrested; since he could not be held guilty merely because he had signed the fatal contract as finance manager, I should not worry. He advised me to go to England with the manuscript of my book. By the time I came back he was sure Arcadi would be free. So he said, perhaps not really believing it, but wanting to ensure my safety and my son's.

I then made my decision. I already had a visa to go to England and return having applied for it through the Institute before Arcadi's arrest. I had even managed to secure permission to exchange rubles for thirty pounds sterling for my trip to England to see *Japan's Feet of Clay* through the press.

I could take Jon out of the country into safety in England and return. All through the long days of anxiety, of traipsing from place to place and person to person, I had feared for our son. Although I had contrived to have his name added to my passport, it was there clearly stated that he was not a British subject.

I knew that the secret police took hostages and frightened men into false confessions by threatening reprisals on their children. I must get Jon out of the country while I could. Arcadi would want me to save him whatever happened..

I left Moscow by train by night ten days after Arcadi's arrest. Before leaving I handed in a letter to the Lubianka prison for him saying I was going but would return. I shall never know whether or not the prison authorities let him have it.

Philip Rabinovitch sent his limousine and chauffeur to take us to the station. I remember nervously endeavoring to get Jon's socks and shoes on at the last moment.

After we crossed the Russian Frontier into Poland, the sick feeling I had had for days began to pass. My heart sang, "Jon is safe, Jon is safe." I could breathe again. Looking after him on the three-day journey without a sleeper took all my energy and thoughts. Jon was excited and restless. In the first days after Arcadi's arrest he had hunted for his father all over the flat in cupboards and even under the beds.

In Berlin, where we waited three hours between trains, I gave Jon the first banana he had ever tasted and we had a luxurious bath at the station. I remember that bath so well because Jon, in spite of my supporting hand, slipped under the water in the huge tub and came up spluttering "Damn Mamma." This "damn" was his rendering of the Russian words, "Ja tibia dam," meaning "I'll give you what for," an expression he had often heard in the courtyard of our Moscow apartment house where the children played. His speech at this time was a mishmash of English, German and Russian.

It was a strenuous journey, and I was exhausted by the time I took the boat from Holland on the last lap of my return to England. As I was staggering down the steps of the ship to a third class cabin, carrying my son on one arm and clutching a suitcase with my other hand, a friendly voice hailed me. Owen Lattimore, whom I had met shortly before in Moscow relieved me of my burdens and helped me put Jon to bed.

Subsequently in London both Owen and his wife Eleanor became my friends. They were generous to me, not only with their sympathy, but also providing me with clothing for my son from their own boy's outgrown clothes.

I knew that as editor of *Pacific Affairs* Owen Lattimore was closely connected with the Soviet Government and that they were friendly to the so-called "Soviet Socialist experiment." But since they deplored the mass arrests, imprisonments without trial, and other tyrannical features of Stalin's Russia, I believed them to be honest liberals, sincere in their condemnation of the terror from which I had fled.

My confidence at this time in Owen Lattimore, against whom I was to testify fifteen years later before the Tydings Committee in Washington, was largely due to his independent behaviour at the conference in Moscow at which we first met.

Here I should explain that, after the Kremlin switched over to its "Popular Front" policy, the Institute of World Economy and Politics where I was a "senior scientific worker," had become the Russian Branch of the Institute of Pacific Relations (IPR), destined to play an important and pernicious role in the determination of America's China policy in later years. For the benefit of the visiting Americans, a room had been taken in another part of the town and a notice put up saying "Soviet Council of the Institute of Pacific Relations." It was here that E. C. Carter, president of the American I.P.R., and Owen Lattimore were first received by the leading Communists at the Institute. As I had left the Communist Party years earlier, I could not attend their private meetings. But the Americans came to the Institute for a day long session to consult on Far Eastern questions. I was astonished to see how often and completely Mr. Carter (a former head of the International YMCA and a very smooth operator) deferred to the Soviet viewpoint. Owen Lattimore appeared to be more independent in his attitude, since he dared to argue that it was incorrect to designate Mongol society as feudal. From this I concluded that he was not a Communist—an opinion which was fortified later, in London, when he told me he had almost lost his job as editor of *Pacific Affairs* because he had published an article by the Trotskyist Harold Isaacs.

My delay in getting to England had made it too late for Faber and Faber to publish my book until September. Their reader, G. F. Hudson, Fellow of All Souls, who was unknown to me then but was to become one of my best friends, had sent in a most favorable report.

Mr. Geoffrey Faber, head of the firm, who had had sufficient confidence in me to contract for an unwritten book and pay me an advance on royalties the previous year, encouraged me to hope that *Japan's Feet of Clay* would be a big success. My hopes soared that by making a reputation in England I might save Arcadi.

Three weeks after I had left Moscow Vera cabled that they were taking away our flat and I must return immediately.

Mother was unable to look after Jon alone and I had almost no money. The Yeserky's, old Russian Jewish friends of Arcadi's who were "non-returners" meaning employees of the Russian trade missions or embassies who had stayed abroad when ordered to come back to Moscow—drove Jon and me down to Ditchling in Sussex late that evening to a small nursery school they knew, run by a Mrs. Shawcross whose nephew was a Labor Party lawyer. Here I left my sleeping two-year-old son to wake among strangers. I feared that finding me gone he would cry desolately but I had no choice. Arcadi needed me most and Jon would be well cared for.

Next morning I left for Moscow via Berlin, from where, during a few hours stop-over, I wrote Mother on May 10th saying:

> Darling, I felt I loved you very much when I said goodbye to you
> and when I saw you waving to me on the platform. Poor Mother who
> has only me left and I in such a mess. I am not so unhappy now that I
> am going to Arcadi and I shall see him and perhaps be able to help him.
> I do hope Jon is happy. I am glad I left him in England. I know you
> love him, dear, and will look after him whatever happens to us. But I
> hope it will all soon be over and that I shall soon be back.

I wrote Mrs. Yeziersky from the train asking her to get some shirts and shoes for Jon, as she knew the right sizes. I had just been to the cinema and found that "the similarity between Nazi and Communist propaganda was extraordinary."

The rest of my letter to Mother was concerned with code names and phrases for her to understand what I should mean when I wrote from Moscow.

My worries as always were small as well as great. I mailed a hurried pencilled letter from Warsaw saying I had been so stupid as to leave my toothbrush on the boat and could she get her doctor, a Russian-born Jewish friend of ours who was planning to visit Russia, to bring me one to Moscow "because the new English one I bought is for Arcadi." Russian toothbrushes were like almost everything else, of very poor quality. I also asked Mother to try to get Dr. Yates to bring me coffee, but told her she should not give him my address. I would phone him at his hotel. Then I wrote:

> Soon I shall be back in Moscow but no Arcadi to welcome me. Up to
> now I have felt all right but am now getting excited and nervous. I hope
> I shall hear soon that Jon at least is all right.

Vera met me at the station in Moscow and told me that our ever resourceful Emma had barricaded herself in our apartment for three days. She had bolted the door and refused to open it to anyone, but she obviously would be unable to withstand the siege for many more days.

Armed with a letter I secured from Eugene Varga I went to the house management of the block and raised hell. They had intended to take advantage of our predicament to put in a friend of the House Committee Chairman. Once I showed them that I was no cowed wife of a secret police victim, but a foreigner still employed at the Academy of Sciences and able to stand up for our rights, they abased themselves in true Russian Soviet style with profuse apologies.

Our home was saved for the time being, but the news about Arcadi was foreboding. Vera had ascertained that he was now accused of a political offense. What offense they would not tell her, but everyone knew that a political charge was far graver than a mere accusation of having done wrong in business.

There began for me the saddest, gloomiest, most trying and anxious period of my life. Day after day I went to the Public Prosecutor's office and stood in line waiting my turn to speak to an official there. According to the new Soviet Constitution, the State Prosecutor had "supervision of the exact observance of the laws." No one was to be subject to arrest "except under the decision of a court or with the sanction of the Prosecutor."

Actually, when Arcadi was arrested, no warrant or any kind of paper was shown to us. Perhaps the Prosecutor signed batches of blank slips for the NKVD to fill in, but such a formality, if it did take place, was meaningless.

After, as before the promulgation of the new Constitution with its ostensible safeguards against arbitrary arrest, the power of life and death was left in the hands of the Secret Police which continued to imprison anyone it pleased. The only difference that the "inviolability of the person" clause in the Constitution made was that citizens might try to ascertain at the Public Prosecutor's office why an arrest had been made, and had to send appeals through him instead of directly to the secret police.

Each time I finally got to see an official at the Prosecutor's, I was told to come back in four days or in a week's time. When I came back, and had again spent hours standing in line, I was told that the case was now in the hands of another official. When I got to the other official the process was repeated.

After five weeks of this I managed, through the help of an influential Party member to get to one of the Assistant Prosecutors, called, as far as I remember, Levine. He spoke German, and our conversation was brief:

"Ihr Mann hat im Ausland gearbeitet?"

"Ja."

"In Japan?"

"Ja."

"Nun, er hat dort was gesagt dass er nicht sagen sollte."

That was all: Arcadi was in prison because of something he had said which he ought not to have said six or seven years before in Japan.

Perhaps Anikeev was right. Perhaps it was one of Arcadi's jokes which had been reported and filed away in his dossier which had brought him under suspicion.

I started to appeal. I wrote to the Prosecutor, to Yezhov, then Assistant Commissar of the Commissariat of the Interior, (NKVD), and finally to Stalin himself. I never received any acknowledgement of any of my letters. Meanwhile I went twice weekly to the NKVD to fill in a form asking to be permitted to visit my husband. Nothing ever came of this either.

In May Arcadi had been moved from the Lubianka to the Butirky Prison. This meant either that his examination was completed or that the Lubianka was so full that he had been transferred while awaiting further examination.

We could not know which of these alternatives it meant. If he were already condemned we had to go to the prison every three days to see if his name was yet posted on the list of those being sent away to a concentration camp.

The NKVD did not inform the relatives of arrested persons of their fate. The family had to watch the lists posted on the prison walls. It might be days or months before husband, son, wife, or father was sent off condemned without trial. The only way to know was to watch the lists.

Vera had a friend who knew a woman whose husband was a trusty among the condemned political prisoners in the Butirky Prison, and was allowed a visit from his wife once in twelve days. Through this old comrade of hers we found out that Arcadi was not among those already condemned. He was therefore evidently still in solitary confinement, or with others still under examination.

No one in the queues at the prison and at the Prosecutor's expected that anyone would be given a trial. It was taken for granted that all would be condemned in secret, or, if a miracle occurred, released similarly without trial.

The articles in the New Constitution guaranteeing trial in open court "with participation of the people's associate judges" (Articles 103 and 111) were a dead letter from the beginning, for they contained a joker: "with the exception of cases specially provided for by law," or "except in special cases."

These articles were only intended to delude gullible foreign "Friends of the Soviet Union," who failed to appreciate the significance of the addition of the words "except in special cases." No citizen of the USSR took the New Constitution for anything more than was intended, a thin facade to cover the naked police regime, a cruel mockery of the millions condemned without trial.

After Arcadi was transferred to Butirky Prison, food could be delivered to him every eight days and change of linen every sixteen days. To do this I went early in the morning with a sack or pillowcase and stood in line after filling in a form stating exactly what it contained. If anything forbidden, such as cigarettes, was included, everything might be rejected.

The first time I went, a friend of Vera's, an old Social Revolutionary from Siberia, went with me to help. For the form had to be carefully filled out, and I might make a mistake over some of the Russian words.

Vera's friend was a Socialist of the old school. For hours that morning she helped poor illiterate women who could not write and feared their pitiful supplies of black bread and onion might be rejected unless they could sign their names on the form.

Many of the women with their breadwinners arrested and children to support were obviously half-starved themselves, but they had trudged the streets to bring bread for their husbands.

There was no poor relief in Russia. Neighbors and relatives were too poor to help or too afraid to help. Even if their children were old enough to leave alone, it was almost impossible for women whose husbands had been arrested to get any kind of work.

There were different days for different letters of the alphabet. As far as I can remember, our day included all those whose names began with A, B, C, D.

At this prison it took hours before my turn came to hand in my sack to the NKVD official. Some idea of the huge number of political prisoners in Moscow at this time could

136

be formed from the large numbers standing in line each day to deliver food to their relatives.

Strangely enough, there seemed more good will and friendliness among these people than in other line-ups in Moscow—a comradeship of the damned. They had little left to fear or hope for. The worst had befallen them already.

On May Day, while I was still in England and Vera had stood in line for me, she heard a man ahead of her say, "Half of the population of Moscow is demonstrating today, while the other half is either in prison or waiting like us at the prison gates."

On my first visit to the Butirky prison, a boy eleven or twelve years old ahead of me, seeing how ignorant I was of the procedures, exclaimed with some scorn mixed with pity, "Is this the *first* time you have brought food to a relative in prison?" I then remembered the "humorous" story Arcadi used to tell about the kid who got up early to take bread to his mother in the hospital and then to his father in prison. Arriving panting at school a few minutes late he was asked by the mistress of the science class, "How many back teeth does a frog have?" And the boy, sighing deeply, says: "Teacher, I wish I had your troubles."

Often in future years in the West, I recalled this Russian Jewish expression when, hearing people complain of minor troubles, or considering themselves poor or underprivileged when actually they were incomparably more fortunate than the great majority of the Russian people. All values, as also all sufferings, are relative. The most 'underprivileged' people in the Western world are fortunate in comparison to the subjects of a Communist totalitarian tyranny.

In this connection, writing now in 1968 in the United States where, despite the great advance in my time in civil rights and equal opportunities for Negroes, dissatisfaction abounds. I recall the showing in Moscow of an American film picturing the Negroes as oppressed. The Moscow audience, however, was more impressed by the good shoes worn by the Negroes in the film, unobtainable in Russia by all but the privileged.

At the prisons we waited for the proof given us that husband or father, brother, or sister, son or daughter still lived, when in the late afternoon, we were given a receipt, signed by the prisoner for the packages we had handed in that morning. Every sixteen days we were allowed to send in clean clothing and receive back the soiled linen of the prisoners. When I got Arcadi's dirty underwear back for the first time I broke down and cried. It was five weeks since they had taken him away, and this was the first opportunity Vera or I had had to supply him with a clean shirt, underwear and socks. The stuff we got back was filthy, sweat-stained, black with grime. This brought home to me more vividly than anything else what he must be suffering.

The prisons were terribly crowded, and I pictured Arcadi in the heat and dirt of a crowded cell. There would certainly be bugs. He would be sleeping on a plank bed, and the room would be airless. Arcadi who was so fastidiously clean had had to wear the same underwear for weeks.

Yet I comforted myself in remembering his philosophic spirit, and his gift for understanding men and never losing his self control. I hoped he would know from the foreign chocolate and soap I had sent him that I had been to England and had come back and was still at liberty. That should give him good heart to endure.

He might guess that I had left Jon safely in England. In any case, he knew I would provide for our son, and that I could fight for myself. The NKVD would not be able to force him to a false confession through threats against us.

One day in the street I met Berkinghof's wife. He had been taken off the train to prison on his arrival from Mongolia, where he had been the Soviet Trade Representative. She and their young son had been brought to Moscow by the lure of a false telegram purporting to come from him. They had lived well for years as top ranking members of the Communist Party but practically everything they possessed was in Mongolia. Varya was haggard and white, fearing most for the future of their small son, whom they adored. She was trying to get a job, but was refused employment everywhere.

I heard of one arrest after another among our friends and acquaintances. The scythe was sweeping ever wider and higher. Very important people were being arrested and disappearing without trace. Everyone I knew looked afraid. Panic spread. It was clearly hopeless to try to get anyone to help. All were consumed by fear for themselves.

The radios in the street blared out, "Life is happy! Life is joyous!" Varya Berkinghof and I smiled bitterly as we said goodbye to each other for the last time on Tverskaya street.

Vera did all she could to save her brother, showing the same bold spirit as in her youth when she defied the Tsarist tyranny. But she was as helpless as I was. She bravely assured me that no innocent man such as her brother Arcadi would be condemned, and surely soon would be set at liberty, but I doubted whether she believed it. Poor Vera was still clinging to her belief in the good intentions of the Communist Party. A year later, in April, 1937, she was herself arrested when nearly all those who belonged to the proud category of those who had been condemned to hard labor as political convicts in Tsarist prisons were purged or liquidated by Stalin, who suspected all the revolutionaries of the past.

Emma, my friend rather than servant, looked after me, forced me to eat the meals she cooked for us and tried to keep my hopes alive. A descendant of German farmers induced by Catherine the Great to emigrate to Russia to teach the ignorant Slavs agricultural skills and animal husbandry, my red-haired, blue-eyed and muscular Emma, like other "Volga Germans" had retained not only her militant Protestant faith, but also the steadfast courage which was the hallmark of the Teutonic tribes, described by the Roman historian Tacitus as unconquerable by reason of their bravery, loyalty, and love of freedom.

It was a perfect summer in Moscow. One lovely day succeeded another. In the evenings I would sit reading on our sixth floor balcony, my eyes leaving the printed page at frequent intervals to look down on the courtyard below in the hope of seeing Arcadi come walking along. I imagined the smile and the light or joking words he would surely use when he came home, and shut my mind to the terrible fears which returned with the darkness.

Seeking momentary escape from Giant Despair, I read many books during those long, lonely, beautiful evenings of my last summer in Moscow. The one I remember best is Somerset Maugham's *Of Human Bondage*. Maybe I still remember this best of all Maugham's books because it enabled me to escape for brief periods from my own anguish, by reading a sadder story than my own. I could identify myself with the main character in the novel distilled by Maugham from his own life as a poor student in London, because I had experienced poverty, loneliness and youthful longings for love in a similar situation. But Somerset Maugham's alter ego as portrayed in this book was never warmed by the "durable fire" of true love "in the mind everburning" which had made my life with Arcadi so happy, despite disillusionment and privation. Even as my eyes smarted in reading *Of Human Bondage* I could account myself fortunate among women for the love and companionship and understanding I had known even if I had lost Arcadi forever.

All through those months in Moscow of fear and hope for Arcadi I was also consumed with anxiety for my son and my mother, separated from each other as from me. They both needed me to look after them, while I stayed on in Moscow unable to do anything to help Arcadi or them. My heart ached for my son, alone in a strange place, too young for anyone to explain to him why both his mother and father had vanished from his life. As also for my mother, lonelier now than ever since the death of Temple only a year before. On June 6, 1936, a few days before Temple's birthday I wrote:

> There is nothing new since I wrote you last. I am just waiting and waiting. I am working as much as I can at the Institute and still trying to find out what Arcadi is accused of. I think I told you in my last letter that they said I could not be told for another month or perhaps three weeks. I am very lonely but not worrying too much as I feel certain it will be all right in the end.
>
> I have had no letter from you since the one written May 25th. I had hoped to hear that you had seen Jon. I do so long to know how he is. I do not like it that they think he is very quiet. It must mean that he feels strange and shy.
>
> You and Rab, I expect, will drink to Temple's memory on the 10th. I think of him very often and remember his courage and his sunny temperament and wish he were alive with all my heart. I would give much to have him with me now. I love you, dearest, and know you love my son. I hope these dark days will pass soon and that I shall be with you again.

Late in July I received a cable from my publishers in London that I must come at once to correct final proofs of my book due then to go to press. It was impossible to tell how long Arcadi's examination would last. It might be months before his case was decided and I had come to the conclusion that the only way I could help was to go to England and try to exert pressure on Moscow from there.

Standing in line at the Public Prosecutor's and sending in appeals was clearly useless. Moreover, my son had to be provided for in England. I must make some money. I had plenty of rubles, since the thousands we had received from the sale of the typewriter were only partially spent, but they could not be exchanged for English currency.

I decided to fly to England and come back after my book was published. This time, I could not secure a return visa. The Soviet authorities, no doubt glad to be rid of me, gave me an exit visa, but told me to get my return visa in London because my British passport was about to expire.

This was a valid reason, but I could not be sure that it was the real one. However, I had no choice. I had to go to England and could only hope it was true that a visa to return to the Soviet Union would be procurable in London.

During the anxious last months in Moscow I saw my friend Mark Kazanin more frequently than anyone else. I had not been dismissed from the Institute of World Economy and Politics where we were both "Senior Scientific Workers," and I believed that he was a friend I could trust. But after I left Moscow for the last time the seeds of doubt were to be sown in my mind even about Mark.

Arcadi while not liking him much had thought it was a good thing that I had such a friend and adviser at our place of work, and I had not understood until after Arcadi's arrest that Mark really was, or thought he was, in love with me. He had a most loyal and very nice Irish wife whom I had imagined he loved as much as I loved Arcadi. But now, while Arcadi was in prison, Mark wanted to make love to me, and said that if only I would forget Arcadi and live with him he would manage to escape from Russia to join me in the West.

I was both shocked and greatly worried and began to avoid Mark's company. Such is the dreadful atmosphere of suspicion and fear in a police state that no one can ever be sure that friends will not betray you, either from compulsion to save themselves, or for their own advantage. A year later in England I had a cryptic message from Vera given to an English friend visiting Moscow, which implied that Mark had been a secret informer against Arcadi.

A few years ago I learned from Jane, visiting Moscow briefly for the Royal Institute of International Affairs, that Mark Kazanin and his wife were still alive but she had not seen them. This suggested that Mark never was such an uncompromising opponent of Stalin's tyranny as he convinced me that he was. Or maybe he was merely quietly discreet, and thus escaped liquidation. I prefer to believe that his temporary infatuation or imagined love of me, or his fears for his own survival, never in fact led him to become an informer against my husband.

This all sounds very melodramatic, but life in Russia was of the essence of horrible melodrama with too many villains or weaklings and cowards and few heroes. As I have already related, on the terrible night of Arcadi's arrest a bad moment had come when the secret police came across a manuscript on the life of Pushkin, written by Mark under a pseudonym, which I had undertaken to convey to England.

When I left Russia with Jon soon afterwards I carried Mark's ms with me and it was eventually delivered to his brother in America, who was a psychiatric doctor. It was apparently never published and Mark's brother died before I came to the U.S. or soon after. But for a long time I felt guilty about that ms, since I took a risk which might have further increased the mortal danger which threatened Arcadi. And since Mark and his wife survived the war and the worst years of the Stalin era and lived on into the somewhat more "liberal" Khrushchev era, yet never communicated with me through his many foreign friends, the suspicion which I originally refused to entertain concerning my erstwhile dear friend, Mark Kazanin, has come back to me now in writing my Memoirs.

All this time the treatment I myself received encouraged the hope that they were not going to imprison Arcadi indefinitely. True that I was English, but other foreigners had been arrested. Surely if they were trying to frame Arcadi they would do something to implicate me as well.

I had the terrible feeling all along that perhaps he was suffering for my sins. I had never *done* anything against the Soviet Government, but I had *thought* a lot against it. And I had not always been sufficiently cautious in expressing my opinions when on trips to England or meeting English friends visiting Russia.

Occasionally I had revealed a little of the truth on conditions in the USSR to friends who visited me in Moscow. Arcadi, had been more discreet, never openly expressing "dangerous thoughts," contenting himself with relating the jokes current in Moscow. He had accepted the realities of life in the USSR and convinced himself that no changes for the better were possible through any change in the composition of the Soviet government. He had continued to work extremely hard giving all his knowledge, energy and talents to his job, convinced that this was the only way for conditions to be improved.

Being a Jew and a Russian, he was far more of a fatalist than I; more resigned and philosophical concerning ills that could not in his view be cured, but could be ameliorated if everyone tried to do his own job as well as possible. Indignation and anger were in his view unnecessary and futile.

140

I left everything we possessed behind in Moscow: books, clothes, linen, furniture and money. The money I left with Vera, telling her to continue to pay the 200 rubles a month we always allowed to Arcadi's former wife, Anna Abramovna, and their son Vitia. Anna Abramovna had had a job for some years past, and Vitia was now in his teens, but I knew that Arcadi would wish me to continue the financial assistance he always provided despite his former wife's enmity.

To keep the flat safe and occupied, I installed in it a man and his wife whom I knew to be decent people who would vacate it if and when Arcadi was set free. They were glad to take Emma on as their servant. In the second room I placed Vera's son Shura and his wife and child, leaving Emma the smallest room as hers by right, whether employed by the other inmates or not.

The last night I did not go to bed at all. After packing, I sat down to write a long letter to Arcadi in case he should come home or be sent away before my return—or in case I never got back.

I assured him that whatever happened, even if I did not see him for years, I would continue to love him. Life without him was unbearable and unthinkable and I promised that if he were condemned, I would return and try to be near him, but would leave Jon in England. I left the letter with friends, but it is unlikely that Arcadi was ever allowed to receive it.

I left Moscow by airplane at four o'clock in the morning. Emma tried to see me off but was not allowed to come to the airport. She wept and clung to me, saying goodbye forever. I assured her I should come back. She was certain that I would never return.

Emma was right and I was wrong. I myself feared that she might be right as I said goodbye to Moscow, where I had known such great happiness and profound sorrow.

Lovely Moscow in the dawn of a glorious summer day with the blue sky over the red Kremlin walls and the risen sun's rays brightening the golden church towers and cupolas. Once a beacon to the world in the hope it had seemed to offer of a just social order and brotherhood of all mankind; now the grave of the Communist ideal which had inspired me to dreams of a better world.

Nine years before, almost to the day, I had stood in the Red Square for the first time, my heart full of enthusiasm and faith. Now I was flying away to the West leaving the dearest person in my life to a fate unknown. Tears blinded my eyes as the plane rose higher and higher and I looked down for the last time on the city where my youthful hopes were buried.

Chapter 16
RETURN TO THE WEST

For years after I left Moscow for the last time on that cloudless July morning in 1936, I lived suspended between two worlds. I had returned to the West but my heart was in Russia with my husband. Although I gradually abandoned hope of being allowed to return to the unhappy land where Arcadi was incarcerated, I could not kill my irrational belief that one day, somehow, he and I would be together again. So even after I burned my bridges in 1940 by writing *The Dream We Lost*, I neither acted nor felt as if I had lost Arcadi forever.

Gradually I adapted myself to reality and the knowledge that I had to start life again alone with our son. But I put down no roots, feeling myself to be only a transient resident in the world outside the vast prison house called the Union of Soviet Socialist Republics. Nor did I, until too late to love and marry again, feel myself a widow.

Looking back across the three decades which have passed since Arcadi kissed me goodbye in the early dawn of the April day which ended our life together, I realize that it was not until my sixties, "with all passion spent," that my heart accepted the finality of our separation. And still today I can see Arcadi as clearly as if he were alive, smiling at me tenderly but with a quizzical expression, encouraging me to go on writing, but doubtful whether anyone could convey to the fortunate Westerners any conception of the realities of life where liberty is not.

The first two years after my return to the West were the hardest. I longed to bear witness to the truth about the Soviet Union, which I had learned by such intimate and bitter experience, but was convinced that if I spoke out publicly I would be signing Arcadi's death warrant. Yet I could not refrain from speaking frankly to old or close friends. Nor could I bring myself to pretend that all was well with the state of Russia when in the company of the deluded liberals who were then falling over one another in joining Popular Fronts with the Communists.

I knew that by lending my support to the false image of the U.S.S.R. current among the liberals and Communist fellow-travellers to whose company I had once belonged, I might save Arcadi. But I could not tell the big lies required of me. Nor did I think he would wish me to do so. Still an agnostic, I was more certain than ever after my life in the Communist jungle that one destroys oneself and others by denying one's convictions either in order to save oneself and those one loves or for the sake of an ideal.

So, for the most part, I kept silent, but even my silence was all too eloquent. Thus, I found myself increasingly cut off from my own kind, meaning my liberal socialist contemporaries who had rejected Communism in the late 20's when I had embraced it, but who were now following my own footsteps down the well-intentioned path which leads to the totalitarian hell.

Back in the 20's when at London University Labor Party and University Labor Federation meetings we had lightheartedly, and usually amicably, debated concerning the way to establish the socialist order of society from which we expected all blessings to flow, we had all been as innocent as Adam and Eve before they ate of the bitter fruit of knowledge. During the intervening years I had learned that "socialism" far from ensuring an improvement in the human condition could mean, and perhaps inevitably entailed, the establishment of a more stultifying and soul-destroying system than any previously experienced by the sons of men. Meanwhile, many of my old friends in England had been travelling in the opposite direction.

Since the political world would seem to be as round or elliptical as the earth itself, my increasing alienation from my own kind was due to my having travelled further and faster around its spectrum than most of my contemporaries. While I had been drawing further and further away from the Communists, they had been moving ever closer, thanks to the world economic crisis of the early 30's, the Nazi menace, and the Kremlin's successful democratic masquerade.

Few among my former friends had any understanding of my predicament, political, moral or material. Those to whom I dared speak frankly looked upon me askance as an unwelcome returned adventurer who ruffled the calm surface of the sea of complacency on which they sailed. Having plunged deeper and voyaged further than they had dared to do, I had come back from the Promised Land with the unwelcome information that it was a desert. They had preserved their security and their innocence by not taking the ultimate step of joining the Communist Party as I had done long before it was popular to be Red, or at least pink. Now they wanted to be both secure and "progressive" by joining hands with the Communists in Popular Fronts against fascism. The tide of success was running their way. I must have seemed to them like a skeleton at the feast.

In their anxiety to erect a bulwark against fascists and Nazis, most liberals chose to forget or ignore all they had ever known about Communism. To them the issue seemed all too simple. The growing power of Hitler's Germany constituted a clear and present danger. To combat the Nazi and fascist powers seemed to require an alliance with the Soviet Union. But since liberals are prone to rationalize actions conceived out of a proper regard for the facts of power politics, either in order to preserve the good opinion of mankind, or to salve their consciences, they had to convince themselves that there was only one devil abroad, Hitler, and that Stalin's aims were good, however horrible his practices. Thus they were all too ready to stifle their doubts and many of them displayed an increasingly cold-blooded indifference to human suffering. The argument then and later in both England and America ran as follows:

Admittedly, Stalin has created a cruel police regime and has perverted the first Socialist State, but this is only a temporary phase caused by "capitalist encirclement" or the fascist menace. Since its foundations are socialist, the U.S.S.R. offers hope for the future. It is "progressive" whereas Nazi Germany is a "dictatorship of finance capital" and its aims intrinsically bad.

British imperialists of the Winston Churchill stamp simply said that since Nazi Germany constituted a clear and present danger England should be prepared to take the aid of "the devil himself,"—to use his own famous phrase in cementing the Anglo-Russian alliance. Neville Chamberlain had thought that an accommodation with Hilter was feasible and more likely to preserve the British Empire than an alliance with Stalin. In Lawrence Denis's brilliant aphorism: the choice between the two totalitarian dictators was "Hitler, who wanted to join the Carlton Club, and Stalin, who wanted to burn it down."

It was a moot point and no one today can say with any assurance that Chamberlain, who considered Hilter to be a lesser devil than Stalin, was wrong since Churchill lived to see the liquidation of the British Empire which his alliance with the Communist powers was designed to prevent. One thing seems certain: if only, after Nazi Germany attacked Russia, the West had left the two totalitarian giants to fight it out and bleed each other white, the Soviet Colossus would not now bestride Eurasia.

Beatrice and Sidney Webb were leading the procession of socialists and liberals along the primrose path which was to lead, a few years later, to the unconditional alliance of England and America with "Uncle Joe" Stalin against Hitler, which eventually produced this, our world today. With the immense prestige of their long life of historical research, the Webbs made the Soviet Union not only respectable, but admirable. They hid, under their Fabian mantle, the horrors, the starvation, the misery, the degradation of the human spirit and the barbarous methods of government in "Socialist" Russia. Stalin, it seemed to me, must be rubbing his hands in glee, confident that since it had been so easy to induce the Webbs to present a favorable picture of the U.S.S.R., the whole Western labor, socialist and liberal movement could be expected to excuse or condone the purges and terror which were engulfing Russia in a sea of fear. Confident in this expectation, Stalin could afford, he rightly concluded, to throw off all restraint. Otherwise he would not have dared to execute thousands and condemn hundreds of thousands, or even millions, to his slave labor camps without even the mockery of a show trial. By shutting their eyes to the atrocities committed by the Stalin regime, or excusing them, a host of Western liberals, unintentionally, no doubt, rendered themselves accomplices of these crimes against humanity.

The situation was not yet as bad as it was to become after Stalin became our ally against Hitler. But already in the late 30's there was a growing conspiracy of silence on the Left concerning the dark side of that other world in which I had sojourned. Journals of progressive opinion became increasingly reluctant to publish condemnations of the Moscow purge trials, and began to put new meanings to old words and principles. Some who still called themselves liberals got to redefining liberty to mean "subordination to a common purpose" to quote George Soule in the American *New Republic*. They went so far as to excuse executions, torture, imprisonment of innocent persons, and other violations of human rights, if only it was done in the name of socialism or a planned economy. Cruelties which horrified them when committed by "reactionaries" or "imperialists" or fascists and racists, were condoned or glossed over provided they were socialistically administered.

To an ever-increasing degree, men and women who had been my friends or associates came to behave as if they subscribed to the Soviet concept that "information does not consist in the dissemination of news, but in the education of the masses . . . (it is) an instrument in the class struggle; not a mirror to reflect events objectively."*

Proceeding from their *a priori* belief that "public ownership of the means of production and distribution" is an absolute good, the "totalitarian liberals" managed to maintain their faith in the "progressive" nature of the Soviet system in spite of all its crimes against humanity. Shutting their eyes and closing their ears to realities, or too far above earth to heed the cries of anguish of the millions of enslaved Russians and other subjects of the Communist dictatorship, they continued to argue that it must, intrinsically, be good because it was "socialist." Thus they helped the Communists to keep others enslaved while themselves retaining their safe and free position in the "capitalist world." And

---

Soviet Communism; A New Civilization, Beatrice and Sidney Webb, Longmans, Green & Co., London, 1935.

when the anti-Communist winds began to blow in the '50's, they could truthfully proclaim that they were never, but never, members of the Communist Party.

The human capacity to see what you want to see, even if it isn't there, would seem to be most fully developed among idealists too fearful to test their beliefs in the crucible of experience. As Bertrand Russell had written long before in his 1914 book of essays called *Mysticism And Logic:**

> It is only in marriage with the world that our ideas can bear fruit; divorced from it, they remain barren. But marriage with the world is not to be achieved by an ideal which shrinks from fact, or demands in advance that the world shall conform to its desires.

Today, in endeavoring to understand how and why so many men and women of good will in the 30's and 40's deluded themselves and others concerning Soviet Russia, I have come to the conclusion that it was precisely because they never fully committed themselves to the Communist cause that they continued to believe in it. Those of us who fully engage ourselves in the causes we believe in submit our ideals to the hard test of personal experience. By publicly professing our opinions, we risk being proved wrong, or being defeated, and have to take our punishment. But those who refrain from risking their "lives, their fortunes and their sacred honor" in any cause, either because they do not care enough or because they are too fearful or too proud to fight, have no right to call themselves idealists or liberals.

To quote Bertrand Russell again:

> The essence of the liberal outlook lies not in what opinions are held, but in *how* they are held; instead of being dogmatically held, they are held tentatively, and with a consciousness that new evidence may at any moment lead to their abandonment. This is the way opinions are held in science, as opposed to the way in which they are held in theology.**

To test political opinions or theories about man and society one must find out how they work when put into practice, and to do this some risks must be taken. Instead, the pseudo-liberals who came to exert paramount influence in the press, radio and universities of the West following Hitler's rise to power, remained safe and comfortable in their reinforced steel towers in the rarified atmosphere of theoretical speculation.

Dante consigned to the "anteroom" of hell those who had no opinion. Worse even, it seems to me, are those who profess to have ideals but never risk anything to realize them, preferring security to experience—those whom one might describe as the "demi-vierges" of the political world. But undoubtedly theirs is the kingdom in the democratic world of the West, if not in Heaven.

Those of us who descended to Avernus in our quest for social justice, and came back to the free world with the stigma of "ex-Communist" upon us for the rest of our lives, were attacked from all sides when we proclaimed the truth we had learned by our dreadful experience. Some were bludgeoned into silence by the severe penalties visited upon ex-Communist-anti-Communists by the entrenched forces of the pseudo-liberals who resent those who destroy their illusions, or prove them to have been wrong. But we were the leaven in the free world which saved it by arousing it before it was too late for realization of the Communist menace.

---

*Barnes & Noble, 2nd edition, 1954.

***Unpopular Essays,* Simon & Schuster, New York, 1951.

Describing the harmful influence today of those who still refuse to admit even to themselves how wrong they were about Communism, my old friend Dwight MacDonald wrote in his essay "Liberal Soap Opera":

> The faith of the "intellectuals" has turned sour as Soviet Communism has emerged as a totalitarian system like Nazism. But although this kind of liberalism has disappeared as a political force, it survives as a nostalgic myth, so that in most liberal intellectual circles it is still risky to say a good word for Whitaker Chambers, or a bad one against Owen Lattimore. The myth survives because the liberals have never honestly confronted their illusions in the thirties and forties about Communism, have instead merely counter-posed a disingenuous defense, a blanket denial to McCarthy's sweeping attack. One does not learn from experiences which one refuses to examine. The survival of the liberal myth which glosses over Soviet-Communism's shortcomings and correspondingly exaggerates those of American capitalism, is a big factor in delaying the political reorientation that our liberal ideology has so long needed.*

Those who have "invested" their minds and hearts in an illusion or a false belief are even more reluctant to abandon it than speculators to cut their losses in a business investment which has failed. Or to quote Confucius, a man who makes a mistake and refuses to admit it commits even greater mistakes afterwards.

Meanwhile, the idealists, or extremists on the "Right" or Conservative side, preserve *their* illusion of a past golden age when "free enterprise" was unconfined, by ignoring the sufferings and injustices of that time, just as "liberals" have ignored the cruel realities of the Communist system.

Today, although almost everyone is ostensibly "anti-Communist," there is not much greater understanding of Communism than two or three decades ago when it was as popular to be pink as it is now impossible to be Red. New myths have supplanted the old ones. The days have long since passed when my voice and that of other "premature anti-Communists" was drowned out by the powerful influence of the scribes and pharisees who assured the West out of the depths of their own ignorance that the "economically democratic" Soviet system was better than our own "political democracy." But, as the "power of attraction" of the Soviet myth waned in the light of reality, exaggerated fears of the dread might of the Communist colossus which bestrides Eurasia came to exert a similar baneful influence. Believing that the U.S.S.R. cannot be challenged without risking an atomic war which would make a desert of the world, and misled by an overestimation both of Soviet strength and its appeal among the uncommitted peoples of Africa and Asia, the West dares not raise a standard to which all men ready to fight for freedom can repair.

I was not only politically isolated and finding it more and more difficult to mix with the society to which I had belonged before I went to live in Russia. I was also in dire financial straits during the first year after I left Moscow, before the success of my book, *Japan's Feet of Clay*. My earning capacities as journalist and lecturer were curtailed by my views which prevented me from swimming with the pro-Communist, Popular Front, tide. I had left behind in Moscow all Arcadi's and my possessions and had arrived in London with only a suitcase. My rubles were not exchangeable, and I had left them in

---

Memoirs of a Revolutionist, Farrar, Straus, 1957.

Russia to provide for Arcadi's son, Vitia, and for Emma to send food packages to Arcadi in prison. The £2 or less a week which my mother was now receiving from her father's estate was not enough for her to live on, much less help me, and she was too old and too broken in health following my brother's death in Fiji in 1935, to be able to look after my child while I worked.

I perforce left Jon in the Sussex nursery school where I had deposited him the night before I had returned to Russia for the last time, then still hoping that Arcadi could be saved. I visited him often but it was increasingly painful to leave him there, when he cried at my departure. In later years I could never forget that on my first visit to him after my return from Russia he had stamped his foot and rejected me, no doubt because he felt I had abandoned him. Time was when I feared that Jon had been permanently injured psychologically. But as he grew up and suffered other deprivations due to my being unable fully to fulfill the responsibility of being both father and mother, and on account of my controversial opinions, I found instead that he became more self-reliant, as also more loving and appreciative of me than I deserved.

In this connection I well remember a long and intimate talk I had with Anne Lindbergh in 1949 as we drove from New York to the Lindbergh home in Connecticut. She had been saying some very nice things about my son, whom she had known since he was a little boy. Now fifteen years old, he had escorted her from a party given by my good friends Dick and Virginia Williams to promote my book on Germany.* I told her that I had been disturbed in London while staying with Jon with English friends, when they reproached me for burdening my son with knowledge of my financial difficulties and political struggles. Anne Lindbergh thereupon exclaimed that my English friends couldn't be more wrong, and went on to tell me about the unfortunate upbringing of herself and her much loved brother which had rendered him incapable of facing life. Both of them, she said, had been so insulated from reality by their upbringing that her brother, a most sensitive person like herself, was now in danger of becoming a mental case.

Dear, beautiful and kind Anne Lindbergh, either because she is a poet, or because the female of the species is tougher than the male, escaped his fate. But she too, as I told her several years later when she wrote her best seller about sea shells and personal problems of human relationships, eventually sought escape from the great issues of our time which she had boldly sought to face in her 1940 book called *The Wave of the Future*.

My letter to her on this occasion, to which she never replied, marked the end of my long friendship with this justly famous lady whom I once loved and held in the highest esteem and still admire. She had told me that when she flew with Charles Lindbergh she had known no fear, but when she accompanied him onto *America First* platforms, her heart quaked and it had required all the courage she could muster to do so. As she wryly remarked, she was then condemned by the same people who had hailed her courage in accompanying Charles on some of his hazardous flights which she had greatly enjoyed. A decade later when she wrote *Gift from the Sea* she was warmly praised and widely read by the same people who had rejected her when she dared to stand by Charles Lindbergh in his prescient warnings of the consequences of American involvement in the Second World War on the Communist side. As also by all escapists from the pressing problems of our age who take refuge in personal preoccupations.

* * *

In contrast to my American friends of the future who rallied round to help me in

---

The High Cost of Vengeance, Henry Regnery, Chicago, 1949.

every possible way when I emigrated to the United States with my mother and son in 1939, my erstwhile English friends were for the most part as indifferent to my economic situation as to my loss in Russia of all I had held dear.

Bertrand Russell and his third wife, Patricia, whom we called Peter, were the outstanding exceptions. They understood my agony of heart and mind, and helped me in every way possible, both materially and by moral support. I stayed with them for long periods at Telegraph House at Harting in Hampshire, sometimes together with my small son. Above all, Bertrand and Peter Russell kept my hopes alive and revived my flagging spirits by the reassurance they gave me that there are some people in the world who fight against injustice and cruelty and really care about the victims of tyranny, under whatever mask it disguises itself.

I had hardly known Peter until now, although I had met her during one of my infrequent short visits to England from Moscow, when she was Bertie's secretary before his divorce from Dora. I had known Dora well during and after the time I stayed with the Russells in Cornwall in those far-off days when I was Secretary of the King's College Socialist Society. But I had never known her intimately or come to love her as I came to love Peter who took me to her heart in my distress. I never knew Russell's first wife, a Quaker, and I have only briefly met his last wife whom he married some years after Peter divorced him for infidelity when he was already in his late seventies. But it seems to me that Peter, for all her faults, was the best of them as well as one of the most beautiful women I have ever known. Tall and slim with near classical features, green eyes, a cupid's bow mouth, and lovely luxuriant red-gold hair, Peter was that rare phenomenon: a beautiful woman with a compassionate and loving heart. In my worst moments she brought me out of the valley of despair by her sympathy and fighting spirit.

Bertie was always so generously inclined to regard any woman he married as his equal that he gave them each in turn credit for original thought when they simply echoed his own theories. Thus, he elevated them into a realm of thought and behavior beyond their intellectual capacities in which they found it hard to breathe. Dora, after taking full advantage of her prestige as the wife of Bertrand Russell to win a name for herself, had boxed him in when she challenged him to live up to his unrealistic theories of free love and equality between the sexes by foisting on him the two babies she had conceived by cohabiting with another man, and also requiring him to support them as if they were his own children. The fact that the father of her two bastards was an insignificant little man who was neither handsome, nor intelligent, and whose only claim to fame was having once been a pro-Soviet *Daily Herald* correspondent, and who asked nothing better than to be Russell's pensioner, had put Bertie into a horrible position. He could not completely repudiate his free love theories, but it was a little too much to expect that he would regard as his own a boy who had no Russell blood in him. For deep down in Bertrand Russell is a pride of ancestry which all his liberal theories cannot drown. Dora subsequently proved to be mean and cruel. She not only put Bertie on the rack of his own theories. When the final break between them came she stripped him as bare as she could financially, even to the extent of carrying away linen and furniture. It was not perhaps surprising that she became an avowed Communist *after* the ugly face of Stalin's Russia had been displayed to the world for all who had eyes to see.

Meanwhile, Bertie had married Patricia Spence who was the opposite of Dora Black. Peter had no pretensions to equal or surpass Bertie intellectually. Her relationship with him was perhaps always mainly filial. She was almost young enough to be his granddaughter but she really loved him while also looking after him in a way Dora had never done. Dora had left it to Bertie to attend to such chores as ordering the food and fuel and attending to all the other daily needs and problems of the school which they ran together for a few years at Telegraph House, besides turning out potboiler books to finance the school. Peter, on the contrary, was a real wife to Bertie and looked after him and their son with a devotion which Dora had been too selfish, or too imbued with an exaggerated idea of her own worth, to do.

Eventually Peter and Bertrand Russell would be estranged and divorced. For the moment I want only to recall their harmonious relationship in England when I first came to know Peter. She was so wonderfully kind to me. She fought for me, comforted me, and gave me courage to endure by her loyalty and sympathy and love. Never as long as I live shall I ever forget my debt to Patricia Russell, who was as kind and courageous as she was beautiful, and devoted herself whole-heartedly to the endeavor to save my husband both for my sake, and because of her compassion for all suffering humanity.

Notable among others who helped me to survive both materially and spiritually, were Malcolm Muggeridge and his wife Kitty, a niece of Beatrice Webb's and author today of an exceptionally interesting intimate biography of her famous aunt.* This book, which she sent me after I was nearing completion of this volume of my Memoirs, casts a revealing light on why and how Beatrice Webb became in old age so pernicious an influence on the liberal-labor movement in the West by her *apologia* for Stalin's Russia. Starting like myself as a liberal-socialist but drawn to the Soviet Union by its professed aims, Muggeridge had likewise recoiled in horror after his experience in Russia as correspondent of the *Manchester Guardian* in the early 30's. I had not known him when I lived there. But his book *Winter in Moscow* written with irony, wit and compassion was perhaps the most effective anti-Soviet book ever written.

Kitty Muggeridge's book reveals the callous ultra-cynical views of her famous aunt, Beatrice Webb, whose comment on Malcolm Muggeridge's disillusionment in Russia was: "Why did he imagine he would like Soviet Russia? He ought to have smelt a rat . . . and carefully avoided discovering its stinking body?"

Muggeridge in his account of his last visit to Beatrice Webb shortly before her death wrote in the *Daily Telegraph* that having taken "the stoney, desolate path of those who believe that the salvation of the individual lies in the exaltation of the collectivity," there was only one possible destination for her:

> The last time I saw her she took me upstairs to see a portrait of Lenin . . . .The lighting, arranged from below, exaggerated the cruel mouth, the mongoloid eyes and the cheekbones. It seemed a perfect symbol of the age—this product of Victorian uplift, of Fabian endeavour; this architect of the Welfare State and proponent of 'ethical' religion, now, on the threshold of death, abasing herself before one of the most ruthless and bloody tyrants of history, who had held up to scorn everything she had ever purported to believe in.**

Back in England in 1936-37 Malcolm Muggeridge enabled me to get book reviewing and writing assignments in England, and later on in America when he was correspondent of the London Daily Telegraph in the late 40's he and his wife Kitty and our teenage son and daughter became close friends. Today he is one of the few premature anti-Communists who survived to become a universally known and respected writer and

---

Beatrice Webb: A Life 1858-1943, Alfred A. Knopf, New York 1968.
**ibid.*, p. 250.

television personality. Thanks to his wit, independence of mind and wide ranging knowledge he vies only with William F. Buckley, Jr. as a successful "conservative" commentator.

I would be ungenerous and ungrateful not to remember old friends who helped me before the success of *Japan's Feet of Clay* put me on the way to earning money again. Sybil, my friend from Prior's Field days, supplied me for a month or two with money to hire a woman to relieve me of such time consuming chores as lighting fires, clearing away ashes and cleaning the flat.

Jane Tabrisky was as always a dear and loyal comrade. Having shared the first years of my Russian experience she understood my situation best and was completely in my confidence. Being Jewish, she was naturally more concerned with the Nazi menace than with the Soviet totalitarian tyranny.

Rab Buchanan, my brother's first wife's sister's former husband, continued to be my friend but his political understanding was limited. Like other well to do Britishers of conservative background but with a penchant for Bohemia, he was drifting left with the Popular Front tide. He never actually joined the Communist Party, but after visiting me in Moscow in 1932 he had written to Temple in Tahiti that he was "still a Communist after having been in Russia but that life is very much like London's: talk, drink, women and parties."

This was easy to believe by a visitor keeping company with privileged foreign Communists. I remember leaving a party given by Ralph Fox, (later to die in Spain), in the early hours of a spring morning with Jane and Michael and Rab. As they walked me home along Kropotkin Street we saw a long line of weary men and women outside a store, waiting for it to open at 9 a.m. They were waiting for a small ration of food. We had left a party where caviar, hors d'oeuvres, ham, wine, vodka, chocolates and fruit had been consumed in abundance, and where as we said goodbye the guests were singing revolutionary songs in drunken voices.

In an earlier chapter I have mentioned H. N. Brailsford who like myself had been a defender of the Russian revolution in the 20's and was by now for the same reasons as myself an uncompromising enemy of Stalin's tyranny. He also now endeavored to help me but I never knew him well as a personal friend.

Leonard Woolf, husband of the more famous Virginia, but far more worthy of fame in my estimation, was one of the other few to whom I dared speak freely. His short book "Barbarians at the Gate" by now forgotten, is a work of greater merit to my mind than Toynbee's ambitious attempt to tell the history of the world.

My recollection of Virginia Woolf, whom I met at one of Kingsley Martin's parties, is unpleasant. At the moment when she, arrogant queen of letters, wanted to break it up she said "Home Leonard," in much the same tone as a lady of high degree in the 19th century addressed her coachman. Which attitude of hers perhaps accounts for Leonard Woolf's twitching hands and the affectionate little marmoset which sat on his shoulder in the office where he edited the *Political Quarterly* to which I contributed.

* * *

Japan's Feet of Clay more than fulfilled my hopes. It was a best seller in England and also a success in America. I was elated when seeing the Faber and Faber book delivery van carrying on top a banner advertising my book. A French edition was brought out by the prestigious Payot publishing firm in Paris and translations were also made into Swedish, Danish and Norwegian.

I could now at last bring Jon to live with me with someone to look after him and

150

Mother. I was fortunate to secure the services of an exceptionally nice girl called Rita who being of Baltic origin was now a refugee from both the Communists and the Nazis. She later married an old comrade of mine, Hugo Dewar, then a Trotskyist. They are both still my friends today and I frequently visit them in London.

I was invited to lecture to the Royal Institute of International Affairs, and the Asia Society, and had articles published in journals of repute. Following Japan's attack on China in 1937 I wrote a pamphlet published by the London *News Chronicle*, entitled "Japan Can be Stopped" co-authored by David Wills, today a correspondent in Washington. Published also in a French translation it was circulated at the Nine Power Conference in Brussel which followed the outbreak of the Sino-Japanese war. Which conference was as futile and unproductive of result in halting Japanese aggression as the League of Nations had been in 1931 when Japan took Manchuria. I recall the Chinese Ambassador saying in Brussels: "The sky is dark with chickens coming home to roost." A memorable remark because it so eminently applies to the present situation in the Far East.

In the spring of 1938 I wrote a short book called *Japan's Gamble in China* which I managed to complete in six weeks although also busy with *A Modern Sea Beggar*. Harold Laski contributed an introduction in which he described me as "a distinguished authority upon the economic aspect of Far Eastern politics," and my book as having "that care in documentation which characterizes all Miss Utley's work."

All this led to my being enabled to go to China in 1938 as special correspondent for the London *News Chronicle* in the War Zone, and thus for a while escape from the agonizing decision whether to tell the world all I knew about Russia whatever the consequences for Arcadi if he was still alive. Since I dared not as yet do anything effective against Stalin's total tyranny I could at least help China in her struggle against the Japanese imperialist aggressors.

A year before I went off to the Far East I made a last attempt to save Arcadi.

Chapter 17
BERTRAND RUSSELL, GEORGE BERNARD SHAW, AND THE
CASE OF BERDICHEVSKY

It was not until a year after I returned to England that I decided my only hope of saving Arcadi was to enlist the support of great names among the British liberal elite in an appeal to the Soviet Government. Bertrand Russell had suggested this long before. I had held back for fear that to do so might result only in making my husband's case important enough for the Soviet Government to liquidate him without trace.

By this time I had despaired of securing a visa to return to Russia, but the success of my book, *Japan's Feet of Clay*, and the world-wide acclaim it was receiving had given me some stature, so that it seemed possible that Moscow would pay attention to our plea.

The Russells and I jointly drew up a carefully worded petition to Stalin, the draft of which was submitted to H. N. Brailsford, C. M. Lloyd, Kingsley Martin and Harold Laski, all of whom were in my confidence and anxious to help me save my husband.

Brailsford was one of the very few liberals who, like Bertrand Russell, had no illusions about Communism or the U.S.S.R. He was writing hard-hitting exposures of the Soviet Union counter to the Popular Front tide then already near its flood. So although he helped draft the appeal he had doubts as to whether his signature would not be harmful. Professor Laski, although previously anti-Communist, had become a friend of the Soviet Union following Hitler's rise to power. But he was still, apparently, a sincere liberal and assured me and Russell that we could rely upon him "to do everything I humanly can to clear up this matter." In one of his letters to me at this time he wrote: "I think it is a perfect case for fighting and I am prepared to fight."

The Russells first tackled Sidney and Beatrice Webb whose recently published book, *Soviet Russia–A New Civilization* based on Soviet documents and partly written or revised for them by Communist officials and propagandists, had become the Bible of the Socialist and liberal friends of the Soviet Union. Bertie's mother had been a friend of Beatrice Webb's and he had known her since he was a child. Sidney Webb had known my father who had at one time been acting secretary of the Fabian Society. Webb also knew me slightly from the late twenties when I was a Fellow of the London School of Economics and when he and H. G. Wells had both voted for me to become chairman of the London University Labor Party. But when, one lovely sunny afternoon, we drove over the beautiful countryside from Harting to Liphook in Surrey to visit the Webbs, I was doubtful that even Bertie would be able to persuade them to support our appeal. Nor were my hopes raised when the formidable Beatrice, over the tea table, expounded at length on the "progressive" features of the Union of Soviet Socialist Republics.

She was the outstanding example of those Max Eastman later described as the "plan-mad liberals" who long to see everyone controlled and disciplined for the good of society. A doctrinaire Socialist with a dried-up heart, she had no compassion for the sufferings of the miserable victims of the "Great Experiment" in Russia. "Planning" justified all, excused all, was worth the loss of freedom and the denial of any standard of morality except the good of the State. In the Webbs' own words in their favorable reporting of the theory and practice of the Soviet Socialist state: "Whatever contributes to the building up of the classless society is good; whatever impedes it is bad."

Russians, having never known the blessings of liberty, could very well do without them. They should be well content to live in a socialist state dedicated to the proposition that "public ownership of the means of production and distribution" is the way to prosperity, even if a generation or two starved to prove it.

But, of course, Englishmen were not expected to be subjected to the same ordeal.

Beatrice Webb and other "totalitarian liberals" like her in the Western World never admitted, or failed to see, that their attitude toward the Russian people closely resembled that of British imperialists in their heyday toward "the lesser breeds without the law," who had to be disciplined for their own good by white overlords.

After listening to Beatrice Webb that sunny afternoon in Surrey, I reflected that a century before, doctrinaire British Liberals had been as lacking in humanity or compassion as the doctrinaire Socialists of our time. In the early 19th century, belief in *laissez faire*, leaving the devil free to take the hindmost in the competitive struggle—which was supposed to ensure the greatest good for the greatest number—had caused the progressives of that era to harden their hearts and close their eyes to the abuses of a free enterprise system which consigned women and children as well as men to toil long hours in mines and factories, in worse condition and worse fed and housed than most Negro slaves in America.

In Moscow, not long before I sat drinking tea with the Webbs in their beautiful walled garden, I had seen them drive by in a large automobile on their officially sponsored and conducted "investigation" of conditions in the "first Socialist state." Trudging home at the end of another weary day of work followed by standing in line to buy food, I had then murmured to myself some half-remembered lines from a poem my father wrote before I was born and which I had read in an old Socialist song book:

> The rich man rides by
> > In his carriage and pair.
> What does he care,
> > Why should he care?

Russell had told me that he thought Beatrice Webb's admiration for Soviet Russia was due to its Puritanical aspects and her own pleasure in bossing people. She, of course, conceived of herself as one of those who would give the orders in her ideal planned Socialist Society. This was only natural, since, like John Strachey, J. B. S. Haldane, and other British Left wing intellectuals who were admirers or defenders of Stalin's Russia, she belonged to the British governing class, or what is today called the Establishment.* So, of course, did Russell, and to a higher stratum of it. But here one might recall that it was the Tory Lord Shaftsbury who passed the first Factory Act in England to protect workers from rapacious capitalists when *laissez faire* middle class liberals opposed state intervention to save even little children from inhuman exploitation. As also the fact that Disraeli, another aristocratic conservative, and a Jew, had been far more sensitive to the sufferings of the British poor than the puritanical Gladstone who led the Liberal Party and embodied all the "virtues" of middle class Victorian England.

Bertie's explanation for Beatrice Webb's indifference to human suffering was a Freudian psychological one. She had, he told me, loved Joseph Chamberlain in her

---

*Labor Party and Trade Union leaders of working class origin had learnt too much about Communists by association or conflict to trust them.

youth, but he failed to reciprocate. She had married Sidney Webb as a substitute. Frustrated in love, this brilliant and once beautiful woman had become a formidable Puritan, longing to deny to others the joys she had never known. She had sublimated her unfulfilled sexual desires into love of power and had become a sort of Puritan Inquisitor. Hence, her pleasure in learning in Russia that cosmetics were hard to come by, and their use by the masses frowned upon by the authorities; and in general, by the evidence given her that vanity and carnal pleasures were discouraged. If she ever realized that the Puritanical principles of the Communists were observed more in the breach than in observance by the Soviet ruling class, this may not have disturbed her. Her main concern was to enforce "morality" on the masses in order that by self denial they should build "socialism."

Sidney Webb was a different character. He was a warm-hearted human being, and kind. Although also an intellectual, he was not completely blinded by theories. But he was dominated by his wife. I knew from sources other than the Russells that little goateed and rather rotund Sidney was overawed by Beatrice. My friend Jane's brother, who wrote for the London Times Literary Supplement under the name of Charques, had found it very funny that while staying with the Webbs, he had encountered Sidney in the middle of the night sneaking down to the kitchen for a snack after Beatrice had refused to let him eat as much as he wanted at dinner. Also, Malcolm Muggeridge, who was married to Beatrice Webb's niece, had told me of Sidney's subjection to his wife. This perhaps explains, even if it does not excuse, how Sidney Webb came to lend his name to the monumental fraud perpetrated on the West by the Webbs' "great" book on "Soviet Civilization". Perhaps, as my friend Isaac Don Levine has said, the Webbs were "the most horrendous symbol of the decay of the Western intelligentsia in our time."

Certainly, the Webbs and those other "liberals" who followed in their train, are to a large degree responsible for the errors and miscalculations which led the West to "snatch defeat out of the jaws of victory" during and after World War Two. Had it not been for the false image of the Soviet Union which the totalitarian liberals foisted on the Western World, we should never have trusted "Uncle Joe" Stalin and enabled him to impose his totalitarian tyranny on Eastern Europe.

On that summer day so long ago when Bertrand Russell took me to visit the Webbs at Passfield Corner, Sidney expressed some doubts concerning the rosy picture of the "worker's paradise" his wife painted. His conscience had not yet been atrophied and he was, I think, still a liberal in the original meaning of the word in spite of his wife's influence, or his fear of her displeasure. Yet I hardly expected that his recognition of the darker aspects of the Soviet regime would prevail against his wife's self-induced belief that all was for the best in the U.S.S.R. because it was "Socialist."

I underestimated Bertie's influence over even the formidable and cold-hearted Beatrice Webb; as also the lengths to which he was prepared to go, not simply to help me personally, but to uphold his principles. He gently intimated to Beatrice that if they did not support our appeal he would never speak to her again.

This ultimatum proved effective. The Webbs wrote a separate memorandum to Stalin saying: "We both of us know Freda Utley and her writings. We warmly commend the accompanying memorial, with which we agree, to the kindly consideration of the authorities. We have not the advantage of knowing Miss Utley's husband, and it is for this reason that we sign this separate note."

Bernard Shaw, whom I had confidently expected to be ready to help, proved a harder nut to crack than the Webbs. Finally, after we had both cajoled and bullied him long and hard, G.B.S. gave way. But Bertrand Russell was so disgusted at Shaw's attitude that the "Case of Berdichevsky" led to a permanent rupture of the friendship between these two famous men.

The letters exchanged at this time between George Bernard Shaw and his wife, the Russells and myself, have not until now been published. In publishing them now with Bertrand Russell's permission, I am not simply telling my own story. These letters, together with my accompanying narrative, present a dramatic contrast between the character, philosophy, and personal attitudes of these two intellectual giants of the Western World in our century: Bertrand Russell and George Bernard Shaw.

As I have already related, Shaw and my father were friends in their youth when my father was both assistant editor and musical critic of *The Star and Morning Leader* and G. B. S., its dramatic critic; as also while both of them wrote for the *Saturday Review*, belonged to the Fabian Society and were associated with Annie Besant, Charles Bradlaugh, and other prominent free thinkers.

So, when the Russells arranged to take me to lunch with Shaw and his wife with a view to enlisting their aid for our appeal to Stalin for the release of my husband, I felt confident that G. B. S. would help us.

At that time I was happy to be earning ten pounds a week working at the Royal Institute of International Affairs analyzing and summarizing a mass of papers submitted in French, German and English from many countries for a conference on International Intellectual Cooperation. Bertie and Peter came to 10 St. James Square to fetch me with their baby son Conrad in his crib in their car. Peter was nursing her baby and was therefore taking him with us to Shaw's.

I remember that short ride well. It was a lovely spring day and we had great expectations. Nor did it seem, during lunch with the Shaws and sherry beforehand that they would not be fulfilled.

Shaw welcomed me warmly, recalled his friendship with my father in the days of their youth, and told me what a brilliant young man Willie Utley had been. He seemed so very friendly and sympathetic, and also so ready to recognize the darker side of the Soviet regime, that I was soon telling him without reservation of my experiences in Russia. No doubt I talked far too freely, disregarding Bertie's and Peter's advice to be discreet. Shaw led me on, encouraging me by his sympathy and his seeming realization of the tyrannical nature of the Soviet regime, to assume that he was no more in favor of Communist tyranny than Bertrand Russell or myself. Disregarding the Russells' advice I threw discretion to the winds. Convinced that Shaw actually was what he seemed to be: a clever man who hated tyranny, hypocrisy and cant, and could be counted upon to use all his great influence to save my husband, I told him what I thought about Stalin's Russia.

I was most grievously mistaken.

A few days later, on June 2, Peter Russell wrote to tell me that in reply to her letter to Mrs. Shaw, thanking her for her kindness to me, Shaw's wife had written that G. B. S. would do all he could, but that: "It is difficult, as she is so strongly prejudiced against what we are deeply sympathetic to: the U.S.S.R."

"How could they expect you to be favorable, under your circumstances?" Peter Russell indignantly exclaimed in her letter to me. She had, she wrote, "heard little of what you said to Shaw" at lunch, but when she had "stolen a glance at you both, he seemed to have a sympathetic air."

Bertie was afraid that Shaw had been leading me on to commit myself as an opponent of the Soviet regime, in order to deny his help. Peter wrote that this explanation would seem "too cruel." Her idea was that the Shaws "are Irish, and Irish people cannot resist seeming to agree and sympathize when they don't;—it's their nature."

"Oh, dear Freda," she wrote, "I feel so depressed about it. Still she says he will do all he can. I feel very unhappy today as though all the misery of the world were my fault and as though there were a recipe for curing it somewhere which I had mislaid. And your troubles have lately come to represent all the rest: they are so typical. Do you ever have the silly illusion that if you stopped trying to endure and just rushed out into the street and screamed about it, people might heed and understand?"

"There seem to be just a few people in the world who are vulnerable and permeable. The rest live in cylinders of plate glass through which they see but do not feel."

"I ought to cheer you instead of letting out my weak despair upon you. Sometimes I wish I were one of the unhappy ones, for then I could tell myself I must endure it and try to think of other things, but I cannot get any consolation out of heroic endurance of other peoples troubles, and so I feel guilty if I alone am happy for a single moment—what a world!"

"Dear Freda, if there is anything else I can do, tell me, for I am wretched if I can do nothing."

"Brailsford's article is excellent and very clever. He is one of the few people without plate glass."

In another letter, replying to one of mine in which I said I realized how foolish I had been to unburden myself to Shaw, Peter wrote:

> Don't kick yourself, but kick us when you see us next. I said to be very gentle in your criticism (of Stalin's Russia), but I ought to have realized that it might be all or nothing.
>
> This whole situation between communists and others, which your case shows up so much, makes me unutterably wretched. People become Communists, I suppose, from wishing for human happiness, but very soon they forget about that entirely and care only for fetishes. What the hell is the use of nationalizing the means of production if that is all?

The intimation in Mrs. Shaw's letter to Peter that because I was "prejudiced against" the U.S.S.R., whereas she and her husband were "deeply sympathetic" toward it, G. B. S. was disinclined to help, was not the end, but rather the beginning of Bertie and Peter Russell's efforts to enlist his aid in saving my husband's life.

Peter, who acted as her husband's secretary and as his *alter ego* in working for the causes they believed in, devoted herself unreservedly to the task of softening Shaw's hard heart, or as eventually proved necessary, bullying him into the realization that he could not expect to retain the friendship or respect of men like Bertrand Russell if he persisted in believing, or pretending to believe, that anyone unsympathetic to, or "prejudiced against" Communist Russia was undeserving of help.

I could not bring myself to give Shaw the assurances he required that I was a true believer in the Communist faith, even to save the life of my husband whom I dearly loved. But Peter, caring little for principles or theories but passionately concerned to allieviate suffering and mitigate man's inhumanity to man, was willing gently to deceive Shaw and even to use her charm to save my husband. She sent a letter to Shaw saying that although perhaps I was "a bit prejudiced," she begged him to make allowances for "Freda's grief and growing despair." She herself, she wrote, "should be more than prejudiced—quite mad and irrational—if I were Freda and it was Bertie in her husband's place." She also told the Shaws that I "so rarely spoke of it at all that it was no wonder if I spoke a little wildly when I did speak." Her whole letter was designed, as she wrote to me, "to give them the impression that you would be all in favor but for your personal situation which made a balanced judgment impossible."

Shaw, after reading my *Japan's Feet of Clay*, "with great interest" as also the evidence I had sent him concerning its world-wide acclaim, was, after all "thinking what he can do best to help," according to a letter I received from his wife dated June 20. Evidently he had decided that maybe after all I had a little power and was, therefore, worth helping. A few days later he sent me a copy of a letter he had drafted to the Soviet Government. It was, in general, excellent, since he represented me as an important person and my husband's case, therefore, worthy of consideration, but he ended it by saying:

> I don't know Mr. Berdichevsky personally nor have I any knowledge of the reasons for his seclusion, but unless they are very grave I venture to suggest that he may be doing more harm to the reputation of the Soviet in the Arctic Circle than he could possibly do in England where he would have no claim on public attention or sympathy.
>
> G.B.S.
>
> June 30, 1937

This letter was, as I saw it, too dangerous to use, because Shaw had also written that I was "using every means" in my power "to bring the pressure of public opinion to bear on the Russian government."

I replied, in humble fashion, begging him to delete the above sentence. My letter ran as follows:

> Dear Mrs. Shaw: I am extremely pleased and gratified for what G. B. S. has written and even begin to feel some real hope that I may see my husband again. I appreciate very much the fact that he should have said so much and taken so much trouble.
>
> There is just one small point which I am compelled to write to you about. Could the sentence on the second page marked in pencil be cut out? In the first place, it is not true that I have used 'every means in my power to bring the pressure of public opinion to bear on the Russian government.' I have not written a line or even let it be generally known that my husband is in prison without trial. Only my friends know about it.
>
> My friends who have signed the appeal make a point of saying that I have not written or said things which could be objected to by the Soviet government, and G. B. S.'s letter as it stands flatly contradicts them.
>
> I do so hope that you will both forgive my having to ask you to cut out these lines? I am afraid you must both be heartily sick of me and my troubles by now and beg you not to consider me ungracious.
>
> I know that I spoke freely and frankly to you both that day—this is because as friends of Bertrand Russell I felt I both could and must do so—but generally speaking I refrain from expressing my resentment. And I certainly have never tried to bring the 'pressure of British public opinion to bear'—even now, I am only trying to use the pressure of people friendly to the U.S.S.R. and would not dream of letting people who are hostile know of my grievances.

Shaw replied categorically refusing to change his letter. I thereupon wrote to him again as follows:

Dear Mr. Shaw: However useless it may be to appeal to you again to alter what you have written, since your letter makes it clear that I must 'take it or leave it' I simply must protest at your insistence that I intended publicity when I met you. I did not, and what both I and the Russells told you was in confidence. If you treat our appeal to you for assistance in our efforts to get my husband released as a public matter, and as if we had already let my 'grievance' be publicly known, he may be shot out of hand. I am not exaggerating or being melodramatic about it. There is, if you like, a threat of publicity behind the appeal to the Russian government, but if so, the threat ceases to have any force if the matter has already been made public. If you had written that 'they will seek to influence British public opinion,' instead of 'they are seeking' it would not be dangerous.

If either I or my friends had been doing what you say, should we not have written letters to the press or referred to the matter in articles? Brailsford, for instance, who has written articles about the public trials, has never referred to my husband's case and has promised me not to do so. Bertrand Russell has often said to me how much he wishes he were not precluded from speaking or writing about what I have told him.

Even though I dare not ask you to change what you have written since you have told me it is your final word, and since I realize you must be annoyed with me for having involved you in so long a correspondence and having wasted so much of your time, I must beg you to treat the whole affair as confidential and not public.

I know how valuable your time is and I am sincerely grateful to you for having met me and for having written to help me. I deeply appreciate the kind way in which you and Mrs. Shaw received Bertrand Russell's request that you should help me. Please do not merely think me a nuisance and understand how nervous and worried I am at making this appeal at all and my fears at letting anything be sent to Russia which might jeopardize my husband's life. I cannot consult with him and I am fearful that my efforts to get him released may perhaps only make things worse for him. Although I have lived 5 years in Russia I do not feel that I understand it or know what the government's reaction will be to anything. But I do know that expediency rather than justice is what decides things—not only in Russia of course.

Bertrand Russell and his wife wrote the actual appeal, not me, and they took the greatest care in the wording of it. He wished me to let him send an appeal a year ago, but I did not dare to do so and am only doing so now because I feel desperate and have no other hope. We never, of course, intended to ask you to sign the actual appeal, since you hardly know me—It was only sent to you for reference and to show you who had signed it.

Sincerely yours,
Freda Utley

Shaw's response to this letter was the end insofar as I was concerned. It is reproduced here as a prime example of the ignorance, brutal insensitivity, and inhumanity of so many of the miscalled liberals of our time who were determined to believe that all was for the best in the horrible world of the Union of Soviet Socialist Republics, which they persisted in believing, in face of all the evidence, was the best of all possible worlds.

> 4, Whitehall Court (130) London, SW 1
> Phone: Whitehall 3160
> Telegrams: Socialist, Parl-London
> 8th July, 1937

Dear Miss Utley

Now that you are face to face with what an agitation for your husband's release means, you are probably quite right in deciding that it is safer and wiser to keep quiet and do nothing. If I have helped to bring you to that conclusion I have done you a very useful turn.

But make up your mind hard. Do not keep on trying to do both, like the lady who cried laces in the streets but hoped nobody heard her. The only thing you can do is to make a devil of a row, at some risk of provoking the Russian authorities instead of intimidating them. That is what you have been doing up to the present, though fortunately you have not yet gone too far to withdraw. But now that you have resolved to withdraw, do so completely. Burn all the letters and take comfort in the fact that the five years will not last forever; that imprisonment under the Soviet is not as bad as it is here in the west; and that when I was in Russia and enquired about certain engineers who had been sentenced to ten years for sabotage, I learnt that they were at large and in high favor after serving two years of their sentence.

> Faithfully,
> G. Bernard Shaw

Miss Freda Utley
68 Jessel House
Judd Street
W.C.1

On receipt of this letter, I wrote Shaw a scorching reply in which I let myself go, telling him just what I thought of him and his foolish ignorance about Stalin's Russia. But I took the precaution of sending Shaw's letter and my own to Bertrand Russell, for him to dispatch mine if he approved of it.

Bertie responded immediately with the following letter:

> Telegraph House
> Harting, Petersfield
> 9 July, 1937

My dear Freda:

Shaw's letter is beastly. Peter and I are filled with unspeakable indignation. The odd thing is that Mrs. Shaw writes in the opposite sense. I am waiting till it can do you no harm, and then I shall write and tell him what I think of him.

We posted your letter to Shaw, which we thought excellent. He is a swine.

I hope the letter will prove effective.

All our sympathy,
Yours ever,
B.R.

On the back of Bertie's letter Peter had written:

I have been wondering whether or not to reply to Mrs. Shaw saying that I shall be in London one day soon and asking her whether it would be of any use to call for a moment alone to try and unravel the misunderstanding. I do think there seems to be a genuine misunderstanding as well as sheer willfullness and cruelty, and I think there may be a little hope left through Mrs. Shaw. Also, Shaw did seem to find me rather attractive—I think he likes red hair! And perhaps I could weep on him. Don't think this conceited.

I have written in that sense to Mrs. Shaw. The worst that can happen is for him to refuse to see me. Bertie thinks he might be nice to my face and say something contradictory to Maisky afterwards.

It is Conrad's bath time. I am as angry as everyone else, but I would lick the beast's boots if this would help. I think he must be a bit crazy. It is Mrs. Shaw who gives me still a little hope.

Much love,
Peter

Next day G. B. S. wrote to Peter:—

10th July 1937

Dear Lady Russell:

Charlotte, still much troubled by her cough, is going down to the country today and will be back in London for a couple of days before we have to go to Malverne for a fortnight, after which we are going to spend August at home as a novelty.

I am afraid there is nothing to be done in the Berdichevsky case. When my letter did what it was intended to do: that is bring Freda hard up against the situation, she was terrified, realizing (or imagining) that my attempt at agitation for her husband's release might provoke the Soviet to—as she put it—shoot him out of hand. How far this apprehension is justified we cannot judge, because we don't know what the Soviet has against him. It is presumably something solid, as the Soviet has something better to do than send people to Siberia for fun.

Now the only thing Freda can do is to agitate. A private agitation is a contradiction in terms. You say she has done her best to conceal her situation except from her most intimate friends and the notables whose help she is asking. What more could she possibly do in the way of publicity? I have had to remind her of the celebrated case of the lady who was reduced to crying laces in the streets, but hoped that nobody heard her.

She cannot really frighten the Russian government, and may irritate it. So unless she can get a private letter written by someone who has an influential friend in Moscow, making an appeal *ad misericordiam*, there is nothing for it but to keep quiet and stick out the rest of the five years as best she can.

Can you suggest anything better?

Faithfully, G. Bernard Shaw

Peter, in sending me a copy of the above letter, wrote to me on July 12 saying that Shaw's behavior was only what she and Bertie had expected. She had proposed meeting Shaw only because she "did not want to give up while there was the slightest hope left." Mrs. Shaw had, in Peter's opinion, "genuinely misunderstood and had wanted to help, but Shaw must deceive her."

Shaw's letter, Peter said, "makes clear what we suspected, that he chooses to believe that your husband is guilty of some awful crime, and that he never meant to help at all."

Peter enclosed a copy of the "stinker" she had written to Shaw in reply, of which she "hoped I approved," telling me that "it seemed better for me to write, as he had written to me," but that she had told G. B. S. that "Bertie concurred."

"He is the worst of beasts" she wrote as her opinion of Shaw, as also that "I am rather proud of my letter to Shaw and I do hope you like it?"

"Dear Mr. Shaw," she had written on July 12, 1937:

I thought when I met you that you were kind. Now I realize that it is only Mrs. Shaw who is kind, and that you, as I had often been told, are frivolous and cruel. And if you really believe what you say about Soviet justice you must also be rather stupid. My husband asks me to say that he concurs in what I write.

Yours faithfully,

Patricia Russell

Shaw's response to Peter's insulting letter was immediate. Whereas rational arguments or appeals to his sense of justice or regard for liberal principles had proved unavailing, the accusation that he was stupid as well as frivolous and cruel caused him to surrender unconditionally.

On July 13 he wrote me as follows, addressing me almost affectionately as Freda, instead of formally and coldly, as heretofore, as Miss Utley, or Mrs. Berdichevsky:

Dear Freda:

Very well, have it your own way: cook my letter to your taste and use it as you please.

You are impervious to any ideas but your own: otherwise I should warn you that the Soviet cares nothing for LEFT opinion: it knows too well how politically powerless and unpopular the Left always is, and being itself the established government and therefore the Russian Right, would like to have all the Left revolutionists safe in Siberia.

It is Right signatures that will help you.

Meanwhile I still suspect that Mr. Berdichevsky's exile may be less stormy than his home life.

Exasperated,

G. B. S.

And to Peter he wrote:

My Dear Lady Russell:

Have I to deal with two Terrors instead of one?

I am not, I assure you, making an exhibition of my delicate sensibilities. I am trying, I suppose, to get that poor devil out of Siberia, though I now rather doubt whether his life there is not more peaceful than it would be at home. Freda does not know how to set about it. Get Right help if you can; Left is no use with Governments. Governments are always Right; and the Soviet is ultra-Right. It knows far too much about Left movements to be impressed by them.

I know that Bertrand "concurs." Of course he does: would you have him wreck his home?

Tyrant!

Just as before,
G. Bernard Shaw

In a pencilled note at the bottom of this letter which Peter sent on to me, she wrote:—

Does it mean that he esteems me as formerly or that my attack has failed to annihilate him?

I replied: "I think it means both."

Having won our victory, Peter and I were ready to make peace with George Bernard Shaw.

In a letter she wrote to him dated July 23, she said:

Dear Mr. Shaw,

We have been away, and I have just got your letter and one from Freda Utley. What can I say to you now? Words fail me, and so, though you may think you have been outrageously bullied, the victory is certainly yours.

Whether Freda should have sought "Right" help or "Left" and whether you and the Soviet government are "Right" or "left," and what, if anything, the two terms mean, are questions that interest me very little. It was your help that I wanted, and I have got it, in spite of, or because of, my abominable rudeness; and I am grateful and apologetic as I could be. (And again Bertie concurs!)

Yours sincerely,
Patricia Russell

I, myself, wrote to Shaw on July 14 as follows:

68 Jessel House
Judd St.
W.C.1
14 July, 1937

Dear Mr. Shaw,

I am too happy at your having given permission to delete that sentence from your letter to worry very much about your opinion of my character, or your conviction that I must be an impossible person to live with!

I should be the last to deny the truth of what you say about the Russian government wishing to place all the Left in Siberia, insofar as the Russian Left is concerned. But I don't think this applies to the Left in other countries—an originally revolutionary government must at least keep up appearances and must rely more on the support of the Left abroad than on the Right.

My mother says to tell you that she agrees with your opinion of my character—she lives with me!

Gratefully,
Freda

162

My mother added a postscript to my letter saying, "I always call my daughter Ann," referring to G. B. S.'s character in *Man and Superman*.

Bertrand Russell never forgave Shaw, or rather I should say that his low opinion of G. B. S. as a cruel man who was also rather silly was confirmed by this episode. Many years later the Australian author, Alan Wood, in his book *Bertrand Russell: The Passionate Sceptic** records: "There was a final irrevocable breach with Bernard Shaw, over a question to do with Shaw's admiration for the Soviet regime. Russell said that Shaw was "cruel, narrowminded and silly,' and commented that Shaw 'liked Russia because when he went there it was just as bad as he expected."

In "The Case of Berdichevsky" G. B. S. revealed himself as impervious to the call of justice as subservient to the threat of Bertie's displeasure and all that this might entail in tarnishing his reputation.

Although Shaw had shown a side of his character ignored by his admiring biographers, I had to admit, in view of the failure of our appeal, that he was probably right in his own brutal fashion, when he told me that no private appeal would do me or my husband any good, since the Soviet Government took heed only of threats from the powerful even as Shaw himself did. It was his hypocritical pretense, or stupid assumption, that my husband would not have been condemned to slave labor in Russia had he not been guilty of some substantial crime, as also his ridiculous statement that imprisonment in the Soviet Union was "not nearly so bad as it is here in the West" which was so revolting. Shaw was eminently right in telling me that the Soviet Government being "ultra Right" would like to incarcerate all the Left revolutionists in Siberia, but he was inconsistent and illogical in also telling Russell that my husband would not have been condemned to an Arctic concentration camp unless the Soviet Government had "something solid" against him. Presumably G. B. S. considered "something solid" as a desire for liberty even without evidence of conspiracy against tyranny. One cannot avoid the suspicion that Shaw was mainly concerned with his own self interest in retaining his popularity among the Left-wing liberals and the Communist fellow-travelers who then ruled the literary roost, by professing his "deep sympathy" for Stalin's tyranny.

Gullibility or outdated views of the world caused Socialists everywhere to revere George Bernard Shaw as a "progressive" because he had exposed and mocked all "bourgeois prejudices" and Victorian or early Edwardian taboos. They ignored his affinity to the Nazis and facists as well as Communist totalitarians who shared his reverence for power, or what he called the "life force" which has full rein in the jungle world of teeth and claw. Shaw himself had never disguised his sympathy for the practitioners of power of all political persuasions, as when in Japan he had openly proclaimed his support of the Fascist militarists to the dismay of his liberal admirers who had flocked to greet him at the risk of arrest and imprisonment.

I ought not to have been surprised at Shaw's mockery of my agonizing choice, or willful refusal to understand that I was torn between my hope of enlisting his support in my effort to save Arcadi, and fear that by telling the truth about the Soviet Union I should cause my husband to be shot. He may have given me good advice when he told me not to be like the impoverished lady trying to sell laces in the streets but so ashamed that she hoped her voice crying her wares would not be heard. But he gave me his advice for the wrong reasons. It seemed to me at the time that he was merely trying to shut me up in order to justify his own support of totalitarian tyranny.

---

*Simon & Schuster, 1958.

As I wrote several years later in *The Dream We Lost*:

> The shadow of the O.G.P.U. stayed over me too long. I lacked the courage to proclaim to the world what had happened and risk his death .... I was probably foolish not to have made a public scandal out of the matter. I should have utilized the prestige given me by the success of *Japan's Feet of Clay* (published in many foreign languages as well as in England and America) to raise a fuss in the press. Arcadi's case was so clear a proof of the fact that men are condemned in the U.S.S.R. not only without trial but without any real charge against them. Now I think that I might have saved his life by being bolder, for until the signing of the Stalin-Hitler pact it would have dismayed some, at least, of the "friends of the Soviet Union" to learn that the Soviet Government is even more cruel than the Nazi Government, which does at least allow some communication between its prisoners and their relatives and does inform the latter when a man dies or is shot.

The contrast in attitudes and behavior of Bertrand Russell and George Bernard Shaw goes far deeper than the labels "liberal" or "conservative," "progressive" or "reactionary" which are pasted on philosophers and writers, politicians and poets, whom we like or dislike.

Bertrand Russell belongs to those whom Edith Hamilton called "the aristocracy of humanity." Men such as Euripides and Isaiah who "feel like a personal experience the giant agony of the world." This aristocracy has such a passion for justice, such acute sympathy for human suffering, and so great a fighting spirit, that those who belong to it go all out for what they believe, regardless of the consequences to themselves.

George Bernard Shaw, on the contrary, had a cold heart and seems to have been mainly concerned with his own interest and in showing how very clever he was.

Half genius and half charlatan and a showman above all, he mocked the foolish aspirations of mankind to "sustain the world which his own ideals have fashioned."*

Both Shaw and Russell were self-proclaimed atheists or agnostics who saw no proof of any divine order in this our world where, in Russell's words, "omnipotent matter rolls on its relentless way," indifferent to man's hopes and fears. But Russell, unlike Shaw, saw man's best fate, not in submission to the powers of darkness which encompass us, or in worshiping them in the guise of a 'life force,' but in defying a hostile universe with Promethean constancy, sustaining alone "like a weary but unyielding Atlas the world that his own ideas have fashioned despite the trampling march of unconscious power."**

But then, no doubt, Bertrand Russell and I are romantics, as he long ago accused me of being, and which his recently published autobiography amply proves about himself.

Voltaire said that life is a tragedy to those who feel and a comedy to those who think. To Russell, who both feels and thinks, it is a tragedy that men cannot become rational and save the world from destruction. To George Bernard Shaw it was mainly comedy. True that in such plays of his as St. Joan, he could make his audiences weep, as well as laugh, at his portrayal of noble characters defying the fates or tyranny, and even seemed

---

A Freeman's Worship by Bertrand Russell. An essay written in 1902 and included in "Mysticism and Logic," first published in 1917.

**ibid.

to have compassion for them. But Shaw, unlike Russell, never personally involved himself in the struggle for the emancipation of mankind. And by the time I met him he had become too cynical or too selfish to believe that anything but power counts on earth or in heaven.

Bertrand Russell, now Earl Russell, scion of a noble family, although he, like Shaw, denied the existence of God, or any absolute values, acted as if he believed in the faith of his ancestors. Or, I should better say that Bertrand Russell was unable to deny the godhead within him and therefore risked himself again and again for what he believed. Consequently he was a poor man for most of the many years I knew him, and at times, as during his last years in America, came near to being as destitute as myself. This was not only because he would not compromise his beliefs for the sake of material advantage, but also, I must admit, because even in old age he loved to shock people by expressing extreme opinions sometimes worthy only of a college sophomore. But Bertie's naughtiness was never malicious or cruel or indulged in for personal advantage.

George Bernard Shaw, on the contrary, although a Celt, or precisely for that reason, was a practical man. He never lost sight of his own material and other interests, seeing no sense in sacrificing himself for the sake of the good, the beautiful, or the true, or for justice for all mankind. Thus he profited hugely from his witty exposures of the shortcomings of Western civilization and the futility of human endeavor and died a millionaire.

Whereas Bertrand Russell was as consistent and logical as he was compassionate, George Bernard Shaw contradicted himself and changed the premises of his argument whenever it suited him, if only to make a clever epigram. As when, as I have related, he believed, or pretended to believe, that Communist Russia was a better place to live in, or to be imprisoned in, than the "capitalist" Western World, but also said that Stalin would like to consign all non-conformists to concentration camps in Siberia. Did Shaw think that he would be safe, comfortable and prosperous in the "brave new world" of the Communists because of his readiness to conform to the demands of the powers which were in process of becoming omnipotent, while posing as a champion of liberty by defying the dead or dying powers which could no longer harm him?

My brother Temple, less involved than myself in man's struggle or man's fate, viewed George Bernard Shaw as a rather comic character who had whored around without ever knowing or caring much where he belonged or what he believed in. Writing to my mother from Suva shortly before his death he said:

> Dear, thank you so much for the Shaw book and the Russell. I liked Shaw's book very much—quite different. Nothing new, but delightfully and urbanely written.
> It is rather amusing to think of Shaw ending up in Voltaire's garden. Voltaire would certainly have liked it, but what he would have thought of St. Joan or Back to Methuselah—? It is a pity Shaw cannot meet a few of the illustrious shades who have influenced him. Chechkov would certainly approve of *Heartbreak House*; Nietszche would like *Ceasar and Cleopatra*—with reservations—but on the whole, cold-shoulder him as a renegade, classing him with Wagner. What Wagner or Ibsen would say to him—? Karl Marx would probably receive him as a sort of faithful husband, who had spent most of his life running after exotic

165

mistresses, but who, nevertheless, had always explained to them that he
was really true to his rather plain wife.

I liked Russell's book but I think it is time he started doing some
serious stuff again. The ratio used to be one solid book to one popular
one; now they are all popular.

Chapter 18
RUSSELL IN AMERICA

In the years following Bertrand and Patricia Russell's vain attempt to save my husband's life in 1937, we were to have disagreements, which, although they led to temporary estrangement, were never personal, so that we remained friends. Today I think he is even more wrong than I was, forty years ago, when he vainly endeavored to dissuade me from joining the British Communist Party. He then knew far more about Communism than I. Today I know more about it than he does, or he has chosen to forget or ignore what he once knew so well.

Prejudiced against America by his experiences here; honored in England following his return from America as never before during his long life; winner of the Nobel Prize and darling of the left-wingers (who deplored his original pacifist stand against the Second World War but are delighted that he has reverted to his pacifist principles when it comes to challenging the Communist totalitarian menace) Lord Russell, hedged in by anti-anti-Communists has become difficult to reach.

I venture to believe that, if I lived in England and had remained in as close contact with him as in the 20's, 30's, and 40's, Bertrand Russell would not today be giving aid and comfort to the Communist totalitarian power he has all his life opposed. This conceit of mine is warranted by past experience during my long friendship with Russell.

In 1935 when briefly visiting England from Russia, I had found Bertie hovering on the brink of revising his views on the USSR because, as he told me, he had been impressed by the many favorable reports by western journalists. Of course, Bertie was never so foolish as to believe all the nonsense written about Russia in the 30's and 40's by "liberal" British and American popular journalists. But he had been shaken in his convictions concerning the evil nature of the Soviet regime, by the superabundant "evidence" produced by the most widely read pundits of our time, whose success as columnists and commentators, still today, tends to increase in geometric proportion to the degree to which they are wrong about Russia.

In 1936, he told me that I had come back to England in time to save him from succumbing to the false propaganda of the friends of the Soviet Union which represented that country as in process of becoming a new and better kind of democracy. But in his last years he finally succumbed saying that "Communism is now a very much better thing than it was in 1920 when I condemned it."*

In the spring of 1939 in America, Russell thanked me for restoring his faith in his own beliefs. His vacillating attitude at this time toward the coming war is expressed in a letter, which he wrote to Olivia Holt prior to debating against Maurice Hindus before the Foreign Policy Association in Baltimore. Accepting with "great pleasure" her invitation

---

*As quoted by Peter Scheer in *Ramparts*, May 1967.

to stay with the Holt's, and telling Olivia to "give my love to Freda and tell her I am delighted to have the chance of seeing her," he wrote:

> The debate was arranged without my being consulted, and I don't know exactly what differences there will be between Hindus and me. I still think it was right to try the Munich policy, but it failed, and I no longer feel any hope for peace unless, just possibly, by frightening Hitler. However, perhaps points of difference will turn up. I still think it would be better to let Hitler conquer Europe than to fight him, but that is a Utopian policy.

As it turned out Russell surpassed himself that evening in Baltimore by his refutation of Maurice Hindus' arguments which took no account of the menace constituted by Stalin's Russia, waiting in the wings to take advantage of the coming Second World War. For this I take some credit. Walking in the Maryland woods with Russell and Olivia Holt the afternoon before his lecture I asked Bertie whether he was about to repudiate the views he had expounded in his *Which Way To Peace.**

In the future there were to be times when he would get mad at me for playing back to him the record of his former convictions. But on this occasion Bertie, who enjoyed himself most when shocking people, laughed with me in Maryland when I reminded him of how, not long before at Telegraph House in England, he had dumbfounded poor Emil Ludwig by his approval of Neville Chamberlain's Munich policy. A few days after his memorable debate with Hindus, Russell wrote to thank me for having renewed his faith in his own beliefs at a critical moment.

Nevertheless, after Dunkirk he abandoned his pacifism, as also the conviction which I continued to hold that the result of the Second World War, entailing an alliance between the West and Soviet Russia, could not but lead to the triumph of Communism over a large part of the world, which would prove even worse because more enduring and more universally destructive of liberty over a larger area than German hegemony over Eastern Europe.

As I saw it, Bertrand Russell's "Achilles heel" was his deeply rooted patriotism. To him the salvation of England came first, ahead of all or any principles or theories. He could no more get away from his origins than I could from mine. He was an English aristocrat and nationalist however hard he tried not to be. I was not only not a member of the British governing class by birth but had been brought up and conditioned by my youthful experiences to be fundamentally internationally minded.

I remember Peter saying one evening in Pennsylvania, "Do you notice, Freda, that whereas most people say 'they' in referring to the government, Bertie always says, 'we'?" Such was his instinctive attitude as a member of the English ruling class.

Bertie had a grand repertoire of droll stories about his aristocratic forebears and relations which he loved to tell in anticipation of the laughter they evoked in which he gleefully joined in. One concerned the proud Duke of Bedford whose second wife once dared to put her hand affectionately on his shoulder, whereupon he turned on her and said: "My first wife never did that and *she* was a Percy." A joke perhaps not so funny in America except among those familiar with Shakespeare who remember Harry Hotspur of Northumberland. Bertie also liked to tell about his grandfather, Lord John Russell of the Reform Bill, and his contempt for the upstart Hanoverian Kings who cut no ice in the social circles of the old nobility of England.

---

*M. Joseph Ltd., London, 1936.

168

The second volume of Bertrand Russell's autobiography published after I was nearing the completion of this first volume of my own, has shed light on some dark corners of my knowledge of him. It reveals that his aversion to America was old and deep seated, and leaves an impression that these United States were his milch cow until England took Earl Russell back to her bosom.

In the second volume of his autobiography Russell admits that fear for England has always been his basic motivation. However astute his rationalizations of his changes in outlook and the varying policies he supports, the basic factor in the equation is always England's survival. He confesses that at the time he wrote *Which Way To Peace* his maintenance of his pacifist position had already become "unconsciously insincere." In the face of the "cruel bigoted and stupid" Nazis whom he found morally and intellectually odious "he had clung to his pacifist convictions with increasing difficulty." During the First World War he had never "seriously envisaged the possibility of utter defeat," but "in 1940 when England was threatened with invasion" he found "this possibility unbearable"; and "at last consciously and definitely decided" that "he must support what was necessary for victory" however "painful the consequences!"

The best and worst of the British aristocratic tradition is revealed in another passage from Bertrand Russell's Autobiography in which he writes that "the history of England for the last hundred years is in my blood, and I should have wished to hand on to my son the tradition of public spirit which has in the past been valuable. In the world I forsee there will be no place for this tradition."*

Reading his autobiography makes one aware of Russell's capacity to deceive himself or "rationalize" his changes of course in both his personal and political life. I now understand better what a "thorn in the flesh" I must have been to him in America when as he himself writes "it was a divided self" that favored the Second World War. In his own words his "whole nature had been involved in his opposition to the First World War" and he "never since 1940 recovered the same degree of unity between opinion and emotion as I had possessed from 1914 to 1918."**

It is clear from passages in the letters he includes in his autobiography that Russell as early as the spring of 1940 had already ceased to be a pacifist.

In May 1940 he had written from California to Kingsley Martin, editor of the *New Statesman*, saying that ever since the war began he had felt he could not "go on being a pacifist." And that he now felt he ought "to announce that he had changed his mind," and asking to have this mentioned in the *New Statesman*.***

The Second Volume of Russell's Autobiography (which I have read only since compiling the greater part of this book) affords much supporting evidence for my long held surmise that "England My England," was always a basic motivation in Russell which he rationalized by divergent arguments at different stages of his inordinately long life.

After Russell obtained his sinecure at the Barnes Foundation in Philadelphia and lived at Little Datchett Farm near Malvern in Pennsylvania, I visited him and Peter often from New York, in blissful ignorance of how far we had drifted apart. By 1942 however, our differences on the war led to temporary estrangement despite Peter's efforts to maintain our friendship.

The Autobiography of Bertrand Russell, Volume II, Little Brown, 1968, Page 287.

**ibid.*, p. 289.

***ibid.*, p.357.

I happen to have preserved, although in mutilated form, a letter he wrote me in August 1942 after a flare up:

".......I think it would have been better if, before we met, we had made more sure of the objects of the meeting. By this time it must be clear to everyone that Gandhi's policy means handing India over to the Japanese. You and I differ so completely about the war that we could only have avoided quarrelling by not discussing this disagreement. I begged you to keep off the subject, and so did Peter, but you wouldn't. We both admire your courage, and are sorry that you have made things difficult. I hope that, when the war is over, if we are all still alive, we may be able to meet again as friends. I am sorry I was unjust, but it was the accumulated result of years of irritation and inability to make you understand how much we disagreed, not only in opinion, but in feeling.

Let us try, on both sides, to remember what we thought of each other before the war. For the present no good relations are possible but Peter and I will both continue to have kindly and affectionate thoughts of you, provided the necessity of arguing is removed.

Yours still with affection

(s) Bertrand Russell

I ascribed Bertie's irritation or fury at me on this and other occasions to his unease following his abandonment of beliefs which I played back to him. As I was to write to Lady Rhonda, Editor and Publisher of *Time And Tide*, with reference to Russell, one cannot repudiate the basis of one's lifetime beliefs without loosing one's balance.

Unlike Russell, I had never been an admirer of Gandhi and I had always wanted America to help China against Japan. But at this time no doubt Bertie was just so infuriated that as he admits in the above letter he was unjust to me. In this connection I here quote from a letter written to me by Max Eastman in November 1957.

Didn't Bertrand Russell use (never mind the bad English) to oppose the liberation of India from British rule? I seem vaguely to remember so.

I'm writing a profile of him for my next book, and while I bow down to his having been so early right about the Bolsheviks, and World War I, I would like to call a gentle attention to one or two points where he wasn't so obviously right. In his recent (very charming) book he seems, in an inoffensive way, to say he was pretty right all along about everything. That isn't quite so, is it?

I'd like to show you my essay-portrait when it's done, if you'd have time to read it critically. It begins: "Bertrand Russell is the most readable of living highbrows. He also knows more than any of the rest of them . . . ."

Not long after the above "fare ye well, but let's not meet" letter Bertie and I were friends again while agreeing to disagree. He had by this time lost his sinecure at the Barnes Foundation ostensibly because Peter, who attended his lectures, insisted on knitting and was alleged to disturb the classes. The real reason was in all probability Peter's undisguised dislike of America where she found life very difficult, and Bertie's desire to return to England now that he had become an all out supporter of the war against Hitler.

Neither she nor Bertie, in spite of their straitened means, could reconcile themselves to simplifying the routine of daily existence. In telling me about their search for a house near Philadelphia, Peter had expressed her horror or shock at finding a Pennsylvania Dutch family in their beautiful old house "eating in the kitchen in their shirt sleeves." This to me seemed only natural and sensible, but to Peter it was "appalling."

Servants or not, guests or not, the table had to be properly laid in the dining room with candles, gleaming silver, snowy table cloth, wine glasses and wine. I remember an evening when Peter, exhausted by her efforts to serve a dinner in proper style after the departure of the last couple she had lost, and needing also to attend to young Conrad, started getting hysterical. After she had left the dinner table in a tantrum Bertie took me out for a long walk in the calm countryside in the moonlight and unburdened himself to me concerning his troubles. He loved Peter dearly, but she was becoming very difficult.

If only I had noted down the record of this conversation, I might be able to explain better why Peter and Bertie eventually separated. At the time I felt sorry for him because Peter was behaving so unreasonably. Now I sometimes wonder whether Bertie was not equally or more at fault.

It was not until several years after that sad evening in Pennsylvania that Peter left Bertie and now refuses even to bear his name. I remember that walk in the countryside because it was my first intimation that sooner or later I should have to choose between Bertie and Peter, and at that time I was on his side.

Peter was not really a snob although this was the unfortunate impression she gave to many Americans. She was simply unhappy and maladjusted and became ultra-British in her disappointment at finding life in America as the wife of Lord Russell difficult, disappointing, and dull. Even her accent became a little too ultra-top drawer British U. She told everyone she preferred to educate Conrad at home rather than send him to an American public school.*

It had been easier at the beginning of their residence in America when a nice girl they had brought from England helped to look after Conrad and was a friend and companion to Peter. But she had gone home after refusing to marry their friend Peter Blake because he was a German. A curious sidelight on British prejudices since Peter Blake, today editor of *Architectural Forum* and good friend of Philip Johnson, was of Jewish parentage and educated at Oxford.

I frequently stayed with the Russells for weekends at their house at Malvern and much as I loved Peter, and kind and loyal as she continued to be to me even when I had quarrels with Bertie, I realized by now that he had a stormy petrel on his hands. She was a young and beautiful woman and needed to be courted and entertained as well as loved. While never, I feel sure, unfaithful to Bertie, whom she adored, she needed the society of younger men as escorts to parties and admirers and for youthful companionship. She was totally unsuited to live in a remote house in Pennsylvania often without servants (because few couples stayed long) while expected by herself as well as Bertie to maintain the kind of household which English people of the upper classes take for granted.

However heated the arguments between them, Bertie and Peter got together in blaming America for their troubles. Admittedly America is a difficult country in which to live graciously since domestic help is hard to get and expensive. Admittedly also, Russell had good reason to hate the Catholic politicians and others who in 1939 prevented him from

*Later on in England Conrad went to Eton where he thrived and was no doubt saved from becoming the "spoiled youngster" my son found him to be in 1948 when Jon stayed with the Russells in Wales while I was in Germany.

becoming a professor at New York's City College. On the other hand, there were such people as my friend Sidney Hook, Professor of Philosophy at New York University and one of the most generous, tolerant, principled, and courageous men I have ever known, who were to keep Russell supplied with at least bread and butter by securing him lectures after he lost his stipend from the Barnes Foundation. Nor is there any question that Bertrand Russell owed his livelihood for many years to the success of his popular books in America and the well-paid lectures he had formerly obtained by talking about sex, socialism and pacifism during the years when he could not earn a living in England.

The lectures which Sidney Hook and others of his friends in adversity secured for Russell were, of course, poorly paid. But it shows a singular lack of appreciation that Sidney Hook's name is not even mentioned in the Second Volume of Russell's Autobiography. His only recent reference to Sidney Hook's name is to be found in the aforementioned *Ramparts* article by Robert Scheer recording his interview with Russell in Wales in 1967 in which Russell is recorded as saying, "I can't be bothered with Sidney Hook." Of course, the reason for this churlish attitude on Lord Russell's part is Sidney Hook's intelligent and perceptive criticism of Russell's attitude on Vietnam and his sponsorship of the Communist inspired "war crimes trial" of the USA in Stockholm.

The second volume of Bertrand Russell's autobiograpy, unlike the first, is obviously not his own compilation, but an expurgated version of his Memoirs omitting vital information and important letters repugnant to the "New Left" exemplified by his *eminence grise* Ralph Schoenman, and other mixed-up characters of uncertain motives who have surrounded my old and revered friend Bertrand Russell in his old age.

There is no account, or even a single reference, to Russell's break with Shaw over "the case of Berdichevsky," nor any mention of me. Even when recording the success of his *History of Western Philosophy*, which brought him back to affluence from poverty long before he won the Nobel Prize, Russell fails to mention that it was I who brought him into contact with my friend Quincy Howe and thus secured him a very generous advance from Simon and Schuster after W. W. Norton had offered only a charitable pittance of $500.*

All in all the worst side of Bertie's character was displayed during his last year in the United States. He had by this time conceived such an aversion to America that he was inclined to see some sinister motive behind American generosity. His disposition to bite the hands which wanted to feed him is shown by the following incident.

I was at this time working for C. V. Starr as economic adviser to American International Underwriters after having abandoned hope of earning a living as a writer and lecturer so long as Roosevelt ruled and it was impermissible to oppose the Communists or fail to love "Uncle Joe" Stalin.** Neil Starr, who was both intelligent and generous although he chose to devote his talents mainly to his business empire, had met Bertrand Russell several times at my New York apartment. He now offered to put up a lot of money to provide for Russell's support either by endowing a special chair for him at New York University, or through the Council of Learned Societies. New York University was unenthusiastic in spite of Sidney Hook, but the Council of Learned Societies was happy

---

The Autobiography of Bertrand Russell, Op. Cit., p. 339.

**This was the era when William S. White's *Report on the Russians* was boycotted and condemned by Bennett Cerf of Random House, together with some 30 American newspaper correspondents who viewed any criticism of our wartime ally as inadmissable.

to accept Starr's offer for itself and Russell. Bertie, however, refused the offer unless he could be subsidized in England instead of in America, which, of course, was impossible.

I have a vivid recollection of my argument with Bertie at Pennsylvania Station after he had, as I saw it, let me down, as well as being foolish in rejecting Starr's offer after I had secured it. I argued that it simply was not true that Starr was just another Philistine American millionaire who wanted to "buy" him, but an enlightened and intelligent businessman who wanted to make up to Russell for the grievous affronts he had suffered when first New York's City College and now Barnes had reneged on their contracts with him. As Russell rushed to catch the 5:00 p.m. train to Princeton where they were now living he said to me: "When I disagree with Peter I can't get away from her. But when I disagree with you, dear Freda, I can always escape."

The letter I wrote to Peter at this time, reproduced here, is of interest as showing not only my efforts to help the Russells but my views at this time.

August 20th, 1943

Dear Peter:

I am sorry you should be leaving America without our meeting again, and sorry for the quarrels which have hung over us this past year.

Perhaps you are right to have decided to go to England. There is no point in staying here feeling as you do about America. As you know my own feelings are precisely contrary to yours. Perhaps because, as Bertie once said of me, I am by nature a "social outcast!" In any case I have found here greater opportunity, greater kindness and help and hospitality, and I feel myself far more at ease and at home with Americans than with the English. Of course I do see and appreciate things about England that are better—more political democracy in one sense, and in some ways more tolerance for unorthodox opinions, but even this is mainly true only if one "belongs." The war may have greatly changed things in England: according to my friend Jane who is happier there now than she ever has been, England is now a better place than it ever has been. All the same I fear that you and Bertie are going to be somewhat disappointed because you have been away so long that you remember more of the good than the bad, and I have not forgotten how difficult Bertie found it to get his stuff published those last years in England. I realize that his change of views on war etc. will make it easier but I doubt that he will not again become a heretic. Nor can I see Bertie accepting the idea of a joint British-Russian hegemony of Europe—not that I consider this is likely to happen—a Russo-German entente still seems to me more possible—but it seems to be the current policy. On the other hand, by the way, the possibility of a peace with Germany after Hitler etc. have been ousted seems to me now a slightly more possible outcome than before. But this may be merely wish-fulfilment on my part because I am so afraid of Stalin getting a grip on a large part of Europe. He seems to be playing his cards rather badly at present by making more and more people realize that collaboration with Russia is bound to be impossible if we are to retain any of the values for which we are supposed to be fighting.

I cannot understand the part of your letter about Starr, since I told you and Bertie quite distinctly on the telephone in July that Starr was waiting to hear from Bertie whether he was prepared to stay in America or not; that if he decided to go there was practically no chance of the Council of Learned Societies taking him on; that the matter had been almost fixed up before Bertie signified he would go back to England; that if he decided to stay here Starr was ready to start the whole matter up again. I suggested that Bertie ought to see Starr again and tell him exactly. Did he ever try?

I do feel strongly that you ought not to just go without saying or writing a word.

Dear Peter, I do wish you luck from the bottom of my heart. As I said to you when we had that bitter quarrel last year, I shall never forget your kindness and sympathy during that terrible first two years after I lost Arcadi . . . my love goes with you, and my sincerest hopes that you and Bertie will be happy in England, or at least as happy as anyone can be until this terrible war is over. I hope I shall be allowed to stay here and become an American. Not that I don't realize that awful things may happen here in the future, but I still hope they may be avoided—at least I think that the individualist tradition here is so strong that more economic and therefore political freedom may survive than in Europe. The real test in England will come after the war when national unity is no longer spontaneous in face of danger and when Lend Lease stops and the difficult economic position of Britain has to be faced in a more autarchic or self sufficient world.

The very best to you, Peter, and my love,

Freda

This old letter of mine besides reviving memories of my arguments with Bertie and Peter about America during the years I knew them best, sheds some light on his increasingly hostile attitude toward America in his declining years when, it would seem he has become too prejudiced to be rational.

Prior to his return to England, in May 1944, Russell was re-elected to the Fellowship and Lectureship at Trinity College, Cambridge, which he had lost when he went to prison during the First World War. He soon afterwards became an honored speaker more popular and financially prosperous than ever before and no doubt came to see his difficult years in America as the result of all our faults.

Today he is happy in that he has been able to revert to the pacifist beliefs he abandoned during the Second World War while also advocating what he conceives to be the best policy for the survival of England, regardless of what may be the fate of the rest of the world if America ceases to endeavor to preserve and protect the liberties of other peoples from Communist oppression. Like other, less enlightened, opponents of British imperialism in its hey day, Russell today has become an advocate of submission to the new Communist imperialism.

Commenting on Russell's hostility to America, which was to become more pronounced and increasingly irrational and prejudiced, even vicious, in the ensuing two decades, I wrote to Lady Rhonda, in the March 20, 1945 letter from which I have already quoted:

> I also agree with you in your criticism of Bertrand Russell whom I knew well. I think his attitude about America is prejudiced and unfair, and hardly quite decent after the good as well as bad treatment he

received here. That is another and long story. There are so many Americas and the best of them is what I have always looked for and found here. The trouble is that Americans are still naive about world politics, etc. But they are the most generous people and many tried to make up to Russell for the treatment he received from Barnes and City College. Bertie was one of my best and oldest friends but in the end we disagreed about too many things.

Having known Russell so well so long and also greatly revered him, I have now reluctantly come to realize that he, no doubt unconsciously, shifts his ground when it suits his overriding obsession: the security or salvation of England.

Not long ago Bertrand Russell wrote that the success of non-violent resistence "depends upon the existence of certain virtues in the people against whom it is enforced." And that these British virtues enabled non-violence as practiced by Gandhi in India to prevail, but were of no avail against the Nazis. Yet today Russell ignores his own precepts in equating the United States, where these virtues also conspicuously exist, with the Soviet Union where they are repudiated as "bourgeois prejudices." Obsessed by his own brief experience of "persecution" by the authorities of City College of New York, Russell came to the absurdity of equating his, certainly not underprivileged, experience in America with the terrible persecution in Soviet Russia of heretics and non-believers in the Communist mythology.

Russell's shifts in the policies he advocates are nonetheless usually more logical than either his detractors or his admirers admit. In 1948, following the already apparent disastrous results of World War Two, he said that America should use its atom bomb monopoly to enforce world peace and compel Moscow to let the peoples it had enslaved in Eastern Europe go free. It was only after the West's failure of nerve—or continuing illusions about the nature and aims of the Soviet power, or its humanitarianism or whatever—that Russell, facing the realities of the world situation once Russia had the bomb, began to lead peace crusades, and in effect advocated submission to Moscow as the only alternative to making a desert of the world.

In 1948 in urging a preventative war to destroy Communism he wrote that he had no doubt that America would win in the end, "but unless Western Europe can be preserved from invasion, it will be lost to civilization for centuries" since the Communists would seize Western Europe and we would have to bomb it too. Communism he then argued "must be wiped out and world government established."*

Sidney Hook writes that Russell's moral position is weakened by his former advocacy of preventative war against Russia. But it was consistent for Russell as a realist to accept the logic of the new international situation once America had lost its monopoly of atomic power. Just as in reverse fashion he had come to support the Second World War after the failure of Chamberlain's policy to avert it.

What is both illogical and grotesquely unfair is for Russell now to denounce America for endeavoring in Vietnam to save the people on our side and stem the Communist onslaught in Southeast Asia, after himself having urged us to save Europe by an atomic war two decades ago.

* * *

Despite the growing gap between our views and activities, Russell and I remained friends for a long time. In 1948 he lent me his apartment in London before he and Peter took Jon to stay with them in Wales while I visited Germany.

*Published in the *Saturday Review* of October 16, 1954 and quoted by Sidney Hook in *The New Leader*, October 24, 1966.

The similarity of our views on the cruelty and stupidity of Allied policy and behaviour in occupied Germany, even after Soviet Russia's blockade of Berlin, is shown in the following letter, which he wrote me after Allen and Unwin had refused to publish my *High Cost Of Vengeance*.*

Penralitgoch
Llan Pfestiniog
Merioneth
4.9.49

Dear Freda,

Peter has asked me to answer your letter. I am sorry about Allen and Unwin, and will write to them. But I think you would do better to go to Gollanz. The book is more in his line, and if we bully Allen and Unwin into publishing they will not push the book. If Allen and Unwin can't be budged, shall I write to Gollanz? I will gladly.

The Lit. Sup. is a most dishonest publication. It dislikes me on religious grounds, being Cath. or Angle-Catholic. Its chief argument for Xianity is that it is fashionable.

To the Duchess of Atholl you begin "Dear Duchess." She is virtuous, dowdy, and industrious; you would never guess that she is a Duchess.

You didn't tell me what my mother wrote about to Forbes. Please do.

Your book has just come but I haven't had time to read it yet. I am sure to agree with it.

It will be lovely if you come to England and we see you again.

Yours ever,

BR

It was good to know that without having as yet read my book, Bertie had complete confidence in the similarity of our views concerning the vanquished Germans thanks to our shared basic principles and sympathies for the downtrodden.

His query concerning what his Mother had written about to Forbes, referred to an anecdote told me while I was a guest of Copley Amory on Naushon Island, concerning Lady Amberley's comment on the poor service even in wealthy American families, as shown by the fact that, when she went to bed for the night she had found her bed unprepared by the turning down of top sheet and blanket.

Referring to his mother and father and the book he compiled on their brief lives, *The Amberley Papers*, Russell writes that his parents, not having been faced with modern problems, were confident in their radicalism, and although "they opposed aristocratic privilege, it survived intact and they, however involuntarily, profited by it. They lived in a comfortable, spacious hopeful world."**

A world one might add in which even the most liberal reformist aristocrats expected to live in the greatest comfort without ever performing so slight a chore as turning down their bed covers.

I myself, no doubt, have a complex about "washing up" and all that. To me it seems that aristocrats yesterday and successful intellectuals today are equally prone to assume that someone else will always do the dull or dirty work of the world.

Sometimes as I return home laden with groceries from the supermarket, or when

---

*Henry Regnery, Chicago, 1949.

**The Autobiography of Bertrand Russell, Op. cit., p. 289.

performing household chores which middle-class Europeans for the most part, despite their lower standard of living, leave to servants, I reflect that it is perhaps a good thing that I have never been transported into the world of the privileged, much as I should enjoy its comforts.

I envy the successful writers, professors and bureaucrats, who had never known, or have long since forgotten, what it means to be poor or to count pennies. But I usually pull myself up from wishing that I were one of them by the reflection that freedom from the dull ordinary tasks performed by the mass of humanity insulates the class conscious 'intelligentsia' from reality. As I wrote long ago in an unpublished article written in the days when life was hardest for me thanks to my unpopular opinions, "it all comes down to washing up." The trouble it seemed to me then as now is that most of the would be saviours of humanity always take it for granted that someone else will perform the dirty, dull or disagreeable work which has to be done by someone in any and all systems. And I have always retained my respect for Lenin, as basically a true liberal, in spite of his having led Russia to the hell of totalitarian tyranny, because while in exile in Switzerland he always helped his wife with the washing up. And one of the first favorable impressions I received of America was the fact that even in well to do families the men help with the household chores. One could write an essay on how American mechanical inventions have helped lighten household drudgery precisely because men had to help. For as Temple used to point out to me, women had watched kettles steaming for centuries, but it took a man, Stevenson to notice the potentialities of steam power.

In 1954, after Peter and Bertie were divorced, I visited Russell for the last time in Richmond, a suburb of London, where he was living with his fourth wife. My tea with them was not conducive to any renewed meeting of minds, or a revival of my former close friendship with Bertie. His wife, of course, knew of my friendship with her predecessor. John Russell was by this time an adherent of his mother (Dora) whose favorable view of the Soviet Union was shared to some extent by his second stepmother by reason of her pacifism. The atmosphere was also clouded by the fact that Peter, in her animosity against Bertie had antagonized their son, Conrad, who was refusing to see his father. I got no chance to talk to Bertie alone, except for a brief moment on the steps of their house when after kissing me goodbye he assured me that I should not believe what Peter had written to me about his sentiments toward me. I hope it is the truth despite the letters Peter wrote to me after she had left Bertie which I reproduce here:

18 Dorset House
N.W.L.

October 16, 1949
Dearest Freda,

It is funny that my saying I had not heartlessly abandoned Bertie in his old age should have given you the impression that I had. I wrote without explanation or emotion because of your affection for him. But I ought not to let you think he left me—he still found me useful. I was obliged to say that we must separate unless we could be faithful to each other and honest with each other—it did not seem much to ask from me to him as he assured me to the end that he loved me only and profoundly. But he refused and we separated by my wish a month later. I left it open that I would try again on those terms if he would, but he refused. It is since then that I have learned from several independent sources that he has disliked me intensely for years.

It was necessary to say this to correct any wrong impression I had given. I am sorry I broke and said anything at all.

I do not know how to reply to the rest of your letter, because you see I know things you don't know and you seem to know things I don't know, and it is all far more complicated and horrible than I could explain.

I mind so much that no one told me things I ought to have known that I cannot write to you at all without saying that Bertie's friendship for you does *not* exist. We all found you irritating during the war, dear Freda, but Bertie was horrible about you. I thought at the time that you *must* have seen some of it, as I used to think years ago that Dora must know he hated her, when he came straight to my room from hers, with his face blazing with hatred, as it was when I went to his room when you had just left it and he told me not to let you come any more. But I know now that his face changes in an instant, and that others have seen it like that when it turned away from me when a second before it showed me love and kindness. Dear Freda, Bertie said that everything about you got on his nerves, that he found you physically repulsive, that you made clear to him that you wanted him to make love to you and that the thought of doing so revolted him. Don't be too hurt, my dear, he has said just as bad things of me—worse, since he has said that I was repulsive to him in every way *but* physically—and he has said the same to me of many nice women, including his own daughter. I don't know why he is like that about you. Last summer when you suggested coming to Wales to collect Jon he said I must not let you come (It was always me that had to do these unpleasant things for him) but must make some excuse for taking Jon to London to meet you. He will always pretend to like you except for the occasional outbursts you have experienced, because he can't bear that anyone should not like him. If it hurts much dear Freda, think of the hurt to me, to whom it was so painful that he said these things of others but only went to prove what he said, that he and I were alone in this world in love and understanding. I have had the outbursts too, and the remoteness you noticed towards you last summer, which I attributed sadly to age and thought I must love him the more.

It is a sort of madness: hysteria in the strict textbook sense, but the practical consequences for other people are terrible. By talking against each to each he has always put everyone against everyone else among his intimates, and with women it is dreadful, he collects several at a time who each believe that he loves her and hates the others. The good ones want to rescue the poor darling from his misery (as I thought I was rescuing him from Dora who thought he loved her) and the bad ones cash in.

I didn't mean to say all this when I began and I know it will hurt you dreadfully. But it is too horrible to think of your spreading your affection before him and him accepting it, dear, honest, guileless Freda, as I have done. And for myself, I feel I cannot bear one drop more of deceit and pretense.

Forgive me. I love you though he doesn't. You see, my pet, sex is the least of it.

Peter

Tear this up—no it doesn't matter. Having once broken I cannot go on pretending I haven't said all this to get you away from Bertie—you can tell from my first letter, that I didn't want to do that, but because your talking of your precious friendship with him is an echo of my own agony and I can't bear it. I have been in misery all day on your account added to my own. Some people he only said horrible things about sometimes but you, like me, have been a constant aversion for years.

18 Dorset House

N.W.L.

Feb. 24, 1951

Dear Freda,

Thank you for your card and wishes which I return for you and Jon.

My dear I don't have anything to forgive you except your virtues which are indeed more nuisance to you and sometimes to others than most peoples vices, and when I once love people I don't stop unless I find them insincere. Which I have no fear of with you. But as for being intimate that would be for me rather as it would be for you to try to be intimate with a starry-eyed young Communist. Hopeless I fear. You know yourself the solitude of disillusionment. In my case unlike yours no useful purpose can be served by springing it and my case is insoluble. I'm not open to relief.

I don't know where I shall be when you come to Europe again. Somewhere remote I hope. I am just waiting here still for Bertie to make a financial settlement.

Conrad is at Eton enjoying a classical education thoroughly. He towers above me and is very handsome and good and loves me very much, and also loves a nice girl and grandchildren are the only thing I look forward to (by a different girl no doubt).

I am recovering from a long illness, flu and then complications. I was very ill and I am still weak and stupid. I often wonder about Jon. I like him so much. We are both lucky in our sons if not in all things. I shall look out for the book. Good bye, probably, and love always.

Peter

It would be beyond my competence and the confines of this book to attempt to judge between Peter and Bertrand Russell who parted in anger after I knew and loved them both. I no longer unquestionably believe as I once did everything he told me about his second wife Dora. By the same token I also doubt the veracity of Peter's account in the above letters. But the two volumes of Russell's autobiography reveal enough of his ambivalent attitude towards the women he loved and did, or did not, marry to warrant some credibility to their sides of the story.

As regards Bertie's attitude toward me I can well conceive that in his fury against me when I brought him up against the unresolved conflict in his mind between his former and recent convictions and attitudes, he may have said things which Peter, as emotional and passionate as he, took to be true expressions of his feelings towards me. Our relationship had become what was perhaps akin to a divorce—not of marriage or any

179

sexual relationship, but of minds, or souls, if we have them, equally conducive to intemperate statements expressing the sad fury of alienation from those with whom one used to be attuned.

Whatever Bertie's "real" feelings about me may have been he continued to write to me with assurances of his friendship and trust for years after he left America.

In January 1962 he wrote me a friendly note which reads as follows:

Dear Freda,

Thank you for your letter of December 10. I have no objection whatever to your printing the Shaw correspondence that you write about. It was good to hear from you and certainly I am still your friend.

Yours ever,

BR

Acting on Isaac Don Levine's suggestion that it might be possible to ascertain Arcadi's fate, if Russell got Cyrus Eaton to make inquiries, I wrote to Bertie saying:

Reading yesterday in *The New York Times* that all England will be celebrating your 90th birthday this week, I realize that I should not be troubling you once again with my troubles. But I also know that old age cannot wither nor time destroy your unquenchable spirit, your passionate hatred of cruelty, your love for truth and your concern for all victims of injustice and stupidity. I also venture to believe that it was basically because I believe in the same values as you, and perhaps also on account of some similarity in our temperaments and minds since we both pursue our ideas to their logical conclusion in action, regardless of consequences to ourselves, that our friendship survived for so many years in spite of disagreement and some fierce and even bitter arguments, from the days when you tried to prevent me from making the great mistake of joining the Communist Party in the late 20's, to the time when in America we came to disagree about the Second World War, and now when I disagree with you in your crusade for disarmament at any risk.

In any case, dear Bertie, I know that today as always I can count on you to help me if you can. Arcadi is probably long since dead and if he is still alive he may have married again. I should not feel sad if this were so, indeed I should be happy to learn that he has not been lonely all these years like myself. But even if I have somewhat faded from his memory, if he is alive it would mean much to him and to our son to communicate. And I do not want to die before knowing what was his fate.

Perhaps I should not endeavor to enlist, through you, the help of such a man as Cyrus Eaton who unlike yourself is not one of the pure in heart, or if he is must be very innocent or foolish. I am suggesting that he, rather than you direct, approach the Soviet Government in view of your well known anti-Communist views. But it could be that Don and I are wrong in supposing that an ephemeral political character such as Eaton would have more weight in Moscow than yourself, now that more than ever before you are revered and respected even in

England as well as all over the world. For that very reason Moscow no doubt dislikes you intensely.

I hope that I may be enabled to get to England once again before I die and have another real talk with you after so many years. But, as usual, I have no money, although I may make some out of this book of memoirs, when it is at long last finished.

* * *

Bertie replied promptly telling me of his futile endeavor to save the life of Pasternak's widow and daughter in a letter which made clear not only his unchanged view of Soviet tyranny, but also his actual stand on "the bomb" which he denied meant immediate American atomic disarmament. His letter reads:

29 May 1962

Dear Freda,

Thank you for your letter of May 12. I am sorry to say that I have not any of the letters and papers that you asked about. I am quite glad that you should tell the story of Shaw's brutal refusal to help you. I am writing to Cyrus Eaton as you suggest, but I gravely doubt whether he will be willing to do anything and whether it will be effective if he does. I tried myself to do something for Ivinskaya and her daughter without the slightest success. I must tell you that my policy is not quite what you think. I do not favor unilateral disarmament "by the West" as you will see from the marked passage in the enclosed article. I hope that either through Cyrus Eaton or, if he fails, by some other means you may be able to obtain information as to your husband.

Yours very sincerely,

B R

June 18, 1962

Dear Bertie:

Thank you very much for your letter of May 29, and please forgive my long delay in answering. It was awfully good of you to respond so promptly to my request that you write to Cyrus Eaton. I, myself, doubt whether he will or can, do anything, but Don Levine believes that his wife will. He is going to let me know what he is able to do in that quarter.

I was also glad to read your article which you sent me and to be corrected as concerns the policy you advocate. The main reason why I delayed answering your letter was that I originally contemplated arguing some points with you. But I realize that this is impossible to do by letter as also that I might only start a futile argument to no purpose.

I had also intended by now to have a complete and corrected version of all I have written not only about you and G. B. S. but about you as I have known you through the years. Remembering those days, thirty-five years ago, when I stayed with you at Porth Curno, I am more than ever conscious of the great debt I owe you, both mentally and on account of the kindness you showed me in my youth as well as in later years. I was sorry not to know you were going to be on the Susskind show, so missed that, but have seen you briefly on another T.V.

181

program. I marvel and rejoice that you are still as vigorous as ever, look so very well, and have the same unmistakable and well-loved voice.

I also realize from the account in *Time* of your Susskind interview, that you still indulge in your favorite pastime, "Epatez les bourgeois."

With love,
Freda Utley

It was not until 1963 that I found myself blocked off from communication with him. When I briefly visited England in 1963 and phoned to Wales asking if I might come to visit him, I was first assured by his wife that he would be delighted to receive me, and then put off by the following unconvincing letter:

28 Sept. '63

Dear Miss Utley,

Thank you for your letters to us which have just reached me as Express Delivery is not indulged in the depths of the country where we live. When I spoke to you on the telephone I said that Bertie would, I was sure, like to see you, as of course, he would, if it were possible, but that he had been ill and is under doctor's orders. Unfortunately, I did not get your London address and so could not write you, and after discussing possibilities with Bertie, I asked Mr. Schoeneman, Bertie's secretary, who was in London, to ring you. Long distance telephoning during such a wind storm as we were then having here, is difficult. I am very sorry that he has to give you disappointing news.

Though Bertie is mending well and with astonishing rapidity—as always—he had a very severe cold which left him, naturally, though temporarily, without much energy to spare. It is unfortunate that, at this time of year, especially, when there are a great many visitors from abroad, Bertie's schedule is booked for weeks, even months ahead, and by people who cannot readily be put off. It is not as easy to arrange these matters as it used to be when we lived in London. And there is, added to the normal schedule, the backlog from the fortnight when he could see no visitors. When we discussed what work he has to do and the people he must see during the next few weeks, it became evident that he could not add to either, however much he would like to do so. Perhaps you may be able to consult him by letter about the passages in your ms that you would like to discuss.

I can assure you that Bertie is as you knew him 40 years ago—just as intelligent and sympathetic and delightful as he was then, just as passionate and with judgement unimpaired—but, naturally at 91, his energies are not as phenomenally great as they were then. They are reduced to those of a man of middle age! I can also assure you that he is no more pro-Communist than he was either 40 or 30 or 20 or 10 years ago. None of us who work with him—including Mr. Schoeneman and myself are pro-Communist. Nor Fascist, either, for that matter. He and we too, dislike oppression and persecution and cruelty when and where and under what disguise we find it, just as he did 40 years ago. And I assure you most warmly, that he is disappointed, as I am, that we have got ourselves into such a difficult tangle of work as not to be able

182

to see you. But I am sure that you will understand and I need not go on, and that you will spare us some of your sympathy.

Yours very sincerely,
Edith Russell

P.S. I imagine that Mr. Schoeneman spoke to you of Lord Russell because he had never had the pleasure of meeting you and so, of course, spoke correctly and formally.

Previously I had received a telephone call from Schoeneman, who in an ultra-refined English Oxford accent, told me that "Lord Russell," with emphasis on the title, was far too busy to receive anyone. Again and again I asked whether Bertie himself knew I was in England and wanting to see him. And again and again Mr. Schoeneman refused to tell me, stating only that "Earl Russell" was far too busy with his peace campaign to see anyone.

I gave up although perhaps I should simply have gone down to Wales and breached the castle, sure of my welcome if ever I could reach Russell. But I was 65 years old by this time and it was cold and wet.

Most great men have led too short lives. Perhaps the worst fate, reserved for Bertrand Russell, is to have lived too long. And yet, whatever the historical verdict on him may be, if I survive him, as he nears the full century of his inordinately long life, I will still account him as one of the few great men of our age, worthy to be ranked among the ancient Greek philosophers who took the whole purview of human knowledge as their domain and were not simply observers but also participants in the political struggles of their time.

I have advanced far ahead of my story relating to the ups and downs of my friendship with Bertrand Russell during the last three decades. Hoping that he will still be alive when this book is published and that I may meet him once again before we die, I now resume my narrative back to 1938.

Chapter 19
MY INDIAN SUMMER IN CHINA

Both politically and personally my half-year in China as a war correspondent in 1938 was the Indian Summer of my life. In spite of my experience in Russia, I still harbored sufficient liberal illusions to find myself at one with the American correspondents who now became my friends and companions. Moreover, either because at the age of forty I was in the prime of my life, or because the aura of Arcadi's love still cast its radiance upon me, I found myself to my surprise more attractive than in my youth. The ache in my heart for Arcadi remained, but its haunting pain was for a while anesthetized by my absorption in China's struggle for survival, and also, I confess, by the balm of being made much of as a woman.

The paucity of Western women in the war zone, no doubt, contributed to my popularity. The wives of European diplomats had stayed on in China's beleaguered wartime capital—for as my friend, Madame Georges Picot, wife of the French Ambassador said to me: "Who otherwise would see to it that my husband is properly fed and looked after?" But the families of the American and British Embassy and Consular staffs, as those of the correspondents, had been sent home or evacuated to safe places. This would appear to be customary among the English-speaking peoples when danger threatens. Not, one might surmise solely on account of their chivalrous concern for their womenfolk, but because in societies where women rule the social roost, men enjoy the freedom of their temporary absence. As a young Englishman remarked to me later, on the boat from Shanghai to the United States: "Wasn't Hankow a jolly place last summer with all the Mem-Sahibs away?"

Some missionaries had stayed on, but my American counterpart, Agnes Smedley, correspondent of the *Manchester Guardian*, and I were the only unattached British or American women around, and we were the best of friends.

I suppose it was because I was devoted to Arcadi and had not lost hope that one day, somehow or other, we should be reunited, that love as well as affection and friendship was proffered me in abundant measure. Since I felt myself not to be a widow, but a wife, no one risked anything by courting me, either because there was no one else to assuage their loneliness, or because shared dangers, sympathies, hopes and fears draw human beings together in an affectionate comradeship which verges on love for a moment in time.

In view of the suffering all around me, it may sound callous to record that I had a wonderful time. But everyone who has experienced the heightened awareness of the joy of living war can bring, as also the opportunity it affords of temporary escape from petty cares or the sorrows and perplexities of normal life, will understand why I look back on my experience as a war correspondent in China three decades ago with nostalgia.

All my life I shall remember the last days of Hankow. The blue skies by day, the camaraderie of the *tres gente compagnie* of foreign correspondents, the long talks at evening in the garden of the Navy "Y" where we foregathered to dine and "tire the sun with talking." The free and friendly atmosphere when it was still possible to believe that

184

good and evil can easily be distinguished, and I still belonged to the company of my Western liberal contemporaries. Partly because I had not as yet fully digested my political experience as a subject of the "first Socialist State." Also I think because liberal minded men of good will in the Western world had not as yet been steered off course, by the war propaganda which, following Pearl Harbor, represented only the Axis powers as evil.

Most of the "Hankow Last Ditchers," as I named the small band of Western correspondents, military observers, and foreign service officers who stayed on in China's beleaguered wartime capital until it finally fell to Japan, were Americans. It was now that I first became acquainted with Americans, if I exclude the Communist Party hacks I had known in Moscow, and found I had more affinity with them than with my British compatriots.

The British generally favored Japan, or were not averse to letting her teach the "uppity" Chinese Nationalists a lesson which they foolishly imagined would redound to their advantage by leading to the reestablishment of special rights, privileges and concessions for all the imperialist powers. For this reason, or because Britain was already too exclusively concerned with the Nazi menace, I was one of the very few British correspondents in China. Even the *London Times* had no one in the war zone. Excluding Reuter's ubiquitous news agency and occasional visiting correspondents there were only two representatives of the British press in the war zone both of whom were Americans of left wing sympathies; Agnes Smedley and Edgar Snow, correspondent of the British Labor Party's *Daily Herald*.

The Hankow Last Ditchers included some correspondents from Europe: Walter Bosshard the Swiss photographer for Black Star, Luigi Barzini whose son's book "The Italians"* was a best seller in 1964; and Lily Abels of the *Neue Zuricher Zeitung*, a well-known author, who a decade later interviewed me in Zurich while I was gathering material for my book on Germany, *The High Cost of Vengeance.*

The United Press office in the Lutheran Mission, presided over by the amiable and hard-working "Mac" Fisher was our club. He was the best-tempered and most unruffled man I ever knew, for he never had any privacy. Anyone in Hankow who wanted to know anything walked in, and in the adjoining room there slept not only Fisher himself, George Hogg, an Englishman working with the UP, and their star Chinese correspondent, George Wang, but also anyone else homeless at the moment. During the Munich crisis we all congregated there in the evening for the latest reports, or tried desperately to force Durdin's wireless next door to produce more than indistinguishable sounds.

Mac Fisher was a "Bamboo American" who had lived for years in China and spoke the language fluently. I lost sight of him a decade or more ago, altho I spent a night with him and his wife in Washington in 1945 prior to taking off again for China. But I have found a letter he wrote me when he was unemployed prior to succumbing to temptation or necessity and taking a job in the United States Information Agency where he sank without trace.

Maybe the correspondents of the world press this second year of China's unaided resistance to Japanese aggression were an exceptional group.

Most of them had spent many years in China, years during which, instead of acquiring the narrow prejudices and arrogance of the 'Old China Hand,' they had learnt to love and understand the Chinese, whilst yet preserving no romantic illusions about them. China exerts an influence over all who try to understand her, and their good-natured tolerance,

*Atheneum, New York, 1964.

185

if not the cynicism tinged with pity with which they surveyed the world, had perhaps been acquired from Chinese philosophy.

They had seen the war from the beginning and had been in danger many times, but they rarely spoke of their personal experiences. The sufferings and the constant danger to which the Chinese were exposed loomed too large for any of the foreign correspondents to feel that the moments in which they themselves had been close to death were anything to 'crash into headlines about,' unless one's ego had obscured all sense of proportion.

The visiting special correspondents, who thought they could go home and tell the world all about China after a few interviews with prominent Chinese in Hankow, aroused their amiable scorn. Most of them would probably have subscribed to the views of Far Eastern experts expressed by Randall Gould, the editor of the Shanghai *Evening Post*, who has spent the best part of his life in China:

"Show me a Far East Expert and I will show you a Far East fool or liar or both. Most of the journalistic congregation display enough sense of the realities to sing very small when expertizing is on order for some variety of 'thinkpiece,' otherwise 'situationer,' which compels a hapless correspondent to sweat out a learned discourse. It keeps him trembling for weeks afterwards, fearful that his colleagues will stumble on it and laugh themselves into fits . . . ."

In such an atmosphere as this, one soon lost any illusions one may have had that one could, after a few months in China, write a book which would really analyze, elucidate, and explain China to the world, or give an accurate picture of the future of the war or the future of China. One knew, at least how little one knew and how tentatively one must pronounce judgement.

Received at first with misgivings because I was a woman, expected by the seasoned American correspondents to be a nuisance in war time, and handicapped by the VIP treatment I was given as the author of *Japan's Feet of Clay*, I came to be fully accepted after I had slashed out in an interview published in the Chinese press, against the neglect of the wounded soldiers.

Even Jack Belden, the most woman-despising of all the newspapermen in China, after accompanying me part of the way on my first visit to the front, went so far as to admit that female correspondents might have their uses.

Getting to the front from Hankow was no simple matter. There were no direct roads and little transport except "Shank's Mare." It was so hot that one perspired even while sitting still, and the prospect of walking for many miles through unknown country in which it was doubtful whether one could find any food except what one carried, was discouraging. The Chinese Central Publicity Board, so obliging in other respects, never seemed able to arrange either transport or interpreters for foreign correspondents wanting to visit the front. Chinese officials, themselves averse to roughing it, thought that Westerners, accustomed to luxury, required comfortable transport and accommodations which could not be provided. And the government interpreters assigned to the foreign press had no desire to emulate such energetic and courageous Chinese newspapermen of the Central News Agency as Jimmy Wei and Edie Tseng whom I first met at the front and who are still my friends today.*

There was also the "face" factor. It would have helped China, not hurt her, to let foreigners realize how desperate the situation was, and how badly help was needed. But

---

*Today Jimmy Wei is Information Minister of the National Government in Taiwan, and Edie Tseng is Chief of the Central News in Hong Kong.

"face" precluded any such intelligent public relations policy. Most foreign correspondents who wanted to see the war at close quarters were persuaded to go no farther than Hankow or, if persistent, got shunted off to some inactive and easily accessible sector of the "front" lest they should "eat bitterness"—which is the picturesque Chinese way of saying one would have a hard time.

Such veterans of the foreign press corps as A. T. Steele and Tillman Durdin, Jack Belden, and Lesley Smith of Reuters who spoke some Chinese and were ready to walk and sweat and take the chance of a lift on an ammunition lorry, surmounted all these obstacles. I was one of the few visiting correspondents, and the only "foreign female person" who got to the front lines. I was enabled to do so thanks to Dr. Robert Lim head of the Chinese Red Cross and his friend Dr. Loo Chih-teh, the Surgeon General of the Chinese Army. On two separate occasions they provided me with transport part of the way by permitting me to accompany them on their inspection tours of the "hospitals" and receiving or dressing stations.

All too vividly I still remember the sight and sound, and smells of the hot August night on which, starting out from the much-bombed city of Nanchang, I accompanied Dr. Lim and his Singapore colleagues Drs. Jung and Moe. In the dim light of our electric torches we crept through the ancient, dirty, low-ceiling houses or huts where the wounded lay on the bare floor in filthy, blood-soaked clothing, their wounds roughly bandaged but without nurses to attend them and lucky if an orderly was within call to give them water. Few groaned or spoke, although most of them lay sleepless, their pain-drawn faces coming briefly into sight as the torches illuminated them. As the Chinese doctors bent over to examine them some would murmur: "There is no hope for me, my wound is too bad and I must die." Others, less severely injured, had little more hope of survival, since there was no transport to bring them to a hospital before their wounds turned gangrenous. It was like a scene from Hell redeemed only by the stoical courage and endurance of the Chinese. I was new to war in spite of the air raids I had already witnessed, and the civilian victims in Hankow and Nanchang were far better looked after than the wounded soldiers. I was fearful lest the horror of it all might so overwhelm me that I escape into the beautiful night outside unable to face suffering long enough to alleviate it by describing it to an indifferent world.

We stopped at five receiving stations in all. Some were mere bamboo shelters without walls along the open road; others rabbit warrens in mean streets. The Chinese doctors worked indefatigably. That night some few of the uncounted thousands of wounded in China got temporary relief from pain by an injection of morphine; some lives were saved by the cleansing and dressing of a wound.

Many Westerners hardened themselves to the sight of misery in China by subscribing to the theory that the Chinese nervous system is not the same as ours so that they don't feel the way we do. This comforting theory was manifestly absurd to anyone who had observed the sensitive fine-boned Chinese hand, the mobile Chinese face, and intelligent eyes.

Wounded men who walked for days half starved, somehow went on living. Was it, I wondered, the life-giving sunlight or hereditary selection, or the calm Chinese spirit which neither frets nor fumes, but silently endures?

The courage of the Chinese "common man," as it struck me that night and on many other occasions, is a marvel and mystery. Is it the hardships of his life from childhood which give him an uncomplaining patience, or the fatalism of the most ancient civilization in the world? Fatalism is not I think the right word to describe the Chinese attitude to life which has enabled these exceptionally gifted people to survive famines, wars, conquest and every disaster through the centuries.

Part of the answer came to me some nights later when having succeeded in getting to the front lines I sat with Chinese soldiers around their small campfires, lighted to ward off the ubiquitous mosquitoes.

The countryside in the moonlight was very lovely, the guns were stilled, and there was a queer sense of peace in spite of the war. A strange contentment came to me and I recalled some lines from Euripides:

Men in their millions
Float and flow,
And seethe with a million
Hopes as leaven . . .
But who'er shall know
As the long days go,
That to live is happy
Has found his Heaven.

The morrow may bring death, wounds, famine, or other sorrow, but for the moment one is alive and the world is beautiful. How different from one's usual feeling in the West that it is the morrow which is full of hope.

By a fortunate chance, I had been enabled to reach the front line and see the Chinese Army in action. On my way from Nanchang with Dr. Lim we had been held up at dusk among a crowd of marching soldiers, lorries, pack mules, horses and coolies carrying heavy loads, by a broad river crossed only by a narrow bridge of boats. All wheeled traffic and baggage animals had to wait their turn to cross on a wooden ferry boat propelled by oars. Sitting on the sandy shore to wait our turn with a young moon shedding a little radiance through light clouds, I was watching the animals being urged onto the ferry boat with shouts and cries, and reflecting that in some such fashion Xenophon's Ten Thousand had crossed the rivers of Asia Minor, when I was startled by someone speaking to me in fluent French. A young, handsome, and smartly-dressed Chinese officer introduced himself as Colonel Mok, political officer of the 64th (Cantonese) Division. He had read in the Nanchang paper that morning that the author of *Japan's Feet of Clay* was going to visit the front, and seeing a Western woman sitting in this remote spot, realized that I must be she. He suggested that if I could walk ten miles he would get a coolie to carry my pack and enable me to visit the front line troops with whom he served. This was the chance I was looking for and I rashly told him I could march even 20 miles if necessary. We arranged that he would wait for me later that night at a place called Teian which was on Dr. Lim's route.

Jack Belden, who was one of our party asked if he might accompany me and was soon engaged in animated conversation with Colonel Mok's fellow officers who spoke only Chinese. I produced a precious bottle of whiskey I had secured in Nanchang. None of the Chinese officers drank, but Bobby Lim, who had studied at a Scotch university, kept paces with Jack without the unfortunate results which were to preclude Jack from coming all the way with me to the front.

As we sat on that river bank we talked politics, as one always did in China: Would Chiang Kai-Shek allow the people to be "mobilized;" would Britain and the USA at long last exert economic pressure on Japan? Colonel Mok had spent five years in Paris at the Institute of International Affairs and had a French wife and children in Hong Kong where his family had a factory. He was one of those rare specimens in China, a well-to-do young man who could have been living comfortably in Hong Kong as a British subject but preferred to fight for China.

Jack Belden talked the usual talk of military men in China; why is Chinese staff work poor, why don't the generals cooperate better—but China will win, her soldiers are superb, Japanese morale is fading.

At last it was our turn to cross the river. On the other side was a village and peasants sleeping through the hot night on bamboo tressels outside their houses. Two of them wakened and asked us to sit down while we waited for Bobby Lim and the other doctors who had stayed to cross with the lorry. They apologized for having no tea, but gave us boiled water to drink and spoke of the good harvest, and their hope that the Japanese would not come before they could reap it. I wondered whether anywhere else in the world one could find peasants so well-mannered and hospitable, so calm and cheerful in the face of danger, and so friendly to strangers. A Japanese would have been equally polite but would have displayed a prying curiosity, and the Japanese are neither calm nor philosophical. Jack Belden, usually boorish and tongue-tied with his own people, settled down to talk to our peasant hosts with the utmost ease. Something I said to him as we sat there in the darkness spurred him to explain: "Don't you understand that these people are my people? There are no other people like them. I don't feel myself an American."

Thanks to the Chinese doctors ministrations to the wounded we were hours late at my rendezvous with Colonel Mok but caught up with him at the old walled town of Wushemin (Black Gates) where the road ended and one continued on to the front on foot. He was marching at the head of his men and could only stop for a moment to tell me that he had been unable to contact his general for permission to bring me with him, but if Dr. Lim could suggest any place on his route where I could wait he would send soldiers to fetch me in the morning. Bobby Lim gave him the name of the last dressing station we were to visit, which turned out to be a bamboo shelter without walls, overflowing with wounded men. It had started to rain heavily and Jack, who had been asleep in the car, thanks to my Scotch, said he didn't believe for a moment that Mok really would send soldiers to fetch us. I hesitated, and finally also chickened out at the prospect of sleeping in the open in the pouring rain and perhaps finding myself stranded there in the morning without being able to speak a word of Chinese.

Back in the car I kicked myself for having perhaps missed a unique opportunity to get to the actual front. When Bobby Lim told me he was going to drive direct to Changsha in our truck, but that the car would return to Nanchang, I decided to return there, determined somehow or other to get to Mok's Cantonese division at the front next day. Jack Belden for whom a visit to the front lines was "old stuff" left with Lim who assured him that soon they would stop somewhere where he could sleep off his hangover.

By breakfast time I was back at the Nanchang Hotel and after a bath and a meal, started out to find some way to get to Colonel Mok's division at the front. All I could remember was that Mok served with the 64th Division and that it was at a place that began with an M. At the American Mission I found a Mr. Johnson, the only foreigner left there, who tried to engage me in a long argument about American politics, or was it about the world situation? I escaped at last, too weary to be polite, but with the knowledge that some ten miles from Teian was a place called Mahuiling, and that the Chinese front was somewhere in that direction.

I now knew, or thought I knew, where I wanted to get to. The young man at the desk of the Hotel Burlington produced a "General Chang." No real general he, I imagine, but he was an American-born Chinese who had something to do with aviation, and he was

189

helpful. He would take me to an officer who could arrange things. On the way I remembered a forgotten letter of introduction in my pocket from Mr. Tseng of the Chinese branch of the International Peace Campaign in Hankow to a ranking officer by the name of Ho Shai-li. It had been handed to me at the station in Wuchang when I started on my trek to the front by traveling by train to Changsha by a young man who wrote poems in French. I had stuck it in my pocket and remembered it only at this moment, when it proved to be invaluable.

Miraculously, Ho Shai-li proved to be the aide-de-camp to the general commanding the whole of this war area. We arrived at a lovely country house and a young man appeared who in voice, manner, and appearance was indistinguishable from an English officer. I blinked and wondered if I were still asleep and dreaming in that bumping car on the road back to Nanchang. Soon I learned that Ho Shai-li was the son of Sir Robert Ho-Tung of Hong Kong, knighted by the British. He had been to Woolwich and to the American staff college and had an English mother. I was in shorts and my face was burnt brick red and I looked thoroughly disreputable, but I don't drop my aitches and I had brought a letter from a man with whom he had been at school in France. The fact that I wanted to get to the front on my own tickled him immensely. How would I manage, as I spoke no Chinese. Help me only to get to the Cantonese, I replied. He agreed to help me, but years later when I met General Ho Shai-li* again in Washington he told me had grave misgivings in letting me ride on a Chinese ammunition truck to the front since he would have been held responsible if I had been killed by Japanese planes.

By three o'clock that afternoon I was once more on the road north of Nanchang, sitting between the driver of an ammunition lorry and a thin young man in Khaki wearing glasses who must have been an officer. Insignia of rank were usually absent at the front and the uniforms of Chinese officers were not much better than a soldier's. The same cheap cotton, and in summer sometimes only a vest and no tunic.

This time in broad daylight there was no longer the comforting assurance I had had the night before that the Japanese planes could not bomb or machine-gun in the dark. At the ferry I thought, "What a nasty place it would be in a retreat, or for that matter, now, if the planes came over." However, there wasn't so much traffic by day, and we waited less than an hour to cross.

The only memorable incident of that journey was being stopped by three fierce-looking soldiers, who demanded a lift at the rifle-point. The officer beside me swore at them and pointed at me, no doubt insisting that they must not disgrace the Chinese army by behaving like this. Since he was unarmed, they took no notice, but jumped on behind. One of them pointed his rifle through the hole in the partition between the driver's seat and the back. For a mile or so we drove with a loaded rifle at our backs; but I felt much sympathy with the men who threatened us and tried the effect of a friendly smile. Suddenly an officer in the road cried halt, and pointed a revolver at the soldiers behind. This made them get off, or begin to get off, for I made signs that they were heavily loaded with their packs and ammunition and that there was plenty of room in the lorry. Thereupon all was smiles, and the officer, obviously much relieved, let them stay. The Chinese are above all a reasonable people. Face had been saved by forcing them to obey, the lorry was not heavily loaded, I had no objection; why should not some weary soldiers get a lift?

---

*Today Ho Shai-li is one of the most prominent businessmen in Hong Kong and his son, Robert, publisher of the most widely circulated newspaper there. On my last trip around the world in 1967 he published a long interview with me.

I spent the night at Black Gates where the road ended. The communication officer gave me a plank bed and a mosquito net and by midnight we got Mok on the telephone. Next morning two Cantonese soldiers arrived to escort me and I managed to keep the terrific pace they set for the ten mile trek to the headquarters of the general who was to give me a permit to visit the actual front. He provided me with a horse of sorts, warning me to get off at once if we heard planes since the Japanese took special pains to machine gun anyone riding and therefore presumed to be an officer.

I pass over my experiences at the front as guest of General Li told in detail in my 1939 book, *China At War*. My main problem was finding a secluded place in which to wash.

On my way back from my visit with the Cantonese at the front to Nanchang in an empty ammunition truck I was appalled to find my driver refusing to pick up the walking wounded. When my gestures availed nothing, I yelled and forced him to stop. I got out myself and remounted only when it had been overfilled with the wounded soldiers who scrambled aboard. On arrival at dawn in Nanchang, the American Protestant mission hospital refused to take in the wounded because they had to be "neutral" in the war and care only for civilian wounded. Only the Catholic mission staffed by seven nuns and already so overcrowded that even the cloisters were filled with victims of the war, would accept the wounded soldiers I had rescued along the way. When I asked the French-speaking Mother Superior what nationality she and the others were, she replied, "None, we are sisters in Christ."

I encountered some examples of true Christian charity also among the Protestants. The main difference, it seemed to me, was the fact that most Protestant missionaries in "heathen" lands regard their service abroad as temporary and remain apart, whereas Catholics become a part of the community in which they live.

My last recollection of that long night was being awakened from a short sleep by an air raid and feeling very frightened as the planes circled low over the Burlington hotel. Despite the probability that the Japanese would not destroy the hotel they would need when they captured Nanchang, I felt the front was a safer place to be.

On my return to Hankow I continued to be called "Clayfoot Utley" by the press corps which had greeted me on the first night I dined at the Press Hostel with a witty ditty about "Japan's feet of clay" turning into iron in the mud of China. But once they were convinced that I could "take it," did not demand a woman's privileges, could walk far and fast and above all, that my critical faculties were not atrophied by the warmth of my official reception, I was given every possible assistance.

Regarded in China as a famous author, I was acutely conscious of my inferiority as an untried war correspondent. I had been earning a living by my writings since getting out of Russia and had been a "journalist" of sorts in my university days in London, but I had never before been a reporter. Moreover, my knowledge of Chinese geography was elementary and at the first press conference I attended in Hankow I was as bewildered by the many "fronts" and the multitude of strange names of towns and villages, mountains, rivers, and lakes, as by the complexities of the Chinese political situation.

Everyone helped me.

Colonel "Vinegar Joe" Stillwell, to whom I was referred by the British Embassy which told me they had no military observers comparable to him, personally explained to me the intricacies of both Japanese and Chinese military strategy and tactics.

Bob Murphy of the United Press, a beguiling and precocious nineteen-year-old boy from Kansas City, taught me how to abbreviate words and sling them together in "cablese." This American system of lowering cable costs proved indecipherable to the foreign editor of the *News Chronicle*, who wired me to send my dispatches in straight English. I appreciated Bob Murphy's help just the same, and relished his mid-Western American unselfconscious confidence in his own abilities. I remember a party I gave in Hankow where he met one of the few Sackville-West clan who had never written anything. With brash aplomb Bob proceeded to explain to this scion of one of England's most illustrious literary families that writing is really quite easy and he would be glad to show him how to go about it.

After Pearl Harbor Bob became a Junior Lieutenant in the U.S. Navy conveying ships across the Atlantic, and used to visit me in New York between the trips.

Although I was old enough to be Bob's mother, I still enjoyed dancing and was not averse to visiting night clubs. But I drew the line at accompanying him to burlesque shows which bored me and endeavored to find him a nice young girl friend to go around with. These efforts proved abortive, since he demanded the well-nigh impossible of a politically sophisticated and also beautiful or charming companion. By this time Bob Murphy was no longer the confident brash boy I had known in Hankow, but a very sophisticated young man indeed. Later he was married happily and became an editor of the Encyclopedia Britannica.

Tillman Durdin of *The New York Times* initiated me into the maze of Chinese politics by introducing me to his many Chinese friends of various political persuasions. As a young man from Texas, working his passage to Europe to study music, Durdin had jumped ship in Shanghai. Subsequently he found himself unable to tear himself away and became a "Bamboo American"—an expression then current to describe those who had made China their home and second country. Before Japan's war on China, Durdin had worked on a Chinese-owned Shanghai newspaper, but by the time we became friends in Hankow he was already a top-flight correspondent. He still played the violin for his own pleasure and that of his friends but his favorite recreation was chess, at which game Jack Belden endeavored, usually unsuccessfully, to defeat him.

Scholarly, sensitive and reserved, with a slight physique but great endurance and singular charm, Till Durdin was an "egghead," physically as well as metaphorically. Although only in his early thirties, his thinning hair had already receded far back on both sides of his high wide forehead.

Whereas I am so old fashioned that I am incapable of expressing myself on a typewriter, on which I can do no better than tap out the letters with two fingers, Durdin had almost lost the capacity to write in any other way. He carried a small portable around on his back on long treks to the front when the weight must have made him perspire even more than the rest of us.

Once, after an interview we had together with an important personage in Hankow I gave him my notes to use on account of his difficulty in writing fast in longhand.

I was very fond of Till Durdin in Hankow and years after, in late 1945, when I returned to China as correspondent of the *Reader's Digest* I found him as knowledgeable and balanced as before. He then told me that my arrival and talks with him in Chungking that winter helped him to resist the siren voice of Chou-En-Lai who, by his wit, charm, tact, and avoidance of Communist clichés, was all too successful in persuading most Western correspondents that the Chinese Communists were China's last best hope.

Foremost among my Hankow friends was A. T. Steele, at that time correspondent of *The Chicago Daily News*. Tall and lanky with a thin, angular face, high bony forehead, prominent nose, tight-lipped mouth and a Western drawl, Steele, who came from California resembled the strong, silent hero of a Western movie. But he was a thinker as

192

well as an exceptionally gifted journalist whose caustic humor and hard-boiled demeanor masked the compassion with which he viewed the sufferings and follies of mankind. He was the most objective, self-effacing, kind, and helpful of all the foreign correspondents I have known as well as tireless in endeavoring to ascertain the facts without fear or prejudice.

Arch Steele was my companion on my second visit to the front, begun by accompanying Dr. Loo Chih-teh, Surgeon General of the Chinese Army, in his car on an inspection of the field hospitals as far as the bomb-destroyed city of Yangsin, from where we proceeded on foot to the front lines.

Walter Bosshard, Steele's Swiss friend, started out with us, but although built along the lines of an Alpine guide, he had a tender stomach, and gave up half way because he could not stand the Chinese Army food upon which Arch and I managed to keep healthy. Before returning to Hankow, Bosshard, a photographer for Black Star of New York as well as correspondent for Swiss papers, took a lot of pictures which he called his Utliana Series, some of which I used to illustrate my book *China at War.** Later he wrote a novel in German about our Hankow days in which I figure prominently. I was to meet Bosshard again at the Bretton Woods Monetary Conference in 1944, and for the last time in Egypt in 1959 while he was undertaking a cure in the healing waters at Assuan.

Looking at these photographs today, I see myself unbelievably slim, as compared to now, dressed in dark trousers and sleeveless shirt, a white towel for wiping off perspiration hung at my waist like any coolie, with untidy hair, but wearing that insignia of the intellectual, a pair of horn-rimmed glasses. Washing outside a farm house in a tin bowl of cold water, waking at dawn under a mosquito net surrounded by pigs; laughing with Steele and the Chinese doctors as we eat our morning rice; almost in tears as I stand by a truck filled with wounded Chinese soldiers whose stoic endurance on their rough journey made our slight hardships appear insignificant.

On one occasion Arch Steele probably saved my life by pulling me out of a Chinese Army truck and dragging me unceremoniously into a wayside ditch when Japanese planes straffed the road along which we were traveling. Being hard of hearing, I often did not realize the danger I was in. As we lay together in the ditch Arch trembled more than I did, thanks to my disability.

There are compensations for one's physical handicaps. Ever since childhood, my instinctive response to danger or violence has been to save my glasses from being broken. On my previous journey to the front with Dr. Robert Lim, after he had rushed Jack Belden and me to a field outside the much-bombed city of Nanchang during an air raid, I found myself more concerned with the risk of having my glasses shattered than with death, as I buried my face between my arms prone on the ground, with the bombs falling close. Most recently in Vietnam in 1967, both in the Delta and with the Marines close to the D.M.Z. line, I could sleep comfortably because the deafness I then suffered from precluded hearing the mortar attacks of the Viet Cong.**

On our way back from the front lines a few days later Arch Steele did me another great service. I had sprained my ankle by stepping into an unseen hole on the path along which we were walking in the dusk toward a road on which we hoped to find a truck returning

---

*Faber & Faber, London, 1939. John Day, New York.

**After the ms. of this book had already gone to the printers my hearing, which had steadily deteriorated over the past three decades, has been miraculously restored, by an operation performed on me at the age of 71 by Dr. Di Biasio at Georgetown University and thanks to Medicare!

to Wuchang. We had three miles to go and without Arch's arm to lean on, his jokes and stories to distract me, and his bolstering of my ego by his confidence in my ability to overcome the pain, I would never have made it. When we finally reached the road and managed to flag down a truck after a long wait, Arch insisted that I keep my foot in perpetual motion instead of succumbing to sleep. So that, by dawn I no longer had a sprained ankle!

I was younger then and doubt that today this rigorous cure would work. Or maybe it's all in the mind and some physical ailments are curable if one is not debilitated by the easy way out afforded in the Western World, where endurance or fortitude, or the necessity to struggle for survival have been all but eliminated by soft living and easy escape from pain.

Balanced, calm and cheerful under stress, Arch Steele was always ready with a dry witticism which made one feel that although life is grim, it is also comic, and that in any case, there is "nothing to be done about it." This was his translation of the Chinese expression, Mei yu fatse—which he kept on repeating to allay my impatience as we sat waiting a whole night on a river bank to take our turn to cross over on the single ferry which was transporting a Chinese regiment to the front.

Steele sustained me in other ways on this never to be forgotten trek to and from the front. He tactfully ignored my feminine weaknesses whether it was a question of physical endurance, as we clambered up steep hillsides with Chinese soldiers and a Russian Tass correspondent who, impervious to the heat picked flowers for me by the wayside which I had no breath with which to thank him; or, when I found it beyond my capacity for endurance of other people's pain to witness and attempt to write about the agony of the unsung soldiers of China fighting and dying in a war concerning which "the West" couldn't have cared less.

Among my memories of my experiences of China at war 30 years ago the ones I shared with Arch Steele are most vivid. Held tight on his lap on the sidecar of a motorcycle rushing at breakneck speed along a rutted road with two passengers behind, before depositing us to await an escort to proceed on foot to the front lines; lying amid the stench of death in the moonlight, with the crickets singing; welcomed with the treat of captured canned pineapple by the Chinese military; sleeping on doors removed from farmhouses; borrowing Steele's comb after mine was lost in order to appear less like a tramp or camp follower. It was then that I comprehended Temple's appreciation of the good life as one of struggle and anxiety with fear of death adding zest to life, followed by periods of ease and enjoyment. On returning to Hankow it was wonderful to throw off one's sweat stained clothing, soak in a hot bath, don silk or fine linen and enjoy a good dinner, wine, and an evening of dancing at "Rosie's," run by a charming Chinese lady married to a Portuguese, and possessing the only dance floor in town. Here you met consular and embassy officials, their Chinese lady-loves, naval officers from the American, British and French gunboats in the river, a few businessmen, an occasional young missionary feeling himself rather daring, a group of Russian (Tass) correspondents consuming vodka, and those Chinese, young and old, who paid no attention to Chiang Kai-shek's disapproval of luxury and dancing in wartime. Here also you might see, on leave from the front, the slender, picturesque form of Wang Hsiao-ling, a German girl with the rank of major in the Chinese Army Medical Service, who sported her elegant khaki riding-breeches and tunic even in the dance hall. Married to a Chinese, and looking not more than twenty-one, she spent most of her time at the front and had been seen by various correspondents operating on wounded soldiers on bare wooden tables, and extracting bullets with a penknife. She was not really a surgeon, but she had had a year or so of medical training in Germany, and that meant she was as well or better trained than most "doctors" in the Chinese Army.

On the whole, few Chinese officers or war-workers were to be found at Rosie's. Here was the Chinese *jeunesse dorée* of both sexes, who would dance with the Japanese at the gate and also after they had captured the city. Today the same *genre* in infinitely greater numbers, fills the bars and dance halls of Saigon.

Rosie's was respectable; Hankow's houses of ill-repute were on "Dump Street," some way farther on.

On the whole we were pretty abstemious. Life was too interesting, there were too many people we wanted to talk to and get news from, for us to have much time or need of drinking or dancing. Most of us lived at the Lutheran Mission and had lunch and dinner at the Navy YMCA, where a crowd of Chinese and foreigners would gather to eat the cheapest Western-style food in Hankow. The greater social equality of American life as compared with English struck me forcibly at the Navy Y where American officers ate with us and our Chinese friends at the same tables with the sailors. It is true that sailors did not flock to the Navy Y in droves, for, as one of them explained to Agnes Smedley, "what would a sailor go ashore for but to drink?—and you couldn't get alcohol there."

If at any time one hungered for company one could be sure to find someone or other imbibing cool drinks or milk shakes or ices made of powdered milk at the Navy Y soda fountain, or gossiping under the colored lights in its spacious garden.

* * *

Steele and Bosshard had befriended me from the beginning. They shepherded me through the Wuhan cities following the bombing raid which occurred the morning after my arrival in Hankow and they got me through the ordeal of seeing burnt bodies and hearing the screams of wounded men, women, and children for the first time in my life. These air raids were not to be compared with the mass bombings of the Second World War. But the dead are dead, and even the hundreds of men, women, and children killed or wounded in air raids in China suffered as much individually as the hundreds of thousands killed or wounded later in Europe. Day after day, unless the weather was cloudy, the Japanese planes, many of them bought in America and most of them fueled by the West in that period of our most unpositive neutrality, came over the defenseless Wuhan cities to bomb and destroy. When the air raid alarms sounded, the foreign correspondents would climb up to the top of the high tower in the Lutheran Mission, to watch within the sanctuary of the former international concession where we lived and enjoyed immunity from destruction from the skies. Often we wasted hours on that roof waiting for raids that never materialized, or seeing the Japanese planes drop a few bombs on the airfield to the north, making holes at great expense, which would be filled up again within a few hours at small expense by a small army of coolies.

But often, also, we heard the bombs fall upon the crowded parts of the three Wuhan cities and saw the smoke rise from burning houses, hovels, workshops, and small factories. Then we would all rush along to the places where the bombs had fallen, in Hankow itself, or across the Yangtze river in Wuchang, or over the Han river in the old town of Hanyang. Crossing by ferry or sampan, making our way through the smoking ruins and burning buildings, seeing the mutilated, the slain, the bereaved, and the homeless, I tried not to be too overcome by the horror and the suffering to be able to describe it and even photograph it, which was harder.* Sometimes the casualties would be a mere hundred or

---

*Some of the photographs I took were used by the London Lord Mayor's Fund to raise money for the Chinese refugees.

two; sometimes a thousand or more. The first-aid workers would usually be on the scene before us, for this air-raid service was well organized in Hankow. But often it would be hours before the living as well as the dead could be extracted from the debris of their homes. Pitiful sights of children searching for their mothers buried under falled walls, or weeping beside horribly mutilated bodies. Dead babies and wailing women, and worst of all, the wounded children. One got used to dead bodies. The sight of the wounded and of those who had lost a child, a husband, a mother, or a son was far worse.

In words from the diary of a dead Japanese officer: "For whom do we inflict this cruelty?" For whom, indeed, as many an American, British, or German soldier in the far greater holocaust to come reflected while dropping bombs on enemy cities.

After a bad raid, the Bund and the streets of the concessions would be crowded for a few days with families camping out. Then they would disappear again to their homes over the river, and the next air raid would wipe out a few hundred more helpless victims.

Up on the Lutheran Mission roof we used to feel it was a little indecent that foreigners could view the raids from the safety of the ex-concession districts, almost like a spectacle at a theatre. Watch for the first sight of those black specks high up in the skies, breathlessly follow the bursting shells of the anti-aircraft, which always just missed the target, see the smoke go up from explosions or burning homes. No Chinese planes rose to defend the cities. Such fighting planes as the Chinese still possessed were busy at the front, protecting the bombing planes that tried, with infrequent success, to hit the Japanese transports. The Japanese planes bombing the Wuhan cities usually flew some ten thousand feet up, on account of the anti-aircraft guns, and their bombs were dropped at random. Dozens of times they would aim at the old arsenal and iron works in Hanyang, but they seldom hit them. Instead, each time more of the miserable shacks of the working class population near the river would be destroyed. Over in Wuchang, across the Yangtze opposite Hankow, the Japanese were clearly trying to demolish the whole city and in particular, hoping to hit whichever house Chiang Kai-shek and his wife were temporarily occupying. Japan's espionage system was good, but not quite good enough. Several times their planes scored a hit on the premises Chiang and his wife had occupied until a day or two before. Once, in early August, they almost succeeded; the dugout to which the Chiangs retreated during the raids had a wall blown down and they both escaped by a miracle.

A month earlier on July 21, I had just arrived for my first interview with Madame Chiang when the air raid warnings sounded. I found myself holding hands with her, wondering if this time the Japanese had pinpointed and would achieve their target. After a suitable interval to show each other we were not frightened, she took me down to their primitive dugout shelter. Under the thunder of the bombs falling ever closer which could by a direct hit have blown us out of this world, we had a very frank talk during which I became almost intimate with the First Lady of China, who did so much both to help and to hurt the Chinese Nationalist cause. We were interrupted when the Generalissimo, unaware that his wife was not alone, entered in a loose robe without his dentures and hastily retreated in disorder after a quick greeting.

Years later in New York John P. Marquand, to whom I told my story of having seen Chiang Kai-shek during an air raid without his false teeth, used this trivial incident fictitiously in his story of a successful American journalist in his book "So Little Time."

On my return to Hankow from my first visit to the front I told Madame Chiang what I had seen and urged her to meet Dr. Robert Lim and give some help to the Chinese Red Cross which was endeavoring to provide a minimum of care for the wounded.

I gave her a written report after she assured me she would translate it for her husband and get him to issue orders concerning the use of empty ammunition trucks to evacuate the wounded. Which she must have done, for on my next visit to the front I found some officers with red flags stationed at points along the road with power to compel lorries to stop and pick up a load of wounded.

She wrote in a letter dated 24 August 1930 from the Headquarters of the Generalissimo:

> Dear Miss Utley:
>
> I wish to thank you for your letter and the report on conditions at the front. The latter particularly was very timely, as it corroborates the report of an investigation I had requested about the time you were at the front, and doubtless your letter will strengthen the efforts of the impartial and fair attitude of the official report. Orders have already been given to reform conditions. As soon as these reforms have time to take effect I shall go myself and take a look at things.
>
> Regarding Doctor Robert Lim, I think I may be able to help him. I have therefore wired him to come to see me and I shall do my best to aid him in his work.
>
> Last Friday, in speaking before a group of well-to-do women, I told them that it is not enough for us to carry out the popular slogan: "Those who have strength should give strength, those who have money should give money," but that since the soldiers are fighting for all of us as well as for the country at large, it is necessary we should change the slogan to: "Those who have strength should give strength, those who have money should give money and strength." Furthermore, I told these women that we should ourselves go to the hospitals to nurse the wounded—and not merely to give souvenirs and comfort kits—but actually to nurse and wash these poor men with our own hands. I propose to take my New Life Staff to the hospitals and shall start doing what I preach as an example to others. I regret that my time is so taken up with all the other duties confronting me that I cannot do this regularly, but I hope at least that a demonstration of my sincerity and willingness "not to be ministered unto but to minister" will help conditions in these hospitals.

Unlike most Americans who imagined that the Generalissimo could reform everything if he wanted to, I realized the difficulties he was up against, thanks to my knowledge of medieval history. No orders from above "to reform conditions" ever had much effect in China.

Nor could one take much stock in Madame Chiang's promised visit with her New Life Staff to "nurse and wash" the wounded in a few selected hospitals far from the stench and misery and neglect of the field "hospitals" and dressing stations. She meant well but she took slogans and pious pronouncements as equivalent to performance.

Despite the circumstances of our first meeting and the brief intimacy it engendered Madame Chiang and I never became real friends, although we met frequently in 1938 and later years. She no doubt disliked my agnosticism and my failure to join the ranks of her uncritical admirers. I came to the conclusion expressed in my books that without his beautiful Vassar educated wife and her wealthy Soong relatives, the Generalissimo would have done better for his country and his people. Her attitude seemed to me to have a "colonialist" taint, or perhaps I should better describe it as missionary Methodist. She so distrusted most of her compatriots that she thought they should be kept in tutelage to the West. She responded to my appeal by meeting Dr. Lim and giving him a substantial donation from the funds at her disposal donated from abroad for Chinese relief. But it was sad and surprising that it had required me, a foreigner, to induce her to do so.

Despite her intelligence and political acumen Madame Chiang placed her trust in "the palace eunuchs"—as we used to call the Chinese Christians in her New Life movement, who talked piously but did very little useful work and were jealous of those who did. I found myself on several occasions in the strange position of arguing with her that the people in America and England who wanted to help China should contribute to the Chinese Red Cross, both because China needed to build up her own social services, instead of depending on foreigners, and because the West ought to be trying to help China win the war instead of salvaging our own consciences by charity. It was hard to convince her that Dr. Lim and his colleagues in the Chinese Red Cross who had given up lucrative positions abroad to serve China in her extremity were better qualified and able to supply more vital services to China than foreigners. Nor did she ever come to realize that the Chinese she trusted most because they were Christians like herself and had joined her New Life Movement were in no way comparable in dedication, honesty, and real performance to Bobby Lim and his self-sacrificing band of doctors and first aid workers, who were not Christians.

Like Eleanor Roosevelt, who was to invite me to tea at the White House in April 1939, Mei-Ling Soong, the First Lady of China, reminded me somewhat of the typical old-style "vicar's wife" in an English village who thinks she knows best what is good for her husband's parishioners. Madame Chiang was more politically sophisticated than Mrs. Roosevelt, but both of them were so sure of themselves and had led such over-privileged lives that they had little knowledge of realities, and were easily taken in by those who flattered their self esteem and belief in their righteousness. Neither of them had good judgment in assessing people who seemed to share their views and aims. Both of them went overboard in their different fashion for phony characters who seemed to share their sincere desire for the betterment of their own people and all mankind. Mrs. Roosevelt trusted Joseph Lash and other Communist fellow-travellers, while Madame Chiang, hating Communism, gave her confidence to Chinese "Christians" many of whom were no better than the Communists in their lust for power, but who seemed to her to be good people because they professed the same beliefs as herself.

Eleanor Roosevelt had so little realization of the infinitely better condition of people under the American system of government and way of life that she gave aid and comfort to the Communist cause by ignoring the terrible realities of Stalin's Russia and seeing only the Socialist ideal. Madame Chiang's attitude toward her own people was not in essence dissimilar, although seemingly the reverse, since she looked to the West as the beacon of progress and had no illusions about Communism. Whereas Mrs. Roosevelt trusted Moscow too much, Madame Chiang had such great faith in Washington that she was to become instrumental in persuading the Generalissimo to accede to American demands for "democratic reforms" which were as unrealizable as harmful in China's desperate situation, both before and after Japan's surrender.

Being more Western than Chinese in education and culture, Mei-Ling Soong's attitude toward her own people was not unlike that of the Protestant missionaries who, despite all their good works were in general aloof to the Chinese people. Her sister Madame Sun Yat

Sen committed herself as unreservedly to the Chinese Communists, and is today the prime exhibit in Peking for Mao Tse Tung's claim to be her husband's legitimate political heir.

Following my first visit with her, Madame Chiang sent me two rolls of Chinese grass linen, one white and one pale blue. I gave half of each roll to Agnes Smedley and had the rest made up into badly needed summer dresses and blouses. The American correspondents ascribed this gift, according to their prejudices, to Madame Chiang's charitable effort to improve my inelegant appearance, or as a "bribe" to keep me friendly to the Chinese Nationalist cause. My endeavor to induce Madame Chiang to invite Agnes to meet her was as unavailing as my attempts to persuade Agnes to so far 'demean herself,' as she saw it, to request an interview with the Generalissimo's wife.

Chapter 20
PORTRAIT OF AGNES

Many of the friends and acquaintances I made in China are lost or forgotten, or have long since been alienated from me by the course of human events which led us to pursue different paths according to the variety of our experience. Others are long since dead, among whom Agnes Smedley is the one I mourn for.

No picture of Agnes can do her justice. A high, broad forehead, with soft brown hair falling over her right temple, a wide, generous mouth, candid pale blue eyes which could wrinkle up in laughter, or look upon the world with passionate pity or fierce and scornful anger. She was one of the few people of whom one can truly say that her character had given beauty to her face, which was both boyish and feminine, rugged and yet attractive.

One of the few spiritually great people I have ever met, Agnes Smedley had that burning sympathy for the misery and wrongs of mankind which some of the saints and some great revolutionaries have possessed. For her the wounded soldiers of China, the starving peasants and the over-worked coolies, were brothers in a real sense. She was acutely, vividly, aware of their misery and could not rest for trying to alleviate it. Unlike those doctrinaire revolutionaries who love the masses in the abstract but are cold to the sufferings of individuals, Agnes Smedley spent much of her time, energy and scanty earnings in helping a multitude of individuals. My first sight of her had been on the Bund at Hankow, where she was putting into rickshaws and transporting to hospital at her own expense, some of those wretched wounded soldiers, the sight of whom was so common in Hankow, but whom others never thought of helping. Such was her influence over 'simple' men as well as over intellectuals that she soon had a group of rickshaw coolies who would perform this service for the wounded without payment.

Born in a mining camp in Colorado, her father an unskilled laborer of part Indian parentage and her mother a washerwoman, Agnes' childhood and youth had been one of bitter poverty movingly described in her first book, *Daughter of Earth*.* The literature of her childhood had been the legends of Jesse James, the imagined "Robin Hood" of Western America, and old songs of revolt sung to her by her drunken and illiterate, but much beloved father. She had not received even a high school education, and in her youth had earned her living as servant and waitress and at other jobs of poorly paid drudgery. Somehow or other she had educated herself, became a Communist, and gone to Germany where in 1928 she secured an assignment to China as correspondent for the liberal *Frankfurter Zeitung*. She had been in China ever since, working at one time for the Communists in their underground in Shanghai, visiting them in Yenan after the long March, and in general collaborating with the Communists who seemed to her to be leading the struggle for emancipation of the Chinese people.

Her husband, an Indian, had as mine, been liquidated in Moscow during the great purge, and when we met in Hankow she knew as well as I that the Soviet Government had

---

*Coward-McCann, New York, 1929.

become a brutal totalitarian tyranny. But she continued to believe, or try to believe, then and afterwards, in the revolutionary Communist Movement. When she finally faced up to the fact that no one of integrity who cared for freedom could remain in the Communist camp, she went to pieces, as I shall later relate.

Self righteous Rightists regarded Agnes as nothing but a Communist, or as one of their fellow-travellers. The Communists distrusted her as an unreconstructed liberal "bourgeois idealist." To me she seems a heroic and tragic figure, doomed to destruction by her virtues, her courage, her compassion for human suffering, her integrity and her romanticism. Knowing her, one appreciated what manner of men and women gave its dynamism to the Russian Revolution. As also the reason why the Social Revolutionaries were liquidated by Lenin after they had helped the Bolsheviks to come to power. Also why long after the Bolsheviks had betrayed the Communist ideal, it has continued to inspire those who hunger for righteousness but will not admit, even to themselves, that there is something wrong with an ideology which leads to totalitarian tyranny and brings to power men indifferent to the sufferings of human beings.

Agnes' whole-hearted dedication to the causes she believed in enabled her to exert influence over all sorts of people and won her the liking and respect of men as different as the British Ambassador, Sir Archibald Clark-Kerr; the Reverend L. H. Roots, Episcopalian Bishop of Hankow; the elegant and facetious U.S. military attache, Captain Frank "Pinkie" Dorn, and his friend John Davies the U.S. Consul whose apartment he shared. As also that of a fat restaurant keeper of unknown nationality in Dump Street in the red light district where you could buy the best dinner in town. Dining there one evening with Captain Carlson of the USMC Agnes persuaded the proprietor to organize a collection in every dubious establishment in the street and within a week he produced $5000 with which to buy blankets for the wounded soldiers.

It is difficult to refuse anything to "the pure in heart" as John Davies said, when, he together with an equally reluctant group of Western journalists, military observers and diplomats, and even some missionaries, were induced by Agnes to come and sing under her direction to the wounded soldiers in a Hankow hospital on September 18, the anniversary date of Japan's attack on Manchuria. Few of us had good voices, and our performance was unrehearsed. It is doubtful whether we gave any solace to the wounded as we obediently followed Agnes in singing old ballads and First World War songs through the wards, under the astonished eyes of the Chinese soldiers. They probably had no appreciation of our singing, but Agnes' point was that we Westerners must show that we cared for these forgotten men, and maybe they got the idea, unaccustomed as they were to any concern for their sufferings.

For the first few weeks in Hankow I lived at the flat of the Reverend Simms Lee, Chaplain to the British Navy. His wife was an American from Georgia, with one of the loveliest speaking voices I have ever heard. She looked like a frail Victorian lady, but she had as great a spirit as Agnes Smedley. Her way was not Agnes's; it was the way of a southern lady and a Christian, but she was as fearless in fighting cruelty and taking up the cudgel for the helpless. She and her husband had once been missionaries but had quarrelled with their group over its racial snobbery toward the Chinese. They had adopted and brought up three Chinese boys, one of whom now held a commission in the Air Force. She was continually picking up ragged and dirty homeless Chinese children off the streets, taking them to her flat, feeding them and bathing them before taking them to the orphanages Madame Chiang had established. She had also rescued two little Russian boys whom a British sailor had seen soliciting in Dump Street and made the long and dangerous journey to Hong Kong on the bombed railway in order to place them in a school there. Their prostitute mothers frequently came to visit her and she was full of sympathy for them. "What can I tell them to do," she said to me, "there is no other way in which they can earn a living." She and Agnes, poles apart in thought, politics, and background, struck up a warm friendship. What mattered for Mrs. Simms Lee was the good work Agnes was doing, not her Communist views which she entirely rejected. When Agnes spoke of the White Terror, Mrs. Simms Lee would blaze out with tales of Communist atrocities. When Agnes condemned Chinese shortcomings, Mrs. Simms Lee would express her faith in China winning the war in her own fashion. Agnes would take criticisms of her beloved Red Army from this gentle and determined woman which from anyone else would have led to her walking out of the house.

Less important than religious beliefs, or any ideology, are the qualities of mind and heart which compel commiseration for the sufferings of the unfortunate and endeavor to alleviate them.

Agnes got everyone interested in the terrible plight of the wounded soldiers, so that press dispatches and articles and appeals started going through to the outside world, and a trickle of help began to reach Dr. Lim's gallant band of doctors and first-aid volunteer workers. Her zeal outstripped her diplomacy, and her intemperate advocacy of the cause of the neglected Chinese wounded soldiers led her upon occasion to such exaggeration that her opponents were easily enabled to discredit her. Nevertheless, she got things done, and it was largely due to her efforts that the International Red Cross, in 1939, at long last began to give some small medical aid to the Chinese Red Cross which had until then been refused by reason of Western "neutrality" in the Sino Japanese war.

John Davies had such a high regard for Agnes and was so very fond of her, that I conceived the foolish notion that he might marry her and save her from the consequences of her reckless and self-sacrificing romanticism by his practical common sense. Arch Steele laughed at me and said it was absurd to imagine that John would jeopardize his promising diplomatic career by a misalliance with a woman who was in any case too old for him. When John, like some others in Hankow, tried to make love to me, I put him off by saying, "You belong to Agnes."

Agnes herself thought she was in love with her male counterpart, Captain Evans Carlson of the U.S. Marine Corps who, after having marched for two thousand miles with the Chinese Communist Eighth Route Army in and out of Japanese occupied territory, had conceived irradicable romantic illusions about them. He even did his best to look like a Communist guerilla fighter. To the amusement of Pinkie Dorn* whose immaculate white suits, cool, clean appearance on the hottest days, were in sharp contrast, Carlson walked around Hankow in shorts, a worn khaki shirt roughly cut above the elbows and heavy marching boots.

Since Evans Carlson, later to become famous in the Pacific war against Japan, thought he was in love with me, and Agnes, who loved him, was my close friend, it was all rather mixed up.

Although Evans Carlson did not attract me as a man, I liked him very much and enjoyed being courted and taken to dine and dance at Rosie's where he would order a bottle of French wine, a rare commodity in Hankow in those days, although he actually much preferred a milk shake at the Navy "Y".

---

*Generally known as Pinkie and now retired with Brigadier General rank, Dorn recently wrote a successful book on Chinese cooking and is now engaged in writing a 2000 year history of the Royal Palace in Peking—from Ming to Mao—which he is also illustrating.

During the days I knew him so well in Hankow and enjoyed his confidence, Evans Carlson was torn between his American and Marine Corps allegiance and his feeling that he must speak out for his convictions, even at the cost of resigning from the Service. After much soul searching he left the Marine Corps, but after Pearl Harbor was enabled to reconcile his divided allegiance. Reinstated as a Major in the USMC he was decorated after he captured an island in the Pacific by adopting the tactics of the Communist guerrillas he had learned in China, and became a General.

Dear, innocent, kind and courageous Evans Carlson. Norwegian ancestry and rugged life had given him a proper "leatherneck" tough, weather-beaten appearance. But he was as incurable a political romantic as Agnes Smedley and less intelligent.

After the war, thanks to his having become a Marine Corps hero, Carlson came to exert considerable influence in America on behalf of the Chinese Communist lobby. He was co-chairman with Paul Robeson of a Communist front called "The National Committee to Win the Peace" which urged the withdrawal of all U.S. troops from China and denial of munitions to the Chinese National Government fighting the Communists. When he wrote to me in September, 1946, asking my support, he was both hurt and shocked to find that I was one of his most articulate opponents.

If Agnes and Evans Carlson had married, the result no doubt would have been disastrous, since they were too much alike. Moreover, as I discovered later in America, he already had a wife. One of the most embarrassing moments I experienced during my first lecture tour in America was to be introduced to a Mrs. Carlson in San Francisco, to whose greeting I responded by saying: "Are you any relative of Evans Carlson?" To which she responded by saying, "Only his wife!"

There could be no greater contrast than that between Carlson and Jack Belden who also went overboard for the Communists during and after the Second World War. In Hankow Jack mocked the idealized picture of the Eighth Route (Communist) Army painted by Edgar Snow, Agnes Smedley and Carlson as dedicated revolutionary soldiers fighting to make a better world. Having seen more of the war at close quarters on several fronts than any other Western correspondent Belden insisted that men fight bravely not for ideologies or patriotism, but to retain or acquire the respect of their comrades in arms by proving their manhood in combat.

When in Hankow, over dinner at the Navy YMCA, or under the hospitable roof of the American Vice-Consul, John Davies, the rest of us argued out the old political issues—socialism and how to get it, could one achieve it without a soul-destroying dictatorship, was Fascism coming everywhere, were the Chinese Communists still Communists or liberal reformers—Jack would listen with a smile. Mankind, in his view, was bound to be wretched and unhappy in any society. A man with the most pessimistic philosophy I have ever encountered, subject to fits of profound dejection during which he snarled at his friends and took refuge in alcohol or the pursuit of danger, he could when in the mood, be a most interesting and entertaining companion. When others spoke of patriotism he would insist that it was the professional "old soldier" who fought best. When one asked him what made the Chinese soldiers go on fighting in the terrible conditions in which they were so often placed, he would speak of the desire to "get at the other fellow who was making things so nasty for you." Jack was, in fact, the supreme debunker, with contempt for loud mouthed patriots, politicians and political theorists; yet he had a real respect for idealists like Agnes Smedley and for men like Dr. Robert Lim of the Chinese Red Cross; a wide knowledge and love of poetry; and insight into the character and motives of men. Lonely, sad, and cynical he had not acquired the contentment of the Chinese, but seemed more Chinese than American in his mental processes, in his mockery at human endeavor, his disbelief in idealism, his scepticism concerning progress, and his loyalty to his friends.

At the time we were friends in Hankow Belden had been dismissed as UP correspondent for disregard of the orders of his home office. Later he was to become a successful foreign correspondent by reason of his book about the Burma campaign, *Retreat with Stillwell,** in which he eulogized Vinegar Joe. Which was curious, because in Hankow he had no admiration at all for this vain publicity seeking general and the dislike was mutual. Stillwell on one occasion wanted to get Belden expelled from the China theater because after he had disappeared for some days, a search had to be made for him by the police and he was found in Dump Street sleeping off a drunken orgy.

I once thought that Jack was a throwback to the old frontier America which believed that courage was the supreme virtue. Some years later, visiting him in a New York hospital after he had been wounded in Sicily, I found that like the liberal innocents he had mocked in Hankow, he had fallen for the propaganda which represented the Red Army as an army of liberation. Later after reading his 1949 book, *China Shakes the World,*** in which he sang the praises of the tough, intrepid, and cruel Communists, I sensed that he actually enjoyed recording the tortures the Communists inflicted, not only upon their enemies but also upon the innocent or neutral victims of the Civil War.

Perhaps today we would understand Communism better if we realized that, although it still continues to inspire some liberal innocents abroad, one of its main powers of attraction is to the same type of people who embraced the Nazi philosophy before Hitler's defeat.

* * *

In Hankow, we "iconoclasts," as Steele called John Davies, Till Durdin and myself, endeavored to prepare Agnes for the inevitable disappointments of the future. But she would not let herself be convinced that revolutionary movements are only self-sacrificing and incorrupt during the struggle for power, never afterwards. On one occasion, when driven into a corner by myself and Durdin, Agnes, whose sense of humor never deserted her for long, exclaimed, "Why do you try to make me lose my faith; do you want me to marry a millionaire?"

Our attempts to prevent her returning to "the wilderness" were unavailing. In October, 1938, on the eve of the Japanese conquest of Hankow, Agnes left to work for the Chinese Red Cross in the barren land south of the Yangtze where the Chinese Communist 4th Route Army guerrillas operated. Her loneliness there during her self-imposed exile from the Western world is revealed in her letters to me in London.

After telling of the misery of the people, of the drought which was destroying hopes of the harvest, of the plight of the thousands of homeless and destitute refugees, and after asking me to endeavor to persuade the China Campaign Committee in London to send some medical aid, she said:

> I only write the bare minimum of an article a month for *The Manchester Guardian* and doubt if any of them appears. The fierce heat makes writing a great difficulty and I am occupied as usual with writing endless letters, reports, and appeals for relief funds and medical supplies . . . . Writing also requires considerable spiritual stimulus and I

---

*Alfred A. Knopf, New York, 1943.

**Harper Bros., New York, 1949.

do not have that here. My life apart from this technical work simply does not exist. Before the radio batteries in the hospital radio were worn out, I used to get some help in this respect from musical programs. Do you know I once even listened to Beethoven's Ninth Symphony broadcast from London. I used to tune in on London almost every night for a snatch of music and for news of the international situation. But we have for long not been able to afford to listen to music, having to save the batteries for the bare news broadcasts. Even so, we now have no more batteries and can get none.

Obsessed by a passionate desire to share the experience and suffer with the people she was trying to help at any cost to herself, Agnes was realist enough to know that no intellectual can ever really understand the feelings of the "masses" or be identified with them. As she wrote in her book *China Fights Back: ***

Tonight as those hungry men sang, and then as they marched away to their beds of straw or cornstacks spread on mud floors, their singing had more meaning to me than ever before. Their voices were like a strong orchestra in the night. I, who have had food this day, realized that I can never know fully the meaning, the essence of the Chinese struggle for liberation, which lies embedded in the hearts of these workers and peasants. I am still an onlooker and my position is privileged. I will always have food though these men hunger. I will have clothing and a warm bed though they freeze. They will fight and many of them will die on frozen battlefields. I will be an onlooker. I watched them blend with the darkness of the street; they still sang. And I hungered for the spark of vision that would enable me to see into their minds and hearts and picture their convictions about the great struggle for which they give more than their lives.

Besides being cursed with as great a desire for martyrdom or self-flagellation as any Christian during the ages of faith, Agnes was a poet. She could bring alive in her writings a vision of grey skies of winter over frozen earth, of devastated countrysides and grey ancient walls of forgotten cities; of men cold and hungry, or thirsting in the fierce heat of summer, who went on marching and fighting, kept alive by faith and hope.

Those who came to know and love her in Hankow also appreciated her lively sense of humor, ironic wit, talent for mimicry, and for the composition of limericks on the spur of the moment, besides poems which were half beauty and half nonsense, and stories to make one laugh and cry.

For both of us, the last days of Hankow were an unforgettable experience—a brief interlude of magic days when we enjoyed a respite from loneliness, and the rare luxury of being popular and cherished. This "brief shining moment," not in an imaginary Camelot long ago, but in war ravaged China in 1938, was more poignant for Agnes than for me. She had spent the previous decade and was once again in "the emotional and human desert of China." I had lived in the purgatory of Communist Russia, but had there also known the wonder and lasting happiness of love which all the terrors of tyranny cannot drown. I had a son while Agnes had nothing to live for except her dreams of a better world. Nor had I as yet been isolated from my own kind, as later came to be the case in America when I was estranged from many men of good will and liberal sympathies such

---

*Vanguard Press, New York, 1938.

205

as those I had known in Hankow, on account of their lack of my knowledge and experience of Communist tyranny. Agnes, who had chosen to isolate herself from her own people like a Christian hermit in the Libyan desert in the days of the decline of the Roman Empire, had no such consolation. I remember her quoting, one evening in Hankow, some lines of poetry about sitting lonely by one's fireside while listening to distant applause.

Among the old and dusty files which I have preserved over the years I have found a long letter from Agnes Smedley written to me in London, in June, 1939, miraculously almost intact although written on the thinnest of thin paper from the desolate Japanese devastated area of China where she had joined the Chinese Communist Fourth Army after the fall of Hankow. I read it now with tears in my eyes for the tragedy of Agnes's life, and with nostalgia for those faraway "magic and illusory days" when we cemented a friendship never to be broken, despite our political antagonism after she rejoined the Communist fold in the United States a few years later:

Dearest Freda

The last days of Hankow still remain in my mind as rare, unusual days from the psychological and human viewpoint. I still think of Shaw's "Heartbreak House" when I recall them. As you remarked at the time, no person on earth is more charming than the American journalist abroad, particularly the cultured, serious-minded ones. But I wonder what it would be like were I to meet those same men on the streets of Chicago. Gone the Magic! The only ones who have maintained some contact with me were Evans and Frank. Evans wrote me a short note from Shanghai and sent it here by Belden who came here for a week. Then Evans remembered to send me a copy of one of his articles in *Amerasia*. And, as Frank Dorn returned to America, he wrote me a long, human letter from the ship. But then a ship is much like Hankow—an island on which one is thrown back upon oneself. I suppose he has forgotten me by this time. Once Durdin asked someone in Chungking where I am—so he remembers I am somewhere in the land of the living.

I sort of pine for the magic of Hankow. It was the bright spot in one decade of my life. There I met foreign men, some of them rotters, but most of them with the charm that belongs to many men of the western world. They themselves do not know how very different they are from the Chinese. Though I have never liked to be treated as bourgeois women are treated, still the foreign men from England, America, and perhaps France, have a deep and unconscious attitude of respect for women; a little feeling of protection for women; of helping a woman; and a kind of gentleness toward her. Often his kindness blended a bit with tenderness or a breath of romance. It is difficult to explain, because it is there as an atmosphere. In the Chinese man this is totally lacking in all respects. There is not even friendship and comradeship between man and woman in China. The foreign word "romance" has been taken into the Chinese language and means promiscuous sexual relations. And "love" means sexual intercourse in its general use in China. For a Chinese man to even touch a woman's arm or hand means something sexual and arouses shock.

206

So for ten years I lived in this desert, and because of this, found Hankow a magical place. Since then I have thought much of this. Shall I return to the western world, or shall I remain here? I fear I must remain in China. Hankow was a rare exception, and I believe all of us felt the same about it. I wish to retain it as a precious memory. I think often of the play in which many persons of different classes are on a foundering ship in mid-ocean. Class distinctions fall away as they face death together, drawn closer by humanity. But when the storm passes and the ship is saved, the old cold and cruel class distinctions returned. I believe that to be Hankow.

Love,

Agnes

Others continued to remember our Hankow days as a brief and shining moment in their lives. In whatever part of the world I meet them again, those who were my friends during that enchanted summer retain its memory as a precious and unique experience.

Agnes, no more than myself, could escape from the early influences which shaped her thought and determined her destiny. Just as I remained a "Victorian" or "Edwardian" liberal, in spite of having embraced the communist faith for a short while, so Agnes was always at heart an old American style radical, a Social Revolutionary, never a Communist believer in all power to the State.

She tried hard but was unable to accept the soul-destroying Communist discipline which required that one renounce one's integrity, and abandon freedom of the mind by subservience to the Communist Party bosses who, like Popes in the worst, most powerful days of the Catholic Church, demanded unquestioning obedience.

In June 1939 she wrote to me: "I retain the right to decide how my life shall be spent. Only backward, stupid people obey orders and recognize 'leaders' and consider that everyone except a Communist Party member is an idiot, or at best feeble minded. Even if such principles as I stand upon should cost me my life, still I will adhere to them."

In the same letter written to me in London Agnes asked me whether I knew of the campaign against her led by an American woman Communist, with whom she had refused to work in Shanghai three years before because this Comintern representative had censored her articles and acted as her "boss." "She was a Party member and I was not," Agnes wrote, "therefore, she set herself up as my 'leader' and I had no voice in the matter. The thing broke on the rocks of my democratic traditions. I told her she could have all the connections I had made in China for a decade; but she could not have me . . . . That woman later went to France and America . . . where she started a campaign against me and even tried to prevent the publication of my last book . . . ."

Expressing her defiance of the Communists who were attempting to control her, Agnes wrote me that she was not ashamed of her American heritage, and that "if this be bourgeois democracy, let them make the most of it." "I only know," she continued, "that to me there are basic life principles about the rights of man which this woman tried to violate."

In another letter after thanking me for the appreciative review of her book, *China Fights Back*, which I had written for *New Statesman*, she wrote:

But as you know, dear Freda, I am not at all the saint you mention.
There is time enough for that later on, and we can discuss it together,
for I suppose we both will go to the same place if the Christian idea is

correct. There will be time enough for halos and wings then, but just now this Army would die laughing if I tried to don them. In fact, I am quite unpopular with two or three of the leaders of this Army. However, I've been unpopular all my life and am used to it. Our Hankow days were the only ones in which I had a little popularity, and those days were magic, illusory days, or was it merely that I felt them to be so because I have lived for a decade in the emotional and human desert of China?

Today I am glad to recall that my friendship with Agnes was never broken, despite our political alienation after Agnes returned to America, and temporarily rejoined the Communist Party in spite of her refusal to submit to the Communist discipline which took no account of the liberal humanitarian aspirations and sacrifices of the best of men and women who enlisted under the Communist blood red banner in the false hope of establishing a better world.

Writing to me from California after her return to the States in 1941, she said she was avoiding reading anything I had written in order not to have to break with me. She trusted in our friendship so much more than in that of her 'comrades' and their totalitarian liberal fellow-travellers, that it was to me she appealed for help when ill and penniless on the West Coast, following her return to the land of her birth. She told me that Theodore H. White of *Life and Time* was endeavoring to persuade her to let him revise and publish under his name a piece she had written with a substantial payment to her. She indignantly refused, although desperately in need of money and in spite of his argument that this article would help her beloved Chinese Communist soldiers more under his by-line than hers.

I had no money myself and was at this time finding it very difficult to support my own family. But I remembered Julian Gumpertz, a German ex-Communist acquaintance of mine, who had become a successful investment counselor in New York and who had many years before secured Agnes' first foreign assignment as the China correspondent of the *Frankfurter Zeitung*. Julian, who was one of Hede Massing's former husbands, was an even older vintage anti-Communist ex-Communist than myself. He too believed that Agnes was not, and never could be, a real Communist, although she still clung to our lost illusions. Moreover, he was a Jew and generous. He immediately responded by sending Agnes a check for $500.

Agnes took the money but never saw him again. No doubt she feared to be defiled, or compromised, by contact with a "renegade" ex-Communist who had become a prosperous 'Capitalist' in the free Western world to which she belonged, but which she continued to reject or distrust.

In her heart and by reason of her intelligence and experience, Agnes knew that her best friends, and those who really shared her aspirations for the emancipation of mankind from the chains of poverty, fear and oppression were to be found in this, our Western world. But she was never able to sever the umbilical cord which bound her to the Communists who falsely claim to be the saviours of mankind even while betraying the original Socialist ideal.

During the war years in America, Agnes and I met occasionally after she came East and until she finally left for England where she died. On the occasion of our last meeting, at Randall Gould's apartment in New York in 1943, I was reluctantly forced to realize that she was no longer the exceptional woman whom I had described in *China at War* as "so lacking in vanity and self-consciousness, and so oblivious of her own material self-interest, as to give her an astonishing influence over all sorts and conditions of men and to win her the respect of almost all who came to know her." Her loss of the faith which had sustained her through all the trials and tribulations of her hard and lonely life were apparent in her behavior and conversation. She was still unmindful of her self-interest or material advantage. But she no longer lacked vanity or feminine weaknesses. It seemed rather as if she were now determined to prove that she was as feminine as the worst of our sex.

Unlike myself, Agnes had no Puritan prejudices or dislike of the smutty jokes and dirty stories which affronted my romantic conceptions of love. In the old days I had considered this merely an aberration, or the result of her desire to identify herself with the "masses" by not registering revulsion to vulgarity. Or because she had a false conception of what was required in order to be accepted as "one of the boys"—or girls—by newspapermen. But that evening in New York her conversation consisted of little else than not very funny, off-color jokes and stories about her love affairs. I was pained and vicariously shamed in listening to her. It seemed to me as indecent as unconvincing that Agnes, already in her fifties, should be boasting of her real or imagined conquests. It was as if she were trying to convince herself that her life had not been misspent in an abortive, self-sacrificing struggle for social justice, by demonstrating that she had also been a "success" as a woman.

This pathetic endeavor was out of character and revealed Agnes' profound and tragic political disillusionment. She was no longer the woman I had described as: "one of those rare people whose faith can breathe again even after betrayal, and who will continue to believe to the end of their lives, in spite of any and every disappointment, that oppression and want and misery *can* be banished from the face of the earth."

The Agnes whom I had known so well in Hankow, and had continued to love and esteem in spite of her return to the Communist fold, was already dead or dying of a broken heart when I last met her. When she died in 1950 in an English hospital in mysterious circumstances, there were rumors that the Communists had poisoned her lest she reveal too much. Some evidence was dug up by Don Surene, one of Senator Joe McCarthy's investigators, which suggested this, and it is possible since the Communists had always mistrusted her on account of her basically liberal attitude and her incorruptibility. But she had been in poor health for a long time and it seems to be more likely that she finally gave up the ghost during her last illness because she no longer desired to go on living.

Today in writing at such length about Agnes I am honoring the memory of an exceptional and gallant woman who was my friend, and whose life and death illustrate the tragedy of the pure in heart overwhelmed and destroyed by the complexities of our era during which it is even more difficult than in ages past to distinguish good from evil; progress from retrogression; wars of liberation from wars of conquest; endeavors to establish heaven on earth from attempts to annul all man's painful progress out of brutishness and return him to the jungle by way of totalitarian tyranny.

Chapter 21
CHINA EXPERTS THEN AND NOW

The case of Edgar Snow, who won fame and fortune by his writings extolling the Chinese Communists, was the obverse of the tragedy of Agnes Smedley's life. Unlike Agnes, who did her utmost to secure aid for the wounded of the Nationalist armies, which were bearing the heat and burden of the main battle against Japan, Edgar Snow was interested only in the Communist guerrilla fighters in the Northwest, whom he had made famous by his best seller *Red Star Over China,** and never even visited the Yangtze fronts.

In Hankow I was on friendly terms with him, believing him to be an honest reporter, because in the original English version of his book he was critical of Stalin's China policy which had led to the massacre of the Chinese Communists in 1927 in Shanghai and Canton. It was not until later that I was to learn how mistaken I had been when I read the 1939 revised edition of his book I discovered that he had permitted the Communist Party to expurgate the Trotskyist overtones. For instance this revised edition omits all Snow's references to the fact that the Communist International had become "virtually a bureau of the Russian Communist Party...(meaning that) the policies of the Chinese Communists, like Communists in every other country, have had to fall in line with, and usually subordinate themselves to, the strategic requirements of Soviet Russia under the dictatorship of Stalin...(and that the) Sino-Russian relationship (reflects) the transition (of the Comintern) into an instrument of the national policy of the Soviet Union."

Later on Ed Snow, according to what fitted Moscow's line at one time or another, was to represent the Chinese Communists either as "real Communists" (as during the period of the Stalin-Hitler and Russo-Japanese pacts) or as liberal agrarian reformers, going so far as to say in the Saturday Evening Post of June 10, 1944, that there has never been any Communism in China, even in Communist areas."**

In Hankow in 1938 I lent Snow the advance page proofs of Harold Isaac's *Tragedy Of The Chinese Revolution*, given to me by Secker and Warburg when I left London. I was never able to recover it. Snow said he had lost it. No doubt he feared that his reputation would be tarnished by Harold Isaac's detailed and documented exposure of just how wrong Snow was in the book which made him famous.

In March 1941, in my review of Snow's *The Battle for Asia**** in *The New York Times* Sunday Book Section, I was still giving him the benefit of every doubt when I wrote:

Edgar Snow is one of those Communist sympathizers who is essentially

---

*Random House, New York, 1937. Garden City Publishing Co. 1939.

**A detailed account of Edgar Snow's contradictions of himself according to the changes in the Party line appeared in an article of mine published in Isaac Don Levine's magazine "*Plain Talk*" in September 1947 under the title "Red Star Over Independence Square."

***Random House, New York, 1941.

a liberal and a humanitarian but who, no doubt because he has lived in the Far East throughout the past decade, is not yet disillusioned. Consequently he is still able to write of revolutionary movements with zest and youthful hopefulness and has no misgivings concerning Soviet Russia's role in the East or in the West. His clear and penetrating account of China's economic and social problems, and the unanswerable case he makes out for democratic reforms, mass mobilization and guerrilla warfare as the only way to win the war, is unclouded by the realization that today the revolutionary dynamic may serve the interests of German and Russian National Socialism instead of the cause of liberalism and reform. For him the desirability of the reforms which have emancipated the peasants in the areas administered by the Chinese Communists is sufficient proof of the genuineness of all Communist professions and of the need to give them more power in China.

In the above passage I may have explained how and why so many of America's leading "experts" on China in the State Department, the press, and the universities, were so tragically mistaken concerning the nature and aims of the Chinese Communist Party as to distort U.S. policy after the war. Long residence in China, or exclusive concentration on the Chinese scene, was not an advantage but a handicap in assessing the realities of the situation. The China experts generally ignored the complication introduced into the Chinese political situation by the fact that the Communists were under the orders of a foreign power. This was acknowledged momentarily by Edgar Snow when he wrote that the first allegiance of the Chinese Communists was to Moscow and that Comintern policy is determined by "its main if not its sole objective: the strengthening of the strategic security of the USSR."

Most of the Americans who came to champion the Chinese Communist cause had no inkling of what Snow knew but chose to ignore or deny when it suited his purpose.

It was all too easy in Hankow to be taken in by the Communist democratic masquerade. In 1938 the Chinese Communists actually were fighting the Japanese and obeying the orders of the Central Government. They had a delegation in Hankow, a newspaper and freedom to publish their views. Then, as again in 1946, when General Marshall came to China, they were represented by the personable, intelligent and persuasive Chou En-lai (Peking's Prime Minister today) who has probably during his remarkably durable political life, made more Western converts to Communism than any other man living.

It was not until after the Stalin-Hitler pact in 1939 and the Russo-Japanese pact in 1940 that the Chinese Communists came to direct their main "war effort" against the Kuomintang.

Even I, disillusioned as I was about Communism, found it easy to believe in the reality of the United Front in China in 1938. I knew from my experience in Moscow that Communists are liars-on-principle whenever it becomes necessary to delude "the masses" in order to achieve the "higher aims" of establishing the Socialist new order. I ought to have known that the Chinese Communists could be no different from any others anywhere and everywhere in the world. But I was temporarily deluded by the seemingly liberal attitude of the Communists who welcomed me in Hankow as warmly as the National Government.

I failed to realize that they could not afford to cold-shoulder me because I was too popular on account of my book *Japan's Feet Of Clay*, which had been widely sold in its Chinese translation and which the Japanese held accountable in large part for the

211

origin of the boycott movement in America. Thus, I imagined that the friendly attitude toward me of the Chinese Communists, as shown when Chou En-lai came to visit me at my lodgings and the Eighth Route Army gave a reception in my honor, proved that they were different from the British and other European Communists who would not have dared even to talk to me. Since they must have known that my Russian husband had been arrested and sent to a Soviet concentration camp, and that I was a fugitive with my Russian born son from Stalin's tyranny, I reasoned that the warm welcome given me by the Communists in China indicated that they really were a different breed.

Hence the passage in my 1939 book *China At War* often quoted against me in later years by the Chinese Communist lobby in America, which reads as follows:

> Moreover, the Chinese Communist Party long ago abandoned the dream of establishing its own dictatorship. Now that its social basis is amongst the peasants of the most backward provinces in China, and amongst the middle-class youth and the liberal reformers, its aim has genuinely become social and political reform along capitalist and democratic lines. The Chinese Communists have become radicals in the English nineteenth century meaning of the word.

In writing this passage I thought I was endeavoring to be fair and objective, and not let my hatred of Stalin's tyranny blind my judgment of the character and aims of the Chinese Communists who still seemed to believe in the values and aspirations which had led me to join the Communist Party. Or so it seemed to me at that time. Today, in attempting to be honest with myself and my readers, I realize that I was then still infected with the liberal disease of wishful thinking.

It takes time for anyone to cut their losses, ideological or material, by admitting that their fundamental beliefs or assumptions have been wrong. Despite my Russian experience I had not as yet reached the point of acknowledging that the basic Marxist theory, not simply the Russian practice of Communism, was false and cannot but lead to totalitarian tyranny everywhere in the world.

Also, my longing to belong to the liberal community which was my natural habitat, from which I had for so long been exiled in Moscow and into which I was welcomed in Hankow, helped to warp my judgment. In a word, maybe at the bottom of my heart, or in the recesses of my mind, I did not really believe everything I wrote in my 1939 book *China At War*, warmly praised by liberal reviewers for its "objectivity."

I ought to have known that the Chinese Communists were playing the same opportunist role in 1938 as in the 20's, when they collaborated for a while with the Chiang Kai-shek forces against the Western imperialists with the intention of flinging him away "like a squeezed lemon" once he had served their purpose.*

Chiang Kai-shek in 1927 had become the squeezer instead of the lemon. Stalin's scheme to deny the fruits of victory to the Chinese Nationalists by a proletarian

---

*On April 5, 1927 Stalin delivered a speech to the Communist Academy in Moscow in which he said:
"The peasant needs an old worn-out jade as long as she is necessary. He does not drive her away. So it is with us. When the Right is of no more use to us, we will drive it away. At present we need the Right. It has capable people who still direct the army and lead it against imperialists. Besides this, the people of the Right have relations with the generals of Chang Tso-lin and understand very well how to demoralize them and to induce them to pass over to the side of the revolution, bag and baggage without striking a blow. Also, they have connections with the rich merchants and can raise money from them. So they have to be utilized to the end, squeezed out like a lemon, and then flung away!"

revolution backfired. Having used the mass movement of peasants and workers organized for him by the Communists to sweep victoriously from Canton to Shanghai, Chiang turned on them. After using the Communists to frighten the Western powers and bring them to terms Chiang checked the revolutionary momentum which had swept the Kuomintang to victory. The Generalissimo, or Gimo as he came to be known, was one of the few or only national leaders who bested Stalin at his own game. Which explains why he was never forgiven by the Kremlin which eventually succeeded in so discrediting him in Western eyes that the Communists were able to take over China by our default.

This historical dissertation is necessary because of the bad image of Chiang widespread in liberal circles as the "betrayer" of the Chinese Revolution, and as a no good "fascist" dictator. The real betrayal was done by Moscow which wanted to eat its cake and have it too. Stalin sacrificed the Chinese Communists who, at that time included within their ranks some of the best of China's idealistic youth, by his policy of telling them to submit to the Kuomintang under Chiang's leadership while openly proclaiming Russia's intention of ditching him when the time was ripe.

Today the Kremlin displays far greater sagacity in its alliances with Nationalist movements in the "Third World," which give it the strength to challenge the United States. It may intend to liquidate Nasser in the unlikely event that the Communist Party should ever become a potent indigenous force in the Arab world. But it does not say so. Moscow today is content to acquire positions of strength from which to undermine the West by alliances with national movements, confident in the assumption that sooner or later the "Third World" will be compelled to become as national socialist as Soviet Russia.

In China yesterday, as in the "underdeveloped" or "Third World" today, the fundamental issue was whether to take the Moscow road of national "socialist" economic development under a dictatorship, forcing sacrifices by the "masses" to accumulate capital for industrial development and military strength; or to seek friendship, credits and technical aid from the Western powers which, after having voluntarily or unwillingly relinquished sovereignty and privilege in their colonies, are ready to collaborate on terms of equality for the mutual benefit of all.

The shadow of the past era of "colonial exploitation" still hangs over us, enabling the Communists to misrepresent America in Vietnam as an imperialist aggressor. Even more destructive in stymieing American policy is the legacy of misunderstanding and misinterpretation of Communist policy and aims everywhere in the world inherited from the Popular Front era.

It is hardly surprising that those who lacked the benefit of my experience in Russia were taken in by the Communists in China since even I was temporarily deluded in 1938. It is harder to understand why they persisted in this error long after the United Front was broken in China by the Stalin-Hitler pact of August 1939, and the 1940 Russo-Japanese pact, following which the Chinese Communists ceased fighting against the Japanese, and proclaimed that "with the liquidation of the Nazi anti-Soviet, anti-Comintern policy, the distinction between Fascist and Democratic countries has lost its validity."

"The center of the anti-Soviet movement," Mao Tse-Tung then proclaimed in an interview he gave to Edgar Snow in January 1940, "is no longer Nazi Germany, but among the so-called democratic countries."

After Germany attacked Russia in June 1941, the Chinese Communists as suddenly as every other Communist Party, reversed themselves again, eating their former words and proclaiming that the war in Europe was not the imperialist struggle which they had

213

formerly denounced, but one in which England and America were the children of light. Unfortunately, for the Chinese, the breakup of the Nazi-Soviet alliance was not followed by the reestablishment of a United Front against the national enemy. Japan had carefully avoided going to war against Russia, so that the Chinese Communists continued to direct their main "war effort" against the Chinese Nationalist Government.

The actual situation in China remained generally unknown to Americans. Interested mainly in the European theater of war, they were kept in ignorance by the "China Experts" and the newspaper correspondents who derived their opinion of the Chinese Communists from the Popular period Front when many books favorable to the Communists were published. Some were distributed in paperbacks in an Armed Service edition, notably Edgar Snow's 1944 book *People On Our Side*.* Correspondents in Chungking devoted themselves mainly to exposure and denunciation of the National Government whose shortcomings were all too plain to see. Few newspapermen in China had either opportunity or inclination or the language capacity to observe what the Chinese Communists were actually doing and saying. Moreover the Kuomintang Government, generally inept in propaganda, and also in too desperate straits to dare to offend the American President and the State Department, failed to do anything effective to challenge the distorted American view. Here again "face" was at stake. It was true that the Chinese National Government was riddled with corruption, inevitable anywhere when inflation and the rising cost of living makes it impossible for honest officials to provide for their families on their meager salaries. Above all there was the fact that "hope deferred maketh the heart sick." The Chinese Nationalist armies having fought so long without help from us against Japan, were gradually demoralized when it appeared that, despite Pearl Harbor, we were mainly interested in defeating Germany, and that American public opinion seemed to be favoring the Chinese Communists sitting out the war in Yenan.

Edgar Snow, Owen Lattimore, John K. Fairbank, John Stewart Service and other China experts who knew the score, for one reason or another had no interest in revealing it. The voices of such "premature anti-Communists" as myself were to be drowned out in the 40's by the powerful Chinese Communist lobby in America which included some basically decent deluded, ignorant liberals as well as true believers in the Communist faith.

The case of John Davies is harder to explain than that of others of my friends, associates and companions in Hankow thirty years ago.

He was one of the most intelligent and politically sophisticated Foreign Service officers I have ever met. I trusted him and "Pinkie" Dorn so completely in Hankow that I confided in them without reserve my utter disillusionment in Russia, although I was at this time still "putting a half-hitch on my tongue" as they say in Devonshire, with most people for Arcadi's sake.

In *China At War* I described him as:

> A connoisseur of living, who was also an acute and objective political observer and had spoken Chinese since boyhood. He had a mind of lightning quickness which seized upon one's meaning before one had half expressed it and his astringent mentality was as a cold shower to political romanticism. Agnes Smedley gently mocked him on account of his exquisite flowers, wines, food, and china. But she, like the rest of

*Random House, New York, 1944.

214

us, found an evening in his flat a welcome change from war and the Navy "Y".

Because he was in my confidence in Hankow where we had freely discussed the nature and aims of the Comintern, and since he not only spoke but also read Chinese, it seemed to me incredible that John Davies could have been so unaware in later years of the abundant evidence afforded by the Chinese Communists in their own writings, pronouncements and actions, of their subservience to Moscow as to state, in his reports to the State Department that:

"A coalition Chinese government in which the Communists find a satisfactory place . . . (would provide) our greatest assurance of a strong, united, independent, and friendly China."

Thus it came about that I denounced my former friend, John Davies, in *The China Story* published in 1951, and also testified against him in his presence at the State Department hearings which resulted in his expulsion from the Foreign Service. I did not then or ever, accuse him of being a Communist. I said only that it seemed to me that John Davies was far too intelligent and informed not to know that the Chinese Communists were real Communists, not liberals or democrats or "agrarian reformers." As I saw it, for the sake of his career during the Roosevelt era, when it was popular to be pink, and subsequently under Truman when Dean Acheson and General Marshall wanted to be assured that the Chinese Communists were democrats, he had played along for the sake of preferment, failing to testify to the truth as he must have known it.

Following John Davies' return to America in 1940 or 1941 he told me, after a party to which he had invited me in Washington and at which I had argued intemperately with his State Department friends that Soviet Russia was even worse than Nazi Germany, that I was becoming too dangerous to know. His "boss" at this time was John Carter Vincent whose "cloven hoof" I thought I had perceived on my first meeting with him in Washington:*

Man and his motives are mixed and hard to assess including my own.

Today I conceive it possible that John Davies' misleading advice to the State Department was due to his ignorance of everything outside the range of his China experience. Following his assignment to Moscow he became staunchly anti-Communist and won the trust of Loy Henderson. It could be that he discounted all he had learned from me in Hankow about Russia and Communism as a "view prejudiced by my personal experience." And that having come to despair of Chiang Kai-shek's government he really believed that the Communists were better. That it was not simply for hope of preferment, but out of conviction that he favored the Chinese Communists in his dispatches to the State Department.

Tillman Durdin, in 1946 in Chungking, was to give me what was probably the fundamental reason why so many correspondents fell under the Communist spell in China during the Second World War. "You must understand" he said, "how easy it was to believe in the Communists. It was so utterly hopeless in Free China! The graft, misery, the lack of will to fight anymore. Even I felt that it could not be worse, and must be better in Communist China. You, Freda," he impressed on me, "missed the depressing hopeless years in China following the fall of Hankow. You have got to get the feel of them in order to understand why so many Americans fell for the Communists."

---

*The role played by John Carter Vincent in the determination of America's China policy to the advantage of the Communists is fully dealt with in my 1951 book *The China Story*.

215

The case of General (then Colonel) Joseph Stillwell is easier to explain than that of John Davies. No man was ever more wrongly nicknamed than "Vinegar Joe." His asperity cloaked a soft heart and a sentimental outlook which caused him to react blindly to suffering and injustice. Honest, blunt and courageous, a fine commander in the field who won the loyalty of his men by sharing their hardships, he was politically so uninformed or innocent that he naturally fell under the spell of those who regarded the Communists as the Light of Asia. Despite his "anti-imperialist" and anti-British views Vinegar Joe closely resembled the best type of British Indian Army officers, who had respect and affection for the "sepoys" under their command, but damned the Indian Nationalist political leaders. Stillwell, while despising the Chinese Nationalists and hating Chiang Kai-shek, loved the Chinese "common man" and insisted that, properly trained, equipped and led Chinese soldiers were second to none. He was a prototype of the liberal, or left-wing, neo-imperialists a generation later who want to force "democracy" on peoples unready for it, whose need, above all, is an authoritative government able to curb the strong and protect the weak.

When in 1942 Stillwell was appointed American military representative and Chief of Staff to Generalissimo Chiang Kai-shek, the influences brought to bear on him in Hankow bore their fatal fruit. He had by then irrevocably made up his mind that the Communists were the "white hope" of China. All his subsequent actions and opinions stemmed from that illusion.

I have dwelt so long on my "Indian Summer" in China because it was in 1938 in Hankow that the foundation was laid for the misconceptions concerning the nature and aims of the Chinese Communist Party which were to distort American policy seven years later when, following the defeat of Japan, President Truman and General Marshall denied the Chinese National Government arms and ammunition, unless and until Chiang Kai-shek agreed to share power with the Communists in a "coalition government." This is a later story related in detail in my book *Last Chance In China* (1946) and *The China Story* (1951). The latter was to become a best seller long after it was too late to "save China," or the United States, from the near disastrous consequences of the myths spread by the Chinese Communist lobby in America. Hankow in 1938 leads directly to Korea and to our well nigh insoluble dilemma in Vietnam today.

Back in 1938 in "Hankow before the Fall," as I entitled a chapter in my book *China At War*, we were all bound together by shared dangers, shared sympathies, hopes and fears. We were on China's side and loved the Chinese people without failing to see their less amiable characteristics, or imagining that they were all heroes because China was fighting a war of national salvation. In spite of the callousness of most Chinese toward suffering—a characteristic of all peoples whose life is so hard that they perforce concentrate on personal or family survival—and in spite of the normal or abnormal degree of bureaucratic indifference and incompetence, many of us felt that there were no people on earth so lovable and worthy of respect as the Chinese. Their generosity, their intelligence, serenity in the most difficult, even desperate circumstances, and their unmatched courtesy, endeared them to all who did not prefer robots to human beings.

China, we feared, could not defeat Japan without changing the very nature of her people and losing the pacific and reasonable temper which made them so attractive.

In spite of these handicaps and the aid given to the Japanese by the U.S. and Britain, who continued to sell them war materials until 1941, China was to hold out against Japan for eight long years, with little help from the West. But the effort so exhausted and demoralized her people and the National Government that they had no strength left to resist the Communist onslaught which followed VJ Day. Consequently today the Chinese have been compelled to become, or at least to seem to be, the very opposite of what they once were. Under Communism's stern compulsions, the Chinese are no longer permitted to be Chinese. In 1938 I wrote that it was precisely one's appreciation of the rational, pacific, amiable, smiling, intelligent and individualistic Chinese, so incapable of strict discipline or efficient mass organization, that made one fear that they could never defeat the savage Simian efficiency of the Japanese. Today, under the totalitarian dictatorship of the Communists, the Chinese make the Japanese militarists of yesterday appear almost soft in comparison, as our soldiers learned a decade ago in Korea, and are now realizing with greater losses in Vietnam.

Despite her eventual defeat at the hands of America, Japan succeeded in her basic objective, expressed by the *Oriental Economist* in 1937, and quoted in my 1938 book *Japan's Gamble in China:*

> In any event before Japan could fall in the struggle, China's movement to mould herself into a modern state and her programme of economic reconstruction would both go crashing down, leaving little of such central government as there is at present.

The benefit of Japan's success in preventing Nationalist China from developing into a modern state was to be reaped by the Communists who succeeded in imposing their own stultifying dictatorship on China following Japan's defeat.

The end is not yet. The Japanese, despite or because of, their defeat have learned lessons as yet unlearned by their conquerors. Pulling themselves out of ruin largely by their bootstraps (meaning their capacity for hard work and dedication to their national interests) and also helped by General Douglas MacArthur's enlightened policy, the Japanese may yet come to achieve the aim of their militarists to create an Asian "co-prosperity sphere" strong enough to become the defenders, instead of the exploiters and oppressors of Southeast Asia. History works out in curious and unforeseen ways. Untrue as it was that Japan by attacking China and seeking to dominate the Far East by force of arms was resisting Communism, it may come to pass that she will in the future be the defender of the non-Communist world of Southeast Asia.

I made many Chinese friends in 1938, some of whom I have already briefly mentioned, and others whose names will recur in the Second Volumes of my Memoirs relating to the post-war period. Here in recalling the view from Hankow of the political situation in China, I remember best Hu Chiu-Yuan, renowned today in academic circles as a scholar, philosopher and editor of an independent journal in Free China and something of a thorn in the flesh of the National government which he supports but frankly criticizes, immune from reprisals by reason of his being a member of the Legislative Yuan. He had been a political officer of the famed Nineteenth Route Army which came to be called the Ironsides for its gallant defense of Shanghai against Japan in 1932. Subsequently he had taken part in the 1933 "Fukien Rebellion" against Chiang Kai-shek, and had spent a year and a half in Moscow "as a consolation prize" he said "for the way the Communists let us down." I shall not here attempt to explain or analyze all the ramifications of the relationship between Moscow and the dissident Chinese in the mid-thirties. The interesting thing was, as I recorded in *China at War*, that Hu Chiu-Yuan had "not been impressed" by the USSR. Nor had he much use for the Kuomintang and Chiang Kai-shek. He was "all for the oppressed bourgeoise" in China. The trouble, he said to me thirty years ago, was that the poor bourgeois never got a chance to be one, since if he made a success of an enterprise the Government or the

217

bankers took it over and they were one and the same. "Let us only manage to get a capitalist system in China," was his line, "and put an end to the system which enriches only officials and bankers and hinders our industrial development." Innoculated against Communism by his sojourn in Moscow, this is still his view. It is of course anathema to most latter day liberals or "progressives" who fail to see the close connection between big government and great wealth which strangles free private enterprise. Thirty years ago in Hankow his views were more perceptive and prescient than I then realized, although they impressed me sufficiently to record them.

After long talks with him and Dr. Y.C. Koo, retired Vice President of the World Bank, in Taiwan in 1967, I have come to appreciate the wisdom of Chinese scholars who view the course of human events realistically in the light of their people's thousands of years of experience.

Americans, "born yesterday" in terms of historical existence and experience, are all too easily misled by their own best aspirations which cause them to suppose that their own system of government is suitable for everyone else, however backward their economy and level of political development. They were unable to understand China's problems and needs on account of their general ignorance of history prior to 1776. Still today they believe in "democracy" as a surefire remedy for all inequalities even in countries where the basic need is for law and order and a central government which can curb the centrifugal forces and create a climate in which progress toward self-government becomes possible.

When I left Hankow on October 2 an atmosphere of impending doom hung over the city. The weather had turned cold and rainy and troops were no longer marching to the front but retreating Westwards. The summer during which we had dared to hope that the Wuhan cities would not fall was over. China would go on fighting her lone war for many weary years, but Hankow was about to be abandoned and occupied by "the dwarf robbers from the East" as the posters called the Japanese.

Chiang Kai-shek, together with most of the officials of the ministries of the National Government, had long since departed for Chungking proclaimed as China's temporary capital following the fall of Nanking. A general exodus was in progress from the three Wuhan cities in the Central Yangtze Valley generally known to foreigners as Hankow. One curious fact I then learnt was the value of postage stamps. Refugees departing on foot from the doomed city unable to carry with them heavier objects of value, were paying inordinately high prices for stamp collections.

My farewells were prolonged because night after night the plane expected from Hong Kong failed to arrive, and yet another last farewell party was arranged for me. The Press Corps staged a mock trial of Captain Evans Carlson and myself for abandoning the Hankow Last Ditchers. Arch Steele presided, impressive as the Judge with a wet towel for a wig. A chorus of jurymen sang songs composed by Agnes Smedley in which I was mockingly arraigned for breach of promise to various suitors supposedly seeking for my hand. Steele had told me before the show started that they all knew I could "dish it out" but could I also "take it?" It was a hilarious, sad and happy evening and the apogee of my "Indian Summer." For a moment I could almost believe it was true that, as one of the Americans said to me, I had been "the flame around which they had gathered."

Never had I known, or would know again, people I liked so well, felt so akin to and from whom it was so sad to part. When I finally left they all came to the airport to bid me Godspeed on the lecture tour I was headed for in America. Arch Steele advised me to call myself "Lady Utley" when I got to America, to ensure that I be heard and given my due.

As it turned out it was the Japanese who were to make a huge success for me in the States by refusing to let me land in Yokohama and making me newsworthy all over the world.

Chapter 22
I DISCOVER AMERICA

Waiting at the airfield until the Eurasia plane came in at midnight with only one small light to guide it down, I became acquainted with Walther Stennes, the German World War One hero who had become Captain of Chiang Kai-shek's Bodyguard after repudiating Hilter and escaping from the Third Reich. In later years in Germany after her defeat he became a close friend. That night, while pacing up and down the airfield, we found that we had a mutual friend in Captain Charles Boxer, the British Intelligence officer in Hong Kong with whom I had become acquainted on my arrival there thanks to Major Vinden in Singapore, a friend of my sister-in-law Emsie. A few days later in Hong Kong we all three got together for champagne cocktails and lunch and I almost missed the boat to Shanghai. In the intervening days I had lectured and given press interviews and was asked by Eugene Chen to carry with me an article for the Double Tenth issue of the *Shanghai Evening Post* to deliver to its editor, Randall Gould. This led to my being invited to a dinner in my honor by C. V. Starr, the prominent American tycoon in China who published this large circulation newspaper. At this dinner I first met Emily Hahn, who insisted that I come and stay with her in Shanghai. She was then the "concubine" of Sinmay, a Chinese poet of a formerly rich family in Peking which had lost everything in the Japanese takeover.

Sinmay had a wife and several children living close by "Micky" Hahn's house and Emily was supporting them all by her articles in the *New Yorker*. We became good friends and have remained so until now. I liked her from the beginning on account of her fearless frankness. Far from hiding her liaison with Sinmay she openly proclaimed it, and such was her personality, beauty, charm and talent that she was generally accepted in such diplomatic society as that of the British and American Ambassadors and Admirals. She was also politically intelligent and clear sighted. Despite her good standing in the American liberal literary establishment, she made fun of the ignorant and misleading reporting on China as when she wrote:

> The average American is full of hooey through no fault of his own. He thinks guerrillas are the only soldiers who do any fighting at all in China. He thinks the woods are full of them. Actually, the great burden of resistance has rested on the regular army. The situation is due to the peculiarity of most American newspapermen in China, who are nearly all of them inclined to be Leftist, out of a frustrated sense of guilt, a superior viewpoint of things as they are, and a tendency to follow the crowd—of newspapermen. Most newspapermen don't know any more about the Communists in China that you do. They hear rumors . . . but the chances of seeing what goes on among the Chinese Communists are even less than those of seeing the inside of Russia. If you live in Chungking, you can always interview Chou En-lai. That is what he is

there for. But if you think he is going to give you all the answers you are as innocent as an American newspaperman.*

After leaving Shanghai by ship for the United States I wrote to Charles Boxer in Hong Kong telling him that whoever else he failed to see on his next visit to Shanghai he must surely visit Emily Hahn generally known as Micky by her friends. A long distance introduction which was to lead to their marriage some years later, and to Sinmay's desolation. The whole story has been told by Miss Hahn herself who was to escape incarceration in a Japanese concentration camp in Hong Kong, after bearing a daughter out of wedlock to Charles Boxer after he had become a prisoner of the Japanese.

Back in 1938 in Shanghai she was exceedingly kind to me, arranging for her Chinese tailor and dressmaker to fit me out in suitable clothes for my forthcoming lecture tour in America with hurried fittings between talks and newspaper interviews.

In the evenings, or late at night I sat with her and Sinmay while they smoked opium and I drank Scotch, which is perhaps a worse indulgence than opium for those who can break the habit as Emily Hahn was able to do. One of the prominently successful and well known writers of our time, Emily Hahn has never lost her capacity and courage to "tell it as it is" without fear, prejudice or wishful thinking.

When I visit England we always meet although her husband, Charles Boxer, has become more and more of an anchorite immersing himself in their Berkshire retreat and writing learned monographs on such subjects as the Portuguese in Macao in the 17th century. His Professorship at London University on this subject frees him from the necessity of lecturing to students since none are interested in his subject.

Sir George Sansom who, following his retirement from the diplomatic service, was to have a less favorable sinecure at Columbia University in New York where he had to instruct a few graduate students, remarked that he and Boxer wanted to start a society for the abolition of students in universities.

After enjoying myself hugely in Shanghai and making many Chinese friends besides such Americans as Randall Gould, Emily Hahn and C. V. Starr, I took ship for the United States.

I became a small lion, or little V.I.P. in those days, thanks to the success of *Japan's Feet of Clay* and to the publicity gratuitously given me by the Japanese authorities. By refusing to let me land when the ship on which I crossed the Pacific from Shanghai docked in Yokohama and by placing an armed guard outside my cabin door when I was visited by George Sansom, Minister of the British Embassy, they made me newsworthy all over the world. In Honolulu I was interviewed by a crowd of reporters, and on my arrival in the Western Hemisphere I was inundated with invitations for lectures. I addressed audiences from coast to coast, sometimes speaking twice a day, and appearing before such distinguished groups as the Commonwealth Club in San Francisco, the Council on Foreign Relations in Chicago and Cleveland; and Foreign Policy Association audiences all over the place from Denver to New York and Baltimore.

Owen Lattimore, who secured the invitation for me to speak in Baltimore, asked Dr. and Mrs. Emmett Holt to put me up after the one night I stayed at his home. No doubt my increasingly uninhibited criticisms of Stalin's dictatorship had been reported to the friends of the Soviet Union in the United States so that, although willing to make use of me as an ardent propagandist for the Chinese cause against Japan, Lattimore had become wary of too close association with me.

China To Me, Doubleday, 1944.

I reserve to my next volume an account of my subsequent relations with Owen Lattimore whom I had first met in Moscow when he was not as yet subservient to Moscow's ideological dictation. I mention him here because in his *Ordeal By Slander** he falsely states that I spent three weeks at his home in Baltimore, whereas the fact is that on this first and subsequent visits to that city before my immigration to the United States, I stayed either with the Holts or with Frederick and Sylvia Nelson.

I have always accounted myself fortunate that I first entered the United States by its Western "back door." I reached New York only on the last lap of this strenuous speaking tour so that my first impressions of America were of a more open and socially democratic society than any other in the world at any time in history. I also found greater awareness of the importance of the fate of the Far East (actually Far West from America's point of view) than in Europe, or on the Eastern Seaboard which looks toward, or back on, Europe.

Having learned that the Soviet Union was a hierarchical state dominated by a Communist aristocracy, I now discovered that America came close to my vision of the good society.

In Seattle where I stayed with a Doctor's family so well to do that they had two automobiles and two or three bathrooms I was astonished to find there was no servant, and that the Doctor himself helped with the washing up.

Starting in British Columbia at Victoria and Vancouver, taking in Spokane and Tacoma and spending several days in Seattle, I was next rushed down to San Francisco and Los Angeles and thence by way of Albuquerque to Denver, sometimes lecturing twice a day and giving many newspaper interviews.

In San Francisco I was enchanted by the charm of the city and the breathtaking bridges spanning the Golden Gate and the route to the Berkeley area and by the eager intelligent and beautiful young people who looked after me and wanted to help China. Everywhere I was delighted by the unique American atmosphere of social equality, freedom from class prejudices, friendliness and informality.

In Chicago I spoke to a huge audience for the Council on Foreign Relations, then run by Clifford Utley who had phoned me to Seattle on hearing of my arrival in the States.

In Chicago during my hectic lecture tour I spent some happy hours with Bertrand and Peter Russell. He was then happily ensconced at the University which he found "so far as philosophy is concerned about the best I have ever come across."** We agreed in approving Chamberlain's Munich policy which was being forcibly denounced by the American 'liberal' press despite the fact that the United States showed no disposition to do anything to 'stop Hitler.' As Bertie then wrote:

> Here in America nine people out of ten think we ought to have fought
> but America ought to have remained neutral—an opinion which annoys
> me.***

As Bertie then also remarked it was "odd that in England the very people who in 1919 had protested against the unjusted frontiers of Czechoslovakia (incorporating the Sudentenland Germans) were the most anxious in 1938 to defend them."

I also remember remarking in Chicago my astonishment at the ease of telephonic

---

*Little Brown & Co., Boston.

**The Autobiography of Bertrand Russell. Volume 2 (1914-1944). Allen & Unwin. London. Page 246, In a letter to Gilbert Murray.

***ibid. page 225.

communication over the vast territory of the U.S. as contrasted with the rotten postal system, and Bertie saying with a chuckle that this was because America had to demonstrate the superiority of private enterprise over "socialism" by having an appallingly bad postal service.

By the time I got on the train from Chicago to Washington and Baltimore I felt that I was coming near to the end of my journey. Chicago in the Midwest seemed East to me, so huge were the spaces I had already traversed. Most eastern seaboard Americans had less conception of the vast size of their country than I had acquired. The Committee in New York which had arranged my speaking tour was so oblivious of the vast extent of America's Western territories that it had arranged for me to lecture one day in Spokane and be in Oakland the next in days when air travel was yet in its childhood.

I even had tea with Mrs. Roosevelt at the White House which proved a disappointing experience. I had met her daughter Anna Boettinger in Seattle where after hearing me speak at a luncheon she invited me to her house for tea together with Mrs. Norman Littell and said I simply must meet her mother and tell her what I had told them. So when I arrived at the White House for my appointment with the "First Lady" I expected to interest her in the terrible plight of the Chinese wounded soldiers and enlist her great influence in getting help for the Chinese Red Cross. But I found the liberal humanitarian Eleanor Roosevelt more interested in some folk songs of the Southwest which a man called Valiant was telling her about. And her reference in her column the next day to my visit and my endeavor to awaken her interest in Chinese relief was so wishy washy as to be useless. Her readers were told nothing at all about the neglected wounded. Instead she uttered some platitudes to the effect that, of course Americans help those in need throughout the world and have "a sentimental interest in China." A few weeks later she was reported to have publicly purchased a lot of Japanese Kimonos. And I well remember how shocked and angry I had felt at her reply to my query "Why are most Americans only worked up about the Nazi crimes and atrocities and care little about the horrible things the Japanese do to the Chinese?"

"Well you know," said Eleanor Roosevelt with her toothy smile and vicar's wife superior mein, "we never expected those oriental people to be civilized."

Years later, visiting Berlin during the 1948 Russian blockade, my original low opinion of Mrs. Roosevelt was reinforced. While touring German cities devastated by our bombing she had remarked that the Germans could not really be in dire straits because they looked so clean and were growing flowers in the ruins of their homes. Instead of appreciating the sterling qualities of the German people who under almost any circumstances keep up appearances, Mrs. Roosevelt reserved her compassion for the black or white derelicts who had lost their self respect.

It was all very exciting, absorbing, exhausting and stimulating. I was exhilarated by the feeling that I was promoting a good cause while enjoying myself hugely, relishing my success as a speaker and enjoying my semi-VIP status.

As I now realize but did not then understand, my success was in large part due not so much to my eloquence or to the convictions I expressed but because my line and that of the Comintern were for the moment running parallel.

As Jane had once expressed it: Draw a line from any one point to another and sooner or later the Communist Party line will cross it.

Because Moscow at this time feared Japan and was therefore in uneasy alliance with Nationalist China, my campaign to stop war supplies to Japan met with the approval of the fellow travellers and camp followers in America who already exerted a great influence on the climate of American public opinion by way of the news media, the universities and the lecture forums.

Before sailing for England from New York on the Queen Mary I lectured in Cleveland and Boston and was invited by the Feakins Lecture Agency to return for a commercial tour early in the New Year.

One big chance I then missed was to speak at New York Town Hall because I was determined to get home to Jon for Christmas. Later on in America, after my anti-Communist views had become known, the invitation was not repeated. On the Queen Mary travelling back to England from New York in December 1938, I endeavored to secure an interview with Anthony Eden in his deluxe accommodation in the futile hope that I might persuade him that China's struggle for national existence against Japanese aggression was as important as his exclusive preoccupation with the German Nazi menace. He must have known who I was in view of the success of my books in England. But either because I was travelling Second Class or because he had no more interest in the aspirations of Asiatics than of Arabs twenty years later, he refused to receive me.

Vincent Shean, on the contrary, also travelling de luxe, invited me up to the First Class bar lounge and restaurant. I then first met his wife, daughter of the famous English actor, Forbes-Robinson. I was to remain friends with this intelligent attractive woman after she and Vincent Shean separated.

On my return to England, thanks to my dispatches published in the *New Chronicle*, as well as the reputation I had established by *Japan's Feet of Clay* and *Japan's Gamble in China* I was afforded opporties to speak to such prestige organizations at The Royal Central Asian Society.

Photographs I had taken in China of the refugees and the wounded or killed victims of Japan's war machine were used by the London Lord Mayor's Fund to raise money for Chinese relief. I was as before active on the China Campaign Committee presided over by Victor Gollancz and tangled with him only on the question of identifying support for the Spanish Republican Government with support to China.

China At War published in June 1939 in England was received with less enthusiasm, no doubt because of the credit it gave to Chiang Kai-shek's fighting forces on the Yangtze front, at a time when Edgar Snow and other popular "experts" on China presented the Chinese Communists as the heroes of the national resistance of China against Japan. But it won me a considerable measure of respect for its objectivity, and it might have become a success had not the gathering storm of World War II riveted attention on Europe.*

---

*Faber and Faber, London. The American edition published by the John Day Co. came out later in the year after the outbreak of the Second World War. The delay in American publication was due to my having delivered the ms. to the Brandt Literary Agency which sat on it several months.

Chapter 23
AWAY TO THE NEW WORLD

By 1939 I was finding it more and more difficult to hold either my tongue or my pen concerning the Soviet Union and Communism. In March of that year I wrote an article suggesting the likelihood of a Russo-German alliance which I tried to get published anonymously in the *Spectator*. The editor rejected it on the ground that the idea was fantastic. A month or so before in the U.S., at a Foreign Policy Association dinner in Baltimore at which I sat next to Loy Henderson, I had found he had the same idea. Both of us thought it a distinct possibility, suggested by the topsy-turvy, Alice-through-the-looking-glass evidence afforded by the latest demonstration trials in Moscow in which Britain had been restored to the position of villain-in-chief which she had occupied before Hitler came to power. Not only did the terms of the indictment of the latest purge victims suggest a reorientation in Soviet foreign policy. A Trotsky-like statement made by Stalin before the trial to the effect that the final victory of Socialism is possible only on an international scale, also foreshadowed an attempt to make friends with Nazi Germany in order to encourage her to launch a Second World War.

It was on that evening in Baltimore that I began an enduring friendship with Loy Henderson, the wise and courageous State Department official who later got "kicked upstairs" by the Roosevelt Administration on account of his warnings not to trust "Uncle Joe."

That same spring of 1939, Krivitsky, in a series of articles published in *The Saturday Evening Post* gave proof that Stalin had for years been trying, by secret negotiations in Berlin, to get an alliance with Hitler, and that all his overtures to the Democracies and his action in Spain were but moves toward this end. A little later Demarie Bess, who at that time was one of the few foreign correspondents sending in objective reports uncolored by prejudice or wishful thinking, suggested in *The Saturday Evening Post* a coming Russo-German pact. But such was the influence and power in those days of befogged and bemused "Friends of the Soviet Union" that such warnings went unheeded.

When the Stalin-Hitler pact came, I crossed my Rubicon, destroying by my writings all hope of returning to Russia and seeing my husband again. A letter I wrote, published in the *New Statesman* of September 30, 1939, seems worth quoting from in view of its correct analysis of Communist strategy:

> Mr. Wellock, in his courageous letter, shows the similarity between the German and Russian systems which makes it possible for them to unite in one mighty destructive movement for the overthrow of the "bourgeois democracies." Whilst the Nazis make their frontal armed assault upon the "plutocracies" and their satellites, the Red Army can enter the semi-feudal states of Eastern Europe as the *soi-disant* deliverer of the oppressed peasants.
>
> If by "extreme Left" Mr. Wellock means the Communists and their fellow travellers, I think he is mistaken in assuming that they may be

expected to withdraw their support of the war. The policy of the Comintern is to urge the working class to continue fighting in spite of the fact that Berlin and Moscow are now acting in concert. The Communist idea is that the war will lead to the aggrandisement of the U.S.S.R. and the weakening of everyone else. Stalin's primary motive in making his pact with Hitler was his fear of Germany and ourselves. Peace now between Germany, France and England would probably mean that Germany would turn on Russia and take from her not only the territories she is now occupying but much besides. Hence the fierce abuse of pacifists and all of those who show an awareness of the true situation.

I have long since learnt by painful experience that it pays to be wrong, and that nothing is less conducive to success than to see the shape of things to come when one's vision contradicts popular myths, prejudices, or hopes. Yet I take pride in having realized back in 1939 that Communist policy was based on the correct assumption that the Second World War would lead to the "aggrandisement of the U.S.S.R. and the weakening of everyone else," and that this was the reason why Stalin did everything possible to bring it about and was so abusive of pacifists.

Saying "I told you so" is not only an unpopular pastime, but also a sterile occupation. I had much rather have seen myself proved wrong than have witnessed in the years to follow the fulfillment of my prophecies.

Cassandra, no doubt, would have been much happier if the huge wooden horse against which she warned the Trojans had not been full of Greek warriors who destroyed her city. I, likewise, do not belong to the company of those who would rather be either dead or Red than wrong. Some who, like myself, opposed America's entry into the Second World War as the ally of Soviet Russia, take a macabre satisfaction at the near fatal consequences to the West of having paid no heed to our warnings. I am only too happy today to admit that the results of the Second World War have not proved as disastrous as I anticipated. True it led to the aggrandisement of the U.S.S.R., the subjection of Eastern Europe and China to totalitarian Communist tyranny, and the creation of a lasting Communist menace to the free world. But it did not result in establishing a monolithic Communist Empire threatening all freedom everywhere, because the United States becoming aware at the eleventh hour of the menace of the Communist power it had so greatly strengthened, saved Western Europe although abandoning China.

It was the belief that only the Nazis were vile, and that Russia, because it was "Socialist," must be basically good, which led to such folly as our unconditional alliance with Stalin and Roosevelt's demand for the unconditional surrender of our enemies. This belief among the Western Socialist or liberal intelligentsia survived even the Stalin-Hitler pact, Russia's jackal role in the destruction of Poland and her brutal aggression against her little, but most courageous, neighbor Finland. As soon as Germany attacked Russia and Stalin perforce became the "ally" of the West, all Communist crimes against humanity were forgiven, or forgotten, or excused. And even today, despite the abundant evidence that the Communist powers constitute a greater menace to Western Civilization than Nazi Germany ever was or could have been, the belief persists that an accommodation with the Kremlin is possible and desirable. Thus many of the same people who, yesterday, castigated and smeared Neville Chamberlain as an appeaser are today demanding peace in our time at almost any price with the Communist totalitarian empires. It cannot be only because of their fear of atomic war, since they took the same line before Russia had the

226

bomb. Their basic motivation, it seems to me, is their lingering faith that whereas Nazi Germany was just plain wicked, Communist Russia and China being "socialist" would be good if only we freed them from fear of us, and helped them by gifts and credits to keep their creaky inefficient socialist economic and social systems going.

When Voltaire's character, Candide, discovered that the world did not behave as it should have done according to his teacher Dr. Panglos—prototype of the liberal eggheads of our time—he ascribed his unhappy experiences to his own shortcomings, saying, "There must be something wrong with me!" So also Americans today are continually being told, and have almost come to believe, that if only they were virtuous, peace-loving and self-sacrificing, ready to help everybody in the world to a better life by giving away their substance, while also perfecting their own society, the Communist menace would fade away.

Meanwhile the Communists, having long since learned that they got nowhere by adhering to their professed principles but could advance from strength to strength through a Machiavellian policy of guile and force and fraud, run rings around the bewildered Western democracies.

From world revolution, to champion of democracy against fascism, to collaboration with Nazi Germany, to champion of democracy again after Hitler attacked; to imperialist expansion at the War's end with Western help or acquiescence, to rattling atomic bombs to terrify the world into submission, to pretending to desire peaceful co-existence with us in order to rally their forces for a new attack after we shall once again have given them a blood transfusion of economic aid. This is the Soviet record which unfortunately proves that the American belief that good conquers evil by example is illusion.

The original Communist line under Lenin and Trotsky was honest and sincere and a complete failure. Under Lenin's leadership the international ideal was never lost sight of, and Russia's national interest was subordinated to the final aim of World revolution to establish a new Socialist order everywhere. The policy failed completely, since neither in Germany nor elsewhere did the promised proletarian revolution make headway. Just as today the international ideal of the brotherhood of man which dominates American liberal thinking is getting us nowhere.

Lenin dead and Trotsky exiled, Stalin was free to pursue his own eminently successful, dishonest, hypocritical, cowardly and brutal policy. Russia's national interest, or more correctly the interest of her Bolshevik aristocracy, became the objective of Soviet policy. The safety of the Kremlin tyrants was secured by embroiling the 'capitalist world' in war; by the use of 'Popular Front' movements to impel England and France to fight Germany, instead of continuing the intelligent Neville Chamberlain policy of letting Germany go East and destroy Soviet Russia, or herself, or weaken both of them in a contest of the two totalitarian giants.

* * *

I did not leave England until three months after the outbreak of War in September 1939, although during my first visit to the United States in late 1938 from China, I had learned that America was my country, because it came nearer to my ideal of the just and free society with equal opportunity for all than any other in the world.

I was still tied to the land of my birth in many ways, and had any job opportunities been available I might have hesitated to uproot Mother together with Jon who, in the preceding three years had put down some first tender roots in England.

But despite the success of *Japan's Feet of Clay*, I found myself unable any longer to earn a living by my writings in an England which, now more than ever, was inclined to appease Japan, and was involved in a war against Germany which I feared would result in making the world safe for Stalin.

My good friend Kingsley Martin, editor of the *New Statesman and Nation*, who had formerly published many of my articles, and in his own words, "accepted to a large extent" my views on Russia for the previous three years, now rejected my contributions because he thought that getting on good terms with Russia should be a primary objective of British policy. The letter he wrote to me on November 2, 1939, reproduced here, is of interest as showing the curious workings of the English liberal mind which finds no difficulty in joining hands with conservatives of the Winston Churchill type, to take the aid of the Devil himself to save England.

> The New Statesman and Nation
> 10 Great Turnstile
> London, W.C. 1
> 2nd November, 1939

Dear Freda,

I wish I knew how to write so that you would understand me. The trouble is not at all what you say—I have printed plenty of strong anti-Stalin letters and I have taken an anti-Stalin and not pro-Stalin line in the paper during the last months. I have accepted your view of Russia to a large extent for the last three years. See my views of Gene Lyons and our articles on the purges. The point is that if the war is to go on, and I see no way now of stopping it, no stone should be left unturned to try and get on good terms with Russia. This may prove an impossible project, but we must do what we can about it, otherwise we may find ourselves fighting both Germany and Russia. I approved very much of your first letter in which you urged this danger and suggested that we ought not to go on with the war; the implications of your last letter seemed to me the opposite. In other words, the argument you are trying to put forward is not helped by such a vehement anti-Stalin line and the general impression is not that of a calm observer of the situation but of somebody in a "state of mind." This was the only point of criticism made.

> Yours sincerely,
> Kingsley Martin

In another letter he warned me that "the important position I had built for myself as an authority on the Far East" was being harmed by my "rushing into print" with letters to the press about Soviet Russia giving an impression "of a vehement controversialist which would do harm to your serious work."

How true, how wise and no doubt well meant was Kingsley Martin's advice in this letter which assured me that he would give special attention to any articles I should send from America if only they were not about the USSR. How wrong on the other hand was his view that "Stalin's position is not yet clear nor as fully bound up with that of Hilter as you have suggested."

A quarter of a century later, meeting Kingsley Martin in the Delegates Lounge at the United Nations in New York, we first got together in agreeing on how silly Bertrand Russell had become. But after David Exley, the New Zealander in charge of the UN Press Office, invited us to sit down for a drink, Kingsley and I got involved in a heated argument concerning the Berlin Wall and Western policy. In response to my remark that Khrushchev would not be in a position to threaten the West had it not been for the Roosevelt-Churchill demand for the unconditional surrender of Germany, the by now white haired doyen of the British liberal press, exclaimed: "One of the good things which came out of the war was the partition of Germany."

In general I had found Western conservatives more compassionate, principled and politically intelligent than most self-styled liberals in their attitude toward the defeated enemy. It was nevertheless a shock to find my former friend so imbued with racial, or British, national prejudices that he favored the partition of Germany to the advantage of Soviet Russia. Like many other Englishmen of various political persuasions he was happy to see Russia ruling East Germany as a colony, and had no inclination to do anything to help liberate Germans, or for that matter Eastern Europe as a whole, from Communist totalitarian rule.

Recalling a disillusioning experience I had with Kingsley Martin in England I ought not to have been surprised. Invited to America for a two months lecture tour he generously offered me the use of his large and beautifully furnished duplex apartment in Bloomsbury during his absence. My German-Jewish friend "Hans,"* who figures prominently in later chapters of this book, was at this time homeless and without funds in London. So I asked Kingsley if I might let him occupy the top floor. At first he had no objection but, at the last moment before sailing, he telephoned to say he had been hearing things about Hans and, not wishing to get mixed up in any trouble with the British authorities over German refugees, he must refuse permission. I argued with him that anything he had heard against Hans was undoubtedly the result of the smear campaign against him by the Communist Party which is always intent on destroying anyone who has left it. But Kingsley refused to heed my plea that he should give aid at no cost to himself to a Jew without money who was a victim of both Nazi and Communist persecution. So Hans went to live with my mother in Jessel House while Emsie and I occupied Kingsley Martin's huge place, an outcome which in retrospect was a blessing since Hans became extremely fond of my mother and later in America was to give her love and care and sympathy to the end of her days.

This incident illustrates the basic selfishness, desire for security, or aversion to any unpleasantness, of some of the most prominent liberals of our era who express the finest and most altruistic sentiments in their writings.

That last year in England I helped Hans, whose English was still poor, write his first book, *Germany World Empire or World Revolution.*** This book together with *The Myth of the Total State,**** which he dedicated to "Emmie Utley, my adopted mother and my friend" established him as an author of repute but made little money. He emigrated ahead of us to America after being refused an extension of his English visa; thanks in all probability to the Communists who were adept at slandering their enemies in devious ways. The position of ex-Communist anti-Communists was difficult even for a British subject such as myself.

Sir George Sansom tried to get me a job at the Foreign Office, or at the Royal Institute of International Affairs at Chatham House, but found that my former membership in the Communist Party stood in the way. I was caught between two

---

*His actual name is Guenter Reimann. He adopted a pseudonym while working in the underground under the Nazis. Today he is the editor and publisher in New York of *International Financial Reports.*

**Secker and Warburg, London, 1938.

***Morrow, New York, 1941.

fires: my anti-Communist views were making it increasingly difficult for me to earn a living by my writings while my former membership in the Communist Party precluded Government employment. *Japan's Feet of Clay* had been a best seller and established me as an author of repute, but those who had praised this book most highly in England and America were for the most part the same "liberals" who were friendly to the Soviet Union.

At the beginning of the War I placed Jon in safety with a family in Oxford and sent Mother to Devonshire, staying on myself in the small and pleasant cottage I rented at New End Square in Hampstead for only £2 a week. Several friends came there to stay during the first days when bombs were expected to fall and no one wanted to be alone. Eric Mosbacher,* being the rare type of liberal who practices what he preaches, having opposed Chamberlain's appeasement policy at Munich, had joined the Army Reserve before war came and was immediately called up. His wife Gwenda David, (today as for many years past English agent for Viking Press), asked if she could come over with their baby. I was glad to have her with me since I enjoyed her company, unlike that of Franz Borkenau, an Austrian exile whose books were as excellent as he himself was obnoxious. He was the greatest egotist I ever knew and our friendship ended as far as I was concerned during those first days of the war when after imposing on my hospitality, he refused to do his fair share of household chores, in particular washing up the dishes. Although Jewish, Borkenau was what is supposed to be a typical Prussian.

Years later in America Franz Borkenau once again came to me for help, which I grudgingly rendered him on account of his anti-Communist writings. But by the mid 40's I had grown harder or less comradely, so that I refused him hospitality, and let him exploit me only to the extent of long distance calls at my expense. Borkenau incurred the disfavor even of kind Mary Green of *The New Leader* who, after she had secured hospitality for him in New York had him complaining that the free accommodation provided for him was not good enough. After the war Borkenau became a professor at the University of Marbourg in Germany where he died in the odor of anti-Communist sanctity.

My friendship with Eric Mosbacher and Gwenda David was never broken and we are still friends today.

Although I might not have emigrated to America at the end of 1939, had England had any use for me, I was impelled by my fear that the outcome of the Second World War would be disastrous to the Old World. I was determined to save my son, happily rescued from Russia, by taking him to America lest Europe too become subject to the Communists.

My decision to leave the Old World for the New was the best I ever made. Years before I had failed, by not really trying, to stop Arcadi coming to Moscow from China in 1930 when I already really knew, but had not yet admitted to myself, that once in Russia he would never again be allowed to leave. In 1939 by taking our son to the United States when he was only five years old, I enabled him to become an American, not simply by eventual citizenship, but in heart and mind and outlook. I myself am still rootless in the sense of not really belonging anywhere and being still at heart an internationalist or citizen of the world. There are times when the pull of my origins causes me to regret leaving the Old World. But my son is as American as those born here, and perhaps more like the original Americans who came to the New World from Europe and made the United States great and strong and free, because like them, he knows through my

---

*Eric Mosbacher's sensitive and exemplary translations of Ignatio Silone's works helped make them known all over the world.

experience, better than the native born what it means *not* to enjoy the blessings of liberty.

On leaving England I arranged for Sir George and Katherine Sansom to take over the rent of my cottage at 5 New End Square in Hampstead with the use of my furniture. They promised to store it and my books, manuscripts and other papers in their country house when they left, and to bring some of my possessions to the United States if and when they too came to America. Unfortunately, when they left England, Katherine Sansom put all my stuff in storage together with their own at the Army and Navy Stores in London where it was destroyed in the bombing of Britain. Thus, I lost many precious books and papers besides our few pieces of furniture. Some few of my books had been shipped to America when I left England, and fortunately mother had carried with her an accumulation of letters which are now helping me to write this book. But much was lost, including old articles I had written as well as most of the books I still possessed after losing the greater part of my library in Russia.

Without Katherine's help I should never have managed to get our things packed in time or been able to cope with all the details attendent on our departure to the New World. It was she who secured the local butcher's small delivery van to take us to the station and gaily rode down with us in this inelegant conveyance in order to help me get my family and our luggage on to the boat train. And I left her to clear up all the mess we left behind.

No one understood my problem with my mother so well as Katherine Sansom or was more sympathetic and helpful. Like my mother, she had natural and lasting beauty, dressed elegantly without spending much money on clothes, and had urged me ever since I first met her in Japan to pay more attention to my appearance. But Katherine also realized how very difficult it was for me to do so while providing the necessities of life for my mother as well as for my son, and also attending during my busy life to the requirements of my mother's "toilette."

For many years I had paid storage fees for very old stuff stowed away when we left our Surrey home in 1913, so before leaving England Katherine spent a lot of time going through all the ancient material my mother had preserved for decades. This included, Katherine told me, old bills and bank records, as well as letters which had passed between my parents in their youth and early married life. Unfortunately, these precious letters, which I would give much to read today, and which Katherine separated from the worthless stuff, were destroyed in the bombing of London.

Katherine Sansom remembered their general content and years later in America, endeavored to assuage my feeling of guilt concerning my mother, following her death in November 1945, by telling me what a revelation these letters were concerning my mother's all too possessive love which had evidently been as great a problem to my father as to my brother. From Katherine I learned that my beautiful, charming, and courageous mother, who had been so passionately and wholeheartedly devoted to my father had also been so jealous that she had been instrumental in cutting him off from the company of some of his best friends. She had wanted him to belong exclusively to her, as later on she wanted their son, my brother, to give her a closer allegiance than to any of the women he loved.

Five years later, when my mother died in Belleview Hospital in New York while I lay on my back in a Shanghai hospital with my right arm fractured at the shoulder and strapped to my chest, it was Katherine Sansom whose letters gave me comfort. Understanding better than anyone else what I should feel when mother died, she wrote:

231

My dear, I well know your tender heart and how upset you feel. What I should like to say is this, that in my opinion you have been a perfect daughter—have no kind of feeling otherwise. Your mother was a born charmer . . . . I liked her very much, you know . . . and what I think is that, apart from her devotion to your father, which I know was very real, and she must have been wonderful in his illness, the natural thing would have been for you and her to drift apart, as for instance I have had to with my children. It isn't natural to have to live two generations together. She did her stuff for you as a schoolgirl, you know, and I think she did much for you then. After that, you were the strong one, the clever one, and if life had been kinder to you, you and she would have met occasionally. That is what nature dictates. So don't have any regrets about anything at all.

Katherine Sansom who, like myself, was of Yorkshire origin, was one of the best of the many good friends I have had among all sorts and conditions of people of varying opinions in many parts of the world. Finding and reading her old letters again I record with deep regret that we became estranged a decade later and that the fault was mainly mine.

Both Sir George and Katherine Sansom were tolerant of my views on the War, even while disagreeing with me, and when he was assigned to the British Embassy in Washington we continued to be intimate friends. George defended me against my detractors when, in October 1941, the *Readers Digest* published an article of mine (orginally entitled *God Save England From Her Friends* as published in Alfred Bingham's and Selden Rodman's *Common Sense*) in which I advocated a negotiated peace with the U.S. supporting England, instead of urging her to continue fighting a war which only Hitler or Stalin could win. Without agreeing with me George Sansom, as recorded in one of W. H. Chamberlin's books, had insisted that I had the right to express my controversial opinions.

In the mid 40's I was a frequent guest at the Sansom's apartment in Dupont Mansions on 20th Street, N.W. in Washington, which I myself came to occupy in 1946 after Sir George Sansom managed to retire from the Diplomatic Service and devote himself to his historical studies.

Yet, despite George and Katherine Sansom's tolerance of my views, and our long-standing friendship, after he became a professor at Columbia University, I was most intolerant of what seemed to me at the time to be his, or Katherine's compromising or appeasing attitude toward the powerful Chinese Communist lobby in America. Since George had been of much the same opinion as myself concerning the pernicious influence of Owen Lattimore, Edgar Snow, John K. Fairbank, the Institute of Pacific Relations, and others who had convinced the American public that the Chinese Communists were liberal 'agrarian reformers,' I considered his attitude reprehensible. I failed to take sufficient account of the fact that, despite his eminence as a scholar it would perhaps have been impossible for Sir George Sansom to hold a professorial appointment in the late 40's or early 50's in a leading American University had he not played along with the friends of the Chinese Communists in America. He may have considered it was worthwhile retaining his chair in order to mitigate the influence of the Lattimore-Fairbank school of thought which then predominated in most American universities.

Today I realize that George, who was getting old and had never had much faith in the power of knowledge or reason to influence the course of human events, was simply withdrawing from the political struggles of our time. Like a monk in the Middle Ages retiring to a monastery, he took refuge from the insoluble problems of the world in the Halls of Academe.

Having no illusion as to anything he could do to change the course of history, he preferred to study and write about the past. Katherine had told me years before, that when he had returned to London after his long service in Japan, Lord Vansitart, after hearing George reject various offers of Ambassadorships, had turned to her and said, "What *does* your husband want, Lady Sansom?" And she had replied: "To be a Professor."

George was a kindly and wise cynic who once said to me: "The trouble with you, dear Freda, is that you think a question is something to which there is an answer."

Today, being no longer sure that the right answer to our problems is to be found, I appreciate George's wisdom although I still believe that one must continue to search for the answer until one dies, either physically or mentally.

The final break between the Sansoms and me came after a cocktail party at their apartment at Butler Hall in the early 50's. Olivia Holt, who had originally met the Sansoms through me, had phoned Katherine Sansom to tell her that I was visiting with her in New York. Katherine had said, "Bring Freda along." But when we got there it was embarrassing for everybody. The majority of the guests were Institute of Pacific Relations people and other purveyors of myths about the Chinese Communists being liberal "agrarian reformers" with whom I was at daggers drawn. Poor George was so embarrassed that he neglected to introduce even Dr. Holt to his guests, on account of his association with me. Olivia, being an extrovert like myself who enjoys parties, was at her ease in this gathering as in any other, in spite of the lack of introductions. And I, knowing many of the guests from old times when we had been on the same side of the barricades against Japan, had no inhibitions. Fortified by several Martinis, I rushed into the fray, arguing with all and sundry and no doubt becoming obnoxiously aggressive and insulting to those I regarded as Communist fellow travellers.

Indubitably, I displayed bad manners. I ought to have remembered that it was George himself who, during the long years of our friendship, had once expressed the realistic British view that "you can't teach people morals, but you can teach them manners." I behaved very badly at this party. The Sansoms need not have invited me, and I was embarrassing my hosts.

Today, reading Katherine Sansom's warm and friendly letters written three decades ago, I feel ashamed of myself. She had given me practical aid, sympathy and encouragement at difficult periods in my life ever since she and her husband became my friends in Japan in 1928. They were my only friends in the Western world who had known my husband and been his friend. How could it have come about, I now ask myself, that even if she and George fell short of my intolerant standards of political behavior I rejected them, or caused them to reject me?

I have advanced far ahead of my story, but in saluting George and Katherine Sansom across the years, I am paying tribute to the best of the England I left forever in 1939.

Chapter 24
EMIGRATION TO AMERICA

I landed with my mother and son in New York on a Dutch boat in December 1939 with $500 in cash and few possessions, but great expectations and good friends to welcome me.

Guenter (Hans) Reimann, who had emigrated to America ahead of us, met us at the Hoboken dock and took Mother and Jon off to his one-room apartment at Minetta Street in Greenwich Village while I stayed to see our luggage through Customs.

We had packed everything we took with us in anything that came to hand and had some dozen large and small suitcases and one small trunk. Most of our fellow passengers were Jewish refugees from Germany and Austria who, in contrast to escapees from Russia who were lucky to get out with their shirts, had been permitted to take packing cases of furniture and steamer trunks. My small bits and pieces got lost in the shuffle on the over-crowded dock and it took hours to find them. Having risen at dawn and eaten nothing since breakfast, I was exhausted by mid-afternoon when I finally succeeded in locating all our baggage. I then had one of the wonderful experiences which can happen only in America. I secured the services of a porter who looked and behaved like a character out of a Jack London novel. After passing through Customs, he said: "You look all in; a drink would do you good." I replied that it certainly would, but there did not seem any way of buying one at the Hoboken dock. "Come with me," he said, and depositing my baggage in a safe place he led me to a bar outside and treated me to a couple of whiskies and soda refusing to take any payment when he finally loaded me and my baggage into a taxi.

I was no longer young and that day must have been as disheveled and grubby as when in my childhood Mother reproved me for looking "like a lost gypsy"—one of her favorite North Country expressions. The young man who was so kind to me on the Hoboken dock cannot possibly have found me at all attractive and was simply being kind to an immigrant without money.

Two or three weeks later I was afforded another example of the extraordinary kindness of the misnamed "common man" in America. I had arrived in Philadelphia at dusk on Christmas Eve without a present for my son who was staying there with Mother under the care of Michael Ross and his American wife, while I was in New York arranging a contract for my book on Russia with the John Day Company. After hastily depositing my luggage in their apartment on Pine Street, I was standing shivering in the cold waiting for a bus, hoping to reach a shopping center before the stores closed, when an Italian vendor of Christmas trees offered to drive me downtown in his truck to buy some small gifts at a drug store. On our return to Pine Street my benefactor refused to take any payment, accepting only a glass of wine in Michael's house.

John P. Marquand and his wife Adelaide, who became my friends a year or so later, urged me to write a popular book about my first experiences in America which included frequent encounters with the old gallant and kind "frontier" spirit which still survives in these United States and which had endeared America to me on my first trip from China in 1938. It might have been profitable for me to have done so, but instead of writing a book to express my appreciation of my adopted country, where there is so much more real "fraternity, equality and liberty" than anywhere else in the world, I was to devote myself, for the most part in vain, to alerting America to the Communist menace.

Michael, whose name appears frequently in my book about my life in Russia, had been my comrade in the British Communist Party and had been Jane's lover in Russia for two years. He had left Jane and Russia in 1931 and subsequently emigrated to America where he worked first in the CIO and later for the AFL where he was Foreign Policy Adviser to George Meany at the time of his death in 1964.

After a brief stay in Philadelphia I moved to Baltimore where Dr. and Mrs. Emmett Holt and the Frederic Nelson's had secured for me a small but very nice apartment for only thirty dollars a month on Roland Avenue, next door to one of the best public schools in America.

Remembering my own unhappy experiences at Prior's Field, I feared Jon would suffer because he was a foreigner in speech and dress. Instead, he came home radiant from his first day at school. The teacher told the class that he had crossed the Atlantic Ocean in war time and thus built him up; and American children, like their parents, but unlike the British, are nicest of all to strangers in their midst.

I had first met the Holts and the Nelsons during my hectic six weeks tour of the United States in the fall of 1938 lecturing for The American Committee for Non-Participation in Japanese Aggression, an organization which, under the chairmanship of Henry Stimson, was endeavoring to stop war supplies to Japan, and whose most prominent and eloquent speaker was Dr. Walter Judd, the future Congressman from Minnesota.

Dr. Holt was already well known as a pediatrician who had carried on and revised his father's work as author of the best known baby book in America before Dr. Spock became more famous by his advocacy of 'permissiveness' carried to the n-th degree, the results of which are now apparent in our schools and universities. Dr. Holt, now professor at New York University, is today known internationally for his writings and lectures on nutrition. Olivia Holt at this time was active in arranging Maryland's display at the World's Fair.

Frederic Nelson was at this time an editor of the *Baltimore Sun*. Some years later he became editorial writer on *The Saturday Evening Post* and they moved to Philadelphia. Today in retirement he contributes witty articles to such conservative publications as *National Review* and *Human Events*, but in the early forties he was still a member in good standing of the "liberal establishment." Although anti-Communist, he was an "interventionist," and an ardent Anglophile. His wife Sylvia, one of the kindest women I have ever known, was witty in a delightfully unconscious fashion by reason of her devastatingly candid and perceptive remarks. A southerner with innumerable relatives, she had a particularly soft spot for old ladies and took to my mother at once. The Nelson's large house on the outskirts of Baltimore and their summer place on Cape Cod were always full of visitors so that Frederic found it difficult to find a quiet spot to work. Sylvia was a darling and Frederic was one of my own kind. We were both liberal anti-Communists, a rare combination in those days.

Besides finding the Roland Avenue apartment for us, Olivia Holt and Sylvia Nelson had furnished it. From their own homes and that of their friends, Dexter and Anne Keezer, they had collected old beds and tables, chairs and other furniture which they painted or revarnished themselves. We might have been a pioneer family arriving on the Western Frontier in days gone by, so great was the kindness and helpfulness and hospitality of the Holts, the Nelsons, and their friends. They all liked my mother very much and she felt more at home in the Baltimore atmosphere than anywhere else in America.

Jon spent a lot of time at the Holts and the Nelsons who had large gardens and playrooms and whose children, though older, were as nice to him as their parents were to me and Mother.

I had little or no medical expenses to drain my meager resources as came to be the case later on, since Dr. Holt saw to it that both Mother and Jon received medical attention at Johns Hopkins where he was the professor of Pediatrics. Jon had his tonsils out for free at Johns Hopkins when he was barely six years old, and was also then circumcised because Dr. Holt suggested it might as well be done at the same time. Which was perhaps a bit hard on him although he did not seem to suffer much.

I had wanted to have this operation performed on my son when he was a baby in Moscow because my brother's ideas of hygiene were similar to those now prevalent in America. But Arcadi told me that circumcision in Soviet Russia was frowned upon as a Jewish religious rite, smacking of counter-revolution, so that the only way to have the operation done was surreptitiously by a Rabbi without benefit of anesthetics or antiseptics.

The society into which the Holts and Nelsons introduced us in Baltimore included besides such medical colleagues of Dr. Holt's as Dr. Horsley Gantt, then already well known for his association with Pavlov's experiments in Leningrad and today President of the Pavlovian Society for Research; the *Baltimore Sun* cartoonist, Edmund Duffy and his wife, Anne; Dexter Keezer who soon afterwards went off to head Reed College in Oregon and later became Vice President of McGraw-Hill and his comely wife Anne, both of whom have remained my friends; Leslie Ford, the famous "who done it" story writer; Philip Wagner, editor of the *Baltimore Sun*, now in retirement famous for his Maryland vineyard, and others who gathered at the Hamilton Street Club.

Olivia Holt, to whom this book is dedicated, was to become my ever-present help in time of trouble, as well as an increasingly dear and sympathetic friend in later years.

Our divergent views on the war and their fondness and sympathy for my mother, whom both Olivia and Sylvia thought I treated none too well, were to alienate us for a while following my departure from Baltimore to New York. But they never ceased to help me by inviting Mother for long visits and giving her comfort and love during this difficult period of my life when I was often at my wits ends how to provide for her and Jon.

Mother, whose views were usually the opposite of mine, partly on account of temperamental antagonism but also because she was a British patriot to the core, was naturally an ardent admirer of Winston Churchill, wanted American armed intervention in the war, and saw no merit in my arguments for a negotiated peace to obviate the danger of a Communist conquest of Europe. So she felt very much at home with those of my friends who disagreed with me. And I was far too appreciative of the hospitality and friendship given my lonely and uprooted Mother by the Holts and the Nelsons to resent their disapproval of me during the war. It was just wonderful that they loved her, gave her some happiness and comfort, and took her off my hands for long periods by inviting her to their homes in Baltimore and their summer places in Maine and on the Cape. Had it not been for the Holt's and the Nelson's I should have regretted not having left my mother in England where she belonged.

236

In this Baltimore society, as in England once upon a time, "breeding" or "good manners" charm and wit, counted for more than money or fashionable clothes. My mother had these qualities combined with an enduring beauty of face and form. She had such natural elegance and good taste that she managed to look nice, or what the French call *soignée* even in old or cheap clothes and without benefit of beauty parlors.

One amusing episode in Baltimore in 1940 illustrates my mother's incurably British and most un-American prejudices. Although herself the daughter of a Manchester manufacturer she considered those engaged in "trade" to be inferior to the professional classes, and as far less worthy of respect than even the most impecunious writers, poets, teachers, government workers or even journalists.

So one evening after Olivia had brought a wealthy woman who owned a hotel in Miami to visit us in our little apartment on Roland Avenue, Mother remarked after their departure, "isn't Olivia wonderful; she hasn't a trace of snob in her; she was as nice to that hotel keeper as to any of her friends."

More than 20 years after, a remark made by my "All American" son called this incident to mind. Writing to me in June 1962 from South America where at the age of 28 he had become the Vice President of an American company selling Mutual Funds, he said:

> Someday I'll write you my opinions of all the different nationalities I meet, but the worst in general are the English, still stifled by so much class consciousness they're one group in several who obviously think a salesman is low class. Fortunately, however, we don't bother much with them since they're the lowest paid group of any North European nationality. The Germans, as usual, are the closest in thinking to the Americans, and after Swiss and Swedes who earn more money, are our best clients.

I must here confess that I myself have never quite managed to shed the British prejudices which have always been an anomaly since the British won economic predominance by being the world's most successful traders, and were contemptuously described by Napoleon as "a nation of shopkeepers." In Washington in the 60's when asked what my son was doing in South America I found myself explaining in an apologetic tone that he was in business but surely only temporarily. Jon, who calls himself "a salesman" laughs and says that I preferred to describe him as editor or publisher when for a while he produced the *Bogota Bulletin*, a little news sheet he put out in his spare time and from which he derived only a couple of hundred dollars a month. "I didn't raise my son to be a businessman," I sometimes regretfully remark, feeling a sense of guilt that perhaps I unconsciously did just that. In his childhood and youth my struggle for existence as a writer with unpopular views made such an impression on Jon that he decided to go into business and make enough money to become financially independent while also enjoying himself skin diving in the Caribbean, hunting in the Amazon and in general living the full rounded life which poor children dream about and the rich so often forego. Besides finding competitive business an absorbing game, he acquired experience and knowledge unobtainable in the halls of Academe, and gained greater knowledge of foreign lands than most State Department officials. I comfort myself with the hope that in the end he will make his mark on the world by better writing than mine or by distinguished service in government. But in his view writing is a sweat and making money much much easier.

What'er betide in the future I shall always be glad that I brought my son to the United

States when he was a child so that he is an American in outlook instead of being like myself, in some respects still an alien in thought, sentiment and behavior. I am more at home in America than in the England of either today or yesterday, yet at times I feel a nostalgic longing for the Old World.

For half a year in Baltimore I worked hard on my book earning a little money in between times by occasional lectures, articles and book reviews. It was not easy to work in a two room and kitchen apartment shared by my son and mother, but in those days one could still hire a maid cheaply so that I was temporarily relieved of household chores. Moreover, the landlord kindly let me use a room downstairs in an empty apartment without electricity where I installed myself with a large kitchen table. Here by day while Jon was in school, and by night upstairs with my son sleeping behind me, I wrote *The Dream We Lost*.

Early that summer when it was nearing completion, I moved to New York. Pleasant as life was in Baltimore, I had to make contacts in the Big City to earn money, as also to be near my publisher, Richard Walsh of the John Day Company. I had exhausted the $500 advance on my book and the $500 I brought with me from England, and spent of necessity as it came, the small income I received from occasional lectures and articles contributed to *Common Sense* and *Asia* magazine. I expected soon to be able to make money again having great hopes for the success of my book on Russia, and having been taken on by the Columbia Lecture Bureau for the next season. But for the moment I was almost destitute and Mother was entirely dependent on me having ceased, since we left England, to receive the pound or two a week she had for some years previously been paid as a residuary legatee of my grandfather's estate.

Fortunate as ever in my friends, I was able to survive by depositing both Mother and Jon for long periods during the summer and fall of 1940 with them. Jon spent several months with Alfred and Sylvia Bingham in Salem, Connecticut. They had children of about his age and he was happy there.

One of many sons of the late Senator Hiram Bingham, Alfred was at this time publishing and editing *Common Sense* jointly with Selden Rodman whose sister Nancy was Dwight MacDonald's wife. I had contributed articles to their publication before leaving England and now found their views on the war and its probable consequences similar to mine.

In April 1940 Alfred wrote me the following letter, which I happen to have preserved although I no longer possess copies of any of the articles I wrote for *Common Sense* in 1940-1941:

> I often get facts from reading an article, but I rarely get a whole new perspective—and that is always an exciting experience. Your article gave me that. I had never seen so clearly before the sense in which this is an imperialist war, and the way in which the sins of Britain and France are coming home to roost. Somehow the whole European war takes on a new meaning, and one gets the sense that the Allies must lose without a sort of moral regeneration, not of the slobbering Buchman type, but a new sense of the implications of what is fine in their civilization. They can't win without a new policy in the Far East and toward their colonies. Incidentally I think there are plenty of signs that such a new policy might be adopted, though the "shake-up" in the British Government yesterday would hardly indicate even the beginnings of a

change of heart. At any rate I am enthusiastic about the article. It's really an important piece of work. It cuts through all the fog emanating from the Anglophiles as well as the Russophiles. It's the kind of clean and honest thinking that all of us bewildered "men of good will" need today. It clears a lot of my own thinking. I only wish I had read it before I finished my book on the U.S. of Europe which is now on the press.

Selden Rodman has been away all this week, and I can't tell how he will react, but he ought to be even more enthusiastic than I, at least in so far as it reinforces an isolationist position toward Europe. He may be more skeptical about the call for action against Japan, however, though your cases seem to me wholly convincing.

I do appreciate your doing this for us. It is a distinguished contribution.

Common Sense well deserved its name. With an appreciation of political realities rare among intellectuals and the historical perspective which rendered it immune to war hysteria, this unique liberal journal expressed views consonant with those of the Founding Fathers of the United States. Men, who had eschewed "entangling alliances," not for narrow selfish interests, but because they knew that the quarrels and divisions of the Old World could not be resolved by American intervention.

While others praised the Atlantic Charter, *Common Sense* pointed out that the Roosevelt-Churchill commitment to the total defeat and disarmament of Germany must lead to a second Versailles with even worse consequences.

In contrast to Freda Kirchway in *The Nation* and other "hawks" of that time intent on getting America into the war to save Russia from defeat *Common Sense* asked, "If Moscow rather than Berlin comes to dictate the peace, would America be more secure?" Neither Alfred Bingham nor Selden Rodman were isolationists anymore than Norman Thomas and Sidney Hertzberg* who likewise opposed American intervention in the second war to "save democracy." We were internationalists who refused to believe in the particular wickedness or virtue of any people, race or nation, and had a lively appreciation of the menace of the Communist ideology exemplified by Stalin's terrible tyranny.

We therefore advocated a negotiated peace with America putting her power unequivocably behind Britain's for this purpose, instead of urging her to continue fighting a war she could not win, and would surely lose unless our "English cousins" acquiesced in the extension of Soviet power over Eastern and Central Europe.

Common Sense could afford only small payments for the articles I frequently contributed, but Alfred Bingham was a most generous friend and his wife, Sylvia, as hospitable as himself. I visited often for weekends while Jon was staying with them in Salem and frequently met their neighbor and good friend Chester Bowles.

At this time Chester Bowles was a liberal non-interventionist. In November 1941 he wrote to me from his Madison Avenue Public Relations Office, asking my opinion of an article which Bingham had persuaded him to write for *Common Sense* on "What's Wrong

---

*Publisher and editor together with Cushman Reynolds of *Uncensored* a weekly newsletter whose sponsors included John Chamberlain, Stuart Chase, John T. Flynn, C. Hartley Grattan, Oswald Garrison Villard, Burton Rascoe, Selden Rodman, and whose Washington correspondent was Frank Hanighen.

With the Non-interventionists?" which expressed views similar to my own. Later, however, he joined the "main-stream" of the Democratic Party and became almost as renowned as Adlai Stevenson in expounding a view of the world comparable to that of Mark Twain's "innocents abroad."

Although I still occasionally meet and argue with Chester Bowles today at North Haven in Maine when I spend summers there with the Holts, I have never been able to make up my mind whether he is a romantic liberal capitalist, striving toward a glorious New Frontier, or a very clever politician. Giving him the benefit of the doubt whenever I read his Candide-like public statements I remember Bertrand Russell's essay on the "evil that good men do."

Whereas Chester Bowles has become a national figure, Alfred Bingham has sunk into obscurity although, or because, he was a first class writer, a perceptive political thinker, and a man of outstanding integrity and courage. After Pearl Harbor Alfred, who had always been in favor of the "New Deal," while opposing Roosevelt's foreign policies, convinced himself for a while that F.D.R. was another Woodrow Wilson—a hope which he was to abandon by the time he wrote me the following letter from France in October 1944:

> Some of your criticisms of our commander-in-chief have come to my mind occasionally lately, and I have reached the point where I should not feel it a great calamity if Dewey were elected—and that is a pretty drastic statement! I am extremely pessimistic about the prospects for an intelligent peace. There is almost no really intelligent discussion reaching us from America. It seems as if immature emotionalism had a free field in place of idealism, or even intelligent realism, in the shaping of the peace. The *Readers Digest* has occasionaly had some good articles. And I am very much pleased at the way Sidney Hertzberg has carried on *Common Sense.*
>
> I spent six months in England, and left there feeling reasonably optimistic about the general drift toward a *Common Sense* type of liberation. There is hopefulness and a determination to move ahead in that country. The same is true in France—France has not suffered too much, but enough to prompt a re-thinking of democracy, capitalism and socialism, and there is a surprising degree of unanimity and intelligent reformism—except in the attitude toward Germany where naturally emotionalism is pretty strong. I have been six weeks in France, waiting to move into Germany, where I have a pretty good job as a regional specialist on labor waiting for me. You can get a better idea from the papers of when the job is likely to begin than I have.
>
> My hope is that during the next twenty years there may be a chance of undoing the mistakes that will be made in the next few months. But I suppose I would appear as an extreme optimist if I had a chance at one of those pleasant evenings of discussion with you which I miss these days.

* * *

Others of my friends also came to believe that although at the outset a conflict of 'imperialisms' the war against Nazi Germany was being converted, or could be converted, into a "war for democratic welfare" for all mankind. Geoffrey Hudson* in a long letter written to me on May 21, 1940, expressed the hopes which inspired my anti-Communist friends who came to support the war despite their distrust of Stalin's Russia. "Whatever happens to us now," he wrote, "we are delivered from the all-enveloping complacency of Chamberlain—for better or worse we are now going somewhere and the motion is exhilarating even if it is only to be 'down a steep place into the sea.' "

Commenting that after my experience of suffering in Russia and China I would be fitted to endure what was coming in England, he wrote: "It is going to be terrible for the well-to-do of England who have always thought themselves so inaccessible to the processes of history and have been lapped for years in Chamberlainite self-delusion. We at any rate, whatever dreams we have entertained, have never given ourselves up to *that* kind of fantasy."

Expressing the belief that inspired "those of us on the Left who have been preserved from Communist lunacy" but had by now come to believe that the war had become "our war" he wrote:

> There are only two motive forces which can supersede capitalism; one is the quest of military power and the other is the purpose of democratic welfare. Fascism, being exclusively nationalist and despotic, controls capitalism only for military ends. A democracy at war with a fascist nation must undertake a similar subordination of private vested interests (as Chamberlain would not do, but Churchill will), but in so far as organized democratic forces participate in this control, it can be diverted after the period of temporary military need to democratic welfare.

When I moved to New York Hans arranged for me to become a "lodger" in the 50 dollar a month apartment on Waverly Place in the Village which Dora Shuser, who was to become the closest of all my friends, shared with her sister Rosa and Rosa's husband Ephraim Doner. I occupied their tiny, spare room in which there was barely space to install my bed and the small desk I bought. This was no hardship since I became a member of the family and we lived an amiable communal life undreamed of in Moscow where, in a similar small living space, there would have been continual bickering and quarrels and arguments about who owed who a few kopeks for gas or electricity.

Meanwhile, when Mother was not enjoying the hospitality of the Holts or the Nelsons, I arranged an inexpensive lodging for her in Westport where she was well looked after by Mrs. Oates on Greens Farms Road. Mrs. Oates is one among the many strangers in my life who have been most generous and kind when circumstances were most difficult. Although poor herself, she charged me as little as she could while she looked after my mother there. As also when for a month that summer I arranged for Jon to stay there with his Aunt Emsie to look after him, and was able myself to spend weekends with them out of New York.

My letters to Mother during the summer and fall of 1940 reveal how hectic and busy and worrisome my life was at this time. My situation was rendered all the more difficult by Mother's pride which made her reluctant to reveal to our well-to-do friends just how nearly destitute we were. I had less shame. "In spite of our dignity, etc.," I wrote to her

---

*Author of *The Far East in World Politics*, Oxford University Press 1937. Then a Fellow of All Souls College and today head of the Department of Far Eastern Affairs at St. Anthony's.

in one letter, "we shall have to take advantage of any possible offer of hospitality. Please, dear, for my sake and Jon's, tell Sylvia the exact position." Should she not be able to stay on a while longer with the Nelsons, I continued, "in New York you can live cheaply. Dora is so sweet and really friendly to me that I do not mind our living there rent free. And Hans really loves you and will secure money somehow if I cannot for a few weeks. Please, darling, don't be upset anyhow. In time I shall make money."

On July 30, 1940, I wrote, "I stayed up till 4:00 a.m. finishing the index last night in Westport and caught the 8:16 a.m. train to New York this morning—so am dead tired and this is only a note. I shall return to Westport tomorrow evening, I expect, and stay quietly there till next Monday. Jon looks wonderful and really is swimming. He moves along quite fast."

The postmarks on the envelopes of many of my letters to my mother are illegible, and I all too often datelined them only by the day of the week and the place I was writing from. The following one written sometime early in August 1940 conveys some idea of my difficult financial situation when I was reduced to borrowing a few dollars here and there to provide for Mother's immediate needs.

Thursday

c/o Bingham
Mumford Farm
Salem via Colchester, Connecticut
Dear Mother:

Hans and Dora have just telegraphed me that they are going away on Friday—Dora till the 26th and Hans for about ten days, I understand, but that we are welcome to the flat and she will leave the keys. I am afraid this means, dear, that you will be alone in New York from Saturday night to Tuesday. Will you mind this very much? I am very sorry, dear, but Mrs. Oates is going away with her daughter tomorrow for 3 or 4 days rest so that you could not go there. I will come to New York on Tuesday morning—possibly late Monday night. If you have no money for food, either borrow five from Sylvia or from the Pippetts* at 15 West 8th Street (just beyond University Restaurant). Also dear, I have just had a letter from Sybil who arrived on July 30 with her children and is in New York at 1160 Park Avenue. I am writing to her now to tell her you will be there and to send you a note with her phone number. She is alone there as her friends are away and will love to see you. You could borrow two or three dollars from her till I come, if necessary.

So awfully sorry, darling, but I am sure things will soon be alright. You will keep cheerful, won't you? I hope to send you and Jon here to Mrs. Oates by the end of next week.

My dearest love—also very best love to Sylvia.

Freda

Take a taxi from Penn Station to Dora's flat, 137 Waverly Place. I enclose keys in case difficult for you to get them late on Saturday.

Although concerned about Mother I was happy to be free for a while from her. I loved her and was sorry for her, but she often got on my nerves and I felt most sympathetic

---

*Aileen and Roger Pippet, English friends of mine who did book reviews for various publications.

toward her when she was absent. After leaving her I regretted having been nasty and impatient, and also felt guilty because I was happy to be away from her. In one of many letters I said:

> Thanks awfully for your letter. I am so very glad you are enjoying yourself. I know Emmett and Olivia are both really fond of you and there you are in your best atmosphere. You see, dear, I really do understand how difficult it is for you in my society in New York, or I should say in my world. And once things go wrong it is so difficult to put them right—each becomes nastier and nastier. But I do feel it will be alright when you come back after this break. I wish too, that you could have peace and comfort in your last years. Because I really do love you dear; it is mainly that my whole outlook, experience, attitude to life is quite different from yours.

In those difficult years when I was endeavoring with indifferent success to be both father and mother to my son and daughter to my mother while earning a living for us all, I used half jokingly to say that I badly needed a "wife." My dear sister-in-law Emsie, who was now living in Morris Plains with her American-born mother, could have been just that had it not been for mother's jealousy of Temple's wife even after his death. This made it impossible for Emsie to live with us, although at this time her own widowed mother did not, as in later years, require that she look after her without respite.

Emsie admittedly was tiresome in some ways, as opinionated as myself and very talkative, sharing some of my mother's all too British prejudices but with more understanding and sympathetic respect for my views. She was a most unselfish person who, having started to love Jon and me because of Temple, came to be a dearer friend to me than any sister by birth would in all likelihood have been had I ever had one. She not only loved my son devotedly, but gave him the loving care that I was unable to provide either by temperament or for lack of time. This, of course, only further aroused Mother's jealousy.

Writing to Mother in Baltimore I endeavored in vain to make her understand how much both Jon and I needed Emsie:

> Jon is very well and happy. Emsie is taking very good care of him. His hair looks lovely again, as she brushes it night and morning. You see dear, I cannot be a proper mother and Emsie largely takes my place in giving the little care and attention he needs. He does not even worry about my not being at home because she plays with him and talks to him. Neither you or I are much good at playing with him. I know how difficult Emsie can be and how impolite to you sometimes. But when she loves—and she does love me and Jon—she is quite wonderful. She has already tidied my drawers, she mends for me, unpacks, etc., etc. Don't be offended, dear, but it does make a big difference to me having her and knowing that all responsibilities and little worries at home are off my shoulders. You cannot help it that you are not strong enough—if only I could have you both together at home for my own sake and Jon's.

Chapter 25
FRIENDS IN THE VILLAGE

In spite of nagging money worries and separation from Jon, life in the Village seemed wonderful. After I left Baltimore I was back among my own kind—those whom my brother had inelegantly described as the "bloody intelligents"—and meeting a lot of interesting people.

Dora was a genius at providing good meals for very little money, and she was the soul of hospitality like my long-lost sister-in-law Vera in Moscow. Friends were always dropping in for a meal or just to see Dora who radiated a warmth and kindness and understanding unique in my experience of women. Utterly without malice and all too tolerant of the sins and follies and ingratitude of mankind, she is one of the rare people who really believe that it is more blessed to give than to receive.

How much I owe to Dora can never be told. She sustained me with her encouragement, cheered me, helped me with my mother, fed me for a song, and lent me her best dress to wear when I lectured. I gave her my heart to hold, confiding in her more than I have ever done to another human being, because I trusted her completely and unreservedly and knew that it was inconceivable that she would ever want to hurt me.

I was also most fortunate in having Hans as a comrade then as still today, in the true sense of this word which means more than friend.

Despite differences of opinion which have sometimes become so acrimonious as to lead to temporary estrangement, there is an enduring tie of loyalty between us and such mutual respect and trust that we are always eventually reconciled. During our early penurious years in New York, we always helped one another out, even when barely on speaking terms. Today I count him among my dearest and oldest friends in all the world.

So intricate is the web of life that it was thanks to my brother's chance meeting with an Italian in a pub in Suva that I first met Hans, and came to live with Dora in the Village in New York five years after Temple's death on the other side of the world.

Temple had written shortly before his death, "Life has been more amusing lately, owing to an Italian journalist, Dr. René Paresce, but he leaves today. He is 1/2 Italian and 1/2 Russian and used to be a friend of Trotsky's—before the Revolution. He is a Doctor of Science-Physics, a painter by choice and earns his living as a journalist; English correspondent of the 'Stampa' of Turin."

On the occasion of their first meeting over drinks at Mac's Hotel in Suva, Temple and René had struck up a friendship during an animated discussion of the relative merits of Bertrand Russell's philosophy which my brother favored and the Marxist theories to which René still adhered.

Not long afterwards during my last visit to England prior to Arcadi's arrest and the end of my life in Russia, I had met Hans at Paresce's flat in London. Guenter Reimann, to call him by his right name, was then preparing to risk his life by returning to Nazi Germany, while I was about to return to the prison house which Soviet Russia had become.

Later in England after I had returned to the West, René and his wife Ella, whose father had been a friend of Lenin's, and Hans and I, were continually seeking and enjoying one another's company.

The difference between the Latin and the Teutonic mind, and my own closer affinity to the former was often illustrated during the many evenings when Hans and I and René argued about the failure of socialism in Russia. René and I always wanted to 'escalate' our discussions by omitting many of the intermediate steps between premiss and conclusion in order to get quickly to the point. But Hans insisted on building up his argument, step by step, omitting nothing, even though we all knew the facts, or beliefs or theories, which could be taken for granted in view of our similar background, knowledge and experience. Many years before in tutoring Indians and other students at King's College I had been able to spot the ones who had learned Latin because of their ability to express themselves in shorter clearer terms. And today in America I continually endeavor, with little success, to make Hans abandon his Teutonic style.

René Paresce might well have been chosen for a *Reader's Digest* accolade of "My Most Unforgettable Character." Son of a Russian mother and Italian father, amazingly versatile in his talents and interests, endowed with a quick intelligence and a compassionate heart, he also had an ironic Latin sense of humor and love of life. Strikingly handsome, with a tall slim and lithe figure, Roman nose, light blue eyes and sensitive generous mouth, fair hair going grey as it receded from his broad high forehead, he was as fearless as unmindful of his life and health and soon to die of a neglected cold which developed into pneumonia. After giving up his Professorship of Mathematics at the University of Florence to paint in France, he had been arrested during the First World War because of his association with Trotsky, with whom he had shared an apartment in Paris. Fortunately the Paris Chief of Police had so admired his paintings that he had been permitted to go and live quietly in the south of France for the duration. Later he had become a journalist, and after Temple and he became friends in Suva, toured the United States and wrote a book called *Altera America* describing the poverty of Kentucky mountaineers and other "underprivileged" Americans.

Despite his anti-Fascist sympathies which prevented him from returning to Italy, Paresce's journalistic talents were so outstanding as to enable him to become the London correspondent of *La Stampa*. When I asked him how this was possible, René used to say that Italians never took their politics with such deadly seriousness as Germans and Russians, so that Mussolini's dictatorship was not nearly as total as Hitler's or Stalin's. Another reason may have been that René's brother was a diplomat at the Italian Embassy in London before the Second World War. Afterwards this younger Senor Paresce became Press Counselor of the Italian Embassy in Washington, affording another example of Italian political tolerance, or refusal to go to extremes in persecuting opponents, which is perhaps the hallmark of a very old civilization.

A decade after René Paresce became my dear friend in London I was impressed by the differences in behaviour of the Germans and Italians after the defeat of the Nazi and Fascist regimes. Many Germans were all too anxious to exonerate themselves by denouncing others as Nazi "war criminals." The Italians, although less courageous in war than the Germans—or too intelligent to fight wholeheartedly for their dictator—refrained for the most part from denunciation of others in order to prove their own democratic virtue after their defeat. There were few, if any "war criminal" trials in Italy with the less guilty or unavowed guilty accusing and condemning their compatriots under the aegis of an alien occupation. Italians seem in general to realize that the good or evil men had done

245

under the Fascist dictatorship was mainly the result of varying pressures. Travelling to Italy from Germany by train in 1952 I happened to share a compartment with two young French-speaking Italians who had been friends at school and amiably kidded one another concerning their activities during the war. "I was in the Resistance" one told me. "Only because you hoped to avoid military service that way," the other retorted. "All right, true, but weren't you a member of the Fascist Party because you hoped to get a cushy job absolving you from fighting?" responded the other. And they both laughed in recognition of the truth of each other's argument.

As Dora used to point out, it was a funny thing that Americans hated the Germans for fighting so well and despised the Italians for not doing so. Dora before I knew her had been a buyer at Macy's earning a comfortable income. She preferred to become a social worker on a small salary and has never regretted it. During her affluent days she had been unhappily married to a selfish 'intelligent' and was, as I saw it, still sponged on by some worthless characters in the literary and artistic world who exploited her generosity and sympathy. The daughter of indigent Jewish immigrants, she had the inordinate regard for learning and the arts which is one of the most endearing characteristics of the best of her people but can also mislead them into too great a reverence for "intellectual," good or bad. She has had a hard life but is one of the happiest people I know because of her extraordinary lack of concern for her own interests and her perceptive understanding and sympathy for other people's troubles. Henry Miller once said of her that all the kindness of the Old World was in her face, although why he ascribed kindness to the Old World, I fail to understand. Maybe the pure in heart, even though they will never inherit the earth, are happier even in this world than the self-seekers, the ambitious, and the unscrupulous.

Far from sharing what still remained of my Puritan prejudices, Dora, although faithful to her husbands, saw no sin in "giving herself" without regard to consequences when her heart moved her, or a man badly needed her love and care.

Her second husband was an outwardly hard-boiled American journalist to whom I introduced her one fateful evening in 1941 and whom she married later that year. Wilbur Burton about whom one can read in Vincent Sheean's *Personal History*,* had led an adventurous life as a *Baltimore Sun* foreign correspondent in South America and China. He had at one time been married to the sister of Sheean's heroine, Rayna Proem. In 1927 he was arrested in Peking for his activities on behalf of the revolutionary Kuomintang together with Milly Mitchell, whom I had known in Moscow before she became famous as the wife of the Communist Commander of the American "Lincoln Brigade" in Spain. In spite of, or because of this experience Milly became as anti-Communist as I long before she died in New York.

Digressing for a moment, I must remark here that Milly, who was far from beautiful—in fact, almost ugly—was also evidently a most attractive or sexually desirable woman. She was not, I think, ever a member of the Communist Party although she worked on the Moscow *Daily News*. One day meeting her on Kuznetsky Most in Moscow at a time when she was temporarily taking Walter Duranty's place as Russian correspondent for *The New York Times*, I had stopped to greet her and she, warmly smiling, had said, "Oh, Freda, how happy I am that you, too, are not cutting me dead like so many of my friends because I have temporarily become a correspondent for the capitalist press." Soon after, Milly lost her most recent lover, or husband, a Russian actor,

---

*Doubleday, Doran & Co., New York, 1935.

who was arrested as a homosexual at a time when the Russian concentration camps had driven so many "politicals" to an early death by forced labor under inhuman conditions that it needed new categories of victims to build the roads and railways, work the mines and otherwise fulfill the manifold economic functions of slave labor in the U.S.S.R.

Wilbur Burton had walked into my life on a winter's day in 1941 when he visited C. V. Starr's offices at 101 Fifth Avenue to see Randall Gould, editor of the *Shanghai Evening Post* until Pearl Harbor caused its demise. Finding me working in the room next to Randall he grinned and said, "How typical of Neil Starr to have a 'yes man' and 'no woman' working for him side by side."

Wilbur Burton rarely agreed with me and on the rare occasions when we found ourselves in accord it was usually for different or opposite reasons. But I was fond of him and had a high regard for his sterling integrity, his courage, his scorn for those he called "political whores," and his wide ranging knowledge of literature, philosophy, and poetry. He came from Indiana, where his forebears had emigrated from the South after the Civil War to become poor farmers, and he was self-educated. Despite his rovings in foreign lands he remained all his life an unreconstructed old-style American radical from the Middle West. He had a natural affinity to "wobblies" and anarchists, and as instinctive a repulsion toward Communist despotism as to kings, princes and all types of authoritarian rule.

Seeing no more good in Chiang Kai-shek than in Stalin, opposed to Hitler but regarding the British "imperialists" as no better, he was firmly convinced that the United States should consistently follow Washington's advice to keep clear of foreign entanglements. Thus he chose to go to prison as a conscientious objector soon after he married Dora. He could easily instead have secured exemption from military service, since he was 40 years old and then on the cable desk of the *New York Times*. But he did not choose to take this easy way out and ruined his life's prospects in consequence.

During subsequent years when Dora was endeavoring to get him released from prison in Kentucky, her situation was, to say the least, paradoxical. Burt was kept in prison mainly because he refused to retract the violent diatribe he had written against Roosevelt as a war monger subservient to British and Jewish influences while his wife was working at the Jewish Refugee Relief Center in New York.

Eventually Dora secured Burt's release from imprisonment but only on condition that he become an indentured male nurse in a Maryland lunatic asylum. Here they were at last together again in a lodging in Towson. But he had to work very hard for a pittance, whereas in prison he had had little to do besides talk and organize study groups and debates among the Kentucky moonshiners, Jehovah's Witnesses and other pacifists whose society he had found most congenial. Although a condition for his release from prison was that he should not express his views in print, Burt was able to visit me occasionally in Washington where I had gone to live in 1944, and to pour forth his unreconstructed isolationist views in the letters he wrote me and to his old and loyal friend William Henry Chamberlin. I reproduce one of these letters dated February 18, 1945, because it so well displays Burt's sarcastically cynical style, his rock-bottom isolationism and his realistic appraisal of the shape of things to come thanks to "Roosevelt's War."

17 Alleghany Ave.
Towson 4, Md.
Feb. 18, 1945

Darling Freda: How about la Hahn's "China to Me?" I'm practically dying to read it, and so I expect it by next mail!!!! And did you ever locate a copy of Levine's brochure?

Your Bohemian Brawl was up to the best Utley standard and I enjoyed it immensely—and my entire stay in your domicile. Don't know when I will get to Washington again, but expect me when I do . . . . My Virginia friend was heartbroken not to get to the party; only the serious illness of his sister prevented.

The general press and radio reaction to the Crime(a) Conference reminds me that journalists today perform the same function as the augurs in ancient Rome—but most of our journalists are too naive to smile when they meet.

Anyway, the Crime(a) should have put us in our proper, humble place: America is not God, as some of our more bumptious citizens once imagined; Uncle Joe is God,—but, and our hearts can swell with pride! FDR is his Vicar for America. And through Lend-Lease, we have surely restored the Trotskyist-shaken faith of the Russians in Santa Claus. Now what could be sweeter than for materialistic America's major role in the 20th Century????

Also, the Crime(a) has given us a new definition of "realistic" internationalism as opposed to "perfectionist" internationalism: The Anglo-Americans give multilateral blessing to Stalin's unilateral accomplishments. Thus there are no longer any "spheres of influence brought about in the old-fashioned way of power politics; instead, the Anglo-Ams simply say "Praise Uncle Joe from whom all blessings flow." Of course, Uncle Joe did make one significant concession to his American Vicar: He had, I think now, established his Free Germany Committee in Moscow as a hedge just in case American voters should have proved ungodly enough to not re-elect FDR; now FDR being re-elected, Uncle Joe is willing to go all out for Unconditional Surrender—so that the war may be prolonged, in some fashion or another, to 1948, and thus FDR can again run as Commander-in-Chief and the PAC can again do its stuff. So the Crime(a) may be viewed as a prelude to a Fifth Term—just as Teheran was the prelude to a Fourth Term. (And Uncle Joe may even enter the Pacific war to help his pal in the White House; after all, he has always got Europe at hand—so why should he not take all "realistic" steps to keep FDR looting US for him by Lend-Lease as long as possible?) The only thing I missed at your party was an Englishman to quote my "Epitaph to a GI" to. So I will set it forth to you, without apologies to Kipling:

Walk wide of the Muddler at Windsor, for half of creation he owns.
We've bought him the same with the sword and the flame,
And we've salted it down with our bones.
(Poor GIs!—It's blue with our bones!)
Hands off the lands of the Muddler! Hands off the goods in his shop!
For rival kings must bow, and other imperialists cow,
When the Muddler at Windsor says Stop!
(Poor GIs!—We're sent to say Stop!)
Anyway, I'm not sure that the "poem" is not outdated. Maybe you can

248

compose one in Russian that is more appropriate!!!!

How about coming up to Towson for a *quiet* week-end?

As ever,

Burt

At the end of the war in Europe Burt was permitted to go to the 30 acre farm and ramshackle old house he had inherited near Winchester, Indiana. Having no capital he could not work the land, and life there was pretty grim for both of them while he milked cows and looked after chickens and Dora worked four days a week for a Jewish welfare agency in Indianapolis. After several years of this miserable existence, Dora and I persuaded Burt to return to New York, believing that he would eventually be able to re-establish himself as a newspaperman while she took one of the many jobs open to her there. But none of Burt's former "isolationist" friends would help him to secure employment. When I approached Mary King on the *Daily News*, with whom I was well acquainted, and tried to enlist her help she was uninterested in such a ghost from the past. Wilbur Burton had gone to prison for proclaiming the same isolationist views that she and her husband Joseph Medil Patterson had subscribed to. Now only younger men were of any value on the paper. My friend Batchelor, the cartoonist, was most sympathetic, but had no power to help him secure a job.

In this and my other vain endeavors to help Burt re-establish himself, I was given a salutory lesson as regards "What's-wrong-with-the-Right." It lacks, above all, the comradeship and the loyalty of the "Left," and is generally too heartless, selfish or ungenerous. The only one of Burt's previous friends or acquaintances who made some effort to help him was Norman Cousins who had never had any sympathy with Burt's views, but who believed in Voltaire's axiom that men of integrity should be permitted to speak and to live, however profoundly one disagrees with their views. Cousins failed to secure a job for Dora's husband but he at least tried, unlike those who had shared his views but themselves sacrificed nothing to uphold them. I did not agree with Burt's consistent isolationist views which made him oppose any American action risking war with the Communist powers as strenuously as he had been opposed to our intervention in the Second World War. But I admired his courage and integrity, and I loved Dora. It was very difficult to help them on account of Burt's injured pride which prevented him from making any concessions to conformity and impelled him willfully to outrage people who could have helped him.

The long beard he had grown while he worked his Indiana farm among his similarly hirsute Dukhobor neighbors and refused to shave off, combined with his casual clothes and defiant or positively rude manner, repelled the people Norman Cousins sent him to see who might have employed him. Finding all doors closed to him as a journalist or in any capacity in which his literary talents and diversified knowledge could be used, Burt finally took poorly paid employment as a shop assistant and general handyman at a second hand bookstore on University Place. Embittered and frustrated, he suffered deeply from the affront to his masculine pride at having become partly dependent on his wife, who earned more than he did, who adored him, but to whom he was often mean and nasty because he could not bear his hopeless situation. He reproached Dora for having persuaded him to leave his rural retreat in Indiana where, isolated, hard, and uncomfortable as his life had been, he had been able to earn his own living. Finally, in the fall of 1956, while I was in India, Burt committed suicide. My son cabled me to New Delhi to come home which I failed to do but reached Dora by phone. Rallying to her in my absence Jon said, "How

249

could Burt have done this to you?" Which was as he perceived, young as he was, the heart of the matter.

Burt was the most obstinate and courageous, foolish and uncompromising, old-fashioned radical American I have ever known. He clung to outworn original American concepts long since rendered obsolete by the march of history, while believing that he was in advance of his time. But he was a wonderful guy who deserved a better fate.

Like our friend Lawrence Dennis, who married Dora some years later, Burt was incapable of either forgetting or forgiving the past, or adapting himself to the present and trying to make the best of it. They found infinite satisfaction in saying, "I told you so," in surveying the results of American intervention in both World Wars.

The year of Burt's despair was far off when I lived with Dora in Greenwich Village in the early forties. I there found myself among my own kind, which was not that of the high-class Baltimore society which had been so kind to me. Ideologically and emotionally I still belonged to the "Liberal intelligentsia," although finding many of them deluded or drugged by Communist propaganda. Dora had visited Russia and been the guest there of the playwright Alexander Afenogenov and others in the Russian literary world who belonged to the wealthy Communist aristocracy. But being an intelligent woman of acute human sympathies instead of a cold-blooded intellectual, she had not been blind to the misery of the Russian "common man," and had no more illusions about Communism than myself. She supported me in argument with left-wing friends and her love and loyalty bolstered my courage in sustaining the fight against the ever-increasing strength of the friends of the Soviet Union in America.

When I moved to New York from Baltimore, Huntington Cairns (at this time a high official in the Treasury aspiring to be appointed to the Supreme Court but destined to become Treasurer of the Mellon Art Gallery), asked his friend F. V. Calverton to look after me. George, as his friends called him,* and I "clicked," as the British say, at our first meeting which, as I dimly remember was followed by his escorting me from one to another night spot frequented by the New York literary world.

Calverton and his "wife" Nina Melville lived close to me in the Village and their apartment was a unique meeting place for writers and poets, philosophers, artists, critics and teachers. There I met the elite of the non-Communist intelligentsia as also some who were already travelling along with Moscow's friends and dupes, either in order to advance their careers or because they had convinced themselves that destruction of the Nazi regime was all that mattered.

It was at Calverton's that I first got to know Max Eastman, Norman Thomas, Sidney Hook, Isaac Don Levine, Bertram and Ella Wolfe, Ben Stolberg and Susan LaFollette, Eugene Lyons and other early fighters against Communism who were to remain my friends in the difficult years ahead in spite of differences concerning the war. It may also have been there that I first met Carlo Tresca, the Italian anti-fascist and anti-Communist who was to be assassinated by the Communists without any real effort made by the police to apprehend his murderers.

George Calverton resembled my brother in his aversion to dogma, his wide-ranging interest in such diverse subjects as psychology and sex, anthropology, art, history, science and literature as well as politics, and his tolerance, understanding kindness and sympathy

---

*His real name was George Goetz. He had originally taken the pen name of F. V. Calverton to avoid jeopardizing his teaching job in Baltimore Public Schools when, in 1923, he founded his radical socialist magazine, *The Modern Quarterly*.

for individual human beings. He was one of the best and dearest friends I have ever had. Thanks to him, I soon felt myself more at home in the Village in New York in the forties than in Bloomsbury in London in the twenties.

As Daniel Aaron has written,** even the Communists who became his enemies after 1933, when he published Max Eastman's anti-Stalinist articles, found it hard to hate George. "It was painful to such former friends of his as Mike Gold, Granville Hicks and Joshua Kunitz to have to fight him on the Ideological front because Calverton was kind and considerate and genuinely comradely toward his opponents."

George's heresies were unconfined by fear or prejudice or attachment to Marxist theories. His inquiring mind, perceptive intelligence and courage in recognizing facts which undermined his original beliefs led him to speak out against "radical sectarians" who ignored American realities. "I am disgusted," he wrote to Van Wyck Brooks in 1938, "with the run of Marxists who try to fit America into the Marxist pattern. It won't fit. We need a new terminology, adapted to the American outlook."

He had continued to identify himself with Marxism for a period after he broke with the Communists because he felt that "originally I owe such a debt to Marx, and that a certain number of his theses hold true today." This, I also believe. The Marxist theory has validity in explaining one segment or aspect of the complex nature of man and society. If one can take Marxism merely as a tool for the limited purpose of unlocking the door to understanding our baser nature and some phases of economic history, it has its uses.

The autobiography Calverton had begun to write might have been the best history of our liberal or "progressive" generation.

Whenever I felt in need of good cheer and companionship I walked over to visit George and Nina. Somehow he managed to keep open house for his friends while writing a great many books, giving lectures and editing the *Modern Quarterly* (which had been the *Modern Monthly* before it lost circulation and subsidies and contributors following Calverton's denunciation of the Communists). George maintained another wife and establishment in Baltimore and the strain eventually broke him. Debts piled up and his opposition to U.S. intervention in the Second World War rendered it increasingly difficult for him to make enough money to provide for two wives, and for the entertainment of the friends who enjoyed his unlimited hospitality. One afternoon Nina phoned me to come over at once because George had been stricken. By the time I got there he was already dead.

I went to his funeral with Norman Cousins, who had also loved George and was to remain my friend in subsequent years in spite of our increasingly divergent views on the answers to the problems of our age. Together we wept at George's passing—that of a man who might today be recognized as great had he not dissipated his energies in the writing of too many books on too many different subjects, and spent so much time and effort in helping many people while also expending himself in stimulating talk in convivial company fortified by alcohol.

As he lay dead I felt that we were mourning as much for the doom of what he and the best of our generation had believed in as for the passing of a beloved friend. We belonged to a liberal and hopeful age which believed that it was possible to emancipate mankind from want and injustice, class or race exploitation, war and depressions, but lived to see our best aspirations perverted to become the basis for totalitarian tyranny.

George and I were attuned because we were old style liberals nurtured in the faith of

---

Writers on the Left by Daniel Aaron, Harcourt, Brace & World, New York, 1961.

the Age of Reason. To us it seemed obvious that the radical doctrines of our time needed a thorough re-examination in the light of the experience of our era. In contrast, the attitude of the dominant majority of liberals and socialists in America at the time George died, recalled the famous three stone monkeys of Lincoln Cathedral who shut their eyes, ears and mouth in order not to see, or hear, or speak any evil of the "First Socialist State."

The sad fact was that most "progressives" were denying the basis of their rationalist philosophy by refusing to face facts. They clung to their old faith that socialism *per se* must be good and progressive despite the evidence to the contrary. Their attitude toward the Soviet Union was not unlike that of well meaning Catholics in the Middle Ages who, although horrified by the tortures inflicted by the Inquisition on heretics and dissenters, convinced themselves that these atrocities were necessary for the preservation of the true faith.

We had believed that socialism would mean the emancipation of mankind not its regimentation, brutalization and the denial of individual rights and liberties together with contempt for the power of human reason. We had too late foreseen that the dynamic of revolution might serve the cause of tyranny and that the greatest miseries were to be inflicted in the name of Socialism. George Calverton was one of the few socialists who had the wisdom to perceive and the mental courage to admit that "public ownership of the means of production and distribution" in practice entailed the imposition of a more cruel and soul destroying despotism than any before known to mankind. In my tribute to F. V. Calverton published together with those written by others of his friends in the last issue of the *Modern Quarterly* I wrote:

> We who survive him can only hope that we shall preserve our balance, our values and our integrity as he did, and refuse to accept the easy maxims and doubt-resolving faiths which now sway the world. George never could believe that the end justifies the means, that socialism is only a question of economic forms, that democracy can be preserved by abandoning it, or that Satan can be cast out by Satan.
>
> There is perhaps no solution to the dilemma which confronts us. The dilemma consists in the fact that by combating evil with evil we produce only more evil and become like that which we oppose; and yet that if we refuse to meet fire with fire we appear to condone what we abhor. It is an old, old problem, but to us it seems new because for a generation or more we have believed that capitalism was the root of all evil, and that socialism would put an end to inequality, injustice, poverty, hatred, envy and war. Now we know that the end of the profit system may mean production not for use but for war—may mean tyranny, concentration camps, terror and oppression of the weak at home and abroad, whether such "Socialism" still covers itself with the tattered remnants of nineteenth century humanism as in Russia, or naked and unashamed, proclaims its reversion to primitive values and standards and myths as in Germany.
>
> The hope of a democratic form of socialism fades with each month the war is prolonged, with each rise in the tide of hysteria and hate and unreason and fear. Perhaps there is no hope now of avoiding the Dark Ages upon which we seem to be entering. But it is possible to hope that mankind's need of liberty and beauty and love will prove strong enough

in the long run to start once again the age-old struggle for social justice and liberty under new conditions and by new methods. We know now that the society we dreamed of requires more for its establishment than the abolition of the capitalist system. The capitalist system is already dead or dying but the world is worse, not better off.

"Had he lived," I concluded, "George Calverton would have found life more and more painful and increasingly harder to exist, both materially and spiritually, in an age of unreason, hatred and fear."

Today, a quarter of a century after his death, I imagine that George, could he return from the shades, would, even as I, rejoice that our worst fears concerning the shape of things to come have not been realized. Despite the follies and some crimes of the Western Powers who demanded the unconditional surrender of their enemies at the cost of an unconditional alliance with Stalin, the world today by and large seems to be a better place with greater hope for the emancipation of all mankind from the chains of poverty and fear than when George Calverton was alive.

After his death, life in the Village would never be the same although many of his friends continued to be mine. His spirit hovered over us long after he had passed into nothingness.

Other dear friends of mine have recently in increasing numbers passed into the valley of the shadow of death. Among them "star spangled on the grass" George Calverton is the one who I would enjoy most talking with once again—even if it were in purgatory.

In the Village in the early 40's I also belonged to the circle of Dwight and Nancy MacDonald, her brother Selden Rodman, and their friends and collaborators grouped around *Partisan Review* and *Common Sense*.

Dwight Macdonald then still called himself a Trotskyist but was too independent a thinker and too kind a human being to tie himself down to any dogma. His friends included various types and kinds of disillusioned ex-Communists or anti-Stalinists, liberal socialists, anarchists, pacifists and such unidentifiable characters as James Farrell who was also a friend of Dora's. As also such uncommitted intellectuals as Mary McCarthy who, although she had been a member of the Trotsky Defense Committee had become an anti-Stalinist, as she herself relates, not out of conviction, but in reaction to the threats of the Stalinists then so powerful in the literary world.

The guests at the Macdonald's parties were less diversified than at George Calverton's but there was great argument "about it and about" within the confines of their Socialist ideology, with all of us, to quote the Persian poet once again, "coming out by the same door" as in we went.

Dwight MacDonald himself was a lover of life and good cheer but, unlike George, abstemious. He had already made himself a reputation as a brilliant and witty writer on the *New Yorker*, but was far too interested in politics to spend his time amusing the 'bourgeoisie' and making good money on that smart magazine. He was soon to split with his collaborators on *Partisan Review* and start his own magazine called *Politics*, in which he wrote brilliantly for a season, its contents being mainly his own contributions. Eventually, tiring of subsidizing his own magazine, or realizing that he would be more effective in expressing his views by accepting the many opportunities offered him to write in publications of wide circulation, he jettisoned *Politics*. He rejoined the *New Yorker* and, as its movie critic, helped make *Esquire* into a magazine worthy to be read by "intellectuals."

Not long ago, meeting William L. White again in New York after many years, he embraced me so affectionately that I asked him why. He replied by saying that so many of his old friends who had fought the good fight against Communism are dead, that he loved me and the few others who are still alive. So also today, I retain an affectionate regard for Dwight MacDonald who is not only still very much alive but also more successful in this our world today than anyone else I knew in the Village in the early 1940's, thanks to his wit and style, or perhaps because he has been able to retain his original faith in pacifism, socialism and all that by ignoring the realities of our day and age.

The second Bohemia I lived in, in the Village in New York in the early Forties, was far more congenial to me than the one I had known in London after the 1914 War. It soon became impossible for me to associate with such former friends of mine as Leo Huberman who was moving ever closer to the Communists in spite of his knowledge concerning the realities of life in Soviet Russia. Like other good men among my friends his passionate hatred of Nazi Germany's racist state blinded him to the equally horrible tyranny of Stalin's Russia. But there was not as yet any insuperable barrier between me and those who later came to be designated as the 'totalitarian liberals' on account of their unconditional support and whitewash of the Stalin dictatorship.

It was already unpopular to express dislike, or doubts, concerning the 'Workers Paradise' in Russia in the pseudo liberal circles which were soon to become an entrenched 'Establishment' which a writer defied at the cost of being ostracized. But in 1940-41 one was not yet altogether outside the pale by reason of anti-Communist views. Nor was it until many years later that on account of my testimony against Owen Lattimore before the Tydings Committee, and my book called *The China Story*, that I was consigned to limbo.

Today, neither New York nor London nor any Western city seems to afford any such stimulus or forum for the discussion of divergent liberal or conservative views as "the Village" provided two decades ago. Where, indeed, are not only "the snows of yesteryear" but also the flowers which bloomed so abundantly in the intellectual climate of those days? I wish I were still there, or that it still existed.

Chapter 26
FAILURE OF THE DREAM

In my innocence of what I was up against, I was sustained by hope while writing *The Dream We Lost*. Not of personal happiness, since I was burning my bridges, cutting myself off from any possibility of being permitted to return to Russia and be reunited with my husband if he still lived, risking his life if he were not already dead. But the hope that by telling the story of my life in the U.S.S.R., and analyzing the political and economic lessons I had learned through this experience, I would succeed in diminishing Communist influence in the West.

Other books had been published exposing the true face of the Soviet Union, but they had been written either by Russian escapees or by outsiders surveying the Russian scene from the security of their privileged positions as foreign journalists, diplomats, engineers or tourists. I was the only Western writer who had known Russia both from inside and from below, sharing some of the hardships and all the fears of the forcibly silenced Russian people. In John P. Marquand's words:

> No other Westerner who broke with the Communists had quite her intimate experience with the Russian way of life .... Born an Englishwoman, taught in the best British tradition ... a trained observer and an excellent writer (Freda Utley described) her Russian adventures in terms that are to us here entirely understandable, with reactions close to what ours might be in a similar situation.*

The success of *Japan's Feet of Clay* in America as well as in England encouraged me to believe that my book on the Soviet Union would likewise become a best seller, or at least reach a wide enough circle of readers to dispel the mists of misinformation about Russia and Communism which befogged Western minds.

I was rapidly disillusioned.

Although *The Dream We Lost* had an impact on some of the leading literary, philosophical and political personalities of our time, it failed to break through the sound barrier established by those who controlled the media of mass information. Its reception was for me an instructive introduction to the way in which public opinion, so-called, is formed in America.

As Eugene Lyons was to write a year later in *The Red Decade*:

> In 1940 a remarkable book on her Soviet experiences was published by Freda Utley, an English economist. It was called *The Dream We Lost*. It was at once a deeply touching personal narrative and a detailed, documented analysis. Her books on foreign affairs had in the past been reviewed and always favorably. This one was her most ambitious and intensive work. It was put out by a reputable publisher. Bertrand

---

*In his introduction to the abbreviated version of my book republished in 1948 under the title *Lost Illusion*.

255

Russell, in *The Saturday Review of Literature*, described it as the most important book as yet written on Russia. Not a single one of the regular daily reviewers of the major newspapers, however, even mentioned it! They shied away from it, perhaps because it was too annoying a reminder of their own gullibility and literary power-politics of the years which Miss Utley described so well.*

Only three years before, Robert Van Gelder, in *Books of the Times* had hailed my *Japan's Feet of Clay* as:

> . . . a long overdue book written by an English economist . . . so well and thoroughly documented, so obviously based on solid research that . . . it should be read by all who are interested in getting to the roots of what is happening in the world today.

But when it came to my exposure of Stalin's Russia, George Calverton's repeated efforts to make his friend Ralph Thompson review my book in *The New York Times* were unavailing.

The *Herald Tribune* was equally uninterested in "getting to the roots" of the world situation if this necessitated an uninhibited look at the Union of Soviet Socialist Republics. In 1938, in reviewing my book on Japan it had written:

> Had Dr. Utley's point been driven home during the early stages of the Manchurian crisis it is not inconceivable that the effect on the thinking public of Britain and America might have been sufficient to bring Japan to book.

Lacking any similar interest in bringing Stalin to book, the *Herald Tribune* gave my book on Russia the same silent treatment as *The New York Times*.

The reviewers of the daily editions of *The New York Times* and *Herald Tribune* could explain the blackout by saying that there were other works of greater importance or literary merit than mine. The Sunday editions of these two leading metropolitan newspapers whose "Books" sections could make or break books, could not plead lack of space. Instead of ignoring *The Dream We Lost*, the former damned it with faint praise by giving it to a "White" Russian emigré to review, while the latter smeared and misrepresented it from both the "liberal" and "conservative" angles. Nathaniel Pfeffer in his review accused me of being so motivated by "hatred of Russia" that I wanted to see a Nazi victory in Europe, while Isabel Patterson in her column warned everyone against me as a heretic fit for burning because I had not repented of the sin of believing that a Socialist society could be anything but evil.

Whereas Bertrand Russell praised my book for its combination of "intimate knowledge with extensive economic understanding and profound sincerity" and credited me with "the keenest and most comprehensive intellectual understanding," Isabel Patterson, a self-styled philosopher of conservatism, wrote that "Miss Utley . . . was innately incapable of thinking at all on the subjects to which she has voluntarily devoted her life."

"Hell," says the poet, "hath no greater fury than a woman scorned." I consider this an exaggeration. More potent furies are to be found among "idealists" who resent those who endeavor to bring unwelcome facts to their attention. And perhaps the greatest fury of all is that of the poor in heart who, never having themselves aspired to make a better world, hate those who tried and failed.

It was not until many years later, after my experiences with the "ultras" of the Right

---

*Bobbs Merrill, 1941.

who captured Senator McCarthy and led him to destruction, that I came to understand why conservatives of the Isabel Patterson type were as hostile to me and my book as the Communists. In 1940, wondering why an anti-Communist should be intent on denigrating my exposure of Soviet Russia instead of aligning herself with me against the Communists and their "totalitarian liberal" friends, I sought to talk to this strange woman, thinking that she must have misunderstood, or failed to read my book. Dick Walsh arranged a meeting, which as I recall took place at the Putnam Publisher office. We had a great argument which provoked Miss Patterson to write another column denouncing me again, and further expounding her view that ex-Communists should be treated as untouchables, or as such guilty or stupid people that they ought to be distrusted and silenced forevermore.

Today, reading Ayn Rand's books, which glorify the Communist false image of American capitalism as free enterprise unlimited with the devil welcome to take the hindmost, I have come to understand why the "ultras" of the Right so often agree with those of the Left. The former would have Western society become exactly what Communist propaganda says it is but which it actually is not. The Communists decry the worship of the Golden Calf, while the Ayn Rand type of "idealists" on the extreme right believe that there is no god but Mammon, whom we should worship and upon whose altar we should not hesitate to sacrifice those who fall behind in the struggle for existence. Thus, the extreme Left assails, and the extreme Right extolls the same false conception of a free society as one ruled by jungle law. And both equally reject Christian moral values and those of the other great religions which have tempered man's inhumanity to man.

Ayn Rand's dollar sign neo-Nietzschean philosophy of unrestricted egoism is the antistrophe to the strophe of the Communist philosophy of collectivism unlimited. Hegel, it must be acknowledged, explains a lot by his thesis-antithesis-synthesis philosophy.

Today I realize that I was also up against the prejudice of those who stand on the sidelines against all who dare submit their beliefs to the test of experience. The non-combatant needs to justify himself by asserting his superiority over those who engage themselves wholeheartedly in the struggle to make their ideals come true. His most derogatory adjective is "emotional." Believing that to be detached is to be scientific, he eschews the scientific method of proof by experiment.

A typical example of what might be called "the eunuch's view" of human experience is afforded by the following quotation from a review of *The Dream We Lost* by a certain Frank H. Pardee in the *Boston Evening Transcript*. After acknowledging that it had "more real substance and interest" than most other books about Russia, he wrote: "Unfortunately, for the general excellence of the book . . . the conclusions lose much weight because they are so colored by the author's personal experience."

In referring to this type of critic, Norman Thomas, when introducing me to a New York audience, remarked: "There are many people who think that Freda Utley should not be heard because she knows too much about Soviet Russia through experience."

Bertrand Russell whose burning sympathy for people as individuals stands in striking contrast to those whose humanitarian sympathies are confined to mankind in the abstract, entitled his 1940 review of my book: *The Tragedy of Reality*, and wrote:

> Readers should dwell on the personal side of her story. The personal
> is too often forgotten in a vague way of thinking of history and politics
> in terms of great forces. Tragedies like this are the stuff that tyranny is
> made of, and to know one such tragedy is to know all of them in
> imagination. People who are inclined to think personal suffering is a

257

cheap price to pay for "the nationalization of the means of production," need to be reminded of what personal suffering means.

Various disillusioned books have been written about Russia, but no other known to me combines such intimate knowledge as Miss Utley possesses with such profound sincerity and such extensive economic understanding . . . (Her) detailed, documented and intimate indictment of Stalin's government, with the consequent rejection of the philosophy of which that government is the inevitable outcome, is a very important and valuable piece of work. Like her earlier book, *Japan's Feet of Clay*, it combines the keenest and most comprehensive intellectual understanding with deep and sincere emotion. And in spite of occasional statistics, it holds the reader's attention as intensely as a great novel. Liberals, if they are no longer to be led astray, will, I sincerely hope, read and ponder this book with all the seriousness that it deserves. When at last the Soviet myth is finally dispelled, Miss Utley's account of daily life in Russia will become for historians an invaluable source book.

The above extracts illustrate the contrast between the attitude of a great liberal philosopher and sensitive human being toward suffering and experience, and that of the small men of little understanding and less heart who seek peace of mind by dismissing as "emotional" or "prejudiced" those who endeavor to make them face reality. Reluctance to experience life to the full lest it prove too painful, distrust of emotion, or dread of being singed by the divine fire of indignation against injustice and cruelty and "all the oppressions that are done under the sun," would seem to be the distinguishing trait of critics of our time who form or reflect the climate of public opinion.

Our era is not unique. A century and a half ago in 1817, Shelley wrote:

It is the misfortune of this age that its writers, too thoughtless of immortality, are exquisitely sensible to temporary praise or blame. They write with the fear of reviews before their eyes. This system of criticism sprang up in that torpid interval when poetry was not. Poetry and the art which professes to regulate and limit its powers, cannot subsist together.*

In general, in 1940, I learned some salutary lessons concerning the power of the "Fourth Estate." By selecting news and suppressing views which fail to conform to current stereotyped thinking, or which affront their own prejudices, journalists and columnists, editors, publishers and reviewers of books arrogate to themselves the formation and expression of "public opinion." As Samuel Johnson wrote long ago: " . . . I know not whether more is to be dreaded from streets filled with soldiers accustomed to plunder, or from garrets filled with scribblers accustomed to lie." Of course, nowadays the scribblers and panderers are far better rewarded than in the 18th century and are more likely to live in penthouses than in garrets, thanks to the immensely increased power acquired by the press, radio and television in our time. Today Western civilization would seem to be more endangered by the media of mass communication which enjoy power without responsibility than by its external enemies.

* * *

Re-reading the reviews of my 1940 book on Russia, I see that it was not in fact as badly treated as implied in the passage quoted above from Gene Lyons' book.

---

*Preface to *Revolt of Islam*.

It was a failure to the extent that the boycott imposed in influential quarters prevented it from having a big sale or wide immediate influence. But it was astonishingly well treated by the liberal weeklies besides evoking warm praise from such moderately conservative papers as the *New York Sun*.

Among those who praised it were such distinguished men of letters as Max Eastman, Charles A. Beard, Norman Thomas, Oswald Garrison Villard, Dwight MacDonald, Selden Rodman, Alfred Bingham, Gene Lyons, Ben Stollberg, Isaac Don Levine, and Norman Cousins, who arranged for Russell to review it in the *Saturday Review*.

In *The Nation*, not yet dominated by the baneful influence of Freda Kirchway, Margaret Marshall wrote that because my background, beliefs and hopes were those of a whole generation my story was at times almost unbearable by reason of the reader's sense of identification. And that my indictment was "made tremendously impressive by the respect for fact and the transparent integrity" that informed my book.

Even *The New Republic*, although then edited by the 'totalitarian liberal' Malcolm Cowley, published a fair review by Richard Rovere who expressed sympathetic appreciation of my "comprehensive and destructive criticism" of Russian Communism in what he described as the "curiously calm book" I had written after my experiences. But he could not abide my realistic presentation of the choice before us and described my advocacy of encouraging Hitler to go East as a thesis "hardly better than that of the Tories who invented it."

I have always respected Rovere and even had some liking for him on the occasions we have met in recent years, notably in Berlin during the 1951 Summit Conference. Unlike most liberals in our time, he has not obstinately shut his eyes and closed his ears to unwelcome facts and he has a sense of humor. It was probably due to his generally favorable estimate of *The Dream We Lost* that *The New Republic* gave me the "Red Dean" of Canterbury's eulogy of the Soviet Union to review.* Entitled *Dean in Cloud Cuckoo Land* and published in the January 6, 1941 issue, it was perhaps the most hostile review of a pro-Soviet book published in a liberal journal at that time.

Naturally it provoked a stream of angry letters from "liberals," still faithful friends of the Soviet Union despite the Stalin-Hitler Pact, the dismemberment of Poland and the war on Finland. Such professional anti-anti-Communists as Isodore Scheiller, Ella Winter, and John A. Kingsbury wrote letters challenging my assertion that the German National Socialist system in Germany was not as ruthless as the Communist one. To which I replied: "If Hitler had not been somewhat less ruthless than Stalin the world might be as ignorant of conditions in Germany as it is of the state of Russia; Stalin never let *his* victims out of the country to tell the tale whereas Hitler has allowed thousands of Jews, Socialists and liberals to leave Germany."**

I owed the title of my book on Russia to Pearl Buck, wife of the late Richard Walsh who owned the John Day Company which published it. And I have rarely, if ever, received such tribute to anything I ever wrote as her review in *Asia* magazine in which she said:

> There are books which are to be read for story, others to be read for
> information, some to be read for the revelation of a personality and

---

**The Soviet Power.*

**I am indebted to James J. Martin, for this quotation from my own writings. His two volume documented and authoritative *HISTORY OF AMERICAN LIBERALISM AND WORLD POLITICS*, 1931-41, (Devin Adair, New York 1946) constitutes a valuable source book not only for "revisionist" historians but for everyone who wants and needs to know the true history of our times.

some for their inspiration. (Freda Utley's book) is to be read on all these counts . . . . An English writer well known for her books on China and Japan, all who know her knew that her greatest book would be the one she would one day write about Russia . . . . This is one of the richest books I have ever read. It is more than an unassailable indictment of Russian Communism. It is a strongly dramatic story and one interesting enough to make a major novel, the story of a brilliant mind, rigorously truthful in its working, though born unhappily in the body of a woman.

Some writers might have let the book center about personal tragedy. But this writer is too large for that. *The Dream We Lost* is primarily the work of a free mind searching for truth and recognizing and proclaiming it when found.

I have never quite understood Pearl Buck. A year or two after her enthusiastic endorsement of my views on Russia she had so far succumbed to the ever increasing influence in America of the "Friends of the Soviet Union," that she praised Michael Straight's book eulogizing the Soviet Union in almost as warm terms as my anti-Soviet book.

She used to talk to me about "timing" which is all very well but can be a synonym for opportunism. Perhaps she chose to forget what she had learned from me about Russia, or discounted it, when, after America entered the war she went along with those who, in their zeal to annihilate Nazi Germany, convinced themselves and others that our "ally" Communist Russia, must be better. She was a good friend to me once, but today I sometimes wonder why she, who was so wise about "timing," did not advise me to limit myself in *The Dream We Lost* to my exposure of the horrible realities of Stalin's Russia, reserving my views on the war and American intervention to a subsequent volume.

My book was far too long anyhow and as my English friends Sir George and Katherine Sansom said to me later, I might have had a success had I done so, since in the fall of 1940 during the era of the Stalin-Hitler pact, the influence of the Communists and their fellow travellers was in abeyance.

By including a Third Part in which I showed the resemblance between Nazi Germany and Soviet Russia and concluded that the latter was the greater evil, I ruined my chances of being heard in America. I was so aware of the disastrous consequences which must follow if Russia were to supplant Germany as the strongest power in Europe that I pleaded for a negotiated peace lest we "Make the World Safe for Stalin." Instead of winning friends and influencing people before arguing against American intervention in the Second World War, I had thrown everything into one package and made enemies on all sides. I had gone too far too soon. I had outraged too many prejudices, taken on too many adversaries simultaneously, endeavored to make my readers swallow too large a dose of truth, or reality, at one gulp. Consequently I failed to break through the barriers set up by the stubborn refusal of liberal idealists to see the world as it is, and the equally obstructive belief of reactionaries that the Golden Age lies in the past.

It was not only the Communists and their faithful fellow travellers who wanted to consign me and my book to oblivion. I had ruffled the serenity of all the happy liberal idealists who dwell in ivory towers, or penthouses far from the sight and sound and feel of human suffering, imagining that the world can easily be reformed according to their blueprints without cost to themselves. To them, the Russian people were like so many guinea pigs subjected to an experiment in better living whose sufferings should be no more taken into account than those of animals vivisected to advance scientific or medical knowledge.

One recalls the famous remark made by Walter Duranty, Moscow correspondent of *The New York Times*, during the famine which resulted from the forced collectivization of the peasants and the liquidation of the Kulaks, "You can't make an omelet without breaking eggs."

Whereas the Left disapproved of me for having assailed their calm endurance of other people's sufferings, and because I was an apostate from the Communist Party, the Right distrusted me because I had once been in it. Like other ex-Communists who become the most implacable of anti-Communists by reason of their experience in the Communist hell, I learned that when you leave the Party you run the gauntlet on both sides. I did not quite, even metaphorically, ride into the valley of death like the soldiers in Tennyson's *Charge of the Light Brigade*, shot down by cannon to the right and left of them in a hopeless assault on impregnable positions. My situation was analogous, but happily there were enough Americans on all sides who cheered me on instead of shooting at me.

I had failed to exert any appreciable influence on public opinion by the book I had distilled from the personal and political agony of my Russian experience. Although it took me some while to realize the fact, I had incurred the enduring hostility of the totalitarian liberals who had acclaimed me so long as I confined my denunciation of tyranny to Japanese militarism, thus seriously impairing my capacity to earn a living by my writings and lectures. I was also suspect to the ultraconservatives who are antagonistic to anyone who assails their complacency by seeking to establish a more just and rational social and economic order. But I had won the esteem of a sufficient number of men and women of good will, intelligence, and courage on both the Left and the Right to save me and my book from obliteration.

Besides my loyal defenders among the liberals, who, despite their lingering faith in socialism, would have no truck with Stalin's tyranny, I had the support, and acquired the friendship of such diverse prominent Americans as General Robert E. Wood, Charles and Anne Lindbergh, Colonel Truman Smith, Senators Wheeler, Taft, LaFollette, and Nye, Adelaide Marquand, John T. Flynn, and others who played a prominent part in the "America First" movement endeavoring to keep America out of yet another World War to "save Democracy."

There are others whose names I have forgotten, or who became known to me only many years later, who have assured me that they were powerfully affected by *The Dream We Lost*. Among them I can count the man who became Mayor of Bombay after India won her independence, who wrote to me saying that while he was imprisoned during the Second World War, a copy of my *The Dream We Lost* had been passed from hand to hand among his fellow prisoners and had been instrumental in saving him and other Indian revolutionaries from becoming Communists.

In England I fared far worse. Faber and Faber, publishers of my *Japan's Feet of Clay* and *China at War*, who had given me a substantial advance on my projected book on Russia, chose to lose their investment rather than publish *The Dream We Lost*, although I offered to eliminate the controversial Third Part.

Years later Captain Russell Grenfell R.N. whose books on Naval strategy were renowned, could only find an American publisher for his *Unconditional Hatred—German War Guilt and the Future of Europe*,* criticizing Winston Churchill and Lord Vansitart,

---

*Devin Adair, New York, 1953.

wrote to me: "How Hitler would have revelled in it here. In Germany the Gestapo was needed to suppress criticism; in England the editors and publishers do it automatically."

Among the reasons why there is greater freedom of expression in the United States than in England is the great extent of American territory, its divergent centers of influence, and the large number of independent men of wealth who can afford to refuse to be dictated to by the "establishment" centered in New York.

My most singular failure two decades ago was that of failing to appreciate the dead weight constituted by those who in their search for security, hitch their wagon to what seems to be the winning side. Those who never even contemplate risking "their lives, their fortune and their sacred honor" for any firmly held belief are more likely to "bury us" than the Communists.

More dangerous to me than the ultra's on both Right and Left was the hostility of New Dealers committed to the proposition that the defeat of Nazi Germany would ensure peace, prosperity, liberty and progress "everywhere in the world." Their antagonism was aroused by the concluding chapters of my book in which, besides showing the similarity between Nazi and Communist doctrine and practices I argued that Communism was the greater evil, so that a negotiated peace would be preferable to American involvement in a war which could not but lead to the spread of totalitarian tyranny, black or red. As I relate in the next chapter, after the *Reader's Digest* in 1941 published my article expressing this view, the "totalitarian liberals" almost succeeded in getting me expelled from America, and were to prevent my becoming a United States citizen for many years.

Eventually *The Dream We Lost* came near to fulfilling Bertrand Russell's expectations. In its shortened version, published in 1948 under the title *Lost Illusion*, it won front page recognition in *The New York Times Sunday Book Review*, was widely acclaimed in England, and translated into many languages. In recent years it has also been distributed in paperback by the U.S. Information Service in Asia, Africa, and South America and reprinted in America.

I failed to become a mover or shaker of the world, but maybe I exerted some slight influence on the course of human events.

* * *

I had no premonition of the troubles which awaited me when *The Dream We Lost* was published in September 1940. Richard Walsh and Pearl Buck together with the Columbia Lecture Bureau secured me speaking engagements, and for a while I continued to believe I would be able to smash through the barriers to truth erected by the totalitarian liberal establishment. I was so confident that I prepared to reassemble my family in a home of our own in New York and to concentrate on the preliminaries necessary to secure our immigration visas.

On October 4 I wrote Mother the good news that Caroline Pratt was going to take Jon at the City and Country school for nothing, until I could afford to pay, "probably in a year's time," and that "I am looking for a flat close by the school on 12th street where we can all be together again at last." Other good news was that I had secured a lecture in Illinois for $125, and the Columbia people seemed to be "pushing me a bit now." And, I wrote, "I had a nice note from Lord Lothian on which he had added in his own handwriting that he has read my book with great interest and to come and see him when next in Washington."

I have reason to remember Isabel Scott, Director of the Columbia Lecture Bureau, with gratitude. Believing that I had an important message, this intelligent and quite beautiful Canadian woman worked hard at getting me lectures and defended me against

262

both Left and Right wing prejudice against ex-Communists. On one occasion she forced the Peoria Citizen's Forum to hear me in spite of their wanting to cancel the contract for my lecture on account of a smear review of my book on Russia. And later when I was in danger of being expelled from America on account of my former membership in the Communist Party she wrote the following letter to Congressman Jerry Voorhis of California:

December 9, 1940.

Dear Sir:

Miss Utley has told me that you are very kindly offering a special Bill in Congress which will permit Miss Utley to remain in this country.

I understand that the basic reason for this is Miss Utley's former association with the British Communist Party, and we feel impelled to write you of our very strong feeling that because of this former association and her complete repudiation of all of the concepts of Communism, resulting from her close association with the movement and the complete disillusionment in it, is the greatest possible reason for her being permitted to stay in this country, and to present the evils of this system to audiences all over the country.

No one could possibly be more opposed to the Communistic system than Miss Utley. Certainly, she is in a position to disillusion anyone who might have leanings in that direction, and the fact that she speaks with authority, because of her many years of residence *in* Russia, and not because of personal convictions gathered *outside* Russia, makes her message the more important and compelling.

Miss Utley is a brilliant speaker and has one of the most logical and clear thinking minds I have come in contact with. Recently, I heard Miss Utley speak before the Overseas Press Club, and she gave what I consider one of the most brilliant lectures I have heard in my 15 years of experience in this field. Her response from this club was sensational and she answered questions put to her by the audience in a brilliant fashion.

We feel that what she has to say about the evils of Communism and Nazism, and their similarity, is of the utmost importance to the American audience today. Recently, when she was appearing on the program of the Book Fair in Boston, the Chairman of the committee expressed the opinion that her book, *The Dream We Lost* should be required reading for all members of the Youth Congress. Miss Utley can express more clearly than anyone I know the fundamental dangers which need to be exposed to the American public of the Russian and German systems of government.

I am also enclosing copy of a letter recently received from the Peoria Citizens Forum (Peoria, Illinois), where they had frankly been worried about her previous connection with the Communist Party, and I believe this letter speaks for itself and for Miss Utley more powerfully than anything anyone could say.

We believe that it is vitally important that Miss Utley stay in this country—to talk and write as powerfully as only she can do, in order that we may ward off the hold which Communism particularly seems to have on a large number of our population.

It is our earnest belief that Miss Utley is one of the few powerful influences against Communism in this country today, and I sincerely hope that your Bill will be successful.

Sincerely yours,
Isabel R. Scott

In October 1940 I was invited to speak at the Boston Book Fair. Philip Johnson, today one of the most renowned architects in America and the world, invited me to stay at his house in Cambridge. In later years he helped me to sustain my courage and some measure of confidence in the value and quality of my writing.

Having by chance preserved the letter he wrote me, I reproduce part of it here:

Harvard University
Cambridge

Dear Freda:

I think the idea of your writing fiction A-1. I noticed that Florinsky this morning liked the autobiographical part too. I don't quite know if you realize how awfully good it is, interested as you are in unfeminine things. But you are a woman and if you will only loosen up and enjoy it. Write semi-fiction on China. All your detachment and your intellectuality will bring to it a crispness and objectivity which will make the narrative all the more absorbing.

I talked with Bertie Russell the other day about you. He thinks your hope for the amelioration of Hitlerism absurd. I agree with him, though from a violently different Weltanschauung. He did not argue with me when I said you had sized up present Germany very well in spite of not having been there. He apparently hasn't been there either. He is very epigrammatic these days and lots of fun. I was not much impressed with Lady Russell, as she calls herself here, but I did not get to talk with her . . . .

As ever,
Philip

Reading this old letter of Philip's today while Bertrand Russell in his 90's is denouncing the U.S. for "war crimes" in Vietnam, and pinning his hopes on the "amelioration" of the Soviet System, I wonder whether he recalls his dismissal as "absurd" my hope for the amelioration of Hitler's Germany three decades ago. As also, why he has subjected himself to the advice and influence of Schoenman and other Trotskyist or New Left young men now surrounding him, since he told me long ago that it was political romanticism to imagine that things would have been better if Trotsky instead of Stalin had taken power in Russia after Lenin's death.

* * *

Clothes were a problem for my lectures and I don't know what I should have done had I not then still been slim enough to wear Dora's and Rosa's dresses which they generously lent me whenever it was necessary for me to put on a good front. In a letter answering Mother's request for money for a dress she wanted, I wrote: "Darling, I have hardly any clothes and it is a great disadvantage . . . ."

In another dated October 17, 1940, I say:

Dear, I know you like me to have things—all I ever meant was your

264

insufficient realization of the importance of my being better dressed. My reputation and opportunities here have suffered from the shabbiness and old-fashionedness of my clothes.

The contrast between the company I was occasionally keeping and my almost non-existent income and scanty wardrobe is illustrated by my letter from Boston written on the day after speaking at a luncheon together with Ely Culbertson of Bridge fame:

No time to write you a proper letter, but I enclose a photo of me in paper yesterday. Had quite a success at the lunch and it should help the book. I am living here in great luxury; beautiful room and bath of my own, choice wines and the best cooked food I have eaten in America. The Russells came to dinner last night and it was a success.

Have now got to change and go to dinner with Walshes and Russells and then speak at the Book Fair. Have had my hair done and am wearing a lovely black evening gown of Rosa's which fits me perfectly. Have had to spend a little money on accessories.

I only vaguely remember that Boston Book Fair, where I faced a huge audience in my borrowed evening gown and received a lot of applause, although my talk about Russia and the Communist menace was stronger meat and far more "controversial" than Alice Duer Miller's poem about the Chalk Cliffs of Dover which she recited. Looking through old newspaper clippings I see that I was introduced by Dr. Ernest Hooten, Harvard's Professor of Anthropology, who "asked for 5,000 persons to volunteer to purchase *The Dream We Lost* for presentation to members of the American Youth Congress and American Student's Union to dispel their false illusions about communism." How strange this sounds today when one thinks of Harvard professors as mainly concerned in arguing that the United States should cease and desist from trying to save Vietnam from Communist tyranny.

In the summer of 1945 I was to meet Professor Hooten again when we were guests of Emily Hahn's at Jim Putnam's house on Martha's Vineyard.

My most vivid recollection of the time when he tried to promote my book on Russia is the night when Bertrand Russell and Peter came to dinner. Philip Johnson's friend Professor Hoskins, who later became U.S. Ambassador to Sweden, and his wife were the other guests. I felt mainly responsible for the affair and was delighted to find Russell enormously enjoying Philip's company. Next day Bertie told me how much he liked him. "Your friend Philip," he remarked with a chuckle, "is a diabolist, which is a strange thing for a friend of yours to be, but how much pleasanter it is to spend an evening with a gentleman you disagree with than with a cad you agree with."

I had originally met Philip Johnson with Lawrence Dennis after reviewing the latter's book, *Dynamics Of War And Revolution** in Alfred Bingham's *Common Sense*. At that time I knew nothing about Dennis but had found his book of great interest and importance although disagreeing with his conclusions. I had got along famously with both of them at our first meeting over a champagne and lobster luncheon at "Charles" on Sixth Avenue. I did not agree with their philosophy or "Weltanschaung" since, as Philip still says of me, I have never lost my "liberal illusions." But I liked them both and appreciated the quality of their minds and their courage even though their reasons for opposing American intervention in the Second World War were other than mine. Subsequently we met frequently either in New York or at Dennis's home in New Jersey

---

*New York. Weekly Foreign Letter, 1940.

where he and his wife Eleanor entertained bounteously at Sunday chicken dinners. Driven over by Philip, I there met such active "America Firsters" as Greta Lewisohn, wife to Paul Palmer of the *Reader's Digest*, and Frances, then wife to John Gunther. Both of them were Jewish, which I mention only because of the "anti-Semitic" smear which was undeservedly applied by the "Interventionists" to Lawrence Dennis and others among those who wanted to keep America out of the war.

In an article published in *Life* on January 20, 1941, Dennis was labeled under his picture as "the brain truster for the forces of appeasement" with photographs of Alice Longworth, Charles Lindbergh, Joseph P. Kennedy, General Hugh S. Johnson, and Mrs. Burton K. Wheeler designated as his disciples. Later on Dennis came to be pilloried as a "fascist" and anti-Semite, which he never was, and was insulted and injured by being put on trial as a seditionist together with crackpots such as Elizabeth Dillinger. Today he is the husband of my dear friend Dora with whom I lived in the Village in 1940. Recently Sidney Hook told me that when called upon to take up the cudgels in debate in 1941 against the man described as America's Number One Fascist, he had accepted the challenge and prepared to do battle. But after listening to Dennis's opening remarks he got up and said: "you old social democrat, you." As usual Sidney Hook hit the mark.

Lawrence Dennis's misfortune was that after realizing that international socialism was a doomed ideal, he, like the disillusioned German Social Democrats who became Nazis, believed that National Socialism was the wave of the future. Which perhaps it is, although it will not be so designated by the totalitarian liberals. As Huey Long remarked long ago, if Fascism ever came to America it would be under the guise of anti-Fascism. Those who still want to give all power to the State to enable it to eradicate the inequities of the 'capitalist system' are brothers under the skin to the Nazis even though they abhor Hilter's racial prejudices.

Much confusion was, and still is, engendered in the West by the successful Communist misrepresentation of the Fascists as tools or representatives of what Marxists call "finance capital." Actually the Nazis came to power thanks mainly to the appeal of their perverted socialist theories to the ruined, or threatened lower middle classes, and to the workers without work during the Great Depression. The German capitalists or financiers who backed Hitler on the mistaken assumption that they could use him were quickly disillusioned after he established his dictatorship over all the Germans. But the myth has survived to this day in the Western World. Many Liberals now as yesterday fail to see, or will not see, that National Socialism destroyed in Germany, but very much alive in Russia and China, is the only form of socialism—or communism—which exists or probably can exist.

Lawrence Dennis's designation as a "fascist" was due to the propensity of most Americans to regard any vision of the shape of things to come, as tantamount to wanting it to happen.

Philip Johnson, a rich man's son with a sensitive as well as an artistic temperament and a brilliant intellect, had been impelled by the suffering around him during the Great Depression to turn "right" instead of "left" like most of his contemporaries. He had for a time been associated with Huey Long in Louisiana and also exposed himself to being misrepresented as a "fascist" by going to Germany as war correspondent for Father Coughlin's publication. There he had some arguments with the professional anti-German author, William L. Shirer, who was assigned to the same room in a Berlin hotel.

266

Subsequently, Shirer took pleasure in smearing Philip in the book that made him famous: *Berlin Diary.* *

Basically, Philip was an aesthete, a philosopher, and a sensitive artist although he had the guts to go through the rigors of G.I. training and combat after America got involved in the war he was against. He became, and has remained my good friend although he now professes to have no interest in politics and I know nothing about architecture and am ignorant about art. I appreciate a beautiful poem far more than a lovely building, while Philip says, "Freda, you have a gift with words which I admire and an intellect which I respect—as for myself, my buildings are all I have to say." Perhaps our affection and respect for one another are explained by his remark to a *Time* reporter: "The duty of the artist is to strain against existing style." To me the duty of a writer is to strain against existing prejudices, ignorance or misinformation. We are both non-conformist in temperament.

In the distant days when I knew him best and understood him least, Philip upon occasion aroused all my lingering class consciousness. As, when thinking he had preferred the company of wealthy friends in New York to my intellectual companionship, I wrote as follows on February 3, 1941, to my mother then, as so often, enjoying a visit with the Holt's in Baltimore:

> I was a bit upset as Philip came to New York and kept on phoning to arrange to see me and then putting it off, always for excellent reasons! I have now, however, decided to cut him out of my mind altogether. I suddenly got angry and thought, "Damn him, preferring 'high society' to mine." I was cured last night of thinking about him not only by my own resolutions and pride, but by John Chamberlain taking me to (Oswald Garrison) Villard's to discuss with a lot of people the starting of a new magazine. I met several people there I wanted to meet and who treated me as if I were someone well-known. And I felt, well, after all, rich young men like Philip are not really my society. I must stick to the liberal working intelligentsia.

Philip continued to be a friend whose company I enjoyed greatly, and upon whom I could confidently call to render me such services as meeting my mother in Boston, and putting her up for the night on her way from the Nelsons on the Cape to the Holt's in North Haven, Maine. Imposing as all too often on my friends, in the summer of 1942, I wrote Mother that I was sure Philip would look after her and give her a good time, but that in case he should be absent from his home in Cambridge, I would ask the Marquands in Newburyport to meet her and look after her.

John and Adelaide Marquand were good friends of mine during the difficult years when I was struggling to earn a living in spite of my anti-Communist views, and I frequently stayed with them at Kent Island, Newburyport.

I originally met Adelaide Marquand at a conference in 1940 in the house of Henry Luce's sister, Mrs. Moore. There had been some discussion concerning someone or other who was rejected as no friend of China because he was an anti-interventionist in Europe. As Adelaide told me later, she had been astonished to hear an English voice saying that there was no connection; that one could very well be for American aid to China against Japan without wanting to involve America in the Second World War in Europe. Thus Adelaide Marquand and I discovered one another, she being the only "America First"

*Alfred A. Knopf, New York, 1941.

adherent who, like myself, wanted the United States to go to bat for China against Japan while keeping out of the war in Europe.

Adelaide became my friend from that day and we often met for lunch at her New York apartment together with a few other close non-interventionist friends of hers such as Greta Palmer and Alice King.

John P. Marquand also liked me and warmly praised my book *The Dream We Lost*. When during my frequent visits with them at Kent Island, Newburyport, Adelaide said: "Why do you let Freda say things which you get mad at me for saying?" John would reply, "Because she has earned the right to say them." In March, 1942, as I have been reminded by an old letter, the Marquands jointly offered to adopt my son should anything happen to me.

It was at the Marquand's apartment on Beekman Place in New York that I first met Charles and Anne Lindbergh at a party they gave prior to an America First rally at Madison Square Garden. John Marquand was an "interventionist" albeit with reservations, and was somewhat embarrassed by his wife's enthusiastic support of the "isolationists," as he confided to me that evening. But he admired and liked Charles Lindbergh, John T. Flynn, and others I met that evening who were endeavoring to keep America out of the war. He was a realist who used to say "with what" when the "interventionists" counselled immediate participation in the Second World War to save England.

I got along famously with John Marquand and greatly appreciated his novels which are likely to become as classic a chronicle of the life and times, qualities and defects, of the American "bourgeoisie" in mid-passage as Galsworthy's *Forsyte Saga*, about their counterparts during the heyday of the British Empire. Like Galsworthy, Marquand portrayed as his main characters, anti or reluctant heroes. His most sympathetic characters, like he himself, never dared to go all the way, on account of their overriding concern with security, financial, social, or political.

Marquand's own obsession with security was similar to that of the main characters in all his books, and became more pronounced the older and richer he became.

On one occasion in the early 40's when I stopped off to visit them in Newburyport on my way back to New York from Martha's Vineyard, he disserted at such length on the inequities of the income tax that I teased him by saying: "How much happier I am, dear John, than you since I never earn enough to be concerned with your problem."

Some years later after I had reproached him for sponsoring *Book-of-the-Month Club* choices despite their friendliness to the Communists, or ignorance of the reality of the Communist menace, he got furious and said: "Why can't you understand, Freda, that I'm in this business to make money by publishing popular books."

I owe a debt to John Marquand who tried to help me to write books and articles which would make money and encouraged me to believe I had literary ability. And particularly because he endeavored in 1947 to promote my *Lost Illusion* by his introduction to this cut-down version of *The Dream We Lost*.

Adelaide Marquand of whom I was very fond shared none of her husband's complexes. Born to wealth as one of the "three beautiful Hooker sisters" she was as little concerned with security as with clothes, outward show or conventions, but most generous in contributing money to causes she believed in such as America First. I saw little of her during her last years but could well understand their basic incompatibility which finally caused their divorce. When she died, Adelaide's sister, Mrs. John D. Rockefeller III, whom

I occasionally meet while staying with the Holt's in North Haven, Maine, wrote to me saying:

One Beekman Place
October 17, 1963

Dear Miss Utley,

In case you did not happen to read it in the papers, I am writing you the sad news that my sister Adelaide Marquand died very suddenly last Thursday night, October 10th, in her home in Cambridge. Knowing that you have been one of her dear and long-time friends, I felt sure that you would want to hear about it. Her three children are now all in Cambridge and have been wonderfully brave. I am trying to help them as much as possible to adjust to their loss but we all find it hard to believe that Adelaide is no longer here.

Sincerely yours,
Blanchette Rockefeller

Adelaide Marquand was one of the few people who visited the Soviet Union in the 30's with her eyes open and returned without illusions. She had there met Ivy Litvinov, wife of the Commissar, and been somewhat embarrassed when at a formal luncheon at which she had spoken of seeing a wonderful painting behind the altar of a famous church in Kazan, Ivy exclaimed loudly in shocked tones: "But only virgins are allowed to do so—don't tell me you are *still* a virgin?" Years later when Litvinov was visiting the U.S. Adelaide was invited with John Marquand to meet them in Washington. On which occasion Adelaide told Ivy, "Don't worry about me any more, I'm not a virgin but a mother."

Chapter 27
ORDEAL OF A PREMATURE ANTI-COMMUNIST

Contrast gives savor to life. After having been wined and dined in Cambridge and Boston, had my picture in the papers and my lectures reported, my book acclaimed, and in general accorded a taste of VIP treatment, I returned to my normal life of money worries and work, hurry, flurry and rushing around.

Thanks to Ephraim Doner's invaluable assistance, I found and furnished a $50 a month apartment at 259 West 12th Street. Invaluable because no one else but this impoverished, cheerful, and knowledgeable artist could have shown me how to buy second-hand furniture cheaply enough to provide for our minimum requirements out of the small amount of cash I possessed. I bought three cheap mattresses and a four dollar bed and a table and two chairs, all for $25.

Doner, who now enjoys life in Carmel, California, with his wife Rosa, who teaches school, and their daughter Natasha, was not and perhaps never will be a first class painter, although in recent years he has enjoyed a moderate success. But he had such an engaging personality, merry wit and wide ranging knowledge and interest in literature, philosophy and the curiosities of human behavior, that my friend Sir George Sansom sat for him for a paid portrait mainly in order to enjoy his conversation. Having no interest in security, Doner used to say that man has the right to starve rather than do work he does not like, but Communism denies him even this freedom.

On a late October evening, a day or two after returning to New York from my enjoyment of luxurious living in Philip Johnson's house, as we sat over a glass of beer in a Village tavern to refresh ourselves at the end of our successful bargain hunting in second-hand furniture and junk stores, Doner remarked, "it's hard when you have champagne tastes and only a fresh water income."

Although I had no prospect of ever enjoying a champagne income, brighter days seemed to be ahead when Doner helped me prepare a home for my family on 12th Street. The Columbia Lecture Bureau expected a good season for me and had booked several dates in Canada for early November from which I expected to re-enter the United States as an immigrant on the British quota. Having been notified by the U.S. Consul in Montreal that my documents were satisfactory, I had arranged to be pre-examined by the immigration and naturalization authorities before going there.

On the sunny Saturday morning when I went to Ellis Island with Jon, I had no premonition of the difficulties I was to encounter before I was at long last permitted to become a citizen of the United States.

At Ellis Island I was asked whether I had at any time belonged to an organization advocating the overthrow of governments by violence. I replied "yes," as I was in all truth bound to do since I had at one time been a member of the British Communist Party. A fatal answer, which, to my dismay, appeared to cut me off from any possibility of being admitted to the United States as an immigrant. I made it clear to the Board that I had ceased to be a Communist soon after going to live in Russia in the fall of 1930; that I had not transferred to the Russian Communist Party because of my rapid disillusionment and had let my membership in the British Communist Party lapse after 1931. I also told the Board that my recently published book, *The Dream We Lost*, was an exposure of the Soviet Union and a repudiation of the Communist political philosophy. Finally, I said that it would be unjust to penalize me because I had written a book against Communism, since if I had not written it my membership in the British Communist Party in my youth would not have been known.

I nearly lied that morning. It was obvious that my interlocutors were Irish Catholics who would be prejudiced against me if I told them I was still an atheist or agnostic. So I hesitated before replying when they asked me whether I believed in God. Then I said: " I have no religion but I believe in the power of goodness and truth"—or words to that effect. When Jon asked me afterwards why I had waited so long to answer, I tried to explain to my six year old son that I had to summon up my courage in order not to commit a sin against the Holy Ghost by professing beliefs one does not hold for personal advantage.

The Board appeared to be satisfied that there was no question of my now being a Communist or of having had any sympathy with Communism for many years past, but told me that the provisions of the Immigration Act as amended in June 1940 left them no option. They were compelled by the law to reject me, but I could appeal to Washington.

At this time many known Communists were being freely admitted because they had no scruples in denying the fact which I admitted, namely, that the Communist Party advocates the forcible overthrow of "capitalist" or "bourgeois" governments by revolution. By telling the truth at Ellis Island, I excluded myself from acquiring the citizenship easily obtained by actual active Communists such as Earl Browder's wife who, assisted by Wendell Willkie, was able to enter the United States as an immigrant.

It was to require many years, much struggle, and a private bill in Congress "for the relief of Freda Utley" introduced by Congressman Jerry Voorhis of California, for me and my son to become U.S. citizens. My story illustrates how much greater were the trials and tribulations of premature anti-Communists than any "ordeals" suffered a decade later by Owen Lattimore and others during Senator McCarthy's so-called "reign of terror" when the crypto-Communists trembled, and those who had never had the courage to come clean feared for their government jobs.

I shall never forget with how heavy a heart I returned from Ellis Island that Saturday morning to our newly acquired home on 12th Street. I did not anticipate being immediately thrown out of America where we were living on visitor's visas, but my rejection meant that I could not fulfill the Canadian lecture engagements I had counted on to provide the money I needed to take care of my family. For if I left the United States even briefly I should not be allowed to return.

I telephoned at once to George Calverton and he got going with long distance calls to Washington to save me. Calls which, although they failed to lift the ban which prevented me from fulfilling my lecture engagements, resulted in a review of my case in Washington.

Life sometimes produces comic situations in the midst of adversity: on the Sunday morning following my disastrous interview with the immigration authorities at Ellis Island, I was visited by the brother of my husband's first wife, who came from Philadelphia to ask me to help his nephew, Arcadi's son, get into the United States.

"Sasha" had been studying for his doctorate at the Sorbonne when the Nazis came to Paris and had managed to escape to Portugal on a bicycle. He was now trying to emigrate to the United States, and his uncle, having read reviews of my book, imagined

I was a well-to-do author. After casting his eye around our meagerly furnished apartment he said, "Well, it does not look as if *you* could help." To which remark I replied that although I personally was not in a position to supply an affidavit for Sasha's support in America, I had friends who might be able to help him. I telephoned to Dora who worked at the Jewish refugee office and made an appointment for Sasha's uncle, which he never kept. The following summer my stepson managed to get to America from Lisbon without my help, contacted me and became a member of my family.

In February 1941, I was called before an Appeals Board at the Department of Justice in Washington. Clark Foreman, then at the Department of the Interior, testified that in 1931, when he had known me well in Moscow, I was already anti-Communist, although of necessity keeping my mouth shut on account of my husband who was a Russian citizen. And Frank Hannighen, whom I had originally met in London when he was the European correspondent of the *New York Post*, and who for many years before he died in 1964 was to be editor and publisher of the conservative newsletter *Human Events*, testified to the same effect.

Huntington Cairns in contrast, displaying more discretion than valor or friendship, excused himself from appearing as a witness on my behalf. He was at this time a Counselor at the Treasury and was probably reluctant to antagonize Harry Dexter White and his other fellow travelling associates because he dreamed of being appointed to the Supreme Court.

I myself pleaded that the intent of the Smith Act could not have been to penalize ex-Communists who exposed themselves as I had done by anti-Communist activities. The Appeals Board chairman said they were bound by the letter of the law but that it was not yet established whether past membership in the British Communist Party rendered me liable to the charge of having belonged to an organization advocating the overthrow of the United States Government by violence. Asked whether I would be willing to appear again at Ellis Island to ascertain whether or not the British Communist Party, while I was a member back in 1928-30 had advocated the overthrow of the U.S. Government, I agreed to do so, maintaining that it had not. However, the question would then arise whether the British Communist Party through its affiliation with the Comintern, to which the American Communist Party also belonged, should be held responsible for the latter's acts and policies. This all sounded very legalistic, but in the final outcome my case was not to be decided by "due process" or any judicial decision. It was to be the exigencies of the foreign policy pursued by the Roosevelt administration which finally impelled the Department of Justice to decide against me a year later, after I had written an article in the *Reader's Digest* opposing American intervention in the Second World War.

Some idea of my "ordeal" as an anti-Communist ex-Communist foreigner without money in the Roosevelt era is conveyed by the letters I wrote to Mother from Washington.

> I am waiting in the Congress building to meet someone (a man George used to know) on the Dies Committee about my case, and this seems to be my first chance to sit down and write to you.
>
> The Board yesterday clearly wanted *not* to exclude me, but there is this wretched law of last June which looks almost impossible to get round. They may have a new Board for me at Ellis Island to establish whether or not (a) the British C.P., (b) the Comintern was advocating "the violent overthrow of governments" in 1928-30 when I was a Communist. However, this would only be a slim chance of getting around the law.

It begins to look as if my only chance would be to get a special bill in Congress to exempt me from the workings of the law, which obviously was *not* intended by Congress for people like me, but for those who have pretended not to be Communists when they really are.

* * *

I am awfully tired dear, and my head aches. It is a big strain and I have to keep all my wits about me. So I do hope you and Jon can manage.

Clark was a real friend yesterday. He came with me before the Board and spoke for me and said exactly the right thing so well and convincingly. Really, he was fine.

He and Hanighen (who also came) said I had put my case awfully well—better than a lawyer could have done.

Since the Appeals Board in Washington, while in no way giving me the impression that I was being discriminated against or persecuted, had made it clear that it might be unable to admit me under the law, I went over to Loy Henderson at the State Department for his help and advice. He at once contacted Ray Murphy, Security Chief at the State Department, who arranged for me to meet Dr. J. B. Matthews of the Dies Committee who took me to Congressman Jerry Voorhis of California. On November 30 while staying with Clark and Marie Foreman on Potomac Avenue, I wrote:

Things are looking pretty hopeful. Yesterday I saw a Dr. Matthews who works for the Dies Committee and who is getting a Congress member to bring in a special bill to suspend that Immigration Act re Communists in my case. At least this is the present idea. Nothing is certain yet and I have to stay here a few days to be interviewed and provide documents, etc. I shall know on Monday, I expect, whether it is all straight sailing or whether it is not so simple. Anyhow, it looks very hopeful at present. Let Hans know all this but to others perhaps it will be best to say only that a member of Congress is going to put through a bill, i.e., don't talk about it being done through a Dies Committee member until I know the situation more fully.

Worrying about how Mother could cope with Jon during my absence I enclosed a check for $25 and told her to try and arrange to pay Mrs. Hainey downstairs to come and make breakfast and clean up.

And to Jon, not yet seven years old who, having been separated from me for many months, had expected to be with me all the time after I brought him to New York, I tried to explain my absence in Washington in a postscript for Mother to read to him which said:

Jon, my sweet, I am so sorry to have to stay a few days in Washington. I cannot help it. I hope soon to have everything arranged for us to become Americans. Look after Gran-gran, my darling. I love you. Mother.

Not the least of my worries was having to leave Mother in New York with little money to look after Jon on her own while I was in Washington. I was also afraid that the help of the Dies Committee might jeopardize the backing of my other advocates, who disliked the Un-American Activities Committee of Congress. So I wrote:

Will you phone Abrams and tell him there is no decision yet but that the Board and Seward conducted the enquiry very sympathetically and that there will probably be a rehearing at Ellis Island. *Don't* tell him I am seeing someone on the Dies Committee. Say only I am staying here a few days to see various people who may be able to help in the future. On the whole I don't quite trust Abrams now.

John Davies is going to motor me over to see the Nelsons tomorrow afternoon. He (Frederic) may also be useful in getting me to people.

Hanighen is arranging for me to see Senator Nye (very important Republican and isolationist) on Monday or Tuesday. I expect to get back to you late Tuesday evening.

I shall also try to see Lord Lothian and the Chinese Ambassador (Sunday).

In March Jerry Voorhis introduced a private bill "for the relief of Freda Utley" to suspend the provisions of the Smith Act in my case. He was requested by the Department of Justice to hold up his Bill until a decision was arrived at in my case, since it was still possible that no Special Act of Congress would be necessary to enable me to become a citizen of the United States.

From that time on I came under the protection of the Congress of the United States and no longer had to fear that I might be summarily deported from America by order of the Executive Branch of the U.S. Government.

It was not until a year later when the "interventionists" added their fire power to that of the Communist fellow travelers in high places in Washington that I found myself in a perilous situation.

I was fortunate to have friends who, even though they went along with President Roosevelt's foreign policy, protected me against his totalitarian liberal cohorts who wanted to obliterate me and all other knowledgeable anti-Communists from the political arena. Among these loyal friends I must include Clark Foreman and his lovely and kind Canadian wife Marie, in whose house on Potomac Avenue I sometimes stayed during the "ordeal" of my appearance before the Appeals Board of the Department of Justice in Washington. In later years Clark Foreman came to discount the political lessons he had learnt in Russia where I had first met him, or perhaps he found it necessary to go far Left in order to sustain his reputation as a liberal Southern Democrat. But, in 1941 he was so anti-Communist that he embarrassed Soviet Ambassador Oumansky by publicly asking him questions about my husband's imprisonment without trial when the Soviet Ambassador spoke at the Hamilton Street Club in Baltimore. Eventually Clark Foreman passed out of my ken after he came to keep company with such Communist fellow travellers as Corliss Lamont.

In May 1941 I went before a Board of Special Enquiry at Ellis Island and testified that the British Communist Party had not itself advocated the overthrow of the United States Government. As anticipated, the Board again referred my case back to Washington to decide the issue. Thereafter, my case was kept pending for nearly a year, until suddenly, in February 1942, I was notified that the Department of Justice had decided against me on the ground that I had formerly "been affiliated with an organization which believed in, advocated, and taught the overthrow by force and violence of the Government of the United States," and ordered to leave the U.S. with my mother and son. The real reason why my dormant case had been lifted out of the files and the decision made to expel me from the U.S. was revealed in the Congressional hearings on Voorhis' bill, when my *Reader's Digest* article was cited against me by the Department of Justice. Entitled, "Must the World Destroy Itself?" in the revised and somewhat oversimplified version published by the R.D. in its October 1941 issue, it had originally appeared in Bingham's *Common Sense* under the title, "God Save England from her Friends."

My argument was that the U.S. was urging England to continue a war which she could not win and might lose because if Hitler lost, Stalin would win. As it seemed to me, the longer the war lasted, the more certain it was that the area of totalitarian tyranny would be extended. "Out of universal war on the total scale," I wrote, "no good can come, only perhaps an even worse or a more universal evil than Hitlerism." Since it would be fatal for England to negotiate from weakness, I urged the United States to place its power unequivocally behind England, not for total victory but for a negotiated peace between equals. I also argued that it was possible to hope that if peace were made, Germany, having by her victories wiped out the memory of past defeats and national humiliations and the material privations she had endured between the wars, would rid herself of the gangsters who ruled her and revert to civilized values. Whereas so long as the Germans were fighting for their very lives, the Nazi hold on them could not be weakened. I ended my article by quoting Lord Lothian's famous dictum: "The lesson of the last war is that we get neither democracy, nor liberty, nor peace out of a World War, however noble the end for which it is fought."

My piece was reprinted and distributed in hundreds of thousands of copies by *America First*, and the *Journal American* in three Sunday issues published a longer and better version closer to my original manuscript.

Thus, suddenly, after a long period during which I had only been able to write for such small circulation magazines as *Common Sense*, *The New Leader*, *The Progressive*, and *Asia*, I had become famous, or notorious, by the widespread circulation of my views. This triumph was accompanied by near disaster, since the acclaim my article received evidently caused the Administration's decision to get rid of me.

Wendell Willkie wrote a reply to my article in the November issue of the R.D. which was described by Congressman O'Hara of Minnesota in Congress on November 18 as "no honest reply" but only another example of Willkie's self-confessed "campaign oratory." DeWitt Wallace commissioned me to reply to Willkie in the next issue of *Reader's Digest*. The manuscript I prepared was never published because Pearl Harbor ended the "great debate" of the "interventionists" versus the "isolationists" and those who, like myself and Norman Thomas, were internationalists, who foresaw no good result from the Second World War to "save Democracy."

Thanks to DeWitt Wallace, I had advance warning of the action to be taken against me by the Department of Justice. He contacted me shortly before to tell me that at a party given by the Brandt Literary Agency, Carol Brandt, who also worked for the British Information Agency in New York, had upbraided him for publishing my article and, having had a few drinks been indiscreet enough to say, "We will have her out of the country soon."

"Wally" over a glass of orange juice at the Sherry Netherland Hotel told me to telephone him immediately for his help if I got notice to leave America. Which, of course, I did, whereupon he mobilized all possible help for me, asking William Hard, the *Reader's Digest* representative in Washington to exert himself on my behalf. Meanwhile, Jerry Voorhis had asked Samuel Dickstein, Chairman of the House Immigration and Naturalization Committee, to give immediate consideration to his bill for my relief. Sidney Hook enlisted the support of Adolf Held. Other friends, to all of whom I shall be eternally grateful, rallied around to mobilize support for favorable consideration of HR 312 "for the relief of Freda Utley."

It was to take several years and many Committee hearings by both Houses of Congress for this Bill to become law. During the slow process of its passage, I had to spend much time, and money I could ill afford, visiting Washington either to appear at Committee hearings or to mobilize support for my Bill. But I gained more knowledge and appreciation of the workings of the American system of government than most native-born Americans have the opportunity to acquire. I came to realize that our legislators work harder than anyone else in America, and are, or then still were, genuinely concerned to uphold the principles upon which the Republic was founded. I also met, and in some cases acquired the friendship of many distinguished Congressmen and Senators whom I would otherwise never have known.

Jerry Voorhis was that *rara avis*, a principled and courageous liberal left-winger. I was not his constituent and championing me brought him no votes and consumed a great deal of his time besides being displeasing to the New Deal fellow travellers of the Communists. He was as different as could be to Helen Gehagan Douglas, an outstanding "totalitarian liberal" who, unlike Voorhis, eminently deserved to be defeated by Richard Nixon in California.

As Bertrand Russell told me so long ago, I am incurably romantic about politics. I like brave men who stand up for what they believe come what may. Such a man was Jerry Voorhis who enabled me eventually to become a citizen of the United States.

I have long since lost touch with him, but shall always think of him as the type of American who inspires many people from many lands to emigrate to the United States. Not simply because to be an American is to enjoy the highest standard of living obtainable in the world, but because, thanks to such unsung believers in the American dream as Jerry Voorhis, these United States have gone far to fulfill man's hope for a just and free society.

It was clearly indicated during the hearings on the Voorhis Bill that the real reason why the Department of Justice had finally decided not to permit me to become a United States citizen was not my long-ago short period of membership in the British Communist Party, but my advocacy of a negotiated peace to save Europe from Stalin.

The Communists and their innocent or ignorant New Deal allies were not the only people who wanted to silence me. It was a Southern Democrat Congressman, Gore of Tennessee, who stopped passage of the Voorhis Bill by the House after it had been favorably recommended by the Immigration Committee. (It is here of interest to note that Albert Gore, today a Senator, was an ardent supporter in 1968 of Gene McCarthy's campaign to have America abandon Vietnam to the Communists.)

Republican "interventionists" were also not averse to having me expelled from the U.S. Wendell Willkie, who had intervened to secure the admission of Earl Browder's Russian Communist wife to the U.S., refused to touch my case when Pearl Buck asked him to help me.

On March 17, 1942, she wrote to me saying:

> I managed to get in only a word with Mr. Willkie, but I have sent him the details of your case. He was not able to talk during the meeting, but I did talk to him afterwards. And now I have written to him very fully and earnestly and sent him copies of the Department of Justice letter and Voorhis' letter.

Shortly afterwards she informed me that Willkie refused to help:

> He preferred not to take up any more individual cases just now. He said he worked best when he kept pegging away on a few things, and just

276

now he was absorbed in race relations. I suppose it is inevitable that his political future is beginning to take shape, too, in his mind. How much better the Chinese and Indian notions of government are than ours! They think little of governments and much of their wise men. The result may be chaotic in some ways, but then our way is extremely chaotic. And in China at least it has meant a certain permeation of similar ideals and ideas which accounts for much good.

We had a long talk with the Immigration officer, who was a nice fellow, and we put our best feet foremost for you and were glad to do so. We gathered from him that the whole question of deportation was somewhat academic since no deportation could actually take place during the war. That gives time, at least.

Although Pearl Buck was undoubtedly at this time trying to help me, Wendell Willkie's caution in avoiding conflict with the American friends of the Soviet Union was apparently already having an effect on her for she wrote:

I don't think I can come and testify before the Committee, because I am asked to do this so often and if I do it in one case, even as a friend, it would involve me very much in future refusals. Now we will hope for the very best.

Faced by a formidable coalition of enemies to the Left and to the Right equally hostile to my views, and also finding faintheartedness among the people supposedly on my side, I was saved by those who, whether they called themselves conservatives or liberals, isolationists or interventionists, believed in the basic principles which created the United States and continue to inspire her best citizens. DeWitt Wallace and Oswald Garrison Villard fought for me. Sidney Hook enlisted the support of Adolf Held who wrote to Samuel Dickstein on my behalf. Noah Mason, the Congressman from Illinois who was the ranking Republican on the Committee, said after hearing me testify on my own behalf that he would be ready to sponsor the Bill himself. When it came to the Senate, Russell of Georgia took time to meet me at his office and after hearing me, promised his support. Senators Robert Taft and Bob LaFollette, Wheeler and Nye, Ferguson and Malone, are among those who actively exerted their influence to enable me to become an American citizen.

At the Senate Committee Hearings on the Bill, I brought with me as witnesses John P. Marquand, C. V. Starr, and Sir George Sansom. Marquand's testimony was very useful as also that of my British Embassy friend, but Neil Starr got himself into hot water when he remarked that it was natural for young people critical of the abuses of the capitalist system to become Socialists; that it was easily understood why some went Communist in imperialist England and that he thought if I had been brought up in America I should never have joined the Party. One Senator, who strongly objected to Starr's point of view asked him how long *he* had lived in America; hadn't he spent most of his life in China?

I should not here forget to mention the invaluable help and support I received from my dear friend, John T. Flynn, the fearless liberal opponent of the President he called the "Country Squire in the White House." In October 1944, after both Houses of Congress had at long last passed H.R. Private Law 312 and I was anxiously awaiting news as to whether President Roosevelt would sign it or veto it, John Flynn phoned me at Starr's offices on Fifth Avenue saying, "Citizen Utley, now you can spit in their eye." He had learned ahead of time from his man in Washington that the President had signed the Bill.

At long last I could go to Canada with Jon for re-entry into the U.S. on an immigrant quota and five years later become a citizen. But for many years while my fate hung in the balance, I had been effectively silenced by the friends of the Soviet Union. I was afraid at times to meet people whose views resembled mine. Early in 1941 I was advised by Ray Murphy, the State Department's Security Officer, to refuse an invitation to dinner in Washington by the Finnish Ambassador, Prokope. His other guests included Congressman Hamilton Fish and his wife Grace who in later years in Washington was very kind to me, and endeavored, with indifferent success, to bring me into the circle of the cave dweller society of the capital.

I was not always careful. In a letter dated April 1942 from New Orleans where I had been lecturing at Newcombe College, I endeavored to allay my mother's fears concerning the trouble I might get into by having spent a couple of days visiting John Cudahy, the former U.S. Ambassador to Belgium who strongly opposed Roosevelt's "road to war."

I wrote: "I can't see that it was so terrible. He has been in retirement and never has spoken against Roosevelt as far as I know. Anyhow, no one except you knows I stayed at his house.It was just a nice rest for me. Dennis, I have not seen for a long while. I have realized that I must not any more, but I like him and do not think he is a fascist." "Look, Mother dear," I continued, "I can't help being myself. I mean that however hard I try to be without beliefs and to be reasonable, sensible, look out for my own and your's and Jon's interests, there is something in me which impels me to speak out against or strike against, what I conceive of as disastrous, cruel, terrible, etc. And because it seems to me that most people are madly rushing toward a world which will be as horrible as Russia, it is hard never to talk to, or associate with, the few people who are both intelligent and decent, and have had the experience or insight to see what I see. Of course, I may be wrong in my views, but if I deny what I believe, I will destroy myself."

A decade later, after the tide had turned against the Communists and their totalitarian liberal allies, those who had ridden roughshod over such "premature anti-Communists" as I, came to represent themselves as victims of Senator Joe McCarthy's "witch hunt." "McCarthyism" was to become a byword in America for intolerance of all "liberal" or progressive views. But back in the 40's anti-Communists suffered far worse penalties.

Some few of those attacked by McCarthy were ousted from government service. Most of them suffered little if at all, retaining or securing university appointments or well-paid positions with the Foundations and news media. Owen Lattimore, who pictured himself as an innocent victim of McCarthy in his book *Ordeal By Slander,** had his reputation tarnished by my exposure of the pro-Communist bias of his writings in my testimony before the Tydings Committee; by the speech I wrote for Joe McCarthy to deliver in the Senate; and by the later hearings of the McCarran Committee for which I briefly worked. But he did not lose his professorship nor suffer any financial loss—quite to the contrary. Moreover, although he lost some influence, his views have continued to impregnate the universities and news media with the result that today America's view of Vietnam is distorted by its lack of information of the true story of how we "lost China."**

My ordeal in the 40's as an ex-Communist anti-Communist cannot be compared to that of the victims of Communist dictatorship in Russia, Europe, China or Vietnam. But

---

*Little Brown, Boston, 1950.

**My 1951 best seller, *The China Story*, used in evidence in the hearings of the Senate Committee which investigated the recall of General MacArthur, [published by the Henry Regnery Co. and still available in paperback] gives a detailed analysis of Lattimore's writings and of the pernicious influence they exerted on American opinion and policy.

278

it seems to me the height of absurdity for those who suffered some slight discomfiture by reason of their failure to "come clean" concerning their former Communist affiliations during Senator McCarthy's brief and abortive attempt to expose them, to pose as martyrs.

On the other hand, as I shall relate in detail in the second volume of this book, it is a sad but inescapable fact that many of Senator McCarthy's backers, collaborators and adherents in his heyday, were no better than his opponents. Some were worse, notably, Cohn and Schine, two unscrupulous careerists who led McCarthy to his destruction by their ignorance, arrogance and lack of regard for anything but "winning a case." So ignorant and so uninterested were they in any real effort to expose Communist influences in America that, on their notorious trip to Europe to investigate the U.S. Information Services, they managed to mix up the lists I had given them of books in Amerika Haus libraries in Germany, presenting my compilation of anti-Communist books missing from the shelves as pro-Communist books! A fact of which I was made aware by German friends who sent me press clippings showing that Cohn and Schine had classified my own and other anti-Communist books as pro-Communist. The antics of these two brash and badly behaved ignoramuses were regarded in Germany as proof that McCarthy was himself a clown. I have advanced ahead of my story. But my experience with Cohn and Schine and our mutual dislike, together with my disagreements with the "ultra rightists" and "dumb conservatives" who took Joe McCarthy in tow (causing my break with the Wisconsin Senator after I had given him much unrewarded help) is relevant to my "ordeal" in striving to become a United States citizen in the 40's when the anti-anti-Communists were far more powerful than McCarthy ever was.

It is also of interest today to note that the sins of prejudice or what not leveled at Senator McCarran for the bill he sponsored amending the immigration laws were wide of the mark. It became easier, not more difficult, for ex-Communists to become citizens of the United States afterwards than in my day.

Chapter 28
BACK TO AN OFFICE AGAIN

My son nowadays jestingly suggests that I must have had a guardian angel to preserve me from the consequences of my follies, since time and again when my situation has seemed hopeless I have been saved from destitution at the eleventh hour.

Although I neither believe in angels, nor imagine that I should deserve to have one look after me if I did, I have always felt that if one has the courage to witness to the truth as one sees it, one will not be forsaken by whatever gods there be. Recently I read Mary Renault's wonderful book called *The King Must Die** and there found a passage which echoed in my heart. Theseus in Crete and his companion captive "bull dancers" from Athens have just witnessed the death of a gallant Corinthian whose team had let him down by failing to risk their lives for him. And Theseus says:

> The Corinthian is dead, but so are all his team. They gave themselves to death just when they thought to live a little longer. They know it too. Look at them now. Shame would not weigh so heavy upon them. They are afraid. When you love your life too much in the ring, that's when you lose it . . . . They have lost their pride in themselves. If any of them has had a guardian god, they must hear the music of his passing.

Today, finding myself beginning to enjoy security and ease from strife as old age advances, I have lost, or begun to lose, the single-minded fervor of my youth and middle age. I no longer have much pride in myself and fear to hear "the music of the passing" of the spirit which kept me going through the most difficult years of my life.

A quarter of a century ago my "guardian angel" appeared in the guise of an American "tycoon," Cornelius V. Starr. He had first known me and entertained me in Shanghai in 1938 when I was by way of being a celebrity as the author of *Japan's Feet of Clay*. Meeting me again in New York, in the winter of 1940-1941 at an *Asia* magazine luncheon, he praised *The Dream We Lost* and when shortly afterwards he learned to his surprise that I was having difficulty in earning a living, offered me a job. Writing to Mother in Baltimore on February 3, 1941, I say:

> I have now some really good news to tell you. I spent two hours talking to Starr on Saturday morning. He started by saying that anyone ought to be glad to pay me a salary in order to talk to me!! He is thinking out a way of using me as a kind of research worker. He explained that his success in business was due largely to calculating the course of events in general and so forth. Said my views and knowledge were appreciated by a select few but cannot make money in popular journalism. He may start a sort of information, etc., bulletin or news service. In any case, for the present he says I ask so little ($250) the firm can carry me as a luxury but later if I can be properly utilized he will pay me a good

*Pantheon, New York, 1958.

280

salary. I have to settle the immigration business but I gather that even before that he will start paying me. I shall be at liberty to do other work while on this small salary.

So, darling, this looks like security. I am very pleased, also gratified that a man like Starr really thinks I have such a good brain, etc. He is the type who makes out he does everything for selfish reasons and is quite cynical, but he is really decent and I think kind even. This is about the best kind of job I could get. It will be interesting and allow me scope. And on $250 the rent, girl and food can be paid for. I shall always make some extra.

Neil Starr would certainly have been ready to pay me more than the modest salary I asked, but I was still all too British in some ways and feared to take advantage of what seemed to me a generous offer of assistance in time of need. I failed to realize at this time that as a political-economic advisor I actually could be useful to him and his business associates, so I asked only the minimum to provide sustenance for my family, when he asked me how much I needed. Also there was the consideration in my mind that this small salary left me free to continue writing and lecturing.

Pearl Buck assured me that I could be useful to Starr. In one of her letters she said:

I cannot agree with you that you have no place in the Starr organization. It seems to me that a person with your point of view on the Far East has a good deal to offer to a business organization like that. Things are centering very much these days in the Pacific. It may take some creative thinking to keep up with what is actually taking place there. For instance, have you kept in the organization mind the fact that we do not really know the Indian reasons for the failure of the Cripps mission? There were reasons and we Americans ought to know them. It seems to me you earn your job by keeping their minds open to the full truth about the Pacific situation.

When offering me a job in the offices of Starr, Park, Freeman at 101 Fifth Avenue, Neil told me that if I saved him from "one mistake," my salary would be well worthwhile. He added the gratuitous information that in any case it came off his income tax!

As it turned out I did save him and his associates from considerable loss, since when the U.S. froze Japanese funds in the U.S. in July 1941 I anticipated that Japan would go to war against America when Starr himself was convinced that she would never directly challenge America. I am not claiming that I foresaw Pearl Harbor but I realized that it was too late for Japan to retreat as she might have done had we imposed economic sanctions at the beginning of her war on China. In testifying for me before the Senate Immigration Committee in 1942, Starr said that if he had taken my advice he would have liquidated more assets and saved more of his people in China, but that having paid some attention to my opinion his losses had been less following Pearl Harbor than might otherwise have been the case.

After the war was over Starr came to discount my opinion of the Chinese Communists which conflicted with that of the British, for whom he always had an inordinate respect, as also with the views of the liberal editor of his *Shanghai Evening Post*, my old friend Randall Gould.

They all imagined that it was possible to "do business with" the Chinese Communists and Neil got mad at me and told me I had an anti-Communist complex when I warned him that you could not.

My 1947 book, *Last Chance in China* consequently led to a long break and some acrimonious correspondence. Starr wrote me a nasty letter saying he "gave up" on me: that he had never been my friend as I imagined and had employed me only from motives of self-interest and had found me a failure. A while later he accused me of "gunning for him." I replied that all I had done was to explain that I was no longer associated with the Starr enterprises, when asked how come he was publishing Randall Gould's "silly stuff," described by *Time* as "bubbling confidently over the prospects of communist rule in China."

Joseph Grew* later informed me that he had vainly tried to make Starr listen to me. Neil himself was to make handsome amends in 1956 when I met him in the Philippines and he told his associates there how right I had been when he was wrong a decade earlier. [On this occasion Starr also offered me the use of his lovely house on Repulse Bay on my round the world trip for as long as I wanted to stay in Hong Kong. Thus I lived a life of luxury for a few weeks with several servants to look after me. But I was so ashamed of seeming to be rich that I always stopped his chauffeur-driven Cadillac within a couple of blocks of the Press Club.]

Previous to this brief encounter in Manila I had already been more or less reconciled to Starr thanks to his approval of my 1949 book on Germany, *The High Cost of Vengeance*. By 1958 we were to be at odds again. He wanted to finance me while writing my Memoirs, but I instead, wasted time "ghosting" General Albert C. Wedemeyer's book.** On that occasion Starr was eminently right and I wrong since I not only reaped little financial reward, but had wounding fights with Al Wedemeyer on account of his prevarications, inordinate vanity and conflicting ambitions for fame, wealth, and a political career without the risks involved by taking a bold and unequivocal stand on major issues.

I have advanced far ahead of my story—and China's—to be told in the second volume of my Memoirs. I refer here to my unhappy experience with General Wedemeyer in the late 50's in order to acknowledge the fact that Neil Starr, although like most Americans, politically gullible in foreign affairs, was more astute than I in his judgement of people as witnessed by his original unfavorable estimate of Wedemeyer.

Combined with his appreciation of the political and economic realities of our continually changing times, his ability to judge people no doubt accounts for his phenomenal success in founding and perpetuating a world wide insurance banking and trading business empire. Neil Starr resembled the Chinese, among whom he had spent much of his life, in his loyalty toward his associates, employees and feeling of responsibility for their welfare when first in China and later in Cuba the Communist take-over deprived them of their livelihood.

My respect and liking for Neil Starr endured the vicissitudes of our disagreements and quarrels and I have reason to believe he retained his original regard for me as someone who stood up to him, and was actually of considerable value to him, as witnessed by his appreciation of my contributions during the time I was "economic adviser" to his companies.

I shall always be grateful to C. V. Starr who, whatever his motives may have been,

---

*U.S. Ambassador to Japan from 1931-42 and Under Secretary of State from 1941-45 prior to his retirement.

**Wedemeyer Reports*, Holt, New York, 1958.

bureaucrat, nor a financially successful writer, nor any of the other things I might have been, I remind myself that I have enjoyed to the full the priceless freedom of saying what I think and meaning what I say. Perhaps I have been intoxicated by this freedom ever since I got out of Russia. There I had not dared to speak out for fear of death or imprisonment for my husband and perhaps even for myself. In the Western World the worst I had to fear was some difficulty in earning a living, which seemed a small penalty in comparison with the terrible compulsions which force the subjects of Communist states to conform and obey.

"A slave is he who dares not speak his mind," as Euripides wrote in the 4th Century B.C.

While regularly attending at the offices of Starr, Park, Freeman, although I rarely got there on time, I conscientiously endeavored to be useful. I wrote memoranda on current events and gave my views on the shape of things to come, and was assigned various odd jobs by Starr, including a survey of insurance legislation and conditions everywhere in the world. I had an office of my own and best of all a secretary for the first and last time in my life.

Randall Gould was installed next door putting out the *Shanghai Evening Post*, in exile so to speak, in newsletter form. In 1944 I attended the Bretton Woods Monetary Conference ostensibly as its correspondent. I there hugely enjoyed myself questioning Harry Dexter White at his press conferences, and challenging his assumption that the USSR would collaborate with the Western World in the financial or any other sphere. This Communist-sympathizing U.S. Treasury representative (later to become notorious as the real author of the Morgenthau Plan for Germany), having met me in Washington as a friend of Huntington Cairns invited me to lunch during the first days of the Monetary Conference and continued to be polite even when I greatly annoyed him. His deputy, Frank Coe, today a Chinese Communist propagandist in Peking, displayed his animosity at my effrontery in arguing publicly with the U.S. Treasury representatives.

At Bretton Woods I shared a room and double bed with Sylvia Porter, famous today for her popular but well informed financial column. She had a nice sense of humor and we got along very well together even after she discovered that my name was anathema in liberal establishment circles. I was most impressed at her capacity to come to bed long after midnight and get up again early in the morning looking "as fresh as a daisy" after some quick ablutions and make up. On one occasion I remember her coming to our room about 1 a.m. with Russell of *The New York Times* with a bottle of whiskey and endeavoring to get me out of bed to drink with them.

Much of the news reported from the International Monetary Conference was garnered in the bar where Sir Wiemot Lewis, correspondent of the *London Times*, held court and where more was to be learnt than in the official sessions. Delegates objected when *The New York Times* arrived too late for them to read what had happened the day before.

I, thinking that all Englishmen were now impoverished, often refused to let Lewis pay for my drinks but learnt later that he was married in Washington to a wealthy American.

I greatly enjoyed myself at Bretton Woods making new friends and meeting old acquaintances from the London School of Economics, notably Lionel Robbins, in the British Delegation. His idea of having a party for L.S.E. alumni from many lands who came to Bretton Woods as delegates or correspondents like myself was stymied by the lack of money for entertainment by the British representatives at this first World Monetary Conference.

saved me from destitution during the war years when I was precluded from earning a living as a writer and lecturer on account of my prematurely anti-Communist views. It was with profound regret that I heard he had died shortly before Christmas 1968 without knowing that I was about to finish this book which he had urged me to write a decade ago.

* * *

In 1941 I was not yet in the doghouse. The Foreign Policy Association had cut me off their lecture list in consequence of my anti-Soviet views, as I was informed by Frances Pratt who was friendly to me and regretted the ban imposed by Vera Michaeles Dean, an American of "White Russian" (emigré) origin who may have been motivated mainly by Russian patriotism in her support of the Stalin regime. But I was invited to lecture at the University of Virginia's Public Affairs Institute, a distinguished annual affair, and also participated in the American Political Science Association's symposium on "Defending America's Future," where I first came up against Max Lerner, at that time an ardent defender of Stalin's Russia. The Columbia Lecture Bureau secured me a number of speaking engagements, thanks to Isabel Scott, and the American Friends Service Committee booked me for summer school seminars.

A lecture on Russia which I gave at Princeton caused Professor William S. **Carpenter** to write to Dr. Edgar F. Fisher, head of the Institute of International Education in New York on March 17, 1941, saying:

> Miss Utley gave last Wednesday a splendid lecture before an audience of approximately 450 young men. The lecture was so successful that I am writing to assure you that she is the ideal person to recommend for lectures before similar academic audiences. Her training as an economic historian together with her intimate knowledge of Russia have qualified her in an unusual degree for appearances before college and university audiences.
>
> I hope you will be able to find opportunities for her to speak, and I shall be glad to add my recommendation if it should be required.

Subsequently I was appointed for two three-year terms to be a member of the "Council of the Department of Politics" at Princeton and lectured there once a year. This was the best that Carpenter and Edward S. Corwin, Professor of Law could do for me. Had it not been for the fact that women were not then eligible as lecturers or students at this renowned university, they would, they told me, have given me an appointment on the staff. As it was I greatly enjoyed my yearly visits.

During the war years I also lectured to the Annual Conference of the Industrial Conference Board in New York which rarely if ever had a woman speaker and to the Manufacturer's Association in Chicago.

Besides continuing to write articles for *Asia* magazine, *The New Leader*, *The Progressive* and *Common Sense*, I had an article on Russia published by *Foreign Affairs* and another in the *Washington Post* then edited by Felix Morley who became a good friend of mine.

In October 1941, as previously related, the *Reader's Digest* gave me notoriety by its revamped version of one of my *Common Sense* articles. And in its December issue it condensed under the title "Whither Bound" the transcript of my lecture to the American Political Science Association as published in Volume 216 of its Annals.

During the 1940-41 interlude before the shades of the Soviet prison house closed in on the American literary scene I even reviewed a book for *The New York Times*.

In London I had become well acquainted with Professor Tchernavin and his gallant wife who had escaped to Finland in 1932 from the Solevtsky Island prison camp.* When I left for America they gave me an introduction to Donald Adams who ran *The New York Times Book Review*. He gave me Edgar Snow's *Battle for Asia* to review and published what I wrote on March 9, 1942.

The protests at letting such an anti-Communist as I do a major review in *The New York Times* must have been so vociferous that this was the last as well as the first book which I ever reviewed in this important publication.

I recall a good story which my heterodox American friends used to tell long before Senator McCarthy's adherents accused *The New York Times* of publishing not "all the news that's fit to print," but only all the news which fits.

A young man from the West after writing a best seller is invited all around in New York to cocktail parties. At one of these, given by a publishing tycoon he is taken into an inner sanctum with an enormous machine of today's computer type and informed that it writes books. It had lots and lots of buttons to press depending on whether the book to be written is political, economic or a novel or what-not, and whether it is to be written from this or that viewpoint and in what style. The young author gasps and hardly believing that the machine can really write books asks, "You don't mean surely the kind of books which are reviewed by *The New York Times*?" And his host then shows him another button to push which "writes the review in *The New York Times*."

I have already quoted a passage from my review of Snow's book which shows that in 1941 I was still giving him the benefit of the doubt. But he cannot have relished the excuses I made for him as when I wrote in this same review:

> Mr. Snow's seeming naivete appears to be due to his lack of knowledge of the USSR and his failure to appreciate the significance of the Russo-German alliance (and the) possibility of a Russian betrayal of China . . . . He has never visited the Soviet Union . . . and judges the Comintern on the basis of his knowledge of the as-yet-uncorrupted Chinese Communists.

I also pointed out the contradiction between Snow's condemnation of Chamberlain for having appeased Germany and Japan and his own advocacy of an American alliance with the Russian aggressors. "The only explanation he gives for this inconsistency," I wrote, "is the fact that the USSR pretends to be a democracy."

"A nation's word" according to Snow, "should be taken for the kind of government it says it has." A dangerous and excessively naive—or subtle?—doctrine, which as I then

---

*In *The Dream We Lost* I wrote as follows: "The heroic story of that daring escape has been related by Madame Tchernavin whose book, *Escape From The Soviets* (New York 1935), is a sincere, honest and unornamented account both of the life of the intellectuals in the USSR and of the gallant and seemingly impossible feat of walking with a child (their ten year old son) across Karelia to the Finnish border without a compass." I also quoted at length from Professor Tchernavin's own book, *I Speak For The Silent* which related with restraint, and no trace of self pity or exaggeration, from his personal experience what was whispered all over Russia while I lived there. I then wrote, in 1939: "Accounts of the tortures inflicted by the OGPU and the brutality of the concentration camp guards passed from mouth to mouth in Russia and constituted one of the weapons of terror for keeping the whole population in fear and subjection. No stories that have come out of Nazi Germany are more terrible and whereas Hitler's victims are counted in thousands or tens of thousands, Stalin's are counted in millions."

wrote implied that we should be reconciled with the Nazis if they should start pretending to be democrats.

Also I should add today a doctrine which in part explains the fumblings and errors of American diplomacy in a world where political labels and democratic professions have little relation to realities.

What I wrote about Snow in the 40's is relevant to America's present dilemma in Vietnam. "Liberal" opinion, as voiced by Senators Fulbright and McCarthy, Kenneth Galbraith and other men of good intent who have failed to keep up with the course of human events, echoes Snow long ago.

Ed Snow got back at me in his next book. Adept at confusing cause and effect in order to have it both ways, he wrote about me:

> Miss Utley was a sheep strayed from the Comintern fold, of which she had been a follower for some years before the intervention of a personal catastrophe destroyed her enthusiasm . . . . It seemed to me not much more surprising than it was tragic that the Bolsheviks had found in Miss Utley's Russian husband, if his views at all approximate to hers, a dangerous influence and had removed him somewhere to Mongolia.

Snow, with whom I had been well acquainted in Hankow in 1938, was well aware that I had ceased to be a member of the Communist Party years before my husband was arrested, and that he had not been "removed somewhere" but condemned without trial to a Russian concentration camp in the Arctic regions. But the main point I am making here is his unscrupulous inconsistency in ascribing my anti-Communism to my husband's arrest while also justifying it by my anti-Communist views.

The publication of two of my articles in the *Reader's Digest* so impressed Starr that he offered to finance me by a guaranteed loan from the Schroeder Bank leaving me free to write instead of continuing to perform my ill-defined services at his office. I accepted but not without warning him that it was extremely doubtful whether I would be able to earn a living as a writer in view of my controversial opinions, and that I would in all probability never be able to repay the loan.

After some months, during which I occupied myself in writing a number of articles which were never published, I was glad to return to work for Starr, now at a salary of $400 a month and the impressive designation of "Economic Adviser" to American International Underwriters. At which time Neil remarked with a familiar wry grin on his thin lips, "Freda, if you'll only stop trying to save the world, I'll teach you how to make money."

I should have been well advised to take advantage of the opportunities Starr afforded me to learn enough about the insurance and other business to ensure my financial independence before again challenging the world with my non-conformist views. But although like most people I enjoy spending money, and more particularly appreciate not having to worry about it, I found the pursuit of riches uninteresting.

In the newest American game, "Careers," vying with "Monopoly" among the sophisticated, each player stakes his chips on Fame, Money, or Happiness, or on a bit of each. To me fame has far outweighed fortune if not happiness. Moreover, I suppose my ingrained Socialist outlook incapacitated me for a long time from taking advantage of the transformation of "capitalism" in America into a new economic and social order affording opportunity for almost everyone.

One has to pay for everything in this world; and especially for freedom to say what one thinks. Whenever I start regretting that I am neither a University Professor, nor a

I was fortunate to have dinner once with Maynard Keynes and his wife the famous former Russian ballerina, Lopokovna, whose plain clothes, low heels, hair drawn severely back and lack of makeup reminded one of old daguerreotypes of the social revolutionaries and social democrats who had made the Revolution. Keynes had voted for me in the distant days when I was elected Chairman of the London University Labor Party, and also knew me as the author of *Japan's Feet of Clay*.

At Bretton Woods I also learnt something as regards the reason why even anti-Communists went along with Roosevelt's foolish policy. I became very friendly with a Catholic Congressman from Brooklyn who shared my views and fears concerning Soviet Russia. But when I asked him why he did not publicly oppose the Treasury representatives he replied: "My dear, I have learnt better than to do so. After a speech of mine displeasing to the friends of the Soviet Union I was threatened with an investigation of my Income Tax returns."

Subsequently I collaborated with Starr in writing a pamphlet challenging the assumptions concerning the Soviet Union upon which the first International Monetary Conference based its recommendations. Entitled "Mount Washington Labored" it had a small mouse on the cover to show the result. Printed and privately circulated by American International Underwriters Corporation it enhanced Starr's reputation in the business community. Nevertheless, I never quite got over the feeling that I owed him more than he owed me.

Today reading over copies I still have on file of the memoranda, reports and recommendations I wrote for Starr, I realize that Pearl Buck had been right in believing that I would "earn my job." It could be I now surmise that I more than earned the modest salary I was so grateful to receive.

Thanks to Starr I did not, during the Second World War, suffer anything comparable to the material privations of my life in England during the First. Nor was I ever so lonely, or deprived of the company of my own kind as during the years I worked at the War Office in London. On the contrary, during this period of my life in New York I had a wide circle of friends whom I could afford to entertain upon occasion. I gave parties at which C. V. Starr and some of the top executives of his companies mingled with such diverse company as Bertrand and Peter Russell, Chester Bowles, John and Adelaide Marquand, Philip Johnson, Lawrence Spivak, Quincy Howe, William Henry Chamberlin, Max Eastman and Sidney and Ann Hook, Norman Thomas, Bertram and Ella Wolfe, Don Levine, Alfred Bingham, Dwight MacDonald and his wife together with her brother Selden Rodman; besides of course, Dora, Doner and Rosa, Wilbur Burton before he went to prison, Guenter Reimann and Sheba Strunsky, Norman Cousins, the Chinese Ambassador Hu Shih and many others who stand out less prominently in my memory.

In those days, I was not in the least inhibited by the shabbiness of my furniture or other evidence of my poverty. As I used to say to Mother when she demurred, "People come to see me, not the furniture, to enjoy good conversation and lively argument, not to be lavishly entertained." Of course, drink was necessary, which was not always easy to provide in wartime. On one occasion when William Henry Chamberlin in Cambridge asked me to give a party for him in New York, he offered to "bring the whiskey." He turned up with one bottle. This was, of course, totally inadequate and I was hard put to secure enough liquor for our guests.

William Henry—somehow one always called him by both given names—neither smoked nor drank, but was a great eater of sweets. He was wont to take a paper bag of chocolates with him to munch wherever he went—a habit which had greatly annoyed my old friend Sir George Sansom when Chamberlin interviewed him at the British Embassy in Tokyo.

His teetotalism and other seeming Puritan prejudices proved deceptive. In Shanghai I was told of an occasion when his host finding this *Christian Science Monitor* correspondent uninterested in "wine, women and song," had suggested a card game. When William Henry said he would like nothing better than poker, this seasoned correspondent telephoned other newspapermen telling them that he had a "sissy" guest who would be easy game. To their dismay Chamberlin proved that he could have held his own against professional gamblers in a Western movie. The party had broken up in the wee hours after Chamberlin had cleaned out everyone else.

My stepson, Sasha, resented on my behalf what he regarded as Chamberlin's propensity to make use of me to meet at my apartment with such dangerous-to-know characters as Lawrence Dennis without danger to himself of "guilt by association." But I enjoyed Chamberlin's company and dry sense of humor and wished I had his ability to present unorthodox opinions in such urbane fashion that he was able to contribute articles to such diverse publications as *The New Leader* and *The Wall Street Journal*, besides writing for the *Atlantic Monthly* before he himself severed his connection with this prestigious publication on account of its Stalinist apologetics.

Chamberlin did a great deal by his books and articles to "debamboozle" the Western world befuddled by the illusions spread by the "totalitarian liberals" about Soviet Russia. But he had no inclination to be a hero, crusader or martyr, and made an impression of being cold hearted or callous. Sasha used to do a good imitation or caricature of William Henry, literally twiddling his thumbs and giggling—as the Japanese do when very upset—while recalling some dreadful experience of Soviet callousness, cruelty and deception. Determined to see life as the comedy Voltaire said it is to those who think rather than feel, William Henry is a man of integrity and courage after his own fashion and was loyal to his friends. After Wilbur Burton went to prison for his opposition to "Roosevelt's war" Chamberlin corresponded with him regularly and helped sustain his morale.

Despite the difference in our characters and way of life, William Henry and I were good although never intimate friends. I enjoyed his caustic humor and he evidently relished an occasional dip into the Bohemian atmosphere which was still my habitat. He viewed my disorderly household as comic rather than reprehensive. When one of my old second hand chairs collapsed under Wilbur Burton during some argument, or when the several glass aquariums of tropical fish which divided our living room from Jon's bedroom collapsed, William Henry chuckled with glee and remarked how exciting life was in my home.

Other memories return to me of my life in New York while I had an assured small income as economic advisor to Starr's companies and was friendly with him and some of his top executives. An evening when the nicest and most intellectual of them, Mansfield Freeman, and his wife came to dinner with "Lord and Lady" Russell and the electricity was cut off because I had failed to pay the bill on time and we dined by candlelight. Also the occasion when returning from the office to get ready for a big cocktail party I was giving, I found our dog Jenny's six little puppies had littered the apartment with small messes, and while I was hastily cleaning them up there came a call from the Chinese Ambassador Hu Shih asking if my party was "formal" or informal.

It was at one of these parties of mine, where discussion was free, wide ranging and unconfined by political or ideological commitments that Max Eastman and I faced up to

288

the fundamental question whether, after repudiating Communism, we were still socialists. Max had already in 1940 in his book *Marxism: Is It Science* demonstrated the "unscientific and indeed superstitious character of Marx's whole mode of thought." But as yet he had not decided that "the Socialist hypothesis was disproven." As he records it* I was the catalyst who compelled him to confront facts and make his decision. Remembering "the precise moment" he recalls that it was:

> At a cocktail party given by Freda Utley—I think for her friend Bertrand Russell—during a conversation about some last and most significantly dreadful news that had come out of Russia, she suddenly asked me:
>
> "Aside from these Russian developments, do you still believe in the socialist idea?"
>
> I said, "No."

It takes a long time to discard beliefs which have inspired one's life, and to which one has devoted one's greatest endeavors. Some who are still my friends have never been able to face up to the fact that socialism in practice does not lead to social justice, or to better utilization of the riches of the earth and the energies of mankind in productive endeavor and freedom from want and fear.

As Max Eastman wrote, in recording his spontaneous answer to my basic question in my New York apartment long ago, "it came from the depths of my heart and mind." It seemed perfectly clear, "once the question was boldly put" that:

> if the socialist hypothesis were valid in general, *some tiny shred* of the benefits promised by it would have appeared when the Russian capitalists were expropriated and production taken over by the state, no matter how untoward the circumstances. By the late 30's *everything* in Russia was worse from the standpoint of socialist ideals than it had been under the regime of the Tsar. I did not need any additional experiments such as that in Nazi Germany, or in England, or the obvious drift in other countries, to convince me. I was sure that the whole idea of extending freedom, or justice or equality, or any other civilized value, to the lower classes through common ownership of the means of production was a delusive dream, a bubble that had taken over a century to burst.

Max, no more than I, felt any shame in discarding our original belief in Socialism as the cure-all for the woes of all mankind. He regretted only how long it had taken him "to repudiate in its entirety the whole false Marxist philosophy." Paradoxically, or perhaps naturally, it was now that those who came to be called the "totalitarian liberals" rallied to the defense of the USSR. As Max wrote: "It was a strange experience, for one who had lived through twenty-five years as a Marxian socialist, to see now in proportion as the Soviet regime dropped overboard one by one every vestige of socialism as originally envisaged, the liberal scholars and litterateurs of the world 'came over' to Socialism."**

Today Malcolm Cowley, among others mentioned by Max Eastman in 1940, excuses his former partiality for the Soviet totalitarian state by writing that there was then no evidence concerning the atrocities perpetuated by Stalin except that of "released

---

Reflections on the Failure of Socialism, Devin Adair, 1955, p. 18.

**Stalin's Russia and the Crisis in Socialism*, W. W. Norton, New York 1940.

prisoners and defectors . . . that is from participants who were limited in their point of view and in many cases not to be trusted."*

Ye Gods! Can one imagine anyone describing escapees from Nazi Germany as "limited in their point of view" because of their own suffering? But of course, today as yesterday, the "professional liberals" have double standards in their judgements enabling them to excuse themselves from complicity by default in crimes against humanity.

In his February 1969 *Esquire* review of the Robert Conquest book, Malcolm Muggeridge points out that Stalin's terrorism had been as studied and documented as Hitler's,** but that in contrast to the universal condemnation of the latter, Stalin's terror was almost unanimously approved or justified by the intelligentsia of the West. Even today the professional liberals refuse to acknowledge, or to realize, that terror was and is intrinsic in a Communist regime which can survive only if everybody is kept in a condition of fear; that it was not Stalin's invention but his inheritance from Lenin. I myself, long ago in *The Dream We Lost* had written that although I originally thought Stalin responsible for the horrors of life in Russia and that if Trotsky had won out all would have been well, I had come to realize that the system itself required a Stalin to function.

Max Eastman and I were to continue through the years, until his death in 1969, in basic rapport. Unlike others who, after repudiating Communism have reverted to or been converted to Catholicism, or have become mystically inclined Quakers like the late Whitaker Chambers, Max and I, together with my other old and revered friend, Sidney Hook, have continued to adhere to the original liberal faith in the power of reason which requires evidence of things seen for the validity of any theory.

Others among those who were my friends in New York during the war years, have never been able to bring themselves to examine the basis of their beliefs in the light of recent history. Dwight MacDonald, for instance, who as a pacifist was closer to me than Max during the war years, has not even today succeeded in breaking the umbilical cord which binds him to those who still believe in socialism. He is no longer a Trotskyist but remains an old fashioned Marxist or Leninist who still regards Western capitalism as incurably imperialist despite its change in our time. Despite his knowledge, or the realization I used to think he had of the horrors of Communist rule, Dwight MacDonald today has joined up with the New (or very old?) Left in demanding that we abandon the people on our side in Vietnam to the savage reprisals of ruthless Communist totalitarian tyranny.

As history abundantly demonstrates it is usually the doctrinaire believers in one or another ideology, religious or secular doctrine, who inflict the greatest suffering on mankind.

The trouble as I now see it with such old and good friends of mine as Dwight MacDonald is that the happy circumstances of their lives have prevented them from growing up politically. Despite his intelligence and compassion, Dwight's lack of personal experience of men and politics in action, or of the trials, tribulations and sufferings of the greater part of mankind, stunted his political growth and perhaps explains his affinity with the "New Left" despite his advancing years. Moreover his individualistic tempera-

*Washington Post, "Book World" September 22, 1968. Review by Malcolm Cowley of *The Great Terror* by Robert Conquest.

**Notably in the evidence produced by Kravchenko in his libel action in Paris against the French Communist Party weekly *Les Lettres Francaises.*

ment, which rendered him incapable of collaborating for any length of time with anyone, and led him to establish his own magazine *Politics* after he broke with his friends on *Partisan Review*, indicates his basic affinity with the anarchists, or nihilists, who are today riding high on university campuses led by the S.D.S.

* * *

The diversity of the company I kept in New York is illustrated by the following extract from a letter I wrote to C. V. Starr on April 5, 1944:

> I was asked to a dinner last night by some people called Hoving* and sat next to Herbert Hoover who was very cordial. He said he was glad I had not been made to leave America.
>
> You may be interested to hear that some at least of the British apparently no longer look on me with disfavor! I was surprised to find Sir Louis Beale last Sunday devoting most of his time and attention to me and my views and showing some obvious sympathy for them. Not, of course, that I did not realize he was cleverly flattering me but why should he bother to flatter me—ask me to dinner, etc., unless he thinks of me as useful in some way or at least worth talking to. It was at a party which Ann Paxton, Woodhead and I jointly gave in your apartment—my contribution, however, being only the guests or most of them. W. H. Chamberlin was there and I thought it would be useful for Woodhead to meet Quincy Howe, Spivak, Eugene Lyons, Eastman, Edmund Wilson and some others. And I must admit it is easier to entertain in your spacious halls than in my little room.
>
> Beal made me surmise that what I jokingly said to Woodhead and Duff a while ago may really be happening, viz., that the British line will cross my line.

In October 1941, I had moved to a bigger and better apartment on 11th Street, for which, thanks to Roger Baldwin's wife's agent Judge Dorothy Kenyon, I paid only $72 a month instead of the $90 at which it had previously been rented. It was a walk-up on the fourth floor, which was hard on my mother, but we now had six rooms and Jon had access with other children in the block to the playground yard next door where Roger Baldwin and his wife lived. This move, desirable in any case, had been rendered necessary by the addition to my family of my stepson, Sasha. Maybe had I known what troubles and heartache he was to cause me later, I should not have taken Arcadi's son to live with us. But at the beginning I was overjoyed at being able to help him.

As I have related, Sasha's uncle in Philadelphia, after casting a disdainful glance around my poorly furnished apartment on 12th Street on the disastrous morning after I was rejected as an immigrant at Ellis Island, had not communicated with me.

In the meantime, Sasha in Portugal had made a marriage of convenience with a Polish Jewish refugee who had enough money left to show to the Immigration authorities to ensure their entry to the United States, provided that he, born in Switzerland, could get her included in the Swiss quota by marrying her.

Unhappy as a poor relation in the home of his Jewish "petty bourgeois" maternal relatives in Philadelphia, Arcadi's son had written to me in French in guarded fashion, seemingly unsure of my welcome, but obviously longing to know me. Delighted at the

---

*Walter Hoving at that time Chairman of Lord & Taylor and later of Tiffany's. I still know his wife today. Back in the 40's she showed me her scrapbook collection of my writings and press notices.

prospect of meeting Arcadi's son, and only too glad to help him, I immediately dashed off to Philadelphia to bring Sasha to my home in New York. Subsequently I also brought Blanche, his legal wife, from Chicago where she was staying with relatives, to live with us as housekeeper, cook, baby sitter and what-not in which capacities she proved to be a godsend.

Blanche was the daughter of a well-to-do Jewish family accustomed in Poland to have servants work for her. Now, although I could afford to pay her only a small salary, she cheerfully performed any and all domestic labors required of her. Moreover, since I could completely trust her, she lightened my domestic cares and worries in every possible way, was kind and considerate toward my mother, and looked after Jon when he came home from school.

I had believed Sasha when he told me that Blanche's marriage to him had been only one of convenience to enable both of them to emigrate to the United States. I was distressed when I found that she had for a long time loved my stepson whom she had known well in Lodz before they met again in Lisbon. This made for all sorts of complications in our life together on West 11th Street because Sasha was unkind to her.

Happily, Blanche eventually got over her infatuation for my stepson and married a not unsuccessful New York businessman, with whom, insofar as I know, she has lived happily ever since.

The addition of Sasha to my household and to the number of my dependents added new problems to my life. Mother at first welcomed him but came to resent the fact that by supporting him until he could earn his own living in America I had even less money than before to provide for our wants. Sasha's boorish behavior finally made the situation unbearable. Instead of helping Mother and Blanche, he complained that Mother was treating him like a servant by expecting him to run errands and do chores around the house. Each evening when I returned from the office, wanting only to spend time with Jon, I had to endeavor to compose the grievances of my mother and stepson.

Both of them, having been lonely all day, made demands upon my time and sympathies which compelled me to neglect my own son. Today, I often wonder how Jon survived all these "tensions," which according to the psychologists, should have made him a neurotic when he grew up, instead of developing into a well-adjusted adolescent and an independent and poised young man. He might well have developed all sorts of self-destroying complexes had I not been able to remove him when he was ten years old from both his grandmother's and his half-brother's antagonistic company.

In those distant days when I worried at Jon's clinging too closely to me and at his occasional tantrums, Dora, who loved and understood children, explained to me that this was his natural reaction to hearing my mother criticize me and complain about me so much to him or in his hearing.

Dora supplied a precious antidote in Jon's life to the poison engendered by the supercharged atmosphere created in our home by the conflict between his jealous grandmother and his egotistical half brother. Her unselfishness, cheerfulness, serene temperament and her deep affection for Jon, as contrasted to my mother's possessive love and Sasha's self-love, constituted a beneficial influence in my son's life as well as mine. When he came to manhood, Jon continued to love and repose confidence in Dora, and today in his 30's keeps in touch with her even from distant foreign places.

Physically, Sasha resembled his father, although less handsome and lacking Arcadi's serenity, kindliness and good humor. Like Arcadi he was attractive to women, but unlike his father he had no scruples in using his masculine charms to seduce them or use them.

During two summer vacations, one on Martha's Vineyard, the other in Provincetown, I learned more about women than I had ever known before, thanks to my stepson. Many girls made up to me on the beach in hope of thus securing Sasha's favor even while he ignored or insulted them, or treated them with contempt.

Eventually, Sasha met his comeupance at the hands of my secretary, Connie Hausamann, an intelligent self-respecting independent minded and attractive girl who had been recommended to me by Professor Sidney Hook who esteemed her highly as one of his outstanding students at New York University. Sasha was so much in love with her that he wanted to marry her, and was mortally wounded in his masculine vanity when she decided at the last moment that, although she loved him, she could not face the prospect of union with a man of his character.

For a long time I continued to persuade myself that Sasha must have the same lovable character underneath as his father if only he could be persuaded by my love and trust to drop the large chip on his shoulder which made it so difficult to help him. I excused his faults as the result of his having been a stepchild in his mother's house, and a Jew in Poland where anti-semitism was worse than anywhere else in Europe before the Third Reich in Germany. He was very intelligent and had managed to overcome all his handicaps when, after Arcadi had ceased to be able to send him money, he had got to the University of Paris on a scholarship after having already passed his law examinations in Warsaw.

Like his father and my son, Sasha had an exceptional gift for languages, business sense, political intelligence, and a perceptive understanding of people, which latter gift, however, he used to hurt instead of help the people he knew. He had all that it takes to be successful, except for the complexes which made him resentful or distrustful even of those who wanted to assist him. He also suffered from the defect of most East European and Asiatic "class-conscious intellectuals" who think that they demean themselves by menial or physical labor. A defect which, combined with his arrogant, even rude, behavior caused difficulties for me with Starr who, having himself worked his way through college, considered Sasha to be a no-good intellectual parasite whom I ought not to be supporting instead of doing more for my mother.

Difficult as Sasha was to live with, I appreciated the fact that he spent a lot of time with Jon and loved his half-brother after his own peculiar fashion, although always resentful of my naturally greater love for my own son than for him. He provided a much-needed masculine influence in Jon's life, including games and sports, so that when it came to choosing between keeping my mother or Sasha with us, I decided in favor of my stepson. Since mother was finding it as difficult to climb the three steep flights of stairs to our apartment as to live under the same roof as Sasha, I took a room for her on the ground floor in a lodging house on the opposite side of the street. Here I could send dinner over to her in the evening, and Jon and I visited her every day even if only briefly. My financial situation by this time was sufficiently eased for me to pay for a separate lodging for mother because Sasha was now earning enough to contribute toward his own keep.

The first job I secured for him was at New York University as assistant to Count Coudenhove Kallergi at the European Union. Later Sasha did the research work and analysis of the publications of the Institute of Pacific Relations which helped Alfred Kohlberg to become the leading light of the so-called 'China lobby.'

After I left New York for Washington in 1944, Sasha secured various appointments at universities and eventually accumulated enough capital to become a successful operator in real estate and stock market operations in Seattle where he is married to a teacher. I have not met him or communicated with him for many years, nor has he ever shown the least inclination to repay me even in words for what I did for him when I assumed the burden of his support although finding it difficult enough to provide for my mother and my own son. My stepson could indeed qualify for the title "the meanest man I ever knew." Yet I do not regret having helped him even at the cost of hurting and depriving my own mother. His twisted and perverse character was no doubt at least partly the result of his unhappy childhood and therefore the responsibility of his father, my husband, which I wanted to assume.

The end, insofar as I was concerned came at the time of my son's 16th birthday in March 1950. I had promised to buy him a car as soon as he was old enough to get a license to drive. Having myself never learned to drive a "motor car," it would also be most useful to me to have an automobile which Jon would drive. The spring of 1950 being a period when I was very hard up, because my *High Cost of Vengeance* was producing no royalties to speak of, I asked Sasha, at this time earning six or seven thousand a year as a professor at Bradley University, if he would contribute $100 toward the cost of the $195 I needed to buy an old Ford. And Sasha, for whom I had not only provided sustenance during his first years in America but also such luxuries as a tuxedo to help him mingle with the people who might get him a job; who had taken possession of my typewriter when leaving New York; and for whom in 1942 on Martha's Vineyard I had bought an old Ford for $100, sanctimoniously replied that Jon ought not have a car until he himself earned the money to buy one.

Maybe I should not have diverted my readers' attention for so long to the sad story of my disillusioning experience with my husband's son. But the burden he constituted for me for several years, both materially and psychologically are an integral part of my life's story.

My life has been singularly free of personal experience of ingratitude and meanness; I have been helped by far more people than I have ever been able to help, and have generally found it to be true that the bread one casts upon the waters does return to one eventually even if only in unexpected ways. Sasha disappointed and hurt me deeply but did not fundamentally change my outlook or behavior. Which is perhaps a great defeat for him since he tried so hard by argument and action to convince me that the world is as nasty a place as he insists that it is despite all the acts of kindness from which he has benefited.

During my years with Starr I enjoyed some wonderful summer vacations on Martha's Vineyard and the Cape. It was then possible to rent a cottage in the Chilmark area of the Vineyard for very little money provided one did without electricity or plumbing, cooked on bottled gas, pumped water by hand or fetched water from a spring. Who needed baths when one could enjoy swimming and playing in the surf on the South beach a mile or two away? Days on this unsurpassed vast beach of sand under protecting cliffs where the waves come rolling in from the Atlantic are among my happy memories. Owned by Roger Baldwin's wife Evelyn Preston, they preferred that one bathe naked and it was awkward only when women came with little bits of covering enhancing their sex attributes like today's bikinis. Here Max Eastman's wife Eliena conducted dance classes which were as entrancing to watch as one imagines Nausicaa's games with her maidens naked on a shore in Ithaca watched unseen by Odysseus. Here Sasha, Jon, and I gathered with our friends for long days of swimming, basking in the sun, reading and playing word games until the sun was ready to set and we walked home to gather for cocktails and supper at each other's summer homes. Closest of my friends sharing our primitive life were Bill Lipkind, an anthropology professor and his Italian wife Maria who sang as wonderfully as she cooked, and Aaron, an amateur photographer school teacher who later became a professional. Also Anne Eisner who was Max's secretary before she married Jim Putnam and went off to the Congo where she was to write a memorable book about the pygmies. Karl Wittfegel and his wife Esther and John and Peggy Chamberlain who stayed at the Menemsha Inn had cars to bring them to the South Beach. With John I also sailed and occasionally played tennis.

Max and Eliena Eastman had a beautiful house on Gayhead where I met various celebrities such as the painter Tom Benton and Katherine Cornell.

Never afterwards in my more affluent days in Washington in recent years have I enjoyed such wonderful holidays as on the Vineyard in the 40's. Days bathed in retrospect with the magic glow of summer at the sea in the years when I was still on friendly terms with the largely Jewish intelligentsia of New York.

I spent another unforgettable summer on the Cape where the tenants of the apartment below us on 11th Street in the Village had inherited the Webster House in Provincetown without ever seeing it, and offered me the use of it, warning me it was in bad condition. Sasha and Jon, spending the whole summer there, had cleaned it up before my arrival for a month's vacation. They had made friends with Hilda Patrick who traced her ancestry back to one of the Mayflower settlers, but was married to a Portuguese immigrant who, starting as a fisherman had made money as a rum runner during Prohibition days and was now proprietor of the Flagship, the best restaurant in Provincetown. Hilda was somewhat out of her element, being a former school teacher who reads vociferously and loves the company of 'intelligents.' She is still my friend today and warmly welcomes me on the rare occasions I visit the Cape.

Here in Provincetown, with Frederick and Sylvia Nelson at Truro ten miles away, Edmund Wilson and Mary McCarthy in the same area, and John Dos Passos my close neighbor, I enjoyed a memorable summer holiday. The occasion I remember best is an evening at John Dos Passos's house where the argument between us and George Kent (a *Reader's Digest* editor with whom I had been friendly because his daughter and my son attended the same school in New York), waxed so hot and furious that Dos Passos suggested we all plunge into the sea from his terrace to cool it. After which midnight swim we emerged to continue the argument as zealously as before. This evening marked the end of my short lived friendship with George Kent who had been carried away, or seduced, by Communist fellow travellers and dupes.

I regret that I remember that cold plunge at midnight from Dos Passos's terrace better than all the arguments and varying views expressed that evening in Provincetown.

Edmund Wilson and John Dos Passos were, of course, on my side of the argument, but I remember Mary McCarthy mainly for her beauty. At that time I respected her for her courageous opposition to the Stalinists by her participation in the John Dewey investigation of Trotsky's assassination. Later I came to realize from her own writings that she had done so only out of cussedness and had no serious political opinions or understanding of the fundamental nature and aims of the Communists. Recently she has amply displayed in her articles favoring the Communists in Vietnam her ignorance or callous indifference to the horrible fate which awaits the people on our side should we abandon them. Similarly in the field of sex she has come to ride the popular tide which leads to best sellerdom, as witness her book *The Group* which might be described as a Peyton Place for the upper classes.

There was also an occasion on the Cape when at an evening beach bonfire party hosted by Dwight MacDonald I had a furious argument with his and my former friend, Peter Viereck, son of the Kaiser's propagandist in America during World War I who had defended the German people against the accusation of collective guilt for Nazi crimes when I first met him at Philip Johnson's house in Cambridge, but who later became a "professional anti-German" while teaching at Mount Holyoke College. I don't remember much about this great flare up on the beach that night, but well I remember my son Jon, not yet in his teens, intervening in my defense and Dwight telling him I was strong enough in argument not to need his championship.

How often now, in writing my Memoirs, have I wished that I had kept a diary, instead of having mere reminiscences of episodes, and highlights of conversations long ago which, for one reason or another, have remained etched on the tablet of my mind. Looking back today on the late summer or autumn years of my life in New York in the 40's, I view them with nostalgia for the years when I was not yet alienated from my own kind—or separated from them by living in Washington—those whom my brother long ago in London in the 20's described as the "bloody intelligents."

My move to Washington was partly the result of an article I wrote for the *American Mercury* after my old friend Eugene Lyons became its editor. Entitled "Why Pick on China" and published in September 1944 it made a dent in the solid front of the Chinese Communist Lobby and the Russophiles who then, and for years to come, successfully propagandized a false picture of the situation in China. It had, as I then wrote, become fashionable to excoriate China and denounce the hard pressed National Government, and in general reprimand China for being Chinese, while giving Soviet Russia the benefit of every doubt. The average American, I observed, is no better equipped to judge Asiatic relations than the proverbial visitor from Mars who, if he had only the mass of American editorials and radio comment to go by, would conclude that Russia (which in March had signed an agreement with Japan ensuring her of an enlarged fish supply from Russian waters) was about to enter the war against Japan.

I criticized the double standard applied to Russia and China by such liberal writers as Leland Stowe who, in his book *They Shall Not Sleep* excoriated Free China for the poverty of its people, its dictatorial government, inflation and inequality of sacrifice, but had no words of condemnation for Russia's tyrannical government, secret police, domination of thought and action, concentration camps, and the contrast materially between the privileged position of the rulers and the people.

I admitted all Free China's shortcomings but pointed out that much progress toward reform had been made during the few years preceding Japan's attack in 1937 and wrote that "It would have been a miracle if China with its main ports and cities in the hands of the enemy and without factories to produce goods for the people, had been able to institute democratic government, abolish all the old evil practices and change her economic and political system while resisting a powerful invader," with precious little help from America even after Pearl Harbor. Above all I insisted that far from being a "fascist" state:

> One difficulty in China's war effort is that she is *not* a totalitarian state . . . if Chiang Kai-shek had the same complete power over his country as Stalin and Hitler over theirs he would find it easier to mobilize manpower and resources for war; easier to force the rich to sacrifice, to stop speculation and graft, enforce agrarian reform and abolish age old abuses.

296

Today in Vietnam Americans once again are demanding "democratic government" in conditions which preclude it, in the naive belief that "democracy" is a cure-all pill. Knowing little or nothing of European history before the 18th century, Americans generally fail to realize that elected representative government is a slow growth made possible only after stability and security have been established by a strong authoritarian government.

Dr. Hu Shih (the renowned Chinese philosopher who had been China's Ambassador to the U.S. when I first met him as his guest at the Chinese Embassy on my first lecture tour in 1938) wrote me the following letter:

Sept. 18, 1944

Dear Freda:

The date reminds me of the Japanese "first shot" at Mukden thirteen years ago!

I have been intending to write to thank you, not only for sending me your *Mercury* article, but particularly for your writing it at a time like this when such an article must surely make you very unpopular among the so called "Radicals."

It is a *very fair* article. I especially like the paragraph beginning with "But after the worst is acknowledged . . ." I quite agree with you. I often told my American friends that Chinese totalitarianism is a farce: "Farcism" would be a more accurate name than "Fascism."

I am also troubled by the problem of the future relationship between China and Russia. I have openly advocated some open and fundamental solution of all outstanding problems between these two countries. But after all it takes two to make friends.

With kindest regards.

As ever
Hu Shih

My opinions were also welcomed by Major General Victor W. Odlum, the Canadian Ambassador to China who had visited me in New York for advice and information prior to taking up his appointment. He was among the few diplomats from the Western hemisphere who was able, in his own words, to "adjust his mental binoculars" despite his original revulsion to "the dirt, the smells, the squalor and the awful indifference" in China. Our correspondence at this time is appended to this chapter for its intrinsic and historical interest.

A letter I wrote to Starr from Washington on June 5, 1944 shows my optimism concerning, the, as I thought, receding tide of Communist influence. After telling him that Senator Russell, Chairman of the Immigration Committee, had promised to put the bill enabling me to become an American citizen through that week, and of Bullitt's promise to speak to Biddle on my behalf to ensure that President Roosevelt would sign it, I wrote:

Bullitt was most friendly and his views today *re* the war and Russia seemed almost identical with my own. Indeed, the astonishing thing in Washington seemed to me to be the change of opinion in many quarters. For instance, one man I know in the State Department who was an "interventionist" said to me out of the blue and not knowing that I know (Senator) Wheeler: "Mark my words, Wheeler is the coming man in this country; people are going to remember how right he was in what he said about the War before Pearl Harbor."

You will have heard of Senator Bridges speech, although it was not adequately reported in the press, saying that "this was not and is not our war" if the outcome is to be merely a "reshuffled game of balance of power politics" or a "new-fangled sort of imperialism."

Senator Ball spoke along the same lines in New York a week ago, and there are apparently a large number of Senators urging that we drop "unconditional surrender" and some of them are prepared to advocate peace before Russia becomes the master of Europe.

The President's attempt to conciliate Senator Wheeler is a sign of the times and I should like to tell you privately some of the things Wheeler and LaFollette told me.

In this same letter I told Starr that I had found Clare Luce with a completely changed view of the war, although Henry Luce had not thought things out as fully and they disagreed "quite a lot." She had been very cordial to me, and like Walter Judd shared my fears about China, Russia and Japan. As Judd expressed it to me then:

Chiang Kai-shek is now being pressed by one side in China to make peace with Japan and being told that he has backed the wrong horse in trusting the West; and on the other side he is being urged to build China up as a land power with its center where its raw materials are, and break with the West. But he is trying to stick with us against this joint tremendous pressure from the Japanese and Russian sides. Chiang is in much the same position as Washington was before Franklin got aid from France: if that aid had not come Washington would have gone down in history as a fool who uselessly sacrificed the lives of Americans in a hopeless cause. But since the aid was obtained Washington became the "father of his country."

The sad thing was as I wrote at this time, that "a section of the press here meanwhile, seems to be doing its best to alienate or weaken the influence of America's only natural allies in China: the Western orientated Chinese who have stuck to Chiang and to us."

How apposite today are my remarks about the situation in China in 1944 both to our dilemma in Vietnam since we connived at the assassination of Diem. As also to U.S. policy in the Middle East which has cut the ground from under the feet of the Western oriented Arabs.

Shortly after my article in the *American Mercury* was published I was offered the position of economist and consultant at the Chinese Supply Commission in Washington at a starting salary of $600 a month. My duties were to include "giving assistance and advice in the preparation of published material and speeches," but, as I stipulated, "not the writing of articles under my own name." Nor was I precluded from doing some occasional work for Starr, Park, Freeman, Inc.

C. V. Starr, who ran a sideline for the Office of Strategic Services acting as a cover for some of its intelligence operations, was instrumental in thus enabling me at long last to get into a position to do something effective to counteract Communist influence in Washington. Besides recommending me for the job in Washington he put me on the O.S.S. payroll at a modest salary paid to me through his office for confidential reports to this precursor of the CIA. This was not known to the Chinese Embassy but I saw no conflict

298

of interest since it was all to the good of both China and America that a convinced and knowledgeable anti-Communist such as I should be sending reports analyzing Chinese developments and attitudes for the U.S. Government while helping the Chinese Embassy combat the Chinese Communist lobby in America.

I was also kept on a retainer basis by the Starr enterprises so that for the first time since my arrival in America I had a comfortable income. Altogether I earned about a thousand dollars a month and was able to install my mother and son in a house in Chevy Chase with a resident servant to look after Mother and relieve me of my usual domestic chores.

My affluence did not last long but this was my own fault.

During the summer of 1945 I wrote an article together with Max Eastman for the *Reader's Digest* which owed much to the editing, condensation or encapsulating of its senior editor, Paul Palmer, who had been instrumental long before in getting my first articles published in the *Reader's Digest*.

Entitled "The Destiny of the World Is Being Decided in China" our article exposed the four deceptions which were distorting American policy in the Far East. Namely that: 1) Russia is a democracy and that China could therefore safely be left to Russian influence—a view which gained widest publicity when Owen Lattimore wrote in his book *Solution in Asia* that "all the Asiatic peoples are more interested in actual democratic practices, as the ones they can see in action across the Russian border, than in the fine theories of Anglo-Saxon democracies which come coupled with ruthless imperialism."

2) that the Chinese Communists were not real Communists, had no connection with Russia and in Edgar Snow's words "had renounced any intention of establishing Communism in China in the near future."

Deception No. 3 was that the Chinese Communists were fighting the Japs and that the Chinese National Army was not. In actual fact, as we amply demonstrated, the Chinese Communists after Pearl Harbor had, in Mao Tse-tung's words, "let the S.O.B. Western imperialists" fight the Japanese while they themselves concentrated on fighting the Chinese Nationalist forces, avoiding confrontation with the Japanese.

Deception No. 4 as we saw it was that Chiang Kai-shek was a "fascist" preventing the Chinese Communists from establishing "democracy."

This article published in the June 1945 issue of the *Reader's Digest* had considerable impact on misled and misinformed American public opinion, although we failed to divert the Truman-Acheson-Marshall policy from its set course which eventually led to the "loss of China" to the Communists. It did not bear my cosignature with Max Eastman's because it was thought that it would be more effective if it did not appear under the by line of two such "controversial" old premature anti-Communist authors as Max and myself. I suggested J. B. Powell as the presumed co-author if I myself were not to be given the credit—Powell being the valiant and principled liberal publisher of Shanghai's *The China Weekly* hospitalized with both feet lost as the result of his ill treatment as a prisoner of the Japanese. Powell, whose views coincided with mine, was happy to agree to have the article published as jointly authored by Max Eastman and himself.

I was paid $800 but both Max and Wallace were not happy at the sacrifice of credit I had made. I told them they could amply make up for it by paying my expenses to go to China as a *Reader's Digest* correspondent. With his usual, and in my experience unique generosity among publishers, "Wally" enabled me to take off for China in November 1945. I gave up my salary from the China Supply Commission although they would have been glad to continue paying me. I knew that anti-Communists have to be like Caesar's wife—beyond suspicion. My future writings would be discredited if the Communists could represent me as a paid propagandist. It probably would not have made much difference had I retained my $600 a month salary from the Chinese Supply Commission after I left for China, or had resumed it after my return to Washington and wrote *Last Chance in China*. I should have been smeared anyhow. But, in my old fashioned, or romantic, view I believe in Tennyson's words: "My strength is as the strength of ten because my heart is pure."

My move to Washington, where I have resided ever since except for travels abroad, ended the first phase of my life in America and coincided with the coming end of the Second World War. The years after will be covered in the second volume of my Memoirs.

During the Second World War I felt more and more like a Cassandra able to foresee the fatal consequences of the Roosevelt Administration's mistaken trust in "Uncle Joe" Stalin, but unable to make my voice heard. Not only did it become increasingly difficult to get any articles or books published which exposed the true nature of the Soviet State once it became our "ally" in the fight against Hitler's Germany, it was soon also practically *tabu*, in any respectable American newspaper or magazine, to warn against the host of Communist sympathizers, fellow travellers or dupes, who needed no Trojan horse to enter the citadel of the United States since they were already well ensconced in government departments, press and radio, universities, colleges and schools.

Moreover, respected "liberal" commentators and columnists concerned only with arousing hate against the Nazis, went so far as, for instance Elmer Davis, as to suppress the evidence of such Communist atrocities as the mass murder of Polish officers in the Katyn Forrest. As director of the U.S. Information Service he forbade the Polish language radio service from Detroit to mention the fact that the Russians, *not* the Germans, were responsible for this atrocity.

Worst of all was the fact that the Communists and their dupes were successfully undermining the foundations of the free world by their ability to incite and exploit Western hate and fear of Nazi tyranny to condition America into acceptance of the cruel, stupid and self-defeating demand for the "unconditional surrender" of our enemies. A demand which left the German people with no recourse but to fight on in a desperate endeavor to defend their country from the Red Army, long after they were ready to surrender to us and overthrow Hitler, if only we would let them save themselves and all Eastern Europe from Communist conquest.

To me, who well remembered the 1914 war, it was particularly disheartening to see how "the liberals" who had preserved their sanity and humane values in that earlier struggle to "make the world safe for democracy," became for the most part, the greatest hatemongers and advocates of vengeance on the whole German people during the Second World War. The influence of the Communists and their sympathizers combined with that of the racists-in-reverse who believed in the particular wickedness and collective guilt of the German people exerted a fateful influence on American opinion and policy.

We should not now, thirty years after the beginning of the Second World War, feel compelled to acquiesce in the Soviet enslavement of Eastern Europe, had we not wanted to punish the German "race" by letting the Red Army rape and kill and occupy part of their land. Had we adhered to the principles which made America great and strong and free, and a beacon of hope for all mankind, we should not now be retreating and allowing Communist Russia to consolidate its European Empire for fear of making a desert of the world through an atomic war.

During the war years I tried in vain again and again to get articles published which I now read in manuscript form with some pride and more melancholy in view of my failure to exert any appreciable influence on the course of human events. De Witt Wallace encouraged me to persevere by frequently paying me two or three hundred dollars for articles he felt he could not publish in the *Reader's Digest*, and by letters he wrote me expressing his high regard for my writings. One of these manuscripts with the title "Shall Not the Judge of All the World do Right?" taken from the Old Testament, written in March 1945, expressed views later amplified in my 1949 book *The High Cost of Vengeance* opposing the woe to the vanquished thesis upon which our occupation of Germany was originally founded. And it was "Wally" who was to finance me and give me the prestige of being a *Reader's Digest* Correspondent in 1948 in Germany while I was gathering material for that book.

Chapter 29
THE POLITICAL WORLD IS ALSO ROUND

Three decades ago in *The Dream We Lost*, telling the story of my life in Russia in the 30's, I wrote:

> Disillusionment is a negative process. Unless one is to abjure life one must endeavor not only to learn from experience, but also to face disagreeable realities. Because the hopes of one's youth are dimmed, because history has not worked out in the way one expected, and because certain basic changes are taking place in the world which are distasteful or hateful, one should not ignore them or think one can halt them by force. We can perhaps moderate present historical trends and to some extent control our destinies by a fearless examination of what is occurring. But we cannot bid the world stand still because we dislike its evolution.

In general I have found that whether they stand to the "left" or to the "right" many of my contemporaries, somewhere along the line of their political development, have been frozen into immobility, failing to realize that the world moves even if they do not. Believing that they know all the answers, and have a prescription to cure the ills of all mankind valid at all times and in all places, they imagine they can stand like gods at a fixed point outside the revolving world, with a lever compelling it to accelerate, or reverse, its course. Seeing the world only in one season in the one small part of it they know, they ignore the differences in the political and economic climate of different regions of the globe comparable to the changing seasons of the earth's revolution around the sun bringing birth, springtime, summer, autumn decay, and winter to the cultures of mankind.

Disregarding the stages of mankind's uneven development, they imagine that there is a panacea for all the economic, social and political ills of humanity valid everywhere in the world at any season. Thus, "progressives" and "reactionaries" alike, failing to understand the divergent needs of various people at different seasons of their development, prescribe wrong remedies. The "Right" tells the "underdeveloped countries" whose basic need is law and order and the best possible utilization of meager resources that free enterprise should be unconfined. The "Left" tells them that state ownership of "the means of production and distribution," according to Marx, will set them free, although as all who read must know from the experience of Soviet Russia, China, and Eastern Europe, this is the sure way, not to progress, but backwards into serfdom.

Different remedies are required for different countries or areas of the globe depending on whether they are in the hungry springtime of their entry into the machine age, or in the autumn season like ourselves when the harvest is so abundant that distribution, not production, poses the main problem.

My metaphors have become mixed but perhaps my meaning is clear. On the one hand, I consider it absurd for the "Right" to prescribe unlimited "free enterprise" for economically backward or undeveloped countries where unrestricted competition in a free market leads to the concentration of wealth in the hands of the few and the increasing misery of the many. And it seems to me equally unrealistic and harmful for the "Left," old or new, to insist on the establishment of Western political "democracy" in countries whose primary need is for the order which only a strong authoritative central government can establish. By demanding that all the people on our side should forthwith become western style democracies, skipping over the West's own long historical evolution, western liberals, as ignorant of history as of political realities, pave the way for the establishment of totalitarian dictatorships as the alternative to chaos.

To imagine that the problems of the "underdeveloped" countries of Asia and Africa are the same as our own is like teaching Eskimo's to wear Bikinis, or South Sea Islanders to robe themselves in furs. Yet many who style themselves "progressives" advocate comparable absurdities in their confident prescriptions for the well-being of mankind. Imprisoned within the narrow confines of their own limited experience and knowledge, they equate "progress" with construction of a stucco facade, or cardboard copy, of the edifice built stone by stone by generations of our ancestors, who fought and died and worked to create the citadel of liberty in which we dwell.

The classical world of Greece and Rome, conceived of the Golden Age as in the past, and originally the word progress meant simply moving onward, as does the earth when the season changes from the warmth of summer into the decay of autumn and the bitter cold of winter before the forces of creation are again released in spring.

Since the political world is also round, we should realize that change is not always for the better, but may mean moving into worse conditions in a harsher climate in which one cannot live outdoors warmed by the sun of freedom. But "progressives" seem to ignore the fact that in some climates one should not be concerned with a hot house culture of the plant of freedom, but bend one's efforts to erect a shelter against the stormy blasts of anarchy, and in preserving the seeds of liberty until the season comes when they can burgeon.

Reactionaries, equally blind to realities, ignore the fact that one cannot stay in the same place on the revolving earth without running fast. They vainly imagine that all they need to do to save our liberties is to preserve unchanged, yesterday's institutions and yesterday's world order.

As I write there comes to my mind out of some old recess in my memory two nonsensical lines from a popular song of the 20's which are applicable to the mixed up conceptions of many modern "intellectuals":

> When its nighttime in Italy
> It's Wednesday over here.

Passing from the ridiculous to the sublime I recall verses from Shelley's *Hellas*:

> Worlds on worlds are rolling ever
>   From creation to decay
> Like the bubbles on a river
>   Sparkling, bursting, borne away.

"Oh write no more the tale of Troy," Shelley wrote in this same poem, "a brighter Hellas rears its mountains from waves serener far—a new Ulysses leaves once more Calypso for his native shore." Descending from soaring flights of hope to the pessimism engendered by man's history, Shelley asks at the end of this poem, "Must hate and death return?" knowing they will always be with us to destroy our best hopes of creating a better world. But shutting out pessimism he says,

> Drain not to its dregs
>   The urn of bitter prophecy,
> The world is weary of the past.
>   Oh, might it die or rest at last!

In spite of all his doubts, Shelley wrote in this same poem: "The world's great age begins anew, the golden years return." Hope springs eternal in each generation. If it did not, what sense or purpose would there be in living?

Today I do not know whether in the parlance of our time I am now a liberal or a conservative, a progressive or a reactionary. These words long since became "banner words" debased into stereotyped meanings according to political prejudice, and with little relevance to our era. But in old age as in my springtime I still believe that although mankind plunges back into darkness and cold following each summer of progress, our course has generally been upwards in the endeavor to create a world nearer to the hearts desire.

My experience has ranged over a greater part of the world in space and depth of political experience than most others of my generation. I have both benefitted and suffered because I traveled faster and further than most of my contemporaries who shared my youthful aspirations and illusions.

The knowledge which I acquired too soon, thanks to my experiences in Russia, alienated me from my own kind. As a premature anti-Communist who foresaw the disastrous consequences of unconditional aid to Stalin's tyranny for the sake of "total victory" over Germany, I incurred the enmity of the anti-anti-Communists which endured even after they perforce recognized the truth of what I had written.

For awhile I found myself on the same side as the "conservatives," or isolationists, who, except for a small number of farsighted liberals such as John T. Flynn and Norman Thomas, alone seemed to realize that the end result of the Second World War would be to make the world safe for Communism.

After the war, in my endeavors to awaken America to the Communist menace from within as well as from without, I joined Senator McCarthy's camp but left him after he was taken over by reactionary forces who confused the quest for social justice with Communist treason, and by unscrupulous careerists such as Cohn and Schine.

The inside story as I knew it of Senator McCarthy's rise, decline and fall will be related in the second volume of my Memoirs. As also my subsequent experiences which taught me "What's wrong with the Right" during the brief period of my popularity among conservatives following the success of *The China Story* which made the best seller lists for three months in 1951. I learnt that the extreme, or dumb, "Right" is as alien to me as its counterpart on the "Left" composed of liberals who likewise resemble the Bourbons of whom it was said that they had learned nothing and forgotten nothing.

These experiences, as valuable as my ordeal in Russia in teaching me some political wisdom, brought me back onto an even keel but left me without any political haven.

My temperament and my ideals continued to inhibit me from traveling in the middle of the road, but I realized that one must avoid getting bogged down on either the right or the left soft shoulders of the political highway. I now came to appreciate my prescience so long ago in England when I carved the Greek word *Sophrosune* on my pencil box.

I have incurred the displeasure of the "Right" as well as the "Left" by the opinions I have expressed in the many books I have written since I first endeavored, following my return from Russia in 1936, to awaken the Free World to realization of the Communist menace. A world which, for all its shortcomings and its frequent failures to live up to its basic principles, still deserves to be called "free." Because even the worst political and economic conditions within its orbit seem like Paradise, or at least as a pretty good Purgatory, to all who have experienced the Hell of Communist tyranny.

To me it seemed that I was a liberal in upholding the standard of liberty and justice, or the conception of equality under the rule of law for all mankind, whether I was writing about Russia, China, Germany after her defeat, or the Arab world today. But to my critics I have seemed to be either a defender of 'fascism' or of authoritarian rule *or* as having reverted to my youthful adherence to the Socialist cause, if not actually suspect of harboring Communist sympathies.

As I have learned to my sorrow, those who are most actively opposed to Communism too frequently hate it, not for what it is, but for what it professes to be. Their opposition is not primarily against the soul-destroying tyranny of the Communist dictatorship which reduces its subjects to a new form of slavery, but against the original Socialist ideal of ending the exploitation and oppression of man by the few who owned "the means of production and distribution." Many who call themselves conservatives are in fact reactionaries who would have us go back to the bad old days when the power of capitalists and imperialists was as ruthlessly used and as uncontrolled as that of the ruling hierarchy in a Communist state.

Many self-styled liberals, on the other hand, are still soft on Communism either because they imagine that socialism and social justice are synonymous, or because they fail to realize that state control of the economy carried to the nth degree must make an end of government by consent of the governed and curtail or destroy all our liberties.

Thus policy in the West is all at sea. Some hate Communism not for what it is but for what it professes to be, while others are still attracted to it because they imagine that it is what it is not, or that it could become what its original adherents intended.

There are three lines of the beginning of a poem which I have been unable to find in any anthology and which, I may possibly long ago have composed myself:

> The good lack wisdom
> And the wise lack goodness;
> Thus are all things compounded unto ill.

The "good" I take to mean the many men of good will, today usually calling themselves liberals, or classified as the "Left," who have unwittingly been largely responsible for the spread of Communist tyranny over a large part of the world, thanks to their lack of political wisdom or the knowledge which comes from experience.

The "wise" are those who, with a better understanding of the facts of life and the realities of power, and with a truer, if also too cynical appraisal of the nature of men, lack charity, compassion or sympathy for those less fortunate than themselves. Such men are not truly wise, but merely clever in the pursuit of their short term interests. It is they who give substance to Communism's false claim to represent the poor and oppressed.

Thousands of years ago a Chinese wrote:

> Generous are the gods in granting life, but how
> niggardly when asked of its understanding.

Were he alive today this Chinese sage might reformulate his statement to read: How generous are the gods in letting man learn the physical secrets of the universe, but how niggardly in giving him understanding of his own nature and of the laws which govern the fate of individuals, peoples and states. Today man has split the atom and is already penetrating the regions of outer space, but we have acquired no more, if as much, political wisdom as the ancients, who although unaware that the earth is not flat, perceived from their observation of the cycle of government in the city states that the political world is round. That there are good and bad forms of rule by the one, the few and the many; that monarchy degenerates into autocracy, aristocratic government into oligarchy, and constitutional government into democracy, which means rule by demagogues and leads to dictatorship which may begin well but ends in tyranny.

Old truths are forgotten in the rush of "progress," and those of us who have traveled furthest find ourselves back at our beginnings, having learned how little we know, which is perhaps the beginning of wisdom.

Reviewing my life in retrospect, I find few of the accepted clichés of our time applicable. I accept the truth of the dictum that misfits among rich and poor alike find an irresistible attraction in Communist doctrine because it relieves them of responsibility for their own shortcomings by ascribing all the ills of mankind to deficiencies in the economic and social system. But I did not become a Communist for a brief period of my youth on account of the guilt complexes of the rich or of their children; nor as a result of an unhappy childhood, or as a fugitive from despair at ever finding a place for myself in the free competitive world. Nor out of longing to merge myself in a Communist "fraternity" as a substitute for a Universal Christian Church. Nor because joining the Communist Party or supporting it seemed the way either to acquire powerful political backing, or to enjoy wealth and escape responsibility for using it rightly by posing as a revolutionary. Nor as a means to stifle my longing for lasting love since I had already found it when I joined the Communist Party.

I followed Moscow's star for a few years for the same reasons which impelled me to recoil in horror from Stalin's Russia, once I had learned to know it. As soon as I discovered that Communism, far from being an extension or fulfillment of the liberal ideal, as I had imagined, meant the imposition of a more total tyranny than the world had previously known I rejected it. In a word I was, and have remained, a liberal in the original meaning of this much-abused word.

My outlook being essentially rational, the Communist mystique which justified the horrors of Stalin's Russia was as alien to my temperament as the worship of Moloch or Baal. I could not reject the evidence of my senses, or be convinced by the mumbo jumbo, which the Communists call Dialectics, that all was for the best in the worst of all possible worlds. Nor could I believe that a more humane and just social order would eventually be created by destroying man's humanity and compassion and violating his sense of justice. In a word, that heaven on earth could be established by diabolic means.

So, although I had joined the Communist Party in England in 1927, I left it soon after I went to live in Russia three years later.

Brought up as an atheist and to consider religion as the shield of tyranny, intolerance and cruelty, freedom of the spirit appeared to me as an indispensible condition for the economic and political emancipation of mankind. At the outset I failed to perceive the religious or mystical side of Communism, but later it was my deeply rooted distrust of idolatry and superstition which made it impossible for me to accept Stalin or any other sacrosanct "leader" as a god; and impelled me to recoil in horror from the degradation and enslavement of the human mind which are the predominant features of the Communist World.

Being above all an individualist, taught from childhood to think for myself, the "fraternal passion" or desire to merge oneself into a totality as a substitute for God, which is one of the motive patterns of Communism, was incomprehensible to me. I could not believe that "socialist brotherhood" justified the imposition of torture and death on millions of innocent people, and the excommunication or liquidation of those who dared to protest. As Max Eastman said, those who talk about all mankind being brothers seem often to be thinking of Cain and Abel.*

Like Max Eastman, the concept of human freedom formed the axis of my beliefs. It was such as we who left the Party first and became "premature anti-Communists" because our "motive pattern" was the emancipation of mankind. We could not accept or condone tyranny, cruelty, and oppression as good, because a new set of people were inflicting them upon the mass of the people in the name of a new ideal.

Even in my old age I cannot abandon my rationalist beliefs, despite the abundant evidence supplied in my lifetime that reason has all too little influence on the course of human events. I still believe that "the truth can set men free" but I now realize that even men of goodwill are intent on keeping her down at the bottom of a deep well, whenever she threatens to destroy their illusions, or stands in the way of achievement of their immediate goals.

In past ages it was believers in the divine right of kings, Catholic obscurantists, and Protestant fundamentalists who for one reason or another sought to keep "the masses" in ignorance. Today it would seem to be self-styled liberals or "progressives" who are the greatest offenders. Consciously or unconsciously they use their influence to have printed 'only the news which fits' the prejudices and objectives of their secular religion.

Those whom the French long ago designated as the "Fourth Estate"—the journalists, commentators, columnists and professors who today enjoy the power to shape public opinion without shouldering the responsibilities of power—now constitute a menace to our liberties. To a large extent they have usurped the power of the elected representatives of the people in Congress. In England questions in Parliament are perhaps still more important than Press Conferences. But in America debates in Congress take second place to the opinions of popular columnists and commentators.

Catholics affirm that given the instruction of children in their first six or seven years they will never completely abandon their religion. I, reared as an agnostic, could never like some others who learnt about Communism the hard way by personal experience, join the Catholic Church, nor like Whitaker Chambers, seek consolation by becoming a mystically inclined Quaker. It would have been greatly to my advantage to do so, as was pointed out to me by the late Professor Tansill of Georgetown University who, by reason of his intelligent and principled opposition to American intervention in the Second World War was deprived of tenure and promotion. When over lunch with him at the Cosmos Club in the early 50's he told me that my writing would be more effective by wider distribution if I had the Catholic Church to back me, I answered in Biblical language: "Get thee behind me Satan"—a remark which made us better friends than ever because he was a real Christian of a rare sort who appreciated my dilemma in adhering to Christian values without faith in Christian dogma.

Seeking to reconcile my agnosticism with my conviction all my life that there is a Holy Ghost against which one sins when one fails to bear witness to the truth as one sees it, I find the contradiction resolved by Shelley who wrote that when speaking against: "The erroneous and degrading idea which men have conceived of a Supreme Being," he was not speaking against "the Supreme Being itself."

Hoping that this Supreme Being exists I cannot but believe that he must be just, and will accordingly judge men for good or ill, by their actions, motives, strivings and

*Stalin's Russia and the Crisis in Socialism, W. W. Norton, New York, 1940.

conduct. That He will be charitable toward my weaknesses and forgive my transgressions, rather than condemn me because I am not sure that He exists.

Entering the age of reflection after a life spent in struggle, the lesson I have learned from the battles I have fought, whether won or lost, is that there must be some kind of order in the universe, incomprehensible as it seems to us as we view the injustices and inequalities of the world we know. Atheist or agnostic, as I have been since childhood, my experiences lead me to believe that if one casts one's bread upon the waters in charity or for love of righteousness, it will be returned after many days in one way or another. Or perhaps I mean that whatever you put into life will be what you get out of it.

My reason still rejects the concept of an omnipotent and omniscient God who permits all manner of injustice and suffering in the world He created, and punishes men for doing what He foresees they will do. But I can conceive of Him as a Spirit striving to inspire us with courage to fight for righteousness against the forces of evil.

Despite the disillusionments and vicissitudes of my life, I have never ceased to believe that whether or not any gods exist who care anything for man's fate, his age-old longing for freedom and justice on earth could be satisfied if he acted according to the divine precepts which I hope exist, and which in all ages have inspired man to create gods in his own best image.

As Swinburne expressed it in *"The Last Oracle"*:

> For no thought of man made gods to love or honor
> Ere the song within the silent soul began
> Nor might earth in dream or deed take heaven upon her
> Till the word was clothed with speech by lips of man.

My remembrances of these and other verses of my favorite poets illustrates the curious mixture of faith and disbelief in religion which motivated me and others of my generation. While considering ourselves atheists or agnostics, we believed that life has a higher purpose than its immediate satisfactions.

I did not perceive the contradiction until late in life. Today I realize that liberals of my epoch can be compared to flowers which bloomed while still attached to the parent stem rooted in the culture and faith of the past, whereas today the cut blossoms of liberalism wither and die or become poisonous in decay.

How to maintain "the great truths of Christian faith and conduct" without belief in the Christian God troubled Thomas Huxley as he grew older. Somehow it was necessary to ensure that the ethical standards of Christianity which Huxley respected were not jettisoned along with the Christian dogma he despised. An objective described by Malcolm Muggeridge as "no less difficult than trying to navigate a boat without a sail or compass."

Perhaps old Voltaire expressed it best when he said that if God did not exist he had to be invented.

One of the great Victorian Thomas Huxley's grandsons, Aldous Huxley, perhaps fittingly became "the patron saint of hipsters" in California. In him, as Muggeridge writes, "the wheel turned full circle. What began with Darwin ended with Buddha; the strict disciplines of science turned finally into the fantasies of mescaline."*

Liberalism carried in our time to the nth degree of permissiveness leads to anarchy, as now demonstrated by the violence and irrationality of the "New Left." The old Left which embraced Marxist theory and championed the Communist totalitarian state is dead

---

Esquire, October 1968. Malcolm Muggeridge's review of Ronald Clark's *The Huxleys*, McGraw Hill.

or discredited. But instead of revulsion against it leading to revival of old values which Communism sought to destroy, we have in its place a nihilistic Left which seeks by violence to bring down the pillars of the temple of civilization without any conception of what, if anything, it wishes to construct on the ruins.

Irrationality has succeeded the age of reason into which I was born.

Yesterday in the depression years it was gangs of young Fascists and Nazis who adhered to the cult of violence and saw themselves as courageously revolting against the rottenness of the old order. Today in our age of affluence in the West we have the "new left" emulating them in their determination to destroy our universities, preventing free speech, burning books, ridiculing our institutions and rendering impossible the operation of government under the rule of law.

Extremes meet. Whether they travel left to the North Pole or right to the South Pole the climate is much the same.

In the sphere of international relations and foreign policy the wheel has come full circle. Yesterday's 'war mongers' are today's appeasers. Those who led the hue and cry against Nazi Germany advocate peaceful coexistence now that Communist imperialism threatens the free world. Yesterday's internationalists are today's new isolationists and vice versa.

I am not only among the few who learned about Communism the hard way through personal experience. As the wife of a Russian in Moscow, in the 30's, I also came to know more about human nature under stress, and the savagery which reasserts itself in jungle conditions such as were recreated in Soviet Russia, than is dreamed of in the philosophy of either liberals or conservatives in the West.

Innocent as man before the fall of the ugly realities of the struggle for existence outside their own secure and protected Garden of Eden in the West, most Americans have no conception of what it means to be hungry or cold, or to be driven by the terrible compulsions of a totalitarian state under which men live in constant dread of death or imprisonment for themselves and those they love.

Salvemini defined an intellectual as a man educated beyond his intelligence. I would designate the "progressive" Western liberal "intelligentsia" as men deprived by their sheltered and privileged lives of the wisdom which comes from experience but inflated by the self importance resulting from their superior education and status. The ordinary run of mankind, having to cope with the problems of human existence in a hard world, have more common sense and a better understanding of the trials and tribulations of less fortunate peoples.

Today I realize that man's understanding is limited by his experience. Those who have always known the blessings of liberty are as incapable of understanding the compulsions which drive the subject of a totalitarian tyranny, as those who have never hungered are able to realize what it means to cry for bread. Even the poor, but comparatively free, peoples outside the charmed circle of the prosperous Western democracies, have no conception of what it means to be the subjects of a totalitarian tyranny under which everybody belongs, body and soul, to an all-powerful state. To identify the forcibly silenced peoples of the Soviet Empire and Communist China with the tyrants who rule over them is the height of folly. Yet the politicians and popular publicists of the West, imprisoned within the narrow confines of their limited experience, continue to shape our policies on the same false assumptions as when we identified the German people with their Nazi masters and, by demanding their unconditional surrender, let Communist Russia filch from us all the fruits of victory.

Whether or not any God exists there would seem to be some immutable principles or laws governing the universe which we violate at our peril. It may be only our children or our children's children whose teeth are set on edge by the sour grapes we eat, or plant, and the bread we cast upon the waters may not return until after so many days that we ourselves are already dead. Still the course of human events as well as my personal experience leads me to believe that there is truth in the Biblical saying that men reap as they sow. Reward and retribution are realities even though heaven be only "the vision of fulfilled desire," and hell "the shadow of a soul on fire."

In my lifetime I have seen an unjust peace or the lust for vengeance bring retribution to the victors after two World Wars.

Versailles produced Hitler; and "unconditional surrender" involving unconditional aid to Stalin led to the establishment of the Communist totalitarian dictatorship over a large part of Europe and also to the "Cold War."

Yet one must also recognize that the Communist menace which the West made real by its cruel and stupid 'war aims' has not been without good result. Maybe devils are as necessary as gods for the ensurance of good behavior.

During the Dark Ages of faith fear of the devil and the torments of hell compelled men, to some extent at least, to restrain their cruelty and lusts and ambitions. Today, fear of Communism has induced the prosperous and powerful Western nations not only to let their colonial subjects go free, but also to share their wealth with the poor and formerly down trodden and exploited peoples of Asia and Africa.

In Damascus, which claims to be and perhaps is, the oldest inhabited city in the world, in the summer of 1959, more than two decades after I had left Russia, I had a long talk over tea with the Indian Ambassador to Syria, which helped me to formulate my hitherto dimly conceived conception of the mysterious, or contradictory, ways in which God, if he exists, works his wonders to perform.

This Indian, who was a Moslem from the Persian Gulf, and whom I had gone to visit because I was told he was the wisest diplomat in the Middle East, said to me:

"The French Revolution which burst asunder the chains of feudalism in Europe, did not benefit France, but was an inspiration to the world. So, likewise, the Russian revolution in 1917 failed to improve the lot of the Russian people who are today perhaps even worse off than under the Tsars. But the Communist challenge has so radically transformed the Western, formerly imperialist, world that America today comes nearer to fulfilling the original Communist ideal of social justice and economic progress for the benefit of all than any other state anywhere on earth at any time. And the capitalist system elsewhere has also been transformed, or is in process of changing out of all semblance to the Marxist picture of it, which was once true."

Which tribute from an Indian is worth quoting, echoing as it does my own appreciation of America, my country now by citizenship as well as by choice, and the one which has come closest to being the living embodiment of the hopes which have motivated my life from my youth onwards.

Likewise, or on the other hand, the challenge of Western prosperity and the ever-increasing opportunity which our system is affording to all our people is exerting a powerful corrosive influence on the Soviet Empire, where compulsion in place of the profit motive has failed to create an affluent society and where economic inequality is far greater than in the Capitalist world.

In the process of my wide ranging wanderings in space, time and imagination as well as on the good sound earth I have sojourned in many places, and communicated with many people of diverse faiths seeking by one path or another to establish a Kingdom of Righteousness on earth or to find what our superstitious unenlightened medieval forefathers called the Holy Grail. This quest like that of countless others today as in ages past is perhaps futile. But it has given meaning to my life although my wings were long since broken by my attempt to reach the heavens despite the power of the dark forces of gravity beneath the earth.

INDEX

Aaron, Daniel; 250, 251
Abels, Lily; 185
Abramovna, Anna; 78, 79, 87, 102, 141
Acheson, Dean; 215
Adams, Donald; 285
Afenogenov, Alexander; 250
Amory, Copley; 176
Atlee, Clement; 76
Aveling, Edward; 8

Back, Gilly; 114
Baldwin, Roger; 291, 294
Barzini, Luigi; 185
Baynes, Norman H.; 47, 48
Beard, Charles A.; 259
Belden, Jack; 186-192, 203, 204
Benton, Tom; 295
Berdichevsky, Arcadi Jacovlevitch; 78, 85, 87, 97, 107
    Arrest, Imprisonment and Death, 125-127, 130-141
Berdichevsky, Sasha; 288, 291-294
Berdichevsky, Vera; 125, 134-138
Besant, Annie; 7, 155
Bess, Demarie; 225
Beveridge, Sir William; 75, 104
Bingham, Alfred; 232, 238-240, 259, 265, 287
Blake, Peter; 20, 171
Bluet, Dorothea; 24, 25
Boettinser, Anna; 223
Borkenau, Franz; 230
Bosshard, Walter; 185, 193
Bowles, Chester; 239, 240, 287
Boxer, Charles; 220, 221
Bozell, Brent; 47
Bradlaush, Charles; 7, 155
Brailsford, H. N.; 46, 150, 152, 156
Brandt, Carol; 275
Brockway, Fenner, 45

Brooks, Van Wyck; 251
Brown, Burton, Mrs.; 23, 27, 29, 30
Brown, W. J.; 81, 82
Buchanan, Rab; 114, 150
Buchan-Syderf, Nora; 24
Buck, Pearl; 5, 259, 260, 262, 276, 277, 281, 287
Buckley, Wm. F.; 47, 150
Bullitt, William; 129, 130, 297
Burns, Emile; 104
Burns, John; 7
Burton, Wilbur; 246-250, 287, 288

Cairns, Huntington; 250, 272, 283
Calverton, F. V.; 250
Calverton, George; 10, 250-253, 256, 271
Carlson, Evans; 201, 202, 203, 218
Carnal, Henri; 17
Carpenter, William S.; 284
Carter, E. C.; 133
Chamberlain, Neville; 143, 168, 227
Chamberlin, William Henry; 232, 247, 287, 288, 291, 295
Chambers, Whitaker; 146, 290, 307
Chen, Eugene; 220
Chiang Kai-Shek; 91, 188, 194, 196, 212, 213, 217, 218, 298
Chiang Kai-Shek, Madam; 196, 197, 198, 215, 216
Chilston, Lord; 126
Chou-En-Lai; 192, 211, 212, 220
Churchill, Winston; 74, 75, 143, 236, 261
Clark, Colin; 76
Clark-Kerr, Sir Archibald; 201
Coe, Frank; 283
Cohen, Rose; 111
Cohn, Roy; 279, 304
Cole, G.H.D.; 76, 86
Cole, Margaret; 76, 86

313

Conquest, Robert; 290
Cook, Arthur J.; 70
Cooper, Mary; 25
Cornell, Katherine; 295
Corwin, Edward S.; 284
Cousins, Norman; 249, 251, 259, 287
Cowley, Malcolm; 259, 289
Crook, Beata; 25
Crossland, T.W.H.; 7
Cudahy, John; 278
Culbertson, Ely; 265

Dane, Majorie Clemence; 25
David, Gwenda; 230
Davies, John; 201, 202, 203, 204, 214, 215, 216, 274
Davis, Elmer; 300
Dean, Vera Michaeles; 284
Dédie, Marthe; 17, 19, 21
Denis, Lawrence; 143, 265
Dennis, Lawrence; 250, 265, 266, 288
Dewar, Hugo; 151
Dewey, John; 295
Dickstein, Samuel; 275, 277
Dietrich, Marlene; 104
Dillinger, Elizabeth; 266
Dobb, Maurice; 76
Doner, Ephraim; 241, 270
Dorn, Frank "Pinkie"; 201, 202, 206, 214
Dos Passos, John; 295
Douglas, Helen Gehagan; 276
Driver, Cecil H.; 46
Duffy, Edmund; 236
Duranty, Walter, 246, 261
Durdin, Tillman; 187, 192, 204, 215

Eastman, Max; 77, 152, 170, 250, 259, 287-291, 294, 295, 299, 307
Eaton, Cyrus; 180
Eden, Anthony; 224
Edwards, J. J.; 33
Eisner, Ann; 295
Ellis, Mrs. William; 38

Euler, Liselott; 20
Exley, David; 228

Faber, Geoffrey; 134
Fairbank, John K.; 214, 232
Farrell, James; 253
Ferguson, Senator Homer; 277
Field, Walter; 39, 114, 144
Fish, Hamilton; 278
Fisher, Edgar F.; 284
Fisher, "Mac"; 185
Flynn, John T.; 261, 268, 277, 304
Ford, Leslie; 236
Forrman, Clark; 272, 274
Fox, Ralph; 150
Freeman, Mansfield; 288
Frost, Dr. David; 51, 52, 56
Fulbright, Senator William; 286

Gaitskell, Dora; 51, 52
Gaitskell, Hugh; 51, 52
Gantt, Horsley; 236
Gardiner, A. G.; 54
Gelder, Robert Van; 256
George, Lloyd; 27, 35
Gold, Mike; 251
Gollancz, Victor; 224
Gore, Albert; 276
Gould, Randall; 92, 186, 208, 220, 221, 247, 281-283
Grenfell, Russell; 261
Green, Mary; 230
Green, Russell; 39, 40, 77, 118
Greenwood, Arthur; 76
Gren, Joseph; 282
Cumpertz, Julian; 208
Gunther, Francis and John; 266

Hahn, Emile; 220, 221, 265
Haldane, J.B.S.; 153
Hamilton, Edith; 5, 29
Hannighen, Frank; 272
Hard, William; 275
Harris, Frank; 6

314

Harris, "Stan"; 26, 51
Hausamann, Connie; 293
Held, Adolf; 275, 277
Henderson, Archie, 84
Henderson, Loy; 215, 225, 273
Hertzberg, Sidney; 239
Hesse, Sybil; 33
Hicks, Granville; 251
Hindus, Maurice; 167
Hiss, Priscilla; 61
Ho, Sha-Li; 190
Hogg, George, 185
Holt, Emmett; 221, 225-237
Holt, Olivia; 167, 233
Hook, Sidney; 172, 175, 250, 266, 275,
    277, 287, 290, 293
Hotten, Ernest; 265
Hoover, Herbert; 291
Hoving, Walter; 291
Howe, Quincy; 172, 287, 291
Hu, Chiu-Yuan; 217
Hu, Shih; 287, 288, 297
Huberman, Lee; 254
Hudson, Geoffrey; 134, 241
Huxley, Aldous; 23, 25, 123, 308
Huxley, Julia; 23
Huxley, Julian; 23, 25
Huxley, Margaret; 25
Huxley, Thomas; 23, 308

Isaacs, Harold; 134, 210

Jagan, Cheddi; 111
Jenkins, "Ern"; 26
Joad, C.M.; 55
Johnson, Hush S.; 266
Johnson, Philip; 171, 264, 265, 266, 270,
    287, 296
Joll, Teddy; 51
Judd, Walter; 235, 298

Kalckreuth, Count Joachim; 20
Kallergi, Coudenhove; 293
Kazanin, Mark; 130, 139, 140

Keezer, Anne and Dexter; 235, 236
Kendall, Willmore; 47
Kennedy, Joseph P.; 266
Kenyon, Dorthy, 291
Keynes, Maynard; 287
King, Alice; 268
King, Mary; 249
Kingsbury, John A.; 259
Kirchway, Freda; 239, 259
Kitson, Arthur; 33
Klockner, Irene Von; 15, 16
Koestler, Arthur; 71
Kohlberg, Alfred; 293
Koo, Y.C.; 218
Kunitz, Joseph; 251

Lafollette, Senator Robert; 277
Lafollette, Susan; 250
Lamont, Corliss; 274
Lanchester, Elsa; 52, 53
Laski, Harold; 62, 63, 76, 111, 152
Lattimore, Owen; 125, 133, 214, 221,
    222, 232, 254, 271, 278
Laughton, Charles; 52
Lee, Sims; 201, 202
Lerner, Max; 284
Levine, Isaac Don; 126, 154, 180, 250,
    259, 287
Lewis, Wiemot; 283
Lewisohn, Greta; 266
Lim, Robert; 187, 188, 189, 196, 202
Lindbergh, Anne; 147, 261, 268
Lindbergh, Charles; 147, 261, 266, 268
Linford, Cynthia; 15
Lipking, Bill; 295
Litvinov, Ivy; 126, 269
Litvinov, Maxim; 126, 269
Lloyd, C.M.; 76, 152
Long, Huey; 266
Longworth, Alice; 266
Loo, Chih-teh; 187, 193
Lopokavna; 287
Lothian, Lord; 262, 274, 275
Low, Ivy; 126

Luce, Clare; 298
Luce, Henry; 267, 298
Lyons, Eugene; 250, 255, 258, 259, 291, 296

MacArthur, General Douglas; 217
MacDonald, Dwight; 146, 238, 253, 259, 287, 290, 296
MacDonald, Ramsay; 54
Maisky, Ivan; 79, 81, 99, 125
Malone, Senator; 277
Mao, Tse-Tung; 213, 299
Marquand, Adelaide; 261, 267, 268, 269, 287
Marquand, John P.; 196, 234, 255, 267, 268, 269, 277, 287
Marshall, George C.; 211, 215, 216
Marshall, Margaret; 259
Martin, James J.; 259
Martin, Kingsley; 150, 152, 169, 228, 229
Mason, Noah; 277
Massing Hede; 208
Matthews, J.B.; 273
Maugham, Somerset; 138
Maxton, Jimmy; 45
McCarran, Senator; 279
McCarthy, Eugene; 276, 286
McCarthy, Senator Joe; 209, 257, 271, 278, 279, 304
McCarthy, Mary; 253, 295
Meany, George; 109
Mei-Ling, Soong; 198
Melville, Nina; 250
Menon, Krishna; 111
Mikoyan, Anastasius; 126, 132
Miller, Alice Duer; 265
Miller, Henry; 246
Mitchell, Milly; 246
Morley, Felix; 284
Morrison, Herbert; 76
Mosbacher, Erie; 230
Muggeridge, Kitty; 149
Muggeridge, Malcolm; 99, 149, 154, 290, 308

Murphy, Bob; 191
Murphy, Ray; 273, 278
Muthmann, Gretel; 18, 19
Muthmann, Liligret; 19

Nehru; 111
Nelson, Frederick and Sylvia; 222, 235, 274, 295
Nevinson, Henry; 54
Nixon, Richard; 276
Noulens, The; 92
Nye, Senator Gerald P.; 261, 274, 277

O'Connor, Fergus; 8
Odlum, Victor W.; 297
Oliver, Sir Sidney; 35

Palmer, Greta; 268
Palmer, Paul; 266, 299
Pardee, Frank H.; 257
Paresce, Renè; 244, 245
"Park Avenue Pinks"; 45
"Parlor Bolsheviks"; 45
Patrick, Hilda; 295
Patterson, Isabel; 256, 258
Patterson, Joseph Medil; 249
Paxton, Anne; 291
Pearce, Arno; 103
Petrovsky, Max; 79, 89, 111
Plavnik, Boris; 45, 46, 78
Pfeffer, Nathaniel; 256
Picot, Madame Georges; 184
Pollitt, Harry; 111
Porter, Sylvia; 283
Powell, J.B.; 299
Power, Eileen; 76, 77
Pratt, Caroline; 262
Preston, Evelyn; 294
Putnam, James; 265, 295

Rabinovitch, Philip; 52, 53, 129, 132, 133
Rand, Ayn; 257
Ransome, Arthur; 93, 124

Reimann, Guenter Hans; 229, 234, 241, 244, 287
Reiss, Jimmy; 17, 18, 22
Renault, Mary; 280
Riche, Omar Abou; 12
Robbins, Lionel; 283
Robeson, Paul; 203
Rockefeller, Mrs. John D.; 111, 268, 269
Rodman, Shelden; 232, 238, 253, 259, 287
Roosevelt, Eleanor; 61, 198, 233
Roosevelt, F. D.; 75, 172, 277
Roots, L. H.; 201
Ross, Michael; 109, 234
Rovere, Richard; 259
Russell, Bertrand; 1, 4, 55, 56, 64-73, 78, 80, 81, 101, 145, 148, 152-183, 222, 223, 240, 256, 257, 262, 265, 287, 288
   "Achilles Heel"; 168
   Character Traits; 70, 71, 72
   Early Views on Communist Party; 64, 65, 67
   Favorite Poem; 67
   Marriage Failures; 68
   Letters to Miss Utley; 159, 170, 176, 180, 181
   Meets Miss Utley; 64
   Relationship With His Children; 66
   And Shaw; 71
   Compared with Shaw; 164-165
Russell, Conrad; 171
Russell, Dora; 64, 68, 69, 148
Russell, Edith; 68, 182, 183
Russell, Peter (Patricia); 148, 155-162, 167, 222, 223
Russell, Senator Richard; 277, 297
Ryan, Robert; 26

Sansom, George and Katherine; 100, 221, 229, 231-233, 260, 270, 277, 287
Scheer, Robert; 172
Scheiller, Isodore; 259
Schine, G. David; 279, 304
Schoenman, Ralph, 172, 182, 183

Scott, Harold; 52
Scott, Isabel; 262, 284
Service, John Stewart; 214
Shah of Iran; 17
Shaw, George Bernard; 3, 6, 7, 56, 71, 152-166, 172
   And Russell; 71
   Compared with Russell; 164-165
   Letters to Lady Russell; 160, 161
   Letters to Miss Utley; 159, 161
Shean, Vincent; 224, 246
Shirer, William, L; 226, 267
Shuser, Dora; 241
Silva, George; 45
Smedley, Agnes; 184, 185, 199, 200-209, 210, 218
Smith, Lesley; 187
Smith, Reeves; 34
Smith, Truman; 261
Snow, Edgar; 185, 203, 210, 213, 214, 224, 232, 285
Soule, George; 144
Spivak, Lawrence; 287, 291
Spratt, Philip; 62
Starr, C.V.; 172, 220, 221, 277, 280-283, 286, 287, 291, 297-299
Steele, A. T.; 187, 192, 193, 194, 195, 218
Stennes, Walther; 220
Stewart, Findlater; 62
Stillwell, "Vinegar Joe"; 191, 204, 216
Stimson, Henry; 235
Stolberg, Ben; 250, 259
Stowe, Leland; 296
Strachey, John; 95, 153
Strong, Anna Louise; 99
Strunsky, Sheba; 287
Sun Yat Sen, Madame; 92, 198
Surene, Don; 209

Tabrisky, Jane, 62, 76, 150
Taft, Senator Robert; 261, 277
Tawney, R. H.; 76
Tchernavin; 285

Thomas, Norman; 239, 250, 257, 259, 287, 304
Thompson, Llewellyn E.; 126, 127
Thompson, Ralph; 256
Thorndyke, Sybil; 41
Toynbee, Arnold; 2, 77
Tresca, Carlo; 250
Trevelyan, Sir Hugh; 112
Truman, Harry S.; 215, 216
Tseng, Edie; 186

Utley, Emmie Williamson, 7-13 and elsewhere
Utley, Emsie, 59, 116, 120, 220
Utley, Freda,
   Admitted to U.S.; 277
   Ancestry, 3
   Baltimore Society; 236, 237
   Birth; 6
   Communist Party Candidate; 85
   Crosses USSR on Trans Siberian Express; 89, 90
   Double Standards of "Professional Liberals"; 289-290
   First Romance; 38
   Hitler and Stalin Compared; 143-145
   Husband's Arrest and Death, 125-127, 130-141
   Invited to Spend Summer With Russell; 69
   Joins Communist Party; 77-80
   Joins Labor Party; 45
   Letter from Madam Chiang Kai-Shek; 197
   Letters to Russell; 180, 181
   Letters from Russell; 159, 170, 176, 180, 181
   Letters to Shaw; 157, 158, 162
   Letters from Shaw; 159, 161
   Life in Moscow; 88, 108, 128, 129
   Low Opinion of Mrs. Roosevelt; 223
   Meets Arcadi Jacovlevitch Berdichevsky; 78
   Meets Arcadi in Japan; 94
   Meets Bertrand Russell; 64
   On Partition of Germany; 229
   Petitions Stalin; 152
   Receives M.A. Degree; 75
   Religious Beliefs; 271
   Russell & Shaw compared; 164, 165
   Rand, Ayn; 251
   Shanghai, 1938; 92
   Stalin-Hitler Pact; 225, 226
   Visiting Russells; 148
   Visits to Russia; 80-85

Utley, Jon (John) Basil; 102, 122, 129-134, 147, 151, 234, 237, 262, 271, 273, 293, 294, and elsewhere
Utley, Robert; 59, 114
Utley, Temple; 114-124 and elsewhere
Utley, Willie Herbert; 6-13 and elsewhere

Varga, Eugene; 129, 135
Vickers, Phyllis; 25, 35
Viereck, Peter; 296
Villard, Oswald Garrison; 259, 267, 277
Vincent, John Carter; 215
Voorhis, Jerry; 263, 271, 274-276

Wagner, Philip; 236
Waley, Arthur; 24
Waley, Margaret; 24
Wallace, Dewitt; 275, 277, 299, 301
Wallas, Graham; 76
Walsh, Richard; 238, 257, 259, 262
Wang, George; 185
Webb, Beatrice and Sidney; 7, 61, 105, 144, 149, 152, 153, 154
Wedemeyer, Albert C.; 282
Wei, Jimmy; 186
Wells, H.G.; 152
Wheeler, Mrs. Burton K.; 266
Wheeler, Senator Burton K.; 261, 277
White, Harry Dexter; 283
White, Theodore H.; 208
White, William L.; 253
Williams, Dick and Virginia; 147

318

Williamson, Joseph E.; 8, 10
Willkie, Wendell; 271, 275, 276, 277
Wills, David; 151
Wilson, Edmund; 291, 295
Winter, Ella; 259
Wittfegel, Karl; 295
Wolfe, Bertrand and Ella; 259, 287
Wollstein-Stolberg, Else; 20

Wood, Alan; 163
Wood, Robert E.; 261
Woolf, Leonard; 150
Woolf, Virginia; 150
Wootton, Barbara; 108

Young, Morgan; 100, 101, 102